FRANKLY

'How often has a working-class girl from Ayrshire risen to the highest office in Scotland and become a world leader who stood firmly for the dignity of her nation? Once, so far. Nicola is the first. She not only accompanied us through pivotal, decisive moments in British history, in many cases she was their proponent. In compelling, clear-eyed and self-critical prose, *Frankly* gives us a riveting, deeply human portrait of a woman coming into her power and reflecting on her battles, triumphs and defeats. Sturgeon's voice is an essential account of our time and the collective fate of our nation. I was both enlightened and enthralled'

Douglas Stuart, author of *Shuggie Bain*

'To have been in the room with the First Minister of Scotland during the crises of Brexit and Covid was to have witnessed, at first hand, a political leader at the height of her formidable powers. Now, in this highly personal account, you too can be alongside Nicola Sturgeon on her remarkable journey'

Mark Drakeford, former First Minister of Wales

Nicola Sturgeon

FRANKLY

MACMILLAN

First published 2025 by Macmillan
an imprint of Pan Macmillan
The Smithson, 6 Briset Street, London EC1M 5NR
EU representative: Macmillan Publishers Ireland Ltd, 1st Floor,
The Liffey Trust Centre, 117–126 Sheriff Street Upper,
Dublin 1 D01 YC43
Associated companies throughout the world

ISBN 978-1-0350-4021-6 HB
ISBN 978-1-0350-4022-3 TPB

1 3 5 7 9 8 6 4 2

A CIP catalogue record for this book is available from the British Library.

Typeset by Palimpsest Book Production Ltd, Falkirk, Stirlingshire
Printed and bound in the UK using 100% Renewable Electricity
by CPI Group (UK) Ltd

Visit **www.panmacmillan.com** to read more about
all our books and to buy them.

To the late Iain Ferguson –
uncle, journalist, inspiration.

And to my parents, Joan and Robin,
who have loved and supported me
every step of the way.

Do what you feel in your heart to be right – for you'll be criticized anyway.

Eleanor Roosevelt

Contents

Preface

I've always wanted to write a book, but I haven't always been sure I should write *this* book.

Before putting pen to paper, I had to convince myself that I was motivated by more than the vanity and self-justification that so often characterizes political memoirs. I don't claim that these traits will be completely absent, but I do hope I reach beyond them.

I have tried to reveal the person behind the politician. The seemingly confident, combative woman who dominated Scottish politics for more than a decade, unnerved the Westminster estab-lishment, helped lead Scotland to the brink of independence and steered it through a global pandemic is, underneath it all, painfully shy, an introvert, someone who has always struggled to believe in herself. On many days, even at the height of my political powers, the toughest battle I would fight was with the voice in my head telling me I wasn't good enough.

Like all women, since the dawn of time, I have faced misogyny and sexism so endemic that I didn't always recognize it as such. I have also encountered the snobbery and condescension that conditions many working-class people to believe that power and influence are not for us.

An understanding of the politician I became requires an appreciation of all of that. It also demands glimpses of the child, teenager and young adult I was. In the pages that follow, I will retrace my journey, from hiding under the table with a book at my fifth birthday party to standing on the steps of Bute House and leading my country for the best part of a decade.

I will describe the hurdles I overcame and the sacrifices I made. I will open up about my private life, including the heartbreak and guilt of losing a baby. I will reflect on my achievements and regrets, as well as the many lessons I learned along the way.

———

My story, though, is more than just a personal one. My career on the frontline of politics coincided with the most momentous period in modern Scottish history. As either front-row observer or active participant, I was 'in the room' through all of it.

I don't think anyone has written, in a single volume, the political story of Scotland over these years; certainly no one has done it from my perspective.

I grew up and became politically active in the Thatcher years and stood for Parliament in Tony Blair's landslide election. I campaigned in the referendum that led to the re-establishment of the Scottish Parliament and became one of its inaugural members.

I was the Deputy First Minister and Health Secretary in the first ever SNP government and helped secure our landslide re-election four years later. I negotiated the Edinburgh Agreement which paved the way for the independence referendum, co-authored the White Paper independence prospectus, and was one of the key figures in a campaign that brought Scotland to the brink of becoming an independent country.

I became the first woman to enter Bute House as First Minister, the first female Keeper of the Great Seal of Scotland in more than six hundred years. In 2015, the party I led redrew the political map of Scotland. I won all eight of the elections I contested as SNP leader. I was also a leading advocate for Remain in the ill-fated Brexit referendum.

As First Minister, I interacted with five UK Prime Ministers, from David Cameron to Rishi Sunak, with Theresa May, Boris Johnson and, albeit for the briefest of moments, Liz Truss along the way. I represented Scotland across the globe, at the British–Irish Council and at five UN climate-change summits, including COP26 in my home city of Glasgow.

I led Scotland through the Covid pandemic, the most traumatic and disruptive experience of our generation. I spent hours of private time with the late Queen. I tried, and failed, to secure the second independence referendum that I still fervently believe will happen, and be won, in my lifetime. By the time I stood down as First Minister in March 2023, I was the longest-serving incumbent of the office.

These thirty extraordinary years of Scottish political history demand to be chronicled. This book does so from my unique vantage point.

————

It always takes a while for the dust to settle when a leader leaves office. Early verdicts – especially in the modern media age – can be brutal.

If that is true in general, it has been more so for me.

Events that unfolded after I stood down as First Minister – the stepping up of a long-running police investigation into SNP finances – shook perceptions of me. How could it have been otherwise? However, as much as the opinions of others matter to me, it was my sense of self that took the biggest knock. Over the two years since leaving Bute House, I have endured some of the darkest days of my life. For me, the cloud of suspicion has now been lifted, but the experience has left its mark.

I have always been resilient, and in recent times I have found reserves of strength I didn't know I had. I have also been sustained by the love of my family and the support of a tight group of close friends. However, it is the writing of this book which has offered most solace. It has been a lifeline, a form of therapy in action, grounding me, at times calming me, amidst a constant cacophony of voices claiming to know me better than I do myself.

In these pages, I hope to remind you of who I am and what I stand for.

The fact is I am neither the hero that my most ardent supporters revere, nor the villain that my fiercest critics revile. I have made my fair share of mistakes, but I have always done my best. I have dedicated my life to public service and tried to make Scotland a better place. Along the way I have enjoyed huge privileges and, at times, paid a heavy price for them. I have achieved more than I could ever have imagined and believe I have made an impact to be proud of.

If your opinion of me is already formed, there is no shortage of caricatures out there to reinforce your views. However, if you want to know something about the real me, warts and all, and about how my life has interacted with the recent history of the remarkable country I was so lucky to be born in, then this story is for you.

Nicola Sturgeon
April 2025

CHAPTER ONE

In the Beginning

I am a few months shy of my seventeenth birthday and find myself standing on the doorstep of a large detached bungalow on the curve of a quiet cul-de-sac in Dreghorn, the former mining village in Ayrshire that my parents and I moved to when I was two. My finger is hovering uncertainly over the doorbell.

The walk from my own house to that doorstep took less than ten minutes, but the psychological distance I travelled to get there was huge. The cul-de-sac forms one of the 'posh' private estates in Dreghorn, a busy main road and a whole world away from the social housing scheme I grew up in. The house belongs to Kay Ullrich, the SNP candidate for the constituency I live in. I am awkward, bookish and painfully shy. And yet here I am, about to ring the doorbell of a woman I know only by reputation and offer to help in her bid to become a Member of Parliament. I don't yet realize it but in this moment the course of my life will be set. Everything that has gone before has been leading me here.

———

I was born on 19 July 1970 at sixteen minutes past three in the afternoon at Ayrshire Central Hospital in Irvine. My mum, Joan Kerr Ferguson, was a dental nurse, though she had given up work to have me. My dad, Robert (Robin) Sturgeon, was an electrician.

They named me Nicola, having changed their minds at the last minute from Stephanie. With no offence to the Stephanies of this world, that was a lucky escape. The alliteration would have been a mouthful. I was given Ferguson, my mum's maiden name, as my middle name.

I was born into a world in transition, at the dawn of a new decade. Paul McCartney was leaving the Beatles. The Swinging Sixties were giving way to glam rock. The British Commonwealth Games were happening in Edinburgh. Across the pond, Richard Nixon was in the White House, not yet embroiled in the Watergate scandal, but with anti-Vietnam war protests raging around him. In the UK, a General Election just a month earlier had seen the Tories oust Labour and Ted Heath replace Harold Wilson as Prime Minister.

Economic conditions then were similar to those in the final year of my time as First Minister. High oil prices were driving up inflation. Cost-of-living pressures, stagnant wages and the looming spectre of deindustrialization had sparked significant unrest. In the 1970s, which culminated in the 'winter of discontent', more working days were lost to strikes than in any other decade since the Second World War.

My arrival in the world, though unnoticed by anyone outside my family, wasn't drama-free. My mum, not quite eighteen when I was born, was in labour for more than twenty-four hours and became seriously ill as I was delivered. Two bouts of rheumatic fever in her childhood had left her with a damaged heart valve, so there was panic and alarm when her blood pressure suddenly dropped and she went into cardiac arrest. She recovered, thankfully, but didn't get to see or hold me until I was more than a day old.

Home in those days, when we eventually made it there, was modest: the attic of a cottage in Prestwick belonging to my mum's aunt Jean. We stayed there for the best part of two years while waiting to secure a home of our own. That turned out to be our flat in Dreghorn.

Dreghorn is a former mining village, a couple of miles east of Irvine, one of Ayrshire's biggest towns, situated on the coast of the Firth of Clyde, about twenty-six miles south of Glasgow. Both Dreghorn and Irvine are steeped in history. Irvine was one of the earliest Scottish capitals. It was designated a Royal Burgh in the late fourteenth century by King Robert II, the grandson of Robert the Bruce, who had led the Scottish troops to victory at the Battle of Bannockburn during the First War of Scottish Independence.

Dreghorn is even more historic. The site of a significant neolithic settlement, possibly dating as far back as 3500 BC, it is thought to be Britain's oldest continuously inhabited village. It was the birthplace of John Boyd Dunlop, the inventor of the pneumatic tyre. The Dunlop Hall in the village was the venue for a few of my childhood activities, including a short-lived and not very successful spell of ballroom dancing.

By the time I was born, Dreghorn was part of Irvine New Town. Irvine was the last of Scotland's five new towns to be established and the only one situated on the coast. Many of my friends at school were from families who had migrated from the tenements of Glasgow. In the early part of the 1970s, the town underwent substantial regeneration, most notably with a new shopping mall and leisure centre. The Magnum Leisure Centre, since demolished, was the first of its kind in Scotland. People came from far and wide to visit it. It would later be the epicentre of my cultural universe.

———

The world I inhabited as a child was small and tight-knit.

At its heart was Broomlands Road. A blend of pebble-dashed flats and terraced houses, it was built by the Scottish Special Housing Association in the 1960s. Our flat at number 56 was on the upper floor of a two-storey block. Along the landing lived Auntie Bunty and Uncle Dave (no relation). It was from Uncle Dave that I first learned about death. He was thrown from a horse and killed during the annual Laminar Day celebrations in his home-town of Lanark. I was around six and still remember being utterly dumbfounded by the fact that I would never see him again.

Downstairs was Aunt Pat (also no relation) and her daughters Karen, around a year older than me, and Debbie, a year younger. Karen and Debbie were my best friends growing up. When we weren't playing in each other's bedrooms, we would be 'out the back', running around a paved yard where our mums hung up the washing and sat outside for coffee on those rare Ayrshire sunny days, or on the oblong patch of grass in front of the flats.

We lived there until I was eight, when we moved up the road to a terraced house with front and back door and a garden. A quirk of the door numbering meant that, although we moved half a street away, the change in our address was slight: 56 to 55 Broomlands Road. By the time of the move we were a family of four, with my wee sister, Gillian, arriving on the scene just before I turned five.

My upbringing was loving, and quite traditional for the time. I could not have wished for a better mum and dad. For most of my childhood, my mum was a stay-at-home parent. Later, when I was a teenager, she worked as a cashier in a petrol station and then as an NHS laboratory assistant. Much later still, she would be elected as a local councillor and serve as the Provost of North Ayrshire. My dad worked for a burglar-alarm company, which involved him being 'on call' every two or three weeks. He would regularly have to drag himself out of bed in the middle of the night to reset an alarm that had gone off.

I would frequently wake up when the phone rang and lie with my heart in my mouth, waiting to hear him tell my mum where he had been called out to. If it was somewhere close by, like Irvine or Kilwinning, I could go back to sleep. My childish logic dictated that nothing bad could happen to him on short distances. But when he was headed to one of the further-flung parts of his beat, places like Dumfries, Newton Stewart or Port Glasgow, I would convince myself that disaster was about to strike. Then, I would stay awake until I heard his car pull up again hours later.

An upside of my dad's job was that we always had a car. I loved our regular family excursions, especially shopping trips to Ayr, which in those days was the retail metropolis of Ayrshire. One of my earliest memories is from one of these trips. Aged about four, I was obsessed with the entertainer Cilla Black. I loved her. The Liverpudlian accent, her singing, the bright red hair. I used to plead to stay up to watch *Cilla*, her Saturday night TV show. In Ayr with my mum and dad one Saturday, I had a tantrum in the department store because I spotted a picture of Cilla, on the cover of her latest album. I wanted my parents to buy it for me but they said no. When we met up with my paternal grandparents later, my grandad, wrapped firmly around my finger, took me straight back to the shop to buy the record. I still have it.

My maternal grandparents, Marjory (née McWilliam) and Kerr Ferguson, lived in Prestwick, where my mum was born. They were 'Mum' (I'll keep her in quote marks to distinguish her from Mum) and BoBo to me. The former came from me mimicking my own mum and the latter must have been some childish pronunciation of grandad or papa that just stuck. I was also close to my great-grandfather – my Papa – who also lived in Prestwick. My great-grandmother – Nana – whom my mum adored, died when I was little more than a baby. I have no real memory of her.

Golf was BoBo's passion. He was captain of the junior players at St Cuthbert Golf Club in Prestwick. I enjoyed walking across the golf course with him on the rare occasions I was allowed to. For BoBo, a golf course was hallowed ground. He came alive when he was watching or talking about golf, but otherwise I remember him as quiet and calm. He always seemed to live in the shadow of 'Mum' and her larger-than-life personality. In the final years of his life he became virtually housebound, which cruelly kept him away from the golf club and drained him of any zest for life. His death came suddenly, and shockingly, from a heart attack, when I was at the start of my second year at university. He was only in his early sixties.

In contrast to Bobo, 'Mum' was glamorous and vivacious. She had been a hairdresser in her younger days, with her own salon in Prestwick. She later worked in Hourstons, the department store in Ayr. At her best, she was exceptionally good fun to be around, and Friday nights at 'Mum' and BoBo's were often a highlight of my week.

With 'Mum', though, drama was never far away. She was volatile and had unpredictable mood swings. My mum's relationship with her was complex. Whereas 'Mum' idolized her two sons, my uncles Iain and Scott, she was often hypercritical of my mum and, at times, very harsh towards her. In retrospect, it is obvious that she suffered from poor mental health, but in those days that wasn't easily acknowledged. Though I loved her, my fierce protectiveness towards my mum resulted in my own relationship with 'Mum' being difficult, particularly as I entered my teens. Nevertheless, I was devastated when she also died young. A couple of years after BoBo's death she suffered a stroke and it was discovered then that she had bowel cancer. She died in October 1991, aged sixty-two, just a few hours after I had been formally selected as the youngest candidate in the UK for the 1992 General Election. 'Mum' didn't live to witness my political career, but I like to think she lived long enough to know the path I was on.

The bond with my paternal grandparents was even closer. Margaret (née Mill) and Rob, Gran and Grandad to me, lived in Dunure, a small fishing village about five miles south of Ayr. Like his father before him, Grandad was the gardener at the local estate house, and he and Gran lived in tied accommodation, the Croft.

My gran came from Ryhope, a coastal village just south of Sunderland, in the north-east of England. She lived in Scotland for most of her life and supported Scottish independence – I think she voted SNP before I did – but she was also fiercely proud of her roots. She passed on to me certain attitudes that would shape how I see the world. First, she believed that it doesn't matter where you come from, if you make a country your home it belongs to you just as much as to someone who traces their ancestry back generations. Second, she showed me that identity is complex and multilayered. My gran was English by birth, and proudly so, but she described herself as Scottish by choice. Crucially, she didn't feel that she had to give up one for the other. She was comfortable with both.

———

It is hard to overstate what an idyllic environment Dunure – the Croft in particular – was for a child. The Croft was a smallholding. Hens pecked around everywhere. There were cats and dogs galore, including two black Labradors named Maura and Heidi that I loved, which makes the canine fear I developed later in life even more inexplicable.

Access to the Croft was down a steep hill – the brae – from the main road leading to the village. The house felt hidden away, almost secret, and to me it was a gateway to an adventurous and exciting world. The back garden opened onto a field, and a quick run across it – dodging the cows and the cow pats – led to Dunure beach with its rockpools and hidden 'caves' underneath the rocks. I loved playing there, sometimes with Gillian and my cousins – the children of my dad's siblings, Leslie and Dorothy (also my godmother) – but more often by myself, reflecting the fact that I tended to be happiest in my own company.

If I was forced to choose my favourite place in the world, that stretch of coast, both for its rugged beauty and the special place it has in my heart, would be it. Standing on the shore, looking out at Ailsa Craig – the uninhabited island about sixteen kilometres west of the mainland, home to puffins and gannets, and from which microgranite is quarried to make curling stones – still gives me a sense of peace and tranquillity that I don't find elsewhere.

For a child, Dunure was truly magical. In my primary-school years, I devoured Enid Blyton's Famous Five books. In Dunure, I recreated these adventures. The Croft was my Kirrin Cottage, and I imagined that Ailsa Craig was Kirrin Island. In my mind I was George, of course, the intrepid tomboy. Dunure gave me freedom and fuelled my imagination in ways that wouldn't have been possible elsewhere.

I think it also helped instil in me the hatred of injustice that has always driven my politics. In Dunure I would tag along with my dad to the 'big house' to see Grandad at work. The gardens he tended seemed huge. I would eat strawberries and raspberries, peas from the pod and whatever else was on the go. The people who owned the estate – a family called Morton – were nice, and yet, even though I wouldn't have understood it at the time, let alone been able to articulate it, I was aware of a sense of 'them' and 'us'; that 'they' were, or certainly considered themselves to be, superior to 'us'.

They referred to my Grandad as 'Sturgeon'. Much of the garden was behind a wall, so locals or passing visitors had no access to it, which always seemed to me both unfair and a waste. The kitchen where Grandad had his cups of tea – and where I would sometimes be given an ice lolly or piece of cake – was effectively the servants' quarters. It was only after Grandad died, though, that I became aware of the depth of the inequality. I was only seven, but what happened lit something in me that shaped my outlook on life.

Because the Croft came with Grandad's job, it could be taken away if he was no longer working. Not long after Grandad died, that is exactly what happened. The Mortons decided to sell it.

My gran had lived in that house, or the original gardener's cottage just adjacent to it, for her entire married life. She brought up three children there. Grandad and his father before him had given loyal service to the Mortons for decades, and yet my gran had no security of tenure. No doubt, some of the upset I felt was on my own behalf. I was losing my magical playground. But I was deeply distressed for my gran too. We went with her to view a council house in Ayr. It was in a fairly run-down scheme and I just couldn't imagine her moving from the Croft to live there. Thankfully, she was later offered and accepted a flat in Dunure, further into the village than the Croft, on the first floor of four in a block, with a view of the sea and Ailsa Craig. She lived there, happily it seemed to me, until her death more than twenty years later.

———

The death of my grandad had shattered a world I had taken for granted. The loss of the Croft was part of that, but I think his death also marked the end of the innocent, totally trusting phase of my childhood.

He had gone, very suddenly, from being the fit, healthy, full-of-fun grandfather to someone who was always in bed. His doctor had said it was just a bad flu, and that he'd get better with rest. Except he didn't. He got thinner and weaker and eventually he was diagnosed with cancer.

I visited him in hospital shortly before he died. I didn't understand it at the time but I was being taken to say goodbye. I can see him in my mind's eye even now. Grey-skinned, frail, propped up on pillows. I remember feeling scared. I had never visited a sick person in hospital before. But he made me laugh just as he always had. He was still my grandad. This would be the last time I saw him, but something he said convinced me he was going to be fine. I still remember his words:

'I'll be out of here soon, lass [he always called me lass], and we'll take the dogs for a walk across the field.'

He died a day or so later. He was just fifty-six years old.

I was at Karen and Debbie's, being looked after by Aunt Pat while Mum and Dad were at the hospital. I was playing with them in their bedroom when my mum arrived back. I could hear her and Aunt Pat talking in the hallway outside, and it was clear that my grandad had passed away. I was suddenly full of rage. I screamed and shouted at my mum and later my dad, accusing them of lying to me. Grandad couldn't be gone. He had told me we would take the dogs for a walk. He wouldn't have lied to me.

After this, I was always more questioning of what adults told me.

———

What I loved most as a child was reading. Whereas Karen, Debbie and my sister Gillian were girly girls who liked playing with dolls, I was a tomboy. Dolls bored me and I was much happier with my nose in a book. My mum tells a story of me crawling under the dining table with a book at my fifth birthday party while my friends played games. The book, so I am told, was an Enid Blyton Brer Rabbit story.

My fascination with words started even before I went to school. My parents got the *Daily Record*, the paper of choice in those days for left-leaning working-class Scots. Every morning at the breakfast bar in our kitchen, I would point to words in the headlines and ask my mum and dad what they were. By about age four, I could decipher basic sentences. What confused me most were words like 'some' and 'done' – I knew what they were but couldn't grasp why they had an 'e' at the end. The *Daily Record*'s role in helping me learn to read, and the fact that in later years my Uncle Iain – one of my mum's brothers – would become its assistant editor, meant that, even when it openly backed Labour or encouraged Scotland to vote No in 2014, I still had a soft spot for it.

I was desperate to go to school. One day just before I started primary one, I was sitting with Karen on the concrete steps leading from her flat to ours. With all the wisdom of someone about to enter primary two, she told me sternly that once I was at school, I'd only get to play outdoors for fifteen minutes a day. She was probably trying to scare me, but I recall thinking that fifteen minutes to play was OK, because I'd be learning to read for the rest of the time.

Enid Blyton was an early favourite, not just the Famous Five but also the Secret Seven and later Mallory Towers and St Clare's, both lesser known series set in boarding schools. On rainy days or if I was off school ill, I would crawl behind the living-room couch or hide under my blankets and lose myself in a story. My favourite place to visit was the local library in Irvine.

Reading was everything to me, yet somewhere along the line I started to play it down. I worried that people would think spending hours with my head in a book was a bit weird or not a proper use of my time. I wanted to fit in with other kids but, no matter how hard I tried, I always felt different, a bit apart, and I think others could sense this. As a result, I was occasionally bullied at primary school.

There were some girls in my class, dominant personalities, who would swing repeatedly from being best friends with each other to sworn enemies and back again. Inevitably, and always against my better judgement, I would become a vocal protagonist in their battles. Partly this is because I am, by nature, loyal to the causes I choose. But I think it was also because the girls sensed my desire to be accepted and exploited it by pushing me forward to do their dirty work. When they became bosom buddies again, they would decide it had all been my fault and gang up against me.

On two occasions, both etched in my memory, this led to me being physically assaulted – 'battered' in Dreghorn parlance. Both times, at the end of the school day, they followed me down Dreghorn Main Street, taunting me all the way with what was about to happen and then, just before I was due to turn into my street, one of the girls, who was tall, heavyset, and who weighed much more than me, jumped on my back and pummelled me with kicks and punches. The first time it happened, I kept it from my mum and dad, but the second time, one of my other classmates ran to get them. My parents then complained to the school and the girl got into trouble. Even though I wanted the bullying to stop, I remember being mortified that my mum and dad had got involved.

These experiences had a big impact on me. Not surprisingly, they instilled a visceral dislike of bullies, and a deep disdain for those who abuse the power they have over others. They also brought out in me a natural affinity for the underdog. In any setting or group of people, I'm instinctively drawn to anyone who might be struggling to fit in.

———

From as far back as I can recall, I didn't just have an ambition to go to university but, rather, a certainty that I would do so. No one else in the history of my family had ever studied for a degree, so it is hard to know where that came from. In fact, back then I was a walking contradiction. Alongside shyness, a crippling lack of confidence and a dreadful fear of failure, was a burning ambition, a drive to succeed, a craving to be 'seen'. I had – at risk of sounding daft – a very strong sense of 'destiny'; a feeling that whatever I did in life would not be 'ordinary', that it would attract attention. I occasionally flirted with the idea of journalism as a career – no doubt my Uncle Iain's influence   but this never took hold. In those days, politics wasn't on my radar screen at all.

I had decided that I wanted either to write books like Enid Blyton or be a lawyer. The first of those ambitions was understandable for a kid who rarely had her nose out of a book, but the second was a mystery. When I first articulated it, while still at primary school, I wouldn't even have known what a lawyer did.

In a kind of vicious circle, the strength of my ambition accentuated my fear of failure. As a result, I became ever more determined. I was focused and single-minded. By the time I came to sit exams in secondary school I was an obsessive studier, convinced that if I took an evening off I would be courting disaster.

Although my mum and dad instilled in me the belief that I could do anything I set my mind to – the greatest gift they ever gave me – they never put pressure on me. The pressure came from within. Partly it was fear of letting my parents down. They were young when I was born so I was aware of how much they had sacrificed for me. For my mum in particular, a clever woman who went on to achieve amazing things, having me must have seemed like a full stop to any career ambitions she had. I always felt that I was the custodian of her hopes and dreams as well as my own. I felt a weight of responsibility to succeed, to live up to expectations. To make my mum and dad proud. It was this sense of responsibility I carried with me to secondary school.

———

Greenwood Academy was a metropolis compared to Dreghorn Primary. The two schools bookended the village, the primary at the top and Greenwood at the bottom, on the road out towards Irvine. Greenwood had a roll of over a thousand, taking in pupils from various different primary schools: kids from Dreghorn, neighbouring Springside, the adjacent 'New Town' housing estate of Bourtreehill, and Irvine.

This was the era before induction days. My first day there – in August 1982 – was the first time I had been in the 'big school'. The original buildings have since been demolished, but back then the campus consisted of a trio of three-storey blocks, connected by glass-sided air bridges, with another two stand-alone blocks housing the gym – not my favourite place – assembly hall and music rooms.

Like most kids my age, I had been nervous about going. Rumours abounded of weird initiation rituals, but these scare stories were unfounded. More seriously, I felt that the stakes were high. I firmly believed that how I performed at Greenwood would determine my entire future. As I saw it, secondary school was the next stage in a learning journey that would take me all the way to Glasgow University. I enjoyed the variety of different subjects on offer. I loved English classes in particular. Suddenly my reading habit was being channelled in new and exciting directions.

First I became immersed in Jane Austen and the Brontës. Then, Robert Louis Stevenson, and a bit later Sir Walter Scott and especially Lewis Grassic Gibbon, would open my mind, and heart, to the world of Scottish literature. I read *Docherty* and *Laidlaw*, the seminal novels of William McIlvanney, widely regarded as the father of the Scottish crime fiction tradition known as 'Tartan Noir'. Willie's books resonated profoundly with me – these were stories set in a world I knew, the west of Scotland, told by working-class protagonists whose backgrounds and lives, and ways of speaking, were similar to mine. A few years before I started there, Willie had taught English at Greenwood. I've always regretted that my time at the school didn't overlap with his, even briefly.

As well as English, I enjoyed Latin, a subject that was still compulsory for an aspiring law student. I wasn't much good at putting Latin sentences together and only barely understood the grammar, but I loved what it taught me about the English language. It fed the fascination I had for the meaning and origin of words and, looking back, I think it might also have helped me understand the power of language to shape and move a public mood.

Not surprisingly, given the direction of my life, I also loved

Modern Studies, which is a subject in the Scottish curriculum about politics and current affairs. My teacher in those classes – Roy Kelso – encouraged me academically and was one of the few people who didn't treat my growing interest in politics, especially the SNP part, as a bit weird.

All in all, I enjoyed Greenwood. I was challenged academically in a way that I hadn't been in my final couple of years at primary school, where I had become a bit bored and disengaged. I'm a strong advocate of the comprehensive model of education, but the risk that it becomes a 'lowest common denominator' form of teaching must always be guarded against.

Being at secondary school reignited my enthusiasm for learning, but it also revealed something that discomfited me for a while. I was clever but not a genius. In my first couple of years at Greenwood I did well enough but wasn't topping the class as I had done so easily at primary school. And it gnawed away at me, triggering my ever-present fear of failure. Maybe even dreaming of university made me an imposter.

My response was to become obsessive about studying. Unhealthily so. I spent hours hunched over a desk in my tiny bedroom. Academically, at least, the determination paid off. In the latter half of my time at Greenwood I dominated the annual school prize-giving ceremonies. One of my most cherished possessions is a copy of Lewis Grassic Gibbon's *A Scots Quair*, the trilogy that my favourite book, *Sunset Song*, forms part of. It has a label on the inside cover that reads 'Presented to Nicola Sturgeon – 1st in Modern Studies, 1st in Latin, 1st in English'. Being handed a Nobel Prize wouldn't have made me any happier.

And so began the story of my life. I made up for what I lacked in ability, or confidence, with sheer determination. The need to beat the wee voice in my head telling me I might not be good enough drove me on. By working harder, I outperformed, whether at school, university, or in politics, many contemporaries whose natural abilities and talents were no less, and in many cases much greater, than my own. But the older I've got, the more I've wondered if the price I paid, the opportunities I sacrificed, such as having children, was higher than it would have been if my background or temperament had been different. In short, if I had been more confident.

It is also striking that I was one of only a few of my naturally bright, clever, creative classmates to make it to university. Overall, while we were encouraged by the school to strive for success, there was a sense that it should be within the parameters of our own environment and experiences. There was too little drive to make us reach for a world beyond our horizons.

When I told the careers adviser at school that I wanted to be a lawyer, she looked at me as if I wanted to go to the moon. For schools like mine, it seemed like the job wasn't to raise our aspirations to meet our abilities – it was to lower them to fit our backgrounds. When I later became First Minister, it was important to me that young people from the least well-off parts of Scotland were properly represented in our universities. Getting a degree is not for everyone, nor is it the only path to success, but a young person's opportunity to access a university education should be based on brain power not background.

————

My obsession with studying meant that I sometimes struggled to fit in at Greenwood. However, I found myself becoming gradually less bothered by that. I was even learning to embrace the fact that I was a bit different and to use that to give myself an air of mystery. I had plenty of friends, but spending time with them was less of a priority for me as the months and years passed. My 'best friend' for the first couple of years at Greenwood was a girl called Shelley, who had been in my class at primary school. Back then, 'best friend' was a serious designation, not to be thrown about lightly. It could be taken away as well as conferred. Shelley was lovely. We spent a lot of time together, regularly staying overnight at each other's houses. We were obsessed with the musical television series *Fame*, and so, naturally, fluorescent legwarmers were a staple part of our attire.

But I would increasingly make excuses to go straight home after school, rather than hang out with Shelley, so that I could spend the evenings studying. I still remember the day she 'broke up' with me, telling me that she thought we should no longer be best friends. I was upset, but I think I was more relieved than sad. It meant I would no longer have to make excuses for not spending time with her.

There were other girls that I hung about with over the years, but the one I became closest to was Allison. She lived in what we called the 'Wimpeys', the private housing estate next to our street. She was ferociously clever, much cleverer than me, and very serious. Like me, she was an outsider, a bit of a misfit, so we were naturally drawn to each other. She was one of the few people in my younger years with whom I felt able to be myself. Like me, she wasn't one of the 'cool' kids. With her, I didn't need to make excuses to spend evenings studying.

Boys also featured in this phase of my life. From the end of first year through to about fourth year, between the ages of about thirteen and sixteen, I had an on/off boyfriend called Colin, who had been in my class at primary school. His nickname was Sparky (he wasn't an aspiring electrician).

Sparky wasn't the first boy I kissed, but he was the first who mattered. I adored Sparky. He was beautiful in a very classical sense, with crewcut blond hair, deep blue eyes, chiselled cheek-bones and a perfectly shaped mouth. Why he was my boyfriend was always a bit of a mystery, as all the girls fancied him. I suspect the 'off' phases happened when the mystery confounded him too. During the three or four on/off cycles we went through, it was always him who broke it off. I was always devastated. Hearts are fragile at that age and he definitely broke mine. Thankfully, they also heal easily.

The final time he broke it off, I think he realized I was on a different path, heading towards university and starting to be inter-ested in politics. Our relationship had also been developing physically and was reaching a point I wasn't yet comfortable with. To be frank, I was scared. The thought of teenage pregnancy terrified me.

So, Sparky and I came to an end. I always attached more importance to our romance than he did, as perhaps girls tend to at that age, but it's not impossible that in different circumstances we would have ended up together. Whether we would have lasted is another matter.

———

People often assume I must have had a political upbringing. Nothing could be further from the truth. Politics rarely, if ever, featured in our house. It just wasn't a topic of conversation.

I only really have one memory of hearing my mum and dad talk about what I would later understand to be politics. One morning at breakfast they were animated by what was on the radio. My memory of the disappointed, dejected, angry mood in the room is more vivid than the actual conversation. Later, when I joined the SNP, I realized that this was the morning after the 1979 devolution referendum.

The outcome of 1 March 1979 was momentous. It shaped Scotland, indeed the whole of the UK, and the SNP for many years after. Even though I don't remember it directly, it also influenced the direction of my life. The referendum in 1979 asked the people of Scotland if they wanted a devolved Scottish Assembly – essentially a parliament with very limited powers, significantly less than our current Parliament has. The result was 51.6% in favour and 48.4% against. By any normal standard of democracy those in favour of devolution had won and a Scottish Assembly should have been established. But, as far as Scotland is concerned, Westminster rarely plays fair. Thanks to an amendment tabled by a Labour MP called George Cunningham – born in Scotland but representing Islington – the Act of Parliament paving the way for the referendum contained a poison pill. By virtue of what was known as the 40% rule, it wasn't enough for more than 50% of those who cast a ballot to vote Yes. Those voting Yes also had to represent at least 40% of the total registered electorate. It meant that those who didn't vote were treated as if they'd voted No. It was gerrymandering, plain and simple.

The effect of this on the Scottish psyche – even on those of us too young to participate or understand – is hard to overstate. It's always been part of the Scottish national character – or, at least, the caricature of it – that we talk the talk much better than we walk the walk. We are full of bravado but, when push comes to shove, lack the gumption to follow through. When we find ourselves on the brink of victory, we will usually find a way to engineer defeat, often by turning on each other. It's an age-old story, and not just told by others. We tell it about ourselves too. It is internalized. It flows from, and in turn feeds, a chronic lack of national confidence. No doubt the roots of it lie on the military and political battlefields of history, but it also stems from a sort of 'infantilism' that comes from being a small country governed by a much larger neighbour. There were signs after the establishment of the Scottish Parliament in 1999 and, more so, in the wake of the 2014 independence referendum that we had shaken it off, though it has started to rear its head again. However, no matter its origins or current status, the outcome of the 1979 referendum reinforced it. It didn't help that the referendum was the second in a double whammy of knocks to our national confidence around that time. I remember the first one, the 1978 football World Cup, much more clearly than I do the referendum.

On the path to the finals in Argentina, our national bravado had run away with itself. England had failed to qualify, so the bragging started early. The team manager at the time and also my dad's hero, Ally MacLeod, convinced everyone that Scotland would lift the trophy. Thirty thousand people turned up to wave the team off from Hampden stadium. My dad took me to see the squad bus pass on the way to the airport. Earlier that summer, we had gone on holiday to Ryhope, to stay with my 'English cousins'. I thought it was very funny to prance around singing our World Cup song 'Ally's Tartan Army', which included the immortal line 'England cannae dae it cos they didnae qualify'. Scotland had been on a good run. There were some genuine world-class players in the team, such as Kenny Dalglish. And there were exciting moments along the way; Archie Gemmill's goal against Holland is possibly the finest moment in Scottish football history. But still we crashed out in the first round, mired in scandal and recrimination. The national curse had struck.

I'm telling this story not out of any great love of football, but instead to demonstrate that the national mood going into the referendum wasn't good. But the outcome and what followed from it knocked the stuffing out of the country for a long time. It's not really fair to say, on this occasion, that defeat had been snatched from the jaws of victory – defeat had been baked in by the wrecking ball of the 40% rule. But, even so, the inability to resist or overcome it felt like a failure to those who wanted self-government. The defeat set the scene for the next two decades in Scottish politics. It also created the conditions that made me a political activist.

The SNP blamed Labour for the referendum debacle, both for the insertion of the 40% rule and for refusing to override it in the aftermath of the vote. This led to a politically stupid decision to table a vote of no-confidence in Jim Callaghan's limping Labour government. The Conservative opposition led by Margaret Thatcher quickly got behind the no-confidence move, and a vote was held on 28 March 1979. The government lost it by a margin of just one, with all eleven SNP MPs voting with the Tories against Labour.

It was an extraordinary act of self-harm that the SNP didn't properly recover from for the best part of thirty years. The fact that the Callaghan government was on its last legs made no differ-ence. By tabling and voting for a no-confidence motion, the SNP ensured that a big chunk of the 'blame' for Thatcher's election would be directed at it. The generation of SNP candidates that I became part of, most of us at school in 1979, were still being taunted with the 'Tartan Tory' tag twenty years later.

So, the breakfast table conversation between my parents on the morning of 2 March 1979 may only be vaguely remembered and, at the time, not even vaguely understood by me, but in many ways it formed the backdrop to my early life in politics.

––––

When Margaret Thatcher became Prime Minister in 1979, I remember being pleased that a woman had got the job. The fact her election registered with me at all speaks to the power of representation: the importance of seeing people like us, in this case female, occupy positions of influence and seniority. She might not have set out to do it, and having broken the glass ceiling she certainly did her best to reassemble it, but she also made it possible for girls like me to believe that politics wasn't just for men.

It no doubt helped that she also seemed strong, more than a match for the men around her. Another of my early political memories is the Falklands War. I was terrified that my dad would be called up to fight. That's what I understood 'war' to mean. But it stirred feelings of patriotism too. I vividly remember the TV images of the British Task Force ships leaving Portsmouth, with Union Jacks flying everywhere. I felt certain, and proud, that Britain was the good guy. Who the bad guys were and why we were fighting them I was less clear about, but I had no doubt that Mrs Thatcher would sort them out.

It wouldn't take long for my view of the Prime Minister to harden; for Mrs Thatcher to become 'Maggie', then 'Thatcher' and then just 'that woman'. In parallel, my vague political awareness would turn into active interest and then action. The next time I remember feeling the kind of tribalism I first experienced over the Falklands War was during the miners' strike. This time, I was definitely not on the same side as Margaret Thatcher.

It is not an exaggeration to say that my life in politics was, to a very large extent, motivated and shaped by Margaret Thatcher. The only time in my political career that I properly lost my cool in a TV debate – during the snap 2017 General Election – was when the then leader of the Scottish Labour Party, Kezia Dugdale, claimed that Scotland was starting to feel the same way about me as it had about Thatcher; that when people referred to 'that woman', they were now often talking about me. I saw red and in a moment of madness made what was probably my biggest ever misjudgement in a TV debate. But more of that later.

When I look back now with the wisdom of adulthood (the young me would be screaming 'sell-out' at this point), it is obvious that some of the economic turmoil of the 1980s was unavoidable. Inflation was sky-high, productivity painfully low. Manufacturing and heavy industry in the UK were ruinously uncompetitive. The process of deindustrialization then, just like decarbonization today, was inevitable. But that didn't make the impact of Thatcherism any less painful or alienating. Change might have been inescapable, but the way she went about it was not. That came at a massive human cost.

As I entered my teenage years, unemployment was soaring across the UK, and higher in Scotland than in England. The way the figures were counted and reported had been changed in the early days of the Tory government – in other words, they were fiddled – so the official count was massively underestimated. In Scotland by the mid-1980s it was nudging 15%, and the real figure, based on the old, more accurate, method was closer to 20%. It was even higher in the industrialized central belt where I grew up, reflecting the massacre of manufacturing jobs. At the peak, it was estimated that more than 400,000 people in Scotland were out of work, the highest number since the 1930s. It was brutal.

Back then, I wouldn't have been able to cite these statistics, but I understood the human impact. I was surrounded by it. Behind the numbers were neighbours, friends of my mum and dad, the parents of my own friends, kids in the years above me at school with little or no prospect of getting jobs when they left. There was a sense of hopelessness about the future. A desire to escape was certainly one of the factors driving my ambition to go to university.

My dad never lost his job. But I remember being terrified that he would. There was a sense back then that unemployment was terminal, not temporary. My friends and I firmly believed that if our dads lost their jobs it was likely that they would never work again.

The rights and wrongs of Thatcherism have been debated for years and will continue to be, I am sure, for decades to come. But that it took a massive human toll and that she didn't seem to care is beyond dispute. Communities like the one I grew up in are still suffering problems today that can be traced back to those days.

When I was growing up, strikes were commonplace. But it is the 1984 miners' strike that is most vivid in my memory, partly because of a confrontation close to home. Hunterston Terminal was a bit further up the Ayrshire coast from Irvine, en route to Largs, a popular seaside town where relatives of my mum lived. Coal was being shipped into Hunterston from overseas to undermine the strike. A huge picket of miners tried to stop the coal getting out. They were massively outnumbered by police. Violence broke out, many miners were injured and dozens of arrests were made. The lorries carrying the coal made it out.

I was only fourteen but I knew what side I was on. To me, it was David versus Goliath, the working class fighting for their jobs against a heartless government.

A couple of years earlier, my dad had gone on strike himself. Back then he was a member of the electricians' union, which in later years would become part of Unite. A pay dispute at his company, Chubb Alarms, resulted in a strike that the workers thought would last just a few days before the company would be forced to fold, given the nature of the alarm services it provided. In fact, the strike lasted six weeks. In one visit to my gran's, I remember my mum breaking down in tears, saying that she didn't know how she was going to put food on the table if it went on much longer. I didn't fully appreciate at the time just how difficult it was, but I did feel the impact. For the duration of the strike, my dad had to hand back his work car. Suddenly it wasn't so easy to get around.

I learned that people rarely go on strike on a whim. It comes with a heavy cost: emotional, practical and, of course, financial. That meant that whenever I was faced with the prospect of public sector strikes, occasionally as Health Secretary but more often as First Minister, my instinct was always to get round the table to negotiate and thrash out a deal, rather than to play the hardball game and wait to see who would blink first.

Paradoxically, many of the same people who were going on strike back then and generally railing against the Tories were also taking advantage of some of Thatcher's signature policies, like the privatizations and sell-offs designed to extend share and home ownership. For a whole generation, 'Tell Sid', the line in the advert promoting shares in the newly privatized British Gas, became the catchphrase of our time. For a while, one of the most common sights around our housing scheme was of the identikit wooden front doors installed by social landlords being replaced by fancy new PVC versions, proof that the family behind the door had taken advantage of Thatcher's Right to Buy. My mum and dad never bought shares, but they did buy our house at 55 Broomlands Road.

When I was the Scottish government minister with responsibility for housing, I ended the Right to Buy in Scotland and was accused of hypocrisy. It was an easy attack to make, but it was wide of the mark. For one thing, I wasn't responsible for the decision my parents took. But more to the point, who could blame them? Working-class families, no matter how aspirational they are or how hard they work, rarely get to access the ownership and wealth which society conditions us to equate with success. It was hardly surprising that people like my mum and dad would take advantage of such opportunities. The depletion of the social housing stock, and the rise in homelessness as a result, wasn't the fault of those buying their homes. It was the fault of a government that didn't care enough to replace the houses sold off. The policy was deeply cynical, more about trying to create a new generation of Tory voters than spreading wealth and opportunity for the greater good. It was callous too. Many who bought their homes at a discount under Right to Buy then found out the hard way that they couldn't afford to maintain them when interest rates went up or they lost their job or were hit by an unexpected repair bill. Thatcher couldn't have cared less.

It was all of this – sky-high unemployment, rising poverty, industrial unrest, lack of hope for the future, a clash of values, along with a sense of righteous teenage rage – that drove me into the world of politics.

———

Which brings me back to the doorstep of the detached house in the cul-de-sac in May 1987.

I had joined the SNP a few months earlier. After watching a party political broadcast fronted by the then SNP leader, Gordon Wilson, I phoned the number that flashed up on the screen. As I later became more immersed in the party, these digits – 031 226 3661 – would become as familiar to me as my home phone number.

I am convinced that the person who answered the phone that night was John Swinney. John went on to lead the SNP from 2000 until 2004. He later served as my Deputy First Minister and, of course, became First Minister himself in May 2024. It is certainly possible that it was him on the other end of the line. One of the tasks of the Young Scottish Nationalists at the time was to field calls in party HQ after these broadcasts. Even if I can't be 100% sure, I like to think it was so.

Though it might have been assumed in those days that a budding socialist firebrand would have seen Labour, not the SNP, as her natural political home, it was exactly what my then English teacher, a local Labour councillor, did assume. Aware of my growing political interest, he presented me one day with the form to join Labour. I don't think it crossed his mind that another party might have been in the running. What I saw as his arrogant assumption enraged me and pushed me towards the SNP. In truth, though, it was the path I was already on.

Gordon Wilson was a solicitor by profession, very middle-class, socially conservative, a member of the Free Church of Scotland, with an austere, quite dour persona. Gordon wasn't the type of politician or person I would naturally have identified with. Moreover, while I was growing up in the industrial central belt of Scotland, with a socialist outlook driving my political interest, the base of the party was very much in the north-east of the country, where fishing and farming interests predominated. I still remember our next-door neighbour in Broomlands Road, a gruff man called Davie Watters, ranting about bloody Tartan Tories whenever the SNP was mentioned.

Looking back, the Tartan Tory tag wasn't entirely unfair, and it wasn't just the 1979 confidence vote in the Callaghan government that justified it. Historically, the SNP had never adopted a firm position on either the left or right of politics. It simply supported independence. Its members, including its leaderships, spanned the ideological spectrum. That started to change in the mid-1970s when a younger generation tried to move the party decisively to the left, rightly calculating that it was the only credible position in Scotland from which to challenge the Tories, compete with Labour and paint a picture of what an independent Scotland might be like. This caused major tensions. These came to a head at the 1982 party conference in Ayr. A faction within the SNP – the 79 Group – which had been set up to move the party leftwards was prohibited. Key members, including a young activist called Alex Salmond, were expelled.

However, for all that the SNP, certainly in my part of the world, was seen back then as a bit of an irrelevance, an oddity even, and to the political right of Labour, the reality was fast changing. By 1986, as I was starting to think about joining, the SNP was increasingly defining itself as a social democratic project, firmly of the centre left. The 79 Groupers who had been expelled in the early eighties were back in the party and in the ascendancy. Alex Salmond was a rapidly rising star and would soon become an MP and deputy leader.

Labour was going in the opposite direction. Neil Kinnock had embarked on the process of 'modernizing' Labour, moving it away from the policies of Michael Foot and onto the centre ground. An issue that really stirred the ire of sixteen-year-old me was nuclear weapons. The river Clyde was home to Polaris and later Trident. The USA's European-based nuclear weapons were also sited on the Clyde, at its naval base on the Holy Loch, part of the Cowal peninsula next to the seaside town of Dunoon. CND, the Campaign for Nuclear Disarmament, was therefore highly active in Scotland. I had signed up as a member at one of their stalls in the Mall shopping centre in Irvine sometime before joining the SNP. To me, it seemed simple that weapons capable of wiping out swathes of civilization at the press of a button were morally indefensible. Even though Kinnock didn't abandon a position of unilateral disarmament until after the 1987 election, the signs were there. For the SNP, by contrast, there was probably no issue other than independence more core to its identity than opposition to nuclear weapons.

So, it was these trajectories, the SNP leftwards, Labour rightwards, that made the SNP a much more obvious choice for a young person of my background and opinions than it might have been in years past.

But it was independence that clinched the deal. What enraged me even more than Thatcher's policies was that she was imposing them on Scotland with no democratic authority. Back then, Scotland wasn't yet the Tory-free zone it would later become. Even Ayrshire wasn't Tory free. Although in Cunninghame South, the constituency I lived in, the joke was that the vote for Labour's David Lambie was weighed rather than counted, the neighbouring Cunninghame North was held by the Tories until 1987. Thatcher's Secretary of State for Scotland until early 1986, George Younger, represented Ayr, a seat held by the Tories until their Scottish wipeout in 1997. But the Tories in Scotland were a shrinking minority. At the election in 1983, they won just 21 of Scotland's 72 seats on less than 30% of the vote. Yet they were inflicting huge social and economic carnage on Scotland. The democratic deficit was glaring. Labour was utterly impotent: they had won 41 of Scotland's 72 seats in 1983 and yet they could do nothing to protect Scotland from Margaret Thatcher.

Even if I had agreed with Labour on everything, I would have seen no point in supporting the party. Everyone in Scotland could vote Labour, but if enough people in England voted Tory, it would make no difference. We'd be outvoted. That was the democratic deficit in a nutshell and, while it was ameliorated to some extent by the advent of the Scottish Parliament, it still afflicts Scotland today. It was clear to me then that the only way for Scotland to guarantee governments of our own choosing was to be independent. Even at seventeen years old, I knew that I wanted to be part of winning my country's independence.

———

So I mustered the courage to get myself to Kay's.

There I was, dressed for the part, a tactic to exude a confidence I didn't feel. The armour that in future would be sharp suits and high heels was, back then, jeans, Dr Martens and a donkey jacket with a carefully positioned CND badge on the lapel: the uniform of the 1980s anti-Tory student activist.

As I stood on the doorstep, all the symptoms of a panic attack were brewing within me – racing heart, sweaty palms, dry mouth. Would I press the bell or turn and run home?

I pressed the doorbell. Suddenly the force of nature that was Kay Ullrich appeared before me, hair all bouffant, perfume fumes several steps ahead of her and the cigarette that I would quickly learn was ever-present smouldering in her right hand.

Kay was the SNP candidate for the Cunninghame South constituency. Her daughter, Shelley Jofre, was the year above me in school. She was one of the cool kids, so not part of any gang I would have been admitted to. Kay I knew only by reputation, from photographs on election leaflets or occasional sightings around the village. She was flamboyant and glamorous. She even looked a bit like Joan Collins. I couldn't have been any more star-struck if the President of the USA himself had opened the door.

I don't remember what I said. She would later claim that it was 'Hello, Mrs Ullrich. My name is Nicola Sturgeon and I'd like to help your campaign', which seems plausible, not least in its brevity and banality. What I do remember is her ushering me into the house and introducing me to her 'agent', reinforcing the entirely misplaced sense of Hollywood glamour.

Shortly afterwards, following some not-so-gentle interrogation from 'Agent' Margaret Burgess, who ruled Cunninghame South SNP with a rod of iron, I was plonked into the passenger seat of Kay's car and off we went. Kay drove with a cigarette in one hand, a loudspeaker in the other and, at times, only her knee on the steering wheel. I was terrified. More than that, though, I was ecstatic. I was where I wanted to be, doing what I wanted to do.

CHAPTER TWO

Politics in My Blood

From the moment I pressed Kay's doorbell I didn't look back. For a long time, though, I was quiet and reserved and didn't say much. The other SNP activists I met and campaigned with intimidated me. They all seemed so knowledgeable about politics, and I was worried that if I opened my mouth I'd embarrass myself. All the political theories and strident opinions I'd been spouting at home didn't feel so smart in front of these people.

Despite my shyness, I threw myself into the campaign with an enthusiasm and excitement I'd never felt for anything before. I would go round to Kay's every night and from there we'd go out distributing leaflets and chapping doors – 'canvassing' in the political lexicon. Somehow, the girl who found it almost impossible to chat with people she knew was able to stand on the doorsteps of complete strangers and, however awkwardly, ask them to vote SNP. I was already in character, playing a part to overcome my natural introversion.

There wasn't a huge amount of love for the SNP amongst the public in those days. In Irvine, only around one in ten voters supported us. And some of those who didn't could be pretty hostile. I got chased away from more than a few doorsteps. This was when I first learned that politics, even, maybe especially, at the grassroots level, requires a thick skin. Most people were polite, though often coldly so, but if I'd been put off by the derision, mockery and sometimes nasty abuse of those who weren't, I'd never have come back after the first night.

The act of chapping someone's door to solicit their vote is a precious part of our democratic system. My advice to anyone starting out in politics now is that, no matter how sophisticated online campaigning has become, no matter how accomplished you think you are on TikTok or Instagram, it's no substitute for letting someone look you in the eye, especially if you are the person standing for election.

My favourite canvassing memory is from the 2011 Scottish Parliament election, the SNP's first landslide victory. I was campaigning for re-election in my constituency. At one door, a woman answered and proclaimed, 'Nicola, my man loves you, he's always wanted to meet you, but he's in the bath.' Before I could suggest returning later, she had pulled me into the house and ushered me towards what was obviously the bathroom door. I was briefly terrified. Thankfully, the door stayed closed, and I proceeded to have a delightful conversation with the man in the bath, accompanied by the sound of gently splashing water.

Over time I learned never to jump straight to the politics but to start the conversation on a topic personal to the person answering, noticing their garden or the colour of their front door. This would get easier with experience and confidence, and easier still once I reached the point when people recognized who I was, but in 1987 I had none of this grace or subtlety. I can't imagine what people must have thought to find a child (even at seventeen

I looked twelve) standing awkwardly, staring at her feet, barking, 'Will you be voting SNP?'

One day, we were chapping doors in a housing scheme with a very confusing layout. It was very hard to distinguish front doors from back. I went to one house and was greeted by a woman in floods of tears. It was pretty obvious that she'd sooner have stabbed herself in the eye than voted SNP, but she had also just suffered a family bereavement. She made it very clear to me that I was not welcome, so I mumbled my apologies and let her return to her grieving family. I then turned a corner to what I thought was a new street, and marched up a path, only to find out too late that I was now chapping the back door of the same bereaved household. I scurried away, expletives ringing in my ears, utterly mortified.

I doubt very much that I persuaded a single extra person to vote SNP in that election, but, even so, I loved it. By the end of the campaign, I was hooked. I'd never choose to swap the success of the SNP in more recent times for how it was back then but the thrill of finding a supporter in a street full of Labour voters was intoxicating. When it happened, I'd briefly feel like we were unbeatable, and wanted to keep going until we found the next one.

I also got my first, and definitely not my last, taste of what it is like to lose. I have come to realize that the bitter experience of losing is part of the apprenticeship of winning, but it didn't feel like it at the time. In all my teenage innocence, I thought we must have a chance of victory, after all we had right on our side. If we could just speak to enough people and lay out the evidence, they would change their minds. What I didn't understand then is that politics is not just about facts and figures. It is about sense and sentiment, tradition and tribe, perception and prejudice.

I spent election day, 11 June 1987, going around polling stations with Kay's daughter, Shelley, my yellow and black rosette pinned proudly to a hideous green denim jacket that I loved at the time. Later, I attended my first election count, at the Magnum Leisure Centre in Irvine – a bit different to Frosty's ice disco which I frequented there in my earlier teens – and encountered my first experience of Labour taunts. Labour took election success in Scotland for granted back then.

We came fourth, with 11% of the vote, up a creditable 4% since the last time. Labour got 60%, though, up by even more.

I was crushed. We went back to Kay's to watch the national results on TV. It was a mixed night for the SNP. We won three new seats, including Alex Salmond's, but lost the two we already held, including our leader Gordon Wilson's.

Labour won big in Scotland, but the Tories were elected again UK wide. While it proved something of a turning point in the long and winding home-rule journey, it was nevertheless a tough introduction to elections for me. Far from putting me off, though, it made me more determined. Campaigning for the SNP and independence was what I wanted to dedicate myself to. I had found my mission.

––––

I also made great friends.

Being the underdogs fostered a sense of camaraderie, of us against the world, that I had never experienced before. Every night after campaigning, we'd all head back to the home of a couple of local members, Matt and Louise Brown. I didn't say much, probably not more than a handful of words. I listened to the conversations and the debates and learned how broad a policy church the SNP was. Even though I quietly disagreed with some of the views being expressed, I soaked it all up.

Matt and Louise were local lawyers. Their firm, Matthew Brown

& Company, was situated just across the road from their red sand-stone, detached house, which at that time was the biggest and grandest I'd ever set foot in. Its walls were adorned with expensive artwork and a piano took pride of place in the sitting room.

As grand as the house was, it didn't intimidate me nearly as much as the Browns themselves, though I came to adore them both. They were amongst my biggest supporters throughout my career. To coin an Ayrshire phrase, Matt had a good conceit of himself, meaning he loved to hold court, pontificating on the state of the campaign and politics in general. And I loved to listen. Louise, though, was the cleverer of the two. She was also the personification of style.

At the heart of the group was Kay, our candidate. I became ever more fond of Kay as the campaign progressed. She was great fun, a definite and unashamed prima donna, and a jangle of nervous energy. She chain-smoked her way through the campaign and exuded an air of mild chaos everywhere she went. She was also a woman of substance and steel. I loved her. She died in January 2021, her funeral diminished, as so many were at that time, by Covid restrictions. As I sat in a virtually empty crematorium listening to her daughter Shelley talk movingly about her remark-able life, I remember thinking that I had lost one of the most important people in mine.

It was Margaret Burgess, Kay's election agent, who ruled the roost in the campaign. We were all terrified of Margaret. She had given me a bollocking over the front/back door grieving family incident, but underneath the harsh exterior was a heart of gold, and a very funny, clever woman.

Completing the set of the 'older' members of the group was a wonderful woman called Marion McTear, a very old-school, traditional nationalist. I knew her already as Mrs McTear because she had been the school auxiliary at Dreghorn Primary, where she used to patch up my skint knees.

The younger ones in the group, although they were still quite a bit older than me, were Marie Burns and Ricky Bell, now two of my oldest friends. Marie's roots in the SNP went back to the 79 Group, and I was in awe of her grasp of politics. Ricky seemed very confident and was good-looking. He quickly became, for me, the most important person in the group. He worked full-time in the accounts department of the company that owned one of the local papers. He had his own house and a car. He would often pick me up from school to go to party meetings and events. Being in a political party, which had made me appear weird to my friends and classmates at school, suddenly seemed cool and interesting when it involved being picked up by an older boy in his car.

———

I decided I wanted to go to the party conference which was taking place in Dundee in September 1987. I realize now how difficult this must have been for my mum and dad. I had only just turned seventeen and was going with people they barely knew to spend three days in a world that was alien to them. It is to their great credit that they didn't try to stop me. They knew how important the SNP and politics had become to me, and wanted to support me, as they always have.

It was probably also financially difficult for them. Three days away had to be paid for and they covered my accommodation and waved me off with the princely sum of £40 to pay for my food and other expenses. It was a lot of money back then but I remember worrying about having enough money all the time I was there. I quickly learned, though, that fringe meetings at party conferences, even then, were usually accompanied by free buffets. I also struck lucky one evening when we were out for dinner as, like a bad joke, my food had a dead fly in it, and the restaurant said they wouldn't charge me for it. Result.

I had the time of my life at my first conference. I felt I belonged. I soaked up the debates about devolution and independence, Europe, nuclear weapons and industrial policy. I even plucked up the courage to ask a question at a session on nuclear weapons. I was thrilled to watch as Gordon Wilson, still party leader, was being interviewed, and to encounter at the conference ceilidh the legendary Winnie Ewing, victor in the famous 1967 Hamilton by-election and by then a member of the European Parliament. She would be elected party President at that conference.

This was also the first time I saw Alex Salmond in the flesh. He had just become an MP, representing the North East seat of Banff & Buchan. At the Dundee conference, he would become deputy leader of the party. He was a rising star. He was clever, articulate, charismatic, a brilliant TV performer and, certainly compared to Gordon Wilson, left wing. He was also on the gradualist side of the party, which meant in broad terms that he thought we should embrace a devolved parliament as a stepping stone to independence. Those of a different perspective, the so-called fundamentalists, thought this was a trap, and that a devolved parliament would only blunt the appetite for independence.

On this and most issues, my views aligned closely with Alex's. Obviously, I had no conception back then of how close we would later become, of how important he would be to me, politically and personally, nor how fundamentally associated he would be with both the biggest highs and the deepest lows of my life. Also, at that point, I had never met the young man who was about to be recruited as his constituency office manager, Peter Murrell, let alone have any idea that more than twenty years later I would marry him.

At that time, it was another man on my mind. During those three days in Dundee, I realized I had feelings for Ricky, and started to think that he might also have feelings for me. I was staying with Marie, Ricky and a couple of other younger members in a cottage we had booked on the outskirts of Dundee. Marie would drive us to and from conference each day. We'd get back late at night, after the various social events, and have to navigate a muddy path from the car park to the cottage in the pitch dark. There was no lighting, and each night Ricky would take my hand, ostensibly to help guide me, but it felt like more than that. Nothing actually happened between us in Dundee but, naive and inexperienced though I was, I felt then that it was only a matter of time before it did. By early 1988, we were an item. And we stayed that way until the early 1990s.

The relationship was serious for a while. He took me on my first ever trip abroad, to Paris for my twenty-first birthday. My mum and dad, Mum especially, came to adore him. Just as I can't be precise about when the relationship started, I struggle to pinpoint when it ended. It was probably in late 1991, early 1992. We continued to see each other, drifting in and out of the romantic involvement. Our shared political activity, so important to both of us, meant that not seeing each other would have been impossible.

What was obvious was that Ricky and I were on different paths. I had gone to university; he was working full-time and would progress to a senior position in his field. And whereas at the start of our relationship he was a young rising star in the party, with me his acolyte, by the early 1990s I was suddenly being tipped for great things and talked about as a possible future leader. While he was always supportive, this started to cause some tension. A factor that I only came to understand much later, and that was more fundamental, was that Ricky is gay. He now lives in Glasgow with his husband. I danced at their wedding and could not have been happier for them. We are still the best of friends today.

———

By 1988 I was spending more and more time at SNP meetings and campaign events. I was also increasingly involved, at a national level, with the party's youth wing – known at the time as the Young Scottish Nationalists or YSN. Through that, I was getting to know people, like Fiona Hyslop, who would become lifelong friends and future government colleagues. I began to view the case for independence not just as resistance to a Tory government, but through the prism of Scotland's place in the world. In the summer of 1988, the day before my eighteenth birthday, on a hot, sunny Sunday in July, I attended my first big political demonstration, an anti-apartheid march and rally through Glasgow Green. Similar events were happening in cities across the world, to demand, on what was his seventieth birthday, the release of Nelson Mandela. I was happy. I was on a mission. I was going to change the world. I was becoming more confident and learning to overcome my shyness.

I was also just about to enter law school at Glasgow University, where I would be yanked out of my comfort zone all over again. Occasionally, I have been asked why I didn't try for Oxford or Cambridge. Putting aside the implication that Glasgow is somehow second best, it's impossible to overstate what a massive step it was for someone from my background to go to university at all. Glasgow University was at the outer limits of what I was able to imagine, and Oxbridge might as well have been on another planet.

I arrived there for Freshers' Week in September 1988, wearing a new pair of jeans, Dr Martens-style shoes, a fleece, a zip-up waterproof jacket, and carrying a rucksack. I remember my first day vividly. I had to matriculate and sign up to receive my student grant. I was part of the last generation to enjoy full-grant funding prior to the introduction of student loans a year or so later. Had grants and state-funded tuition not been available, it is highly unlikely that I would have gone to university. My parents couldn't have funded me up front and, though I did take advantage of student loans during my studies, tuition fees would definitely have been a barrier. It is because of the opportunities that free (or, rather, taxpayer-funded) education gave to me that I have always been an adamant opponent of tuition fees. My view when I was in government was that, having benefitted from free tuition myself, I had no right to pull the ladder of opportunity up behind me.

On my first day, I met Caroline Summers and Claire Mitchell, who have been close friends ever since. Caroline was from Paisley, and a year younger than me. Her mum was from Singapore, and, through her eyes, I saw the reality of racism up close for the first time in my life. Her Asian features would attract the vilest of abuse. I don't know how she kept her cool. There were occasions when I struggled to do so on her behalf, but she was dignity personified. Caroline is now a partner in a major law firm, specializing in commercial conveyancing.

Claire was from the Southside of Glasgow and also a year younger than me. She is now a leading King's Counsel and an expert in the field of human rights and public inquiries. She is one of my dearest friends and has been a tower of strength to me in some of the toughest times of my life.

Despite making friends, my first term at university was miserable. I felt small, out of place, and younger than I had in a while. My experiences in the election had given me a false sense of maturity, but here I felt intimidated by the privately educated kids who dominated our law lectures. They were all physically bigger than I was and much more confident. They seemed much cleverer too. I felt completely out of my depth and spent that first term thinking that I would drop out or be thrown out when I inevitably failed my exams. It wasn't until the end-of-term exams, just before Christmas, that things started to turn around. I passed all my exams with flying colours – and many of my privately educated classmates did not. It was a big confidence boost, though only up to a point. One of the things I have learned over the years about imposter syndrome is that success isn't a cure, it's a compounding factor. The better I did, the more of an imposter I felt, and the greater the fear of being 'found out'.

While I made forays into student politics, it is fair to say that the issues that dominated didn't seem particularly vital to me. I had a view on whether or not the university should be affiliated to the National Union of Students (it wasn't and I thought it should be), but I didn't think it mattered all that much. I had well and truly caught the bug for what I considered to be 'real-life' politics, so the primary vehicle I had for building links with other young activists was the YSN rather than the Glasgow University Student Nationalist Association or GUSNA, as it was known.

There was plenty of 'real-life' campaigning to keep me occupied in my first year at university. One of the most dramatic and conse-quential parliamentary by-elections in Scottish political history took place on 10 November 1988. There was a sense of destiny about the Govan by-election from the outset. The SNP had won the same constituency, albeit with slightly different boundaries, in a by-election almost exactly fifteen years previously. Margo MacDonald might have held the seat for only three months before Labour won it back in the February 1974 General Election, but both she and the constituency had secured icon status in SNP circles. The sense of serendipity was heightened by the fact that our candidate in the 1988 contest, Jim Sillars, was by then Margo's husband. Jim had been a Labour MP in Ayrshire and started his political career passionately opposed to home rule. But he slowly changed his beliefs, leaving Labour in 1976 to form his own breakaway Scottish Labour Party. He then abandoned that to join the SNP in 1980. Jim oozed charisma and political gravitas.

The by-election had been brought about by the decision of Bruce Millan, former Labour Secretary of State for Scotland, to become a European Commissioner. As a result, it was seen by voters as an unnecessary contest caused by an MP deserting them to further his own career. This put Labour on the back foot from the off. They also picked a candidate, a trade union official, who was not up to the rigours and scrutiny of a by-election campaign.

But it was the politics of the time that proved decisive. Scotland in late 1988 was in uproar over the poll tax. Thatcher had decided to introduce it in Scotland in April 1989, a year ahead of the rest of the UK. Adding to the sense of anger about the inherent unfairness of the tax was cold fury about Scotland being used as a guinea pig. The fury extended to the Labour Party which, despite its fifty Scottish seats, was impotent and unwilling to lead a robust campaign against it. While the SNP supported a non-payment campaign, Labour shied away, adding to the perception that it was more interested in winning power at Westminster than in standing up for Scotland.

I was out on the campaign trail almost every day. The streets I was pounding were unfamiliar to me then but, almost twenty years later, they would be part of the constituency I came to represent in the Scottish Parliament. The wonderful if intimidating woman who was organizing the campaign, Allison Hunter, would become my own election agent in battles of the future, and many of those I was campaigning with would become friends and colleagues in government.

There was a real sense of excitement and anticipation in the final few days of the campaign as momentum built towards a spectacular SNP victory. On the night of the election, I gathered with other activists outside Bellahouston Academy, where the votes were being counted. The SNP overturned a Labour majority of almost 13,000 votes to win by 3,554 votes. It was seismic, and it changed the course of Scottish politics. It forced Labour to set up the Scottish Constitutional Convention which, with further twists and turns along the way, led to the establishment of the Scottish Parliament. On that cold night in November 1988, it felt like the SNP was well and truly on the up.

———

The cross-party Constitutional Convention set up by Labour to coordinate the push for a devolved legislature divided the SNP. In what would be one of his last interventions during his leadership, Gordon Wilson proposed that the SNP should refuse to take part, and Jim Sillars backed him.

Although deputy leader at the time, Alex Salmond hadn't been consulted and was widely believed to disagree. The issue spilled over at our National Council meeting in March 1989, held in the Inverclyde town of Port Glasgow. Most of the YSN, me included, were advocating for participation in the Convention. There was a heated debate but the meeting voted by 191 votes to 41 in favour of Gordon Wilson. Crucial to the outcome was Alex's intervention. Although we knew he disagreed with the Wilson position, he argued for it, no doubt trying to avoid a leadership split. He made a very ill-judged speech in which he attacked one of the leading figures on the other side of the debate. I ended up feeling more disappointed in Alex than in Sillars. Instead of providing the leadership we had been looking for, he had taken a position that I felt to be dishonest.

The SNP did not participate in the Convention, and we were damaged as a consequence, being seen as absolutist, out of touch with mainstream opinion, more interested in our own interests than in Scotland's and, as a result, much less relevant than we should have been.

A by-election in the neighbouring constituency of Glasgow Central in June 1989 was held comfortably by Labour. In fact, the highlight of that contest from my perspective was a nightly 'protest' that my friend Shona Robison and I staged in the pub next door to the SNP campaign office. The Laurieston was, and still is, a very traditional, much loved Glasgow pub situated in what would later be my constituency. There were a couple of bartenders who refused point blank to serve Shona or me, always pretending not to see us as they took the orders of men behind us in the queue. I doubt it was the bar's official policy not to serve women and the staff were probably just trying to put a couple of uppity university students in our place. Nevertheless, Shona and I were indignant. Every night after campaigning, we would perch ourselves on bar stools and loudly demand to be served, usually to no avail, leaving us to drink pints bought for us by our male friends instead.

By this time, I had joined GUSNA. For all that I doubted its 'real-life' relevance, I did think it had a purpose. For me personally, that purpose was experience. Through the campaigns and debates I took part in on campus, I developed skills that would be of use in my wider SNP activity.

I threw myself into GUSNA activity and particularly the Glasgow University Union debating scene. The GUU's reputation in the student debating field was legendary. I was excited about being part of it, but it was the strangest of environments. Glasgow excelled in what were known as parliamentary debates, or parlis. Different clubs – not surprisingly, I was part of the Scottish Nationalist club – debated motions in a mock replica of the House of Commons debating chamber. It took itself very seriously indeed. Notwithstanding the other women involved, it was a bear pit of male, white, middle-class privilege. Debating prowess aside, many of them could have won world titles in condescension and sneering.

Though I wasn't brilliant at debating, I wasn't terrible either, but the barracking and insults were designed to send a message that this wasn't my world. I ploughed on, regardless. In spite of feeling like the imposter they obviously thought I was, I tried to get better, to fit in. It was a losing battle.

For all that, it was in the GUU debating chamber that I added an extra layer to the thick skin necessary for a life in politics. At the start of my second year, I stood for a seat on the Students Representative Council and unexpectedly topped the poll, coming ahead of the Labour candidate. It was little more than chance, and as far as I can recall turnout was less than 10%, but it is the first time I remember trying to 'spin' an election result. I shamelessly used my win to claim to the student newspaper that my success was indicative of growing SNP support across campus and, by logical extension, across the country. It was baloney but, even then, I understood the importance of momentum.

I still viewed student politics as a bit futile and I also still struggled quite a bit with shyness, so I didn't contribute much to the SRC debates. That started to change, slowly but surely, as my time at university wore on. When I stood for SRC President in 1990, I was much more politically confident. That didn't mean I was any wiser. I learned an important lesson in that campaign about the dangers of political complacency. In the election for President the year before, the GUSNA candidate had lost out by just two votes. I thought that meant I was almost guaranteed victory. Of course, I learned that electorates, especially on a university campus, are not fixed, either in their make-up or in their opinions. I lost by more than 200 votes. Had I not taken victory so much for granted, I might have come closer. It's a mistake I have never repeated. Even in more recent years, when the SNP was all-conquering and the outcomes in my constituency probably reasonably certain, I always campaigned as if I was at mortal risk of losing. My advice to any aspiring politician is to always fight elections this way. Apart from anything else, those whose vote you are asking for deserve nothing less than your total commitment.

One of the factors that fed my complacency was the result of another campus election just a few weeks before. Like Scotland's other 'ancient' universities, Glasgow elects a Rector every four years, a position usually held by a known figure in international or domestic politics. When I arrived at Glasgow, the serving Rector was Winnie Mandela. She had been elected – obviously in her absence – as an expression of anti-apartheid sentiment and solidarity. Her term was due to expire in March 1990.

There was a strong sense on campus that a 'working' Rector was needed. Pat Kane was and still is the lead singer of Scottish pop group Hue & Cry. The band was a really big thing at the time, and Pat was also a strong supporter of independence. GUSNA asked him to stand, and he agreed.

Labour's candidate was veteran MP and hero of the radical left, Tony Benn. I was a big admirer of Tony Benn, as were many in GUSNA, so there was a bit of regret that we would be campaigning to defeat him. He quickly helped us get over it. He came to campus to do a hustings event and was appallingly uninformed about Scotland. He appeared to barely know where he was and, astonishingly, seemed unaware that the poll tax had been introduced a year early in Scotland. As far as I was concerned, it was a classic example of Labour arrogance, but it was so disappointing to witness this attitude from someone of Tony Benn's stature.

The campaign foretold in many ways the shape of Scottish politics to come years down the line, a battle between a young, modern SNP and a tired, complacent Labour Party. Pat promised to be a hard-working Rector, who would be present on campus and stand up for the interests of students. That caught a mood, as did his pro-independence stance. While support for independence was nowhere near what it is today, there was a strong home-rule feeling in the air, fuelled in part by the poll-tax anger.

Record-label constraints meant that he wasn't able to do impromptu gigs around the campus, but that didn't stop the crowds turning up. In one public meeting the room was packed, but it was with people hoping to hear a rendition of 'Looking for Linda'. I had a sinking feeling as Pat launched into what became a twenty-minute monologue on existentialism. Slowly but surely, people started drifting away.

It didn't matter though. We won the election and Pat became Rector. He proved to be a brilliant Rector too. His victory fuelled a sense of momentum for the SNP and independence, and I quickly embarked on a spin offensive with the student media to reinforce the wider significance.

For me, the campaign was a big step up. For the first time, I participated in an election contest not just as a foot soldier but as one of those in charge of organization and strategy. From somewhere I found the confidence to put forward ideas and shape how we ran the campaign. I was in my element, and the fact that we won fuelled my confidence even further.

Caroline and Claire were intensely interested in the world around them, but they weren't into party politics. Nevertheless, they were always supportive of my exploits. They were also both much cooler than me and would encourage me to experience some of the social parts of uni life that would otherwise have passed me by. They were great 'clubbers' and it was thanks to them that I frequented some of Glasgow's nightclubs at the time, Fury Murray's being the favourite. One of those in the law-student nightclub scene was a guy in the year above us called Gerry Butler. Caroline knew him from Paisley, where he also came from, which put us in his orbit. He was always the life and soul of the party, the centre of attention, and seemed destined to live a life less ordinary – these days he is better known as Gerard Butler, the Hollywood actor.

Getting a good law degree was important to me. A career as a lawyer was still what I envisaged for the future, not least because whilst my heart lay in politics, there was no obvious route to a career as an elected politician. So I studied hard. Or at least I did until an opportunity I didn't want to refuse came my way.

In the late summer of 1991, just a few months before I was due to sit my finals, I received a phone call from Alex Salmond. By this time he was SNP leader. Gordon Wilson had resigned and an election to choose his successor took place in September 1990. Alex was calling to ask me to be a candidate in the 1992 General Election. My life in politics was about to move to the next level.

CHAPTER THREE

The Youngest

By the time I got the call from Alex Salmond, we already had a relationship of sorts, forged during his 1990 leadership campaign.

I was on the National Executive Committee of the Young Scottish Nationalists at the time and was unpersuaded initially that we should openly endorse him as leader. There was never any doubt that I would vote for Alex, but most of my colleagues on the YSN executive thought we should campaign for him too. My initial scepticism was grounded in two factors. First, the YSN traditionally hosted a hustings for internal party elections and I worried that it would send the wrong signal if we were seen to be partial in the contest. Why would the other candidate even agree to take part?

The more substantive factor was that I thought Jim Sillars, victor of the Govan by-election two years earlier, might throw his hat in the ring. However, it quickly became clear that he wouldn't. Jim's modus operandi, though this wasn't yet clear to his young followers, was hurling criticism from the sidelines, rather than stepping up himself.

Jim was not willing to back Alex and threw his weight behind

Margaret Ewing instead. Margaret was the MP for Moray, and daughter-in-law of SNP icon and 'mother' of the party Winnie Ewing. Maggie was much loved but did not have anything like the leadership skills of Alex. Jim's positioning complicated the early stage of the contest for those of us who hung on his every word. I knew I would vote for Alex, but was I prepared to go against Jim openly? It turned out I was. Partly it was peer pressure, but mainly it was because I knew Alex was the best choice and felt that if I was serious about politics, I had a duty to say so.

Alex played a part in my decision too. At a party meeting he pulled me aside in a corridor and, fixing me with a stare, said that he'd heard I wasn't sure about the YSN endorsing him. I must have mumbled something in response. Still looking at me intently, he then said that if he couldn't win the backing of young people like me, he would withdraw his candidacy. It is quite hard to describe exactly what I felt in that moment. I absolutely knew I was being played and yet I was also completely taken in. This was the first, though certainly not the last, occasion when Alex would work his political magic on me.

With the rest of the YSN, I endorsed Alex and became a driving force behind the Youth for Salmond campaign. Using my recent experience of the Pat Kane contest, I suggested that we get T-shirts, badges and leaflets made and we set about persuading as many party members as we could that he represented the future of the party and Scotland. Alex won more than 70% of the vote at our conference in September (though, in a reminder of how much smaller the SNP was in those days, only 672 votes were cast in total!). He would have won without the YSN endorsement but we helped him project a youthful, future-orientated image. Our efforts put us, and me in particular, firmly in his sights.

———

I was at home at my mum and dad's when the call came. He said he had been impressed with what I'd been doing in the party and that there was a vacancy in the Glasgow Shettleston constituency. He wanted me to put myself forward for it.

There were good reasons for me to say no, though never the slightest chance that I would. The election would coincide with my final-year law exams the following spring. When I told my Adviser of Studies that I would be a candidate, he didn't mince his words. He told me it was a terrible idea, that there would be plenty of time for politics in the future if that was what I wanted, but, by standing now, I was jeopardizing my chances of a First Class degree. He was right. I got a 2:1.

The other reason to decline wasn't obvious to me at the time. I turned out to be the youngest candidate, of any party, in the whole of the UK, which generated a lot of media attention. I was inundated with interview and photo-shoot requests. How I came across mattered more than would otherwise have been the case, and since I was too young to really know who I was, I presented to the world an image of what I thought a politician should look and sound like.

What I thought and what the party thought became one and the same. I wasn't yet confident in my own style or demeanour, so tended to mimic those around me – middle-aged men mainly. As a result, I developed a very serious and austere persona. It was said that I never smiled. I opted for dark, plain clothes, usually trouser suits.

Looking the part and parroting the party line was what my subconscious told me was the best way to be taken seriously. It was also easier and quicker than learning to be myself. For a young man in politics, looking and sounding the part would have been an advantage. As a young woman, though, I was portrayed as being dour and frumpy, unattractive. Of course, had I gone the other way and struck an individualist, highly feminine pose, I'd have been criticized as unserious. Such is the no-win position women in public life often find themselves in, then and now.

This, then, is how Nicola the soundbite, facsimile politician was born. I came across as a personality-free zone. Had I not stood in 1992, I might have had more time to develop as a person before being thrust into the political spotlight. It might not have taken me so long, more than a decade in fact, to feel even remotely comfortable in my own skin. The flipside is that I wouldn't have earned the experience that fighting a national election at such a young age afforded me.

When I went along to meet the local activists in Shettleston, I could tell that they were deeply sceptical about fielding a twenty-one-year-old as their candidate. Who could blame them? I was Alex's choice, not theirs. Indeed, a perception of being Alex's girl, for all the advantages it brought me, dogged my political career for years to come. It created a suspicion, especially amongst my peers, that I was being promoted beyond my ability and experience. There were whispers, off and on, that we must be having an affair. The depressing subtext was: why else would a young woman be successful in politics?

On many occasions, including in Shettleston, it was true that Alex pushed me beyond my comfort zone and, at times, possibly, beyond my capabilities. I think it was because he genuinely saw potential in me, but he also knew that the SNP had to develop strength in depth. For as long as he was our one and only 'star', our prospects would be limited. To their credit, the Shettleston activists put aside any doubts and got behind me. The team, led by my election agent, John Adamson, was small, but I couldn't have asked for a more committed and supportive bunch of people.

Like many SNP campaigns of the time, ours was a fairly ramshackle affair. We chapped doors and delivered leaflets, but there was no science behind it. What I did learn was how to make a splash, attract attention and get under the skin of an opponent. I was determined to take full advantage of the interest I got from being the UK's youngest candidate, and I learned a lot about surviving in the media spotlight.

———

We had a big launch of my candidacy in October 1991, an 'adoption' meeting in SNP parlance. Kay Ullrich spoke and then Alex Salmond, the star attraction, and then me. My mum and dad came but left shortly after the speeches. 'Mum' was by then at the end of her life and my mum wanted to be back by her side. She died later that evening. I have always felt guilty that I was so preoccupied with my own life while my grandmother was taking her last breaths, but then I also know it is what she would have wanted me to be doing.

My Labour opponent, the incumbent MP, was David Marshall. David was twenty-nine years my senior but, in 1992, still only fifty-one, younger than I am now. Even so, I decided that my obvious disadvantage, excessive youth, should be turned on its head. I toured the constituency usually hollering through a loudspeaker that he was past his sell-by date. He must have thought me a thoroughly objectionable pain in the backside.

He had the last laugh. On election day, 9 April 1992, he polled 21,665 votes, just shy of 61% of the total, to my 6,831 votes, 19.1% of the total. It was a predictable outcome, but in my experience every election defeat, no matter how expected, is disappointing and chastening. This was no exception. I took some comfort from the fact that our vote had gone up by more than six percentage points and his had fallen by three. But, still, it was my first taste of personal defeat outside of student politics and it stung.

Against expectations, the Tories had won across the UK and even picked up a seat in Scotland, going from ten to eleven. John Major, who had succeeded Margaret Thatcher in November 1990, would remain as Prime Minister. For the SNP it was a disappointing night overall. Our vote share was 21.5%, up from just 14% in 1987, but we made no progress in our number of seats. We held the three seats we had won five years earlier, but Glasgow Govan, so famously won by Jim Sillars in the 1988 by-election, returned to the Labour fold.

Shortly afterwards, Jim would flounce out of Scottish politics in a huff from which he never fully emerged, accusing the Scottish people of being 'ninety-minute nationalists'. Many of us who had so revered Jim later came to feel let down by him. In recent years, with the exception of a brief period of collegiality during the independence referendum, he has sulked on the sidelines taking pot shots at SNP First Ministers. Though Alex Salmond wasn't spared his criticism, what he levelled at me was often laced with what felt like the kind of 'silly wee lassie' misogyny that some men of his generation, particularly and sadly on the left of politics, are all too prone to.

The election wasn't all we had hoped for, but it did fuel the demand that was building for a devolved Scottish Parliament. A combined 75% of those who voted in Scotland had backed parties supporting the establishment of a Scottish Parliament of some description. The Tories were alone in opposing it, but as the government of the day were able to stand in its way, even though they held just 11 of Scotland's 73 constituencies.

The SNP was now part of the pro-Parliament majority although, for some, grudgingly so. There was still a real fissure in the party between the so-called 'gradualists', of which I was one, who saw a devolved parliament as a necessary step to independence, and the 'fundamentalists', who believed it would dull the demand for independence and make it more difficult to achieve our ultimate objective.

However, with Alex firmly established as leader, the gradualist wing of the party was much more in control. Even though our ultimate aim was to achieve independence as quickly as possible, we now wanted to be part of the push for a devolved Parliament. Not surprisingly, though, given our earlier stance, the other parties were sceptical about our sincerity and motives. In the immediate aftermath of the General Election, through naivety rather than grand strategy, I gave them added reason to doubt us.

———

A mass demonstration was planned for George Square, Glasgow's main civic space, on the Saturday immediately following the General Election, to demonstrate the strength of support for a Scottish Parliament and highlight how undemocratic it was that the Tories, the political minority in Scotland, had the power to block it.

Under the banner 'Scotland United', the event brought together the main opposition parties, trade unions, artists and writers. More than five thousand people were in attendance. I had been picked by the party hierarchy to be our speaker at the event, quite an accolade for someone who was still only twenty-one. For me, the event illustrated both my growing stature within the SNP and the fact that I was still horribly inexperienced, a reminder that my personal development was trailing my political ascendancy.

I found myself atop the double-decker bus that was the make-shift stage for the rally, alongside George Galloway and John

McAllion, Labour MPs who were big names in Scotland at that time (representing Glasgow Kelvin and Dundee East respectively). There were famous Scottish musicians in the line-up too, such as Ricky Ross of Deacon Blue, Donnie Munro of Runrig and Pat Kane.

There was a photo taken that day, which surfaces online from time to time, of me, George and Pat on the top of the bus. As usual I look much younger than I was, and both a bit sullen and detached. Even though I was still so shy that conversing directly with the others on the stage would have been a form of purgatory for me, when my turn came, I gave a barnstorming speech. I had already learned how to stir an audience and was much more comfortable doing that than having a normal conversation. The contradictions of the 'public introvert' never fail to amaze me.

But while my speech was rousing, I utterly misjudged its tone. No one had told me what to say. I'm tempted to suggest that this was another sign of the confidence the party leadership had in me, and there is some truth in that, but it was also a reflection of the amateurishness that still bedevilled the SNP.

Instead of making a speech about the need for all those who wanted a Scottish Parliament to put aside our differences and unite for a common cause, I launched an angry broadside against Labour. I was still in election mode. It went down well with the SNP stalwarts in the audience, but the majority who were Labour, Liberal or politically non-aligned were less impressed. My speech didn't just miss the mark, it risked undermining the entire purpose of the event. My inexperience was all too obvious, and I was lucky to get off the double-decker bus in one piece. As I wound my way through the crowd at the end, flanked by supportive colleagues, I received more than a few disapproving comments that really shook my confidence.

Ultimately, it did me no harm within the SNP, but in wider

Scottish politics it created the impression that I was more tribal than was really the case. It was a reputation that stuck. The experience taught me that building common ground isn't possible without compromise, but also that it is always a good idea to know your audience.

Later that year, in December, a similar though much bigger event was held in Edinburgh to coincide with a European Heads of Government summit taking place in the city. Twenty-five thousand people turned up on Democracy Day, as it was called by the organizers, to demand a Scottish Parliament. The SNP speaker this time was Alex, but it was someone else who stole the show. Willie McIlvanney, who had once taught at my school and whose books I loved, was another of the headline speakers.

In my view, Willie's influence on Scotland and how we see ourselves can't be overstated. As well as being a first-rate novelist, he was a thinker, philosopher and a razor-sharp social commentator. He described more powerfully than almost anyone else of his literary era the impact on the human spirit of poverty, unemployment and lack of educational opportunities. He also managed to take something intangible, the essence, if there is such a thing, of being Scottish, and articulate it viscerally. That came to the fore when he delivered, on Democracy Day, one of the most memorable speeches of modern Scottish history. He electrified the crowd. I can still conjure up the atmosphere in my mind. As far as I know, there is no extant text of the speech he gave that day, but a single phrase captured the imagination of the crowd and it has resonated with me ever since.

He described Scotland as a 'mongrel nation'. It was a phrase that made sense instinctually. It spoke to our past, a melting pot of Picts, Celts and Anglo-Saxons, but much more powerfully to our present and future, a multi-cultural, multi-ethnic nation that values and celebrates diversity. In a political sense, it gave vivid expression to the fact that the campaign for a Scottish Parliament was not based on any notion of racial or ethnic purity or superiority, but on the simple belief – first instilled in me by my English grandmother – that those who live in Scotland, no matter where they come from, should choose how we are governed and by whom.

Fast forward more than twenty years to the independence referendum and it was that sentiment, that touchstone belief, which characterized the Yes campaign. It is also one of the values that underpins my political outlook.

———

The country (or, at least, its political class) was fizzing with democratic fervour and a sense of righteous anger about the Tory refusal to countenance a Parliament, but there was nowhere for all that energy to go. The Tories would be in government for another five years. The prospect of a Scottish Parliament was a dim and distant one at best. That sense of political drift was reflected in my own life too.

I had no doubt that politics was what I wanted to do. It was my passion. My social life was rooted in it. It got me up in the morning and kept me motivated until I fell back into bed at the end of the day. Yet, I still wasn't able to earn a living from it. I had no obvious way of making it my actual job. The only Westminster seats that the SNP held or had any real prospect of winning had incumbent MPs or candidates already established. I didn't have any desire to be a staffer, and in any event those opportunities were limited too.

———

I graduated shortly after the General Election and went on to complete the Diploma in Legal Practice. I secured a two-year legal traineeship with a big corporate law firm in Glasgow city centre called McClure Naismith Anderson & Gardiner. I was miserable there. Even if a career in law had been my aspiration, I would not have wanted to do this kind of law. Representing big companies and wealthy individuals held no interest for me. I did the bare minimum and counted down the hours every day until 5 p.m., when I would run out the door and head to whatever political meeting or activity the evening had in store.

I was representing the party regularly in the media, giving interviews on issues of the day and taking part in radio discussions. I spent hours in taxis going to and from the BBC, at that time based in Queen Margaret Drive in Glasgow's West End. Following the 1992 election, Alex asked me to join his 'Shadow Cabinet', a grand name for his group of spokespeople. Initially, I was given responsibility for employment, which consisted mainly of commenting on the monthly unemployment figures. In September 1992, I was also elected to the party's ruling body, the National Executive Committee. Despite my closeness to Alex, I didn't always take his side in internal discussions. There was one particular episode in early 1993 when I was one of a number who took issue with a decision he made, resulting in quite a serious challenge to his leadership.

Due to the antics of a block of Eurosceptic Tory MPs, the psychodrama at the heart of the Tory party that would eventually climax in the Brexit fiasco, John Major had effectively lost his majority in the House of Commons. As a result, his government had to look for support from other parties to get key parts of its agenda through. Ahead of a House of Commons vote on the European Maastricht Treaty, a play was made for the votes of SNP MPs.

Margaret Ewing was the leader of our small group of Westminster MPs. The leader of our MP group has always been distinct from the actual party leader, which oddly meant that we had two leaders in a team of just three MPs, a situation that would have been a source of much greater tension had Alex not been so utterly dominant. However, on this occasion, Margaret struck a fateful deal with Ian Lang, the Conservative Secretary of State for Scotland. Our three SNP MPs voted with the Tory government on the Maastricht Treaty in exchange for the promise of a seat for the party on the newly formed EU Committee of the Regions.

There was uproar in the party. Voting with the Tories was seen as tantamount to betraying Scotland. Many of us also considered the 'deal' to be a massive own goal. Just as the 'Tartan Tories' jibe was starting to recede, our own MPs had breathed new life into it. Labour made great play of the situation. It also gave them the perfect excuse to cancel the talks that had started between us in the wake of the Democracy Day rally the previous December, to foster joint working in pursuit of a Scottish Parliament. Labour had no real interest in these talks bearing fruit and the Maastricht vote gave them the perfect pretext to call a halt.

To this day, I am not sure whether Alex knew about and actively supported the Tory deal in advance or had been bounced into it by Margaret. I strongly suspect it was the latter, but it didn't matter. He stood by the decision. This paved the way for a showdown at a meeting of our National Executive Committee in March 1993. Unusually, the NEC met in Glasgow that day, in the Copthorne Hotel. The 'deal' was the main item on the agenda and the NEC would vote to either back our MPs or censure them.

Even though I was furious at the actions of the MPs, I had reservations about a censure vote because of the succour it would give to those, like Alex Neil and Kenny MacAskill, who opposed

Alex's leadership and would use any excuse to undermine it. Others, including my close friends Fiona Hyslop and Roseanna Cunningham, shared my concerns. However, we were so exercised about potential lasting damage to the party's reputation, in particular the return of the Tartan Tory taunt, that we reluctantly resolved to back the censure motion. We did so with heavy hearts and a lot of nervousness. The vote was on a knife-edge, and no one really knew what would happen if Alex lost.

Alex was always very cool in such tense situations, always the master tactician. He had done the numbers, knew that he needed to swing two votes to avoid defeat, and honed in on those he obviously thought most susceptible to pressure. In a break in proceedings just before the vote was taken, he quietly took aside a couple of young NEC members, Stewart Hosie and Shirley-Anne Somerville, and told them that if the censure vote passed, he would immediately resign as leader. The party would be in crisis. His intervention worked and he won the day by 13 votes to 11.

I don't blame Stewart and Shirley-Anne for being spooked. I might have been too had he pulled the same trick on me. I was his protégé and yet he hadn't tried to haul me into line. I think this demonstrated, even then, a level of respect. He wanted me to arrive at and learn from my own decisions. Or maybe, in that moment, he just saw me as a lost cause.

The Maastricht row rumbled on for a while. Predictably, or so it felt, those who had always opposed Alex tried to destabilize him. There were resignations from the Shadow Cabinet and calls for Alex to step down as leader. Sillars weighed in from the sidelines. The group I was part of had no truck with this. Instead, we wrote a letter to the *Scotsman*, urging unity. There was plenty to be done.

———

I was heavily involved in the Monklands by-election in 1994, caused by the premature death of Labour leader John Smith. Kay Ullrich was our candidate. Helen Liddell – later a minister in the Blair government – was Labour's. The campaign was marred by sectarianism, with the Labour-controlled council accused by locals of prioritizing funding for the predominantly Catholic town of Coatbridge over the predominantly Protestant Airdrie. There was a 'jobs for the boys' element too, with Labour councillors thought to be wielding inappropriate influence when people were being recruited to council jobs. It made for an ugly and bitter contest. In the end, Labour won by fewer than 2,000 votes – which, in their heartlands, was a massive shock.

A year later was the Perth & Kinross by-election. The Tory MP, Nicholas Fairbairn, had died and the seat was seen as ours to lose. Despite narrowly losing in the 1992 General Election, Roseanna Cunningham was confirmed as our candidate again, but only after we endured the closest thing Scottish politics had to a sex scandal in those days. There had been an attempt to block Roseanna's candidacy over a relationship she was claimed to have had years earlier with Margaret Ewing's ex-husband. The row was ludicrous given that, by then, Margaret had remarried – to Fergus, Winnie Ewing's eldest son. Nevertheless, it gripped Scottish politics for days.

Roseanna and I were close friends. In fact, she was probably my best friend in those days. It was in some ways an unlikely friendship, as she is nineteen years older than me. Roseanna could be hot-headed, but, in my view, her straight-talking, shoot-from-the-hip approach was her strength. I was asked by the party to take two weeks off work and stay with her in Perth for the final stages of the campaign. It was my job to help keep her calm and on an even keel. It was a tough campaign, in the days when by-elections still entailed the daily bear-pit press conferences. In one, Roseanna referred to the monarchy as 'the pinnacle of the class system', which earned her the nickname Republican Rose. The right-wing media intended it as an insult, but she wore it as a badge of honour.

Roseanna won the by-election comfortably, with a majority of more than 7,000. The Tories were beaten into third place by an up-and-coming Labour candidate, one Douglas Alexander, who would later become an MP in Paisley and hold a number of ministerial posts – including Foreign Secretary – in the Blair, Brown and Starmer governments.

———

Despite my frenzied political campaigning, it took me until 1995, when I was selected as candidate for the Govan constituency, to gain a firm sense of direction. The fact we had won Govan twice before, albeit in by-elections and with slightly different boundaries, made us believe we could do so again. In addition, Labour was riven by division in the constituency. Its own bitterly contested selection battle had to be re-run amidst claims of vote-rigging.

I lived in the constituency at the time, on Camphill Avenue in Shawlands. I was selected at a meeting at Langside Halls, just down the road from my flat, from an all-woman shortlist that consisted of me, my friend Shona Robison and another Glasgow activist, Patsy Thomson. Unlike Labour's, it was a good-natured contest. Being selected for a seat we considered to be even potentially winnable really galvanized me. I set my sights on pulling off a third Govan victory for the SNP.

———

In spring 1996, I was offered an experience which served to strengthen my resolve even more. Roseanna had been invited, alongside other MPs and aspiring MPs, to take part in a Commonwealth Parliamentary Association trip to Australia. She wasn't able to go, so nominated me instead. The prospect both excited and terrified me. I had never been outside Europe before, so the thought of a twenty-four-hour flight to the other side of the world was almost beyond my comprehension. The prospect of spending ten days with people I didn't know was also intimidating.

There were four others on the trip with me: Charles Kennedy, the Scottish Highlands MP and later leader of the Liberal Democrats; Shaun Woodward, the Tory candidate for the safe seat of Witney – he would later defect to Labour and be succeeded as MP for Witney by David Cameron; Eleanor Laing, who would later become Deputy Speaker of the House of Commons; and, last but not least, Maria Eagle, Labour's candidate in the safe seat of Liverpool Garston – Maria would later serve as a minister under both Tony Blair and Gordon Brown. She is currently a junior member of the Starmer government. I was the only one of the group who wasn't virtually guaranteed a seat in the Commons at the next election.

The experience of Australia, the sights and sensations, was stunning. I woke up in my hotel room on our first morning, jet-lagged and hungover (we had gone straight to the bar when we arrived the night before), and opened the curtains to the sight of Sydney Opera House. But it was the immersion in politics that had the biggest impact on me.

We arrived just a few weeks after an Australian General Election in which Paul Keating's Labor government had been replaced by a Liberal administration (the equivalent of the Tories in the UK). The new Prime Minister was John Howard. Election posters still adorned billboards, giving us insight into the campaign platforms of the different parties. The Democrats, the small, third party in Australian politics, had the most striking poster. In what was clearly a play for kingmaker status, they had campaigned under the slogan 'Keep the Bastards Honest'. I thought it was genius.

In Canberra, on a visit to Parliament, I met one of the Democrats' young MPs. Natasha Stott Despoja was only a couple of years older than me and already deputy leader of her party.

The trip also gave me the opportunity to get to know Charles Kennedy. Charles – or Charlie as he was affectionately known in Scotland – was one of few politicians with celebrity status at the time. A combination of his relative youth when first elected, his shock of bright red hair and his cheeky chappy personality endeared him to people across the UK.

As the only two Scottish politicians in the delegation, Charlie and I were thrown together quite a bit (although from Paisley, Eleanor was standing for a constituency in England). On our very first day in Sydney, we were dispatched to the home of the 'Clan Chief' of an Australia Scottish society, who was throwing a party in our honour. The 'Clan Chief', who we soon learned had never set foot in Scotland, was resplendent in full Highland dress. He greeted us in Gaelic, which Charlie spoke and I didn't – an early black mark against me in the eyes of our host. The scores were soon evened up when he discovered, to his horror, that Charlie wasn't a member of the SNP and didn't support Scottish independence. The party was a lovely gesture and our hosts showed us great kindness – but it was a bizarre experience.

On another occasion, in Melbourne, Charlie and I decided to escape the rest of the group. We went to the cinema to see *Trainspotting*, the famous film based on the Irvine Welsh novel, which had just been released. There we were, twelve thousand miles from home, the only two Scots in the entire cinema, laughing uproariously at jokes that no one else understood. It was a lovely, bonding experience and a memory I will treasure for ever.

In the SNP's landslide of 2015, Charlie lost his Westminster seat to Ian Blackford, who, a couple of years later, would become our Westminster leader. Obviously I was thrilled by my party's success and by my friend Ian's election. But I wish we could have achieved it without the loss of Charlie's presence in Parliament. His death, less than a month later, was a tragedy. It genuinely pains me to think that our election triumph, however unintentionally and inadvertently, might have hastened his demise. He was, without doubt, one of the most charismatic and naturally talented individuals ever to grace Scottish politics. Those few days I got to spend with him in Australia were a privilege.

The trip was a whirlwind of meetings with State Premiers and ministers, opposition politicians, third-sector groups and think tanks. If I had harboured any doubts that politics was the world I wanted to inhabit full-time, this trip dispelled them. I returned home inspired and energized for the election battle ahead.

Back home, I was in a relationship with a man called Stuart Morrison. We had been together for two years and, not long after my trip to Australia, we moved in together. We met at McClure's, where he was the firm's financial adviser. He was an amateur musician too, playing drums in a couple of local bands. He wasn't particularly involved in politics, but he supported me to the hilt. While we had many happy times together, somehow we were never quite right for each other.

Stuart was twelve years older than me and had been married before. He also had two young sons. I was fond of his kids but, crucially, I knew that Stuart didn't want to have any more. This meant that, for as long as I was with him, there would be no pressure on me to have children. That suited me. This was a relationship that was never going to interfere with my career. Even though Stuart made me feel happy for a while, this was almost certainly the reason I stayed so long in the wrong relationship.

This, then, was how it was for me as the 1997 General Election loomed. A personal life which seemed happy and settled but which was in fact parked in a lay-by, as I focused ever more single-mindedly on the political life I was intent on leading. And a professional life that was prominent and successful in one sense, and yet still deeply uncertain in another, as I continued to rely on my stalling legal career to keep body and soul together.

CHAPTER FOUR

Govan

It's no exaggeration to say that Govan made me. It turned me into a politician, and a person capable of leading a country. In medieval times, it was one of the major centres of the Kingdom of Strathclyde. Govan Old parish church is thought to be one of the earliest sites of Christian worship in Scotland, giving it an importance in Christian history on a par with places like Iona and St Andrews. It is now home to the Govan Stones, possibly the most significant collection of Viking-era sculptures anywhere in Europe, all of them excavated from the Govan Old churchyard where they had lain for more than a thousand years.

In the politics of the early twentieth century, Govan was also at the heart of Red Clydeside, the radical Glasgow-based movement agitating for social and economic change. In 1920, Mary Barbour became one of the first women councillors in the city, representing a ward in Govan. A few years earlier, she led the famous Glasgow Rent Strikes in opposition to crippling rent rises and evictions. When I was First Minister, I had a portrait of Mary on the wall of my office in St Andrew's House. There were many difficult moments when I found myself looking up at her for courage and inspiration.

Govan was also the heart of shipbuilding on the Clyde, making it one of the engine rooms of the Industrial Revolution. Many of the names that adorn its streets and buildings today – Pearce, Elder, Napier – are taken from the magnates of shipbuilding. It may have taken until 2018 for Mary Barbour's statue to be erected in Govan, but Sir William Pearce's has been there since 1894. It is known locally as 'the black man', a reference to its bronze being turned black by years of city soot and grime. Pearce was one of the owners of Fairfield's Shipyard which, in its heyday, was amongst the biggest in the world. Now BAE Systems, it is one of only two remaining yards on the Upper Clyde.

Many well-known names hail from Govan. One of its most famous sons is Sir Alex Ferguson. He has always been a massive supporter of good causes in Govan. I know a few charities who, on hitting tough times, have opened the mail to find a cheque from Sir Alex, sent out of the blue, with no fanfare. Another well-known Govanite, who weaves into my own story, was Jimmy Reid. In 1971, Jimmy was one of the leaders of the Upper Clyde 'work-in'. The Ted Heath government had decided to withdraw state subsidies from what it called 'lame-duck' industries. This pushed the Upper Clyde Shipbuilders into liquidation, threatening the viability of the yards and six thousand jobs, despite a full order book.

The trade unions decided that, instead of going on strike, they would stage a 'work-in' to complete the orders. Mindful that the eyes of the world were on them, Jimmy made a now famous speech warning the workers against hooliganism, vandalism and bevvying. The work-in attracted global attention, including a £5,000 donation from John Lennon. It also succeeded. The government U-turned and the yards survived. Jimmy was elected Rector of Glasgow University on the back of the win and at his installation made a speech for the ages. The 'rat race speech' as it became known was described by the *New York Times* as 'the greatest speech since President Lincoln's Gettysburg Address'.

Jimmy had been a communist but later joined Labour. In 1997, in my first election in Govan, Jimmy publicly backed my Labour opponent, but by 2004 he was in the SNP, symbolic of the drift from Labour to the SNP that was gathering pace at that time. After he joined the party, I got to know him fairly well, listening to his stories and hearing his views on various issues of the day, local and global. He was always captivating.

After my selection as the Govan candidate in 1995, I developed a deep interest in the history and future of shipbuilding. A shipyard is not an easy place for a young woman to walk into, especially a young woman in a political party that some of the workers still derided as Tartan Tories. On the first couple of occasions I met with the workforce, I could feel the scepticism. From some, it was downright hostility. From the clang of metal on metal to the tangible whiff of testosterone in the air, the atmosphere was intimidating. There were more than a few disparaging comments hurled in my direction. Yet, by not being scared away and, instead, proving myself a reliable ally, I won respect, even if it was grudging from some.

The convener of the Govan trade unions was a no-nonsense, very smart man called Jamie Webster. Jamie had worked in the yard since the late 1960s. He was far from a typical union official in that, politically, he was fiercely independent. He wouldn't pull his punches if he thought Labour politicians were letting his members down.

Jamie and I got on well, which over time helped me win the

trust of the wider workforce. In 1999, when the Govan yard and its counterpart across the Clyde at Scotstoun were under renewed threat, I would join the movement to save them. The campaign succeeded (though there would be tough times yet to come) when GEC, later BAE Systems, acquired the yards. When the acquisition was announced, I went to a mass meeting at Govan and was presented with a big bunch of flowers from the unions. There might have been a touch of unconscious sexism in the gesture, but it still meant a lot to me.

Jamie also inadvertently taught me that even the sincerest compliment paid to a woman in politics can be weaponized against her. It was Jamie who first labelled me 'Nippy Sweetie', a nickname that my opponents and parts of the media would use to deride me, suggesting it meant someone who was cold, hard and humourless. Jamie meant it differently. As he said in his book *Back from the Brink*: 'I thought of her as a nippy sweetie. This was meant as a compliment. My view was that she was very much in your face and to the point and was a capable politician.'

Either way, the nickname stuck and I wear it with pride.

———

Although it wasn't my first stint as a candidate, the 1997 election was the first time I had even a remote prospect of winning. I threw myself into the campaign. From my selection in mid-1995, through to polling day on 1 May 1997, with the exception of the week or so I spent in Australia, I campaigned almost every day.

Labour's candidate was a Glasgow City councillor and local cash-and-carry tycoon, Mohammad Sarwar, who was aiming to become Scotland's first Muslim MP. He had won the candidacy in a bitter and brutal contest where the allegations of vote-rigging against his opponent meant that the local Labour Party was deeply divided, with some high-profile members defecting to the SNP. It all served to convince me that we had an outside chance of winning the seat.

Although Govan was at the heart of the constituency, it ranged much wider. It included East Pollokshields, home to many first-generation Pakistani and Indian immigrants to Scotland; West Pollokshields, with leafy avenues and massive mansions; Ibrox, home of Rangers Football Club; Shawlands, the trendy part of the Southside; and Drumoyne, where Glasgow's biggest hospital, the Southern General, now rebuilt and renamed the Queen Elizabeth, is located.

No serious election campaign is easy, but trekking the so-called mean streets of Glasgow, up and down tenement stairwells, night after night, was physically tough. Never knowing what kind of reception might lie on the other side of the door made it a nerve-shredding experience too. Glaswegians don't suffer fools gladly. There is a directness that I love but which is deeply uncomfortable to be at the sharp end of. Even diehard supporters can be brutal in their criticism and questioning. I quickly learned to survive on my wits, to give as good as I got in doorstep discussions, while being respectful and willing to listen. On one occasion, a big, burly guy covered in tattoos set his Dobermann dog on me. I froze, my paralysing fear of dogs kicking in. I thought I was about to be mauled. Thankfully, the guy called the dog to heel just before it jumped on me. He was only having what passed for fun, but I was terrified. I was also fairly certain I wasn't getting his vote.

The campaign was a lesson in life as well as politics. I met probably thousands of people and heard many wonderful stories. I learned just how extraordinary the lives of supposedly 'ordinary' men and women really are. But I had to endure being patronized and abused too. There would usually be men hanging around outside the pubs on the main street in Govan as I made my way from the underground station to our campaign office, having just hotfooted it from work. I would have to thole the lewd comments and sexual innuendo that are the depressing reality for women in all walks of life. Occasionally, there would be a bit of physical intimidation too, with random men, worse the wear for drink, insisting on putting an arm around me. My election agent kept telling me to let him know when I was due to arrive at the station so someone could meet me, but I stupidly refused. I wanted to show I was strong enough to deal with anything. Of course, no woman should ever have to deal with that kind of behaviour. Sadly, even today, most of us still do.

The sexist abuse, however dispiriting, wasn't surprising. What was less expected were the sectarian insults that came my way. Although I had grown up in Ayrshire, I had never experienced the depth of sectarianism I encountered in parts of Govan. I had grown up, nominally at least, as a Protestant in the Church of Scotland, so the fact that it was mainly anti-Catholic abuse being hurled at me was particularly perplexing. It was also horribly eye-opening to what the Irish Catholic community has suffered for far too long. It seemed to stem in large part from the fact that after campaign sessions we would frequent the Govan Arms pub, which was known to be strongly Celtic supporting. I was hopelessly naive back then and it just didn't occur to me that this would be a problem. I was chased away from one door with shouts of 'Fenian bastard' ringing in my ears, but more sinister were the whispers percolating around the constituency, which I knew were being stoked by elements in the local Labour Party, that I was an active supporter of the IRA. It was deeply unpleasant and an unwelcome education in the darker 'arts' of political campaigning.

I also had my eyes opened to a level of poverty and inequality which, despite my working-class background, I hadn't witnessed before. The constituency had pockets of the most acute deprivation and some of the worst housing conditions to be found anywhere in Scotland. However, in the space of five minutes, within the boundaries of just one constituency, it was possible to drive from areas of the most miserable and grinding hardship to streets dominated by million-pound houses, dripping in wealth and prosperity.

———

My campaign team in Govan was small and inexperienced, but also young and highly motivated. My election agent was Mark Coyle, a young man from Drumoyne, around the same age as me, with bright red hair. Mark worked in sales and had the gift of the gab. My campaign manager was Joe Rocks, a social worker from Shawlands, also around my age. Mark was calm and unflappable and Joe was highly strung and excitable, and they made a great contrasting team.

I also had the benefit of the wisdom and strong personal support of some older and more experienced heads. Margaret and Colin Pennycook were both teachers and had been SNP activists since the 1960s. They were stalwarts of this and every subsequent campaign I ran in. Another wise head was John Macfarlane. John was already in his eighties when I first got to know him. He had been a senior executive in the world of bookmaking. By the time he died in July 2006, at the ripe old age of ninety-four, he was one of the last living links to Red Clydeside. It always seemed significant to me that he had come to see the SNP, not Labour, as the true heirs to that tradition. John was too old and infirm by 1997 to pound the streets, but he helped us raise funds for the campaign. He also introduced me to many of the so-called 'great and the good' of the Southside.

There was no shortage of enthusiasm or dedication in the campaign. But it wasn't brimming with professionalism. In those days, outside a few constituencies, SNP campaigns were rudimentary. We didn't yet have established networks to plug into, or the data that would have allowed us to target potential supporters. Our efforts were more unguided missile than precision strike. To coin a good Scottish phrase, the campaign was a bit hand-knitted. The most visible symbols of this were the blue, slightly battered, Transit van in which I was transported around the constituency and our poky campaign office on Govan Road, which had no heating and a toilet that wouldn't flush.

We tried to turn this to our advantage, contrasting my 'woman of the people' demeanour with Sarwar's millionaire status, but Labour must have taken considerable comfort from their vastly superior campaign resources and organization. The biggest factor in Labour's favour, of course, was the context of the election: 1997 was a change election. People were scunnered with the Tories and Tony Blair was the great hope for the future. Despite its distance from Westminster, it would have taken a miracle to insulate Govan from the Labour wave that was about to sweep the UK.

And yet, right up to polling day, there was an acute nervousness around Labour's campaign in Govan and, by contrast, an infectious optimism in ours. In a harbinger of the deep, almost emotional, connection I later made with a sizeable swathe of the Scottish population when I was First Minister, our campaign in Govan, and my candidacy in particular, was resonating. I was seen as a breath of fresh air: straight-talking, fearless and 'real' in a way that many politicians aren't. I was also getting under Labour's skin. I had embarrassed Sarwar into doing hustings around the constituency, which I then bested him in. The negligible numbers attending meant they had little impact on the outcome, but they struck a psychological blow. My status as the young rising star of the SNP also gave me a media platform that I wouldn't otherwise have had.

There was one particular factor which undoubtedly benefitted our campaign but which made me deeply uncomfortable. Sarwar's Pakistani origin and Muslim faith meant that racism lurked around like a bad smell. There was a limit to what I could do about it, but I made a promise to myself that I would not collude with racist sentiment in any way, even implicitly or by omission. I carried a degree of guilt about potentially blocking the election of Scotland's first Muslim MP. I knew how important, in a historical context, his election would be. And I knew that the election of someone from Scotland's minority ethnic communities was long overdue.

A trap that every politician falls into at times is believing that the ends justify the means. I have not been immune to it over the years, but it is an aspect of politics I've always felt queasy about. An SNP victory in Govan would have been seismic. It would have been all too easy, quietly and subtly, to have played the race card, or to have stayed silent while others played it for me. I am ashamed to say there were a few on the margins of my campaign who thought we should, and possibly even some who did. They even attached a kind of moral equivalence between this and the fact that we thought elements in the Labour campaign were behind the sectarian abuse I was receiving. I made it crystal clear that I would not tolerate it, and that anyone caught behaving in such a way would be booted out. Furthermore, whenever I encountered people who said they might vote for me because of Sarwar's race or faith, I made it my practice to reply that if prejudice was the motive, I didn't want their vote.

Overall, I am very proud of the campaign we fought in Govan. We took it by the scruff of the neck and gave it a real go. The result when it came devastated me. I had always known deep down that winning was unlikely, but I had allowed myself to believe a little too much. In the end, Sarwar won with a majority of 2,914. He got 14,216 votes to my 11,302 – in percentage terms, 44 to 35.

We had lost, but we had swum against the national tide and recorded a swing against Labour. I have never deluded myself that this was all down to me and our campaign. There is no doubt that prejudice against Sarwar's race and faith played a part. But we deserved credit as we had injected energy, passion and purpose into what, even with the nasty racist element, would otherwise have been an easy Labour victory.

For me, the campaign represented a political coming of age. I hadn't been just a token candidate, going through the motions in a no-hope seat. I had been a genuine contender. And I had managed not just to cope with but thrive under the burden of expectation that came with that status.

———

As the morning after the night before dawned, I was deeply despondent. I spent much of the day wallowing in bed. A combination of bitter disappointment, anticlimax and exhaustion floored me. I also knew that I would likely be looking for a new job soon. I had moved from McClure's to Bell & Craig, a small general practice in Stirling. The partners, George Craig and Fergus Bell, were good guys who had given me a chance, but my heart wasn't really in it. Shortly after the 1997 General Election, it was decided that it would be better if I left. They needed someone who would commit to the firm, and they knew as well as I did that that wasn't me.

When I did eventually get up and venture out, there was a palpable sense of relief at the political demise of the Tories, coupled with a hopeful belief in the new, youthful Prime Minister. It was hard not to be affected by it, and my mood lifted a bit, as even I was slightly intoxicated by the aura of positivity that surrounded Tony Blair.

There was, of course, good reason to feel optimistic in Scotland. Labour had promised to establish a devolved Scottish Parliament. Blair's pre-election decision to put the issue to a referendum, with two separate questions, one on the principle of a Parliament and the other on whether or not it should have limited tax varying powers, had sparked fears that Labour might ditch the devolution commitment altogether. The fears were unfounded. Having a referendum turned out to be absolutely the right move – it gave the Parliament a legitimacy and permanence that it would otherwise have lacked.

The date for the referendum was set for 11 September 1997. The campaign was one of the strangest I've ever been involved in. The cross-party nature of it contributed to the weirdness, but there was also an atmosphere of acute anxiety in the SNP. For all that the demand for a Parliament seemed to be the firmly settled will of the Scottish people, the ghost of the 1979 referendum still cast a dark shadow, even for those of us whose memories of it were hazy at best. There was a fear all the way to polling day that a long-held dream, finally so close to becoming a reality, might yet be snatched away.

It was never likely that Scotland would vote No to having a Parliament. But the question on tax varying powers, dubbed the Tartan Tax by the Tories, was much more in the balance. The SNP had joined forces with Labour and the Liberals in what became the cross-party Yes/Yes campaign. Incredibly, this still caused some controversy within the party. There were still some who thought we should campaign against devolution, or at the very least sit it out. While it wasn't a point of view I shared, I could just about understand the fear that a devolved Parliament might stymie support for independence, in that it would satisfy the demand in Scotland for greater democratic accountability. But, for the life of me, I couldn't understand the argument that if the SNP managed to block devolution, people would flock instead to the independence cause. It was deluded. It was far more likely that people would be angry with the SNP, and rightly so, and lose faith with the case for constitutional change altogether.

Thankfully, common sense and political reality prevailed. Alex campaigned side by side with Donald Dewar, then Labour's Scottish leader and, later, Scotland's first First Minister, and Jim Wallace, Scottish leader of the Lib Dems.

Bizarrely, given how invested I was in the outcome and how hard I was campaigning on the ground, I don't remember much about the nuts and bolts of the national Yes/Yes efforts. Although I was on the NEC sub-committee charged with steering the SNP's contribution to the campaign, I wasn't close to the decision-making of the cross-party organization. Another explanation is related to events in Govan. No sooner had Sarwar been elected an MP than he found himself embroiled in a corruption scandal, accused of bribing one of the other Govan candidates. He was later cleared in the High Court of any criminal conduct, so I won't rehearse the detail of the allegations. But a parliamentary by-election, in which I would have been the certain SNP candidate, seemed a distinct possibility, and as a result, my campaign efforts, including for the referendum, were very locally focused.

However, there was one major event in the course of the campaign, just eleven days out from polling, that is embedded in my memory. I was at home on the evening of Saturday, 30 August. Stuart had taken his kids to see his parents in Cairnryan for the weekend, and I spent a happy few hours on the sofa, belatedly reading *Bridget Jones's Diary*. I read it cover to cover that night – and consumed most of a bottle of wine along the way. Helped, no doubt, by the wine, I slept soundly. In those days, there wasn't a phone next to the bed, so Stuart's first few attempts to call didn't waken me. When he finally did rouse me, it was with the dreadful news that Princess Diana was dead. Like most of the rest of the country, I sat in front of the TV for what felt like hours, utterly transfixed, unable to process what I was hearing and seeing. It was beyond words or comprehension.

The SNP's referendum campaign committee was scheduled to meet that afternoon. I called Mike Russell, then the party Chief Executive, to check if it was going ahead. It was, so I got myself ready to head to Edinburgh. I'll never forget the contrast between walking across Glasgow's George Square on the way to Queen Street station, and the return journey a few hours later. On the way there, a couple of bunches of flowers had been laid at the foot of one of the monuments in the Square. When I got back, the Square was completely carpeted. There were crowds of people quietly milling about, hugging each other and crying. I stood for a while too, trying to absorb and make sense of the atmosphere. Like most people, I had never before experienced such a raw and visceral outpouring of public grief.

Our meeting in Edinburgh had been sombre. We were as shocked and sad as everyone else. But there was also a real concern about the impact Diana's death would have on the remaining days of the referendum campaign. Would or could the vote go ahead? And though it might sound horribly cynical, we discussed whether postponement would, in fact, be our preference. It simply wasn't possible to know what effect Diana's death might have. Campaigning would be suspended for a period. People would be distracted. It wasn't impossible that the response would be an impulse for unity rather than devolution.

We mulled it over that afternoon and ultimately took the view that the referendum must go ahead, and that we would argue strongly for that to be the case. For all the uncertainty about the impact of Diana's loss on the outcome, we worried that once postponed, the referendum might never be rescheduled. There was more than a touch of paranoia in that concern, but it was founded in deep, lingering distrust about the strength of Labour's commitment to devolution. There were behind-the-scenes discussions between the different parties in the Yes/Yes campaign. I wasn't involved in these, but knew we were making the case for the campaign to resume following Diana's funeral and the vote to proceed as planned on 11 September.

That is what happened, but I think it easily might have gone the other way. There was certainly pressure for a postponement, confirmed years later when it emerged through the release of archived papers that William Hague, then Tory leader, had written to Blair formally requesting that the date be changed. Had it not been for the fact that this would have required the recall of Parliament during the period of official mourning, I suspect demands to postpone would have been difficult to withstand. And what would have happened then to the course of Scottish history is impossible to know.

Thankfully, events took the course we had hoped for. The campaign restarted after Diana's funeral on 6 September. The final five days were frenetic. If the tax question had generated a No vote, the legitimacy and authority of the new Parliament would have been badly damaged, possibly irreparably. Had the people of Scotland rejected even such a limited revenue-raising power, the message would have been clear that while a Parliament of our own might be a nice symbol, it wasn't to be trusted with any real financial power. Had that happened, devolution would have been strangled at birth.

On 11 September – a day of destiny for Scotland – I spent the day cajoling voters to the polls in Govan. Later, I was in the Edinburgh International Conference Centre for the declaration of the results. The tension in the air was palpable, and so was the relief when the final tallies were confirmed. Scotland had voted for a Parliament by 74% to 26%. The margin on the tax question was tighter but still overwhelming – 63% to 37%.

We were overjoyed. At SNP HQ celebrations went on well into the next day. Scotland had voted for a Parliament of its own. It was, without doubt, a watershed moment in Scottish history. It would change the country for ever, in ways yet to be understood. It also catapulted the SNP into a different league. No longer just a fringe party at Westminster, we would become a major player in a domestic Parliament.

It redefined the arguments for and against independence. And it changed the lives of many activists who, until then, had seen little prospect of achieving elected office. One of those activists was me. In that moment, it became more likely than not that I would become a Member of Parliament. It felt like the life I had wanted for such a long time might finally be in reach.

———

In the first Scottish Parliament election, I was once again the candidate in Govan. The Holyrood seat was more or less identical to the Westminster version I had fought two years before. I was also chosen by fellow members to be the top candidate in the party's regional list for Glasgow, in the PR system used for Scottish Parliament elections. This meant I was virtually guaranteed election as an MSP, even if I didn't win the constituency. It wasn't the route into the Parliament that I wanted though. I was determined to win Govan. My opponent this time was one of Scotland's leading criminal defence lawyers, Gordon Jackson. As with Mohammad Sarwar, I got on well with Gordon personally. His laid-back personality would have made him a very difficult person to dislike, even if I had wanted to.

The campaign was long. The period from the referendum through to May 1999 seemed interminable. At the outset, we were brimming with optimism, with the polls showing that we were well and truly in the race.

On 29 January 1998, I made my first of many appearances on the panel of the BBC's *Question Time*, alongside the comedian Eddie Izzard, the Labour minister Gavin Strang and leading Scottish defence advocate Donald Findlay. It was a massive step up for me. *Question Time* was still the UK's pre-eminent political programme, and I wasn't yet an elected politician. In a sign of just how basic the SNP operation still was, no one tried to prepare or brief me in advance. Other than a five-minute call that afternoon with the party Chief Executive, Mike Russell, I was left entirely to my own devices. It was up to me to decide what I was going to say about the various issues of the day. Even though it was nerve-wracking, I felt that I acquitted myself well and got lots of audience applause. Labour wasn't even a year into government at this point and Gavin Strang seemed shell-shocked by the negative audience reactions to the positions he was taking on issues like university tuition fees. It was a big confidence boost for me. Perhaps the memory that lingers most, though, was chatting to Eddie Izzard in the green room about the beautiful thigh-length boots he was wearing.

As 1998 gave way to 1999, the campaign got much tougher. I don't think any of us appreciated just how challenging the following few months would be. For a start, in theory at least, we were now a potential government of Scotland. That meant far more scrutiny than we were accustomed to. Alex bore the brunt of it. Throughout the campaign, there were whispers that newspapers were spending vast amounts of money trying to dig the dirt on him. He was characteristically bullish, but some of us were nervous that there might be some skeletons in his cupboard. He was a known gambler, though, as far as I was aware, always a canny one. There had also been periodic rumours about affairs at Westminster, though of a consensual nature – there was no hint then of the kind of allegations that emerged in later years.

There was suddenly much more pressure on all of us. By now, I was working full-time at the Law & Money Advice Centre in Drumchapel, one of the four social-housing estates developed in Glasgow after the Second World War. I represented clients who were in debt, threatened with eviction or struggling to get the welfare support they were entitled to. It was work I cared about, and was similar in nature to what would later dominate my constituency surgeries.

My boss at the Law Centre, Jim Gray, was a member of the Labour Party and we had many good-humoured discussions about the best future for Scotland. Despite our different party affiliations, we agreed about more than we didn't, and he was always very supportive of me. But I was being pulled in too many directions.

Since the early 1990s, I had been pushed beyond my experience and maturity. I had got away with it, but during the Scottish Parliament election I struggled not to wilt. I had become known for being a capable and combative media performer, but suddenly my confidence deserted me. I was terrified of making a blunder, of being the one to torpedo our campaign. I became tentative and robotic in interviews. I also wasn't sleeping well, so I felt sluggish and off the pace. But it was the ever-present anxiety gnawing away at me that I remember most.

There wasn't much in the way of support for those at the hard edge of SNP campaigns. The party had limited staff resources. It also wouldn't have crossed my mind to tell anyone I was struggling, or to ask for help or guidance. The culture of politics then, and possibly still today, was to cover up any signs of weakness or vulnerability. This was compounded for me by a fear of letting Alex down. I also still carried the niggling doubt that I wasn't good enough. So, I soldiered on, trying to live up to the responsibilities I had, but feeling increasingly inadequate.

As well as focusing on winning Govan, I was the party's education spokesperson, and on one occasion I was fronting a press conference, alongside Mike Russell, to talk about our education policies, one of which was to extend the teaching of modern languages in schools. Press conferences were brutal affairs. By the final few weeks, there was a sense that our campaign wasn't meeting the expectations that had built up over 1998, when we had been flying high in the polls. The media scented blood and enjoyed the daily sport of trying to skewer us. On this particular day, I made it easy for them.

Brian Taylor, the political editor of BBC Scotland, asked me a basic question. Which modern languages would we prioritize? Instead of coming up with the obvious answers of French, German, Spanish, I froze. My mind went blank. I could say it was stage fright, though by this time I'd done plenty of press conferences. In truth, I just hadn't prepared well enough. It wasn't laziness – I was just doing too much. I had been in Govan until late the previous evening and hadn't given myself enough time to think through the obvious, and not so obvious, questions I might be asked. By the time I pulled myself together, Mike had stepped in to answer for me. I felt utterly stupid. I was convinced that the journalists in the room were suddenly wondering if this person they had long been told was the rising star of the SNP was actually a dud, an imposter. In that moment, what little confidence I had evaporated.

Never again in my entire political career did I go into a major interview or press conference without doing my homework. I have given many imperfect answers over the years, and been caught out on occasion, but the person who always over-prepared, who worked harder than she had to, often harder than anyone else around her, came back with a vengeance. Unfortunately, for a while, this obsessive 'work ethic' made me seem even dourer than I had been before. It eclipsed any personality that might have been starting to emerge. It would take me a few years to find, let alone project, any balanced sense of who I was amidst all the angst and anxiety.

———

My personal struggles in 1999 had their echoes in our campaign at large. Newspaper coverage was almost universally hostile, and we were unprepared for the onslaught against us. Alex did his best to breathe life into what was, by mid-April 1999, a badly flagging campaign. Following a particularly dire opinion poll showing us twenty points behind Labour, he decided to scrap press conferences and wage our campaign entirely on the streets. It was 'jaickets aff' he proclaimed, as he and I launched the new 'offensive' in Govan. In a move designed to appear daring, but which reeked of desperation, we launched our own daily newspaper, *Scotland's Voice*. The brainchild of Mike Russell, it was to be distributed, free of charge, by activists across the country.

All of this frantic activity did earn us a bit of a bounce in the polls but it didn't make any significant difference.

Given the disappointment that surrounded our performance, it is easy to forget just how much we did achieve in 1999. We scored our best share of the vote since October 1974, polling around 28%. We also elected thirty-five MSPs, more parliamentarians in a single day than we had done in every Westminster election combined up to that point. Labour and the Liberal Democrats would go on to form a coalition in what was then called the Scottish Executive, but we became the principal opposition in a Parliament based in Edinburgh, with all of the influence and resources that entailed.

But, whilst we donned a brave face, we knew we had fallen short. And, of course, I failed to win Govan. Gordon Jackson won with a majority of 1,756 – 43% to 37%. I would enter Parliament as a regional MSP, but my failure – and I saw it very much as *my* failure – to win the constituency was hard to bear. In 1997, I had been the plucky underdog, scoring a victory of sorts just by coming close. By contrast, in 1999, I was the front-runner, widely tipped to win; the rising star, with a high profile, up against a Labour candidate who had given the impression that his heart wasn't really in it. And still I lost. I felt that I must be as unlikeable and unappealing to voters as the media narrative was making out.

Could we have done better in 1999? Perhaps, but we were outgunned financially, strategically and organizationally. Our operation was amateur in comparison to Labour's.

Perhaps most significantly, we were a party arguing for independence before the Scottish people had experienced the devolved Parliament in action. That was always going to jar. When we talked about independence, we sounded out of touch, and when we tried not to, we sounded evasive, as if we were trying to hide our real agenda. We could have handled that better, making it clearer that we intended to be patient, that our immediate priority was to build confidence in devolution. But while it is easy to see that in retrospect, it would have caused turbulence in the party at the time.

There were two other developments in the campaign that were seen to have damaged our prospects. In his spring budget, the Chancellor, Gordon Brown, had announced a 1p cut in the basic rate of income tax. Alex, after very little consultation, decided that we should reverse it. He announced that we would use the so-called Tartan Tax power to increase the basic rate by 1p, effectively cancelling Labour's cut and raising an estimated £700 million for public services. Conventional wisdom judged that the policy, later dubbed the Penny for Scotland, was a mistake. The assumption was that for all the talk of protecting public services, when push came to shove, people would not vote for higher taxes. As it happens, I don't think the Penny for Scotland hurt our campaign at all, but it didn't help much either. When the policy was first announced, we had nothing at all to say about how the revenue would be invested, beyond vague mutterings about extra money for health and education. And that was a big failure, because, had it been thought through more carefully and handled better, the Penny for Scotland might actually have captured the imagination.

The lesson I learned from this episode was that no matter how important high ideals and principles are in politics, there is always a need for a retail offer too, an answer to the question most voters will ask: 'What is in this for me?' We couldn't answer that question in 1999. We wouldn't start winning until we could.

The other major development during the campaign was the NATO bombing of Yugoslavia, which was engaged in a brutal campaign of ethnic cleansing against the largely Muslim, Albanian population of Kosovo. As is normal when UK troops are engaged in combat, the Prime Minister gave a televised address to the nation, with the leader of the opposition replying the following day.

Unusually, on this occasion, because of the ongoing election campaign, Alex was also offered a broadcast slot on the evening of 29 March.

The basic argument he made in the broadcast was that a bombing campaign alone, without boots on the ground, would not have the desired effect of destabilizing the Milošević regime and protecting Kosovars. Even though the argument was valid, there was a risk in making it at all in a moment when the public expected unity. In times of conflict, criticisms directed at governments are all too easily heard as slights on the servicemen and women carrying out the orders. But, still, it is an argument that might have cut through had Alex not cast it in language quite so incendiary.

He accused the NATO allies of 'unpardonable folly' and, in so doing, cast doubt on their motives. To Muslim ears, it even sounded as if he thought protecting Muslim lives wasn't a worthy enough objective. He also made a crass comparison between the NATO bombing of Yugoslavia and the Nazi bombing of Clydebank during the Blitz. It was disastrous and it blindsided the rest of us. He had filmed the broadcast at the Highland home of Dennis MacLeod, a Canadian Scot and party supporter who had made his millions in mining. As far as I know, with the possible exception of Mike Russell, he had consulted no one other than Dennis about what he intended to say.

I know that he didn't intend to cause offence, but I do believe that the provocation was to some extent deliberate. Our campaign was flagging, and he saw an opportunity to inject life into it, to play the international statesman and win kudos as a result. He always had a bit of a blind spot on foreign affairs, believing himself to be more expert than was the case. He gambled at the wrong time and definitely on the wrong issue, and we paid the price.

I was out on the doorsteps when the broadcast aired. The first I knew of how badly it had landed was when I chapped a door in Ibrox to be told by the person who opened it, 'Fuck off, yer man's an arse.' From that point on, something shifted in the atmosphere of the campaign. It had already been difficult but there was now a chilliness from some, especially older people and those in the Muslim community.

The moment I realized it had done us real damage was at a public meeting organized by Scots Asians for Independence in Pollokshields, part of the Govan constituency. Alex and I were both scheduled to speak. Until then we had been making real progress in the Muslim community. A couple of weeks earlier we would have been cheered to the rafters. Instead, we arrived to stony silence, followed by tough questions. As the meeting wore on, Alex did well to win the audience round, but I remember thinking that if the mood in the hall was reflected in the community at large, I had no chance of winning Govan.

Whatever the impact it had, or didn't have, on the election result, the Kosovo episode was a reminder that, in any strong leader, the line between brilliance and stupidity can be a very fine one. I fell on the wrong side of it myself often enough, but it was definitely part of Alex's character to believe that no matter how weak the fundamentals of a campaign might be, he could always turn it with a clever wheeze. In my experience, these wheezes failed more often than they succeeded. We started winning, and kept winning, when we fixed the fundamentals.

CHAPTER FIVE

Nicola Sturgeon, MSP

The next four years were not the happiest, politically or personally, for me, and it is tempting to skip over them. But they are an important part of my story. In many ways, they were a bridge I had to cross to become someone capable of leading.

I had worked my whole life to be in Parliament, for most of it with no real expectation that the ambition would ever be fulfilled, and now here I was, a Member of the Scottish Parliament. Yet, no matter how hard I tried, I couldn't shake the sense of failure. My election as one of the Parliament's fifty-six regional MSPs was part and parcel of the PR system. Of the SNP's thirty-five MSPs, twenty-eight of us had been elected in this way. In theory, our places in Parliament were no less legitimate than those of MSPs elected first past the post in a constituency, but it's not how I felt. I had not been good enough to win Govan. I didn't deserve to be there.

I had gone suddenly from being the standout rising star of the SNP to just one of the crowd. Other young MSPs were less well known and therefore more of a novelty. They commanded more media attention. Were they smarter and more able than me?

During this period, there was the occasional anonymously sourced story in the media about how I wasn't cutting the mustard, that I was a disappointment to Alex. I should have shrugged it off, but it ate away at me, confirming my own doubts.

———

The new Scottish Parliament opened in a blaze of glory and sky-high expectations. The first sitting took place on 12 May 1999. I was officially sworn in, alongside the other 128 MSPs. Pending the election of a Presiding Officer (Holyrood's version of the Speaker), the session was chaired by Winnie Ewing as the oldest member, the 'mother' of the Parliament. On that day she uttered words that will be carved for ever in the annals of Scottish history: 'The Scottish Parliament, adjourned on the 25th day of March in the year 1707, is hereby reconvened.'

The formal opening ceremony took place a few weeks later, on 1 July. It was a star-studded affair. The Queen was in attendance. She gifted the new Parliament its mace, inscribed with the words 'wisdom, justice, compassion, integrity'. The celebrity guest of honour was Sir Sean Connery, a long-time supporter of the SNP and independence. MSPs and guests proceeded up the Royal Mile in Edinburgh to the Parliament's temporary home in the Church of Scotland's General Assembly building on the Mound. The streets were lined with people. The atmosphere was one of celebration, achievement, hope.

In the precinct to the General Assembly building there is a statue of John Knox, the sixteenth-century Calvinist preacher who had been one of the leaders of the Scottish Reformation and the founder of the Presbyterian Church of Scotland. One of his most famous publications was *The First Blast of the Trumpet Against the Monstrous Regiment of Women*, in which he argued that rule by women was contrary to the Bible. Women accounted for 37% of the members of the new Parliament. In fact, more women were elected to the Scottish Parliament on 6 May 1999 than had been elected in total to the House of Commons since women had first been allowed to stand in 1918. Gender equality in Scotland, as in most countries, is still a work in progress, and female representation in our Parliament has ebbed and flowed over the years, but there is no doubt that 1999 represented a significant leap forward. I'm glad John Knox was there to watch.

The Queen acknowledged, openly and graciously, that 'this new Parliament, and the symbolism of this opening ceremony, are rightly anchored in the history of Scotland'.

And yet some of her words seemed more pointed, intended to convey that the Parliament had been an accommodation granted by the UK rather than Scotland's to claim as of right:

'Over the centuries the British have sought to acknowledge and promote that pragmatic balance between continuity and change as we have forged new political structures to respond more effectively to democratic aspirations.'

Donald Dewar's speech was one for the ages. Indeed, no account of the day would be complete without it being quoted at length:

This is about more than our politics and our laws. This is about who we are, how we carry ourselves. In the quiet moments today, we might hear some echoes from the past:

The shout of the welder in the din of the great Clyde shipyards;

The speak of the Mearns, with its soul in the land;

The discourse of the enlightenment, when Edinburgh and Glasgow were a light held to the intellectual life of Europe;

The wild cry of the Great Pipes;

and back to the distant cries of the battles of Bruce and Wallace.

The past is part of us. But today there is a new voice in the land, the voice of a democratic Parliament. A voice to shape Scotland, a voice for the future.

Walter Scott wrote that only a man with soul so dead could have no sense, no feel of his native land. For me, for any Scot, today is a proud moment; a new stage on a journey begun long ago and which has no end. This is a proud day for all of us.

A Scottish Parliament. Not an end: a means to greater ends.

If the subtext of the Queen's words was 'this far and no further', Dewar's speech seemed to signify the opposite. His description of a journey with no end was taken by independence supporters to mean that the devolved Parliament of 1999 was not necessarily the end of the process, and that it was up to the Scottish people to decide the course it took, up to and including independence. It is an interpretation that I am certain Dewar did not intend. He was saying that it was what the Parliament did, now and in the future, to improve life in Scotland that mattered and that this would always be a work in progress. Either way, his words resonated. For a man not normally known for soaring rhetoric, he had staked his claim as the author of one of the finest speeches in Scottish history.

It was a great day. The blues that I had been suffering since the election were suspended and, with the formalities over, it was time to party. The evening was rounded off with an open-air concert in Princes Street Gardens, headlined by the rock band Garbage, whose lead singer is the Scottish singer/songwriter Shirley Manson.

I went to bed that night more than slightly drunk, and feeling excited for what lay ahead. For the briefest of moments, it seemed that the whole nation felt the same way.

———

The best parties, however, often result in the worst hangovers. And so it proved now.

It didn't take long for the feeling to fade, for me and for the nation. Scotland had been waiting for a Parliament for three hundred years. So many of the hopes, dreams and aspirations of the country had been invested in its potential. There was a sense that all of our social and economic ills could now be fixed at a stroke. Against that backdrop of unrealistic expectations, it is perhaps not surprising that a feeling of disillusionment would soon set in. But the extent and depth of it could not have been foreseen. Nor was it inevitable.

A series of missteps and misjudgements quickly steeped the new Parliament in a stench of scandal. A new, permanent home, to be designed by the Catalan architect Enric Miralles and built on the site of the old Scottish and Newcastle brewery directly across the road from Holyrood Palace, had been formally commissioned in 1998. The project was quickly beset by delays and costly overruns which escalated over the early period of devolution and served to undermine faith in the new legislature's competence.

New MSPs were also cast into the invidious position of setting our own pay and expenses, giving the impression that we were more interested in feathering our nests than delivering for the country. Another bad judgement in the days leading up to the formal opening ceremony struck a particularly sour note. A decision was taken to commission special commemorative 'medals' to mark the occasion and issue one to each MSP. This immediately caused a fuss about politicians awarding themselves gongs before we had actually done any work.

All of this sapped enthusiasm for the new Parliament, and it was the SNP which bore the brunt. We had suffered in the election from a perception that our commitment to devolution was half-hearted; that, for us, it was just a stepping stone to independence. Now, as the party most identified with constitutional change, we were being disproportionately blamed for devolution's perceived failures.

Our MSPs were also divided and dysfunctional. For the first time ever, we had a large number of elected politicians. But only nine of our thirty-five MSPs had any prior parliamentary experience. The rest of us were novices, with varying degrees of willingness to recognize that fact. There were several big egos in our ranks, and they clashed frequently with the leadership. As a part of the wider leadership, I quickly found myself in conflict with some larger-than-life personalities, including Margo MacDonald, the 1973 victor in the Govan by-election, who had been elected in 1999 as an MSP in Edinburgh.

There were also lingering divisions over tactics and strategy, most notably how we should be using our position in the new Parliament to best advance the case for independence. Alex never really took the time to try to work through and resolve these differences, a criticism that would also be levelled at me during my leadership. He essentially decided what our policy, tactics and strategy would be.

He was also not one to pass up a political opportunity, even if it involved a sacrifice of principle. As a result, an issue which dominated the early days of the new Parliament also created tension between him and me.

———

In early 2000, the Labour/Liberal Scottish Executive confirmed its intention to repeal Section 28, the clause inserted into a Local Government Act in 1988 to ban the 'promotion' of homosexuality. The clause stated that councils 'shall not intentionally promote homosexuality or publish material with the intention of promoting homosexuality' and, specifically, that schools should not 'promote the teaching . . . of the acceptability of homosexuality as a pretended family relationship'.

The message it intended to send was that while gay relationships might be legally acceptable, they were not morally so. It was a wicked piece of legislation and, in perpetuating and intensifying the stigma and prejudice suffered by those in the LGBTQ+ community, it damaged many lives. Repealing it was absolutely the right thing to do, and I had expected the SNP to be enthusiastically and unequivocally behind the move.

It didn't quite work out like that. A furious and deeply unpleasant campaign was launched to 'Keep the Clause'. It was spearheaded and funded by Brian Souter, the owner of Stagecoach and long-time SNP supporter and friend of Alex – and someone I like a great deal despite fundamental disagreement on issues like this one. Brian was backed by the Catholic Church and given a media platform by the *Daily Record*. The focal point of the campaign was an unofficial 'referendum' to ask the public whether Section 28 should be repealed or not. Unsurprisingly, given how the campaign was pitched and promoted, most who took part voted for retention of the clause. But less than a third of the ballot papers that had been posted out were returned. Most of Scotland ignored it.

Those behind it pitched the campaign as all about the protection of children. They maintained that it was not anti-gay. However, it was clearly implying that gay people and their relationships posed a risk to children. Whether intended or not, it was deeply homo-phobic. As education spokesperson, I led for the SNP group on the issue. There was no doubt in my mind where I stood. I backed repeal wholeheartedly and wanted us to be firm in our support.

However, Alex took a different view. He was by instinct a social conservative, but on Section 28, no doubt influenced by Brian, he also sensed an opportunity to embarrass Labour and build support within the Catholic and other faith communities. He initially wanted us to oppose repeal outright. I was adamant that I couldn't and wouldn't support that. Partly as a result of my stance, but also because he knew there would be significant unrest within the party if we argued to retain the clause, he shifted position to one of 'finding compromise'.

We ended up arguing that Section 28 should be repealed but replaced with statutory guidelines for teachers which explicitly recognized the value of traditional marriage. This was ultimately the compromise the Scottish Executive agreed to. The legislation repealing Section 28 imposed a general duty on education author-ities to 'have regard to the value of stable family life'. This was a compromise that many thought necessary at the time, but it doesn't remove the guilt I feel for having gone along with what was essen-tially a concession to bigotry.

It reflected my inability – at that time – to stand up to Alex even when I thought he was pandering to prejudice. I am not proud of that, but I did learn from it.

———

In the early months of the new Parliament, it was clear that Alex wasn't firing on all cylinders. He seemed tired and ill at ease. He had honed his skills in the cut and thrust of the House of Commons and found the style and atmosphere of the Scottish Parliament difficult to adapt to. He was being regularly bested in debate by Donald Dewar, which rankled deeply with him. The cocksure confidence that was his trademark had gone and we all noticed.

Even so, no one expected his dramatic resignation as SNP leader. He phoned me at home on the evening of 17 July 2000 to tell me that he intended to announce the following day that he was stepping down. He felt he was becoming a drag on the party's fortunes and that it was time for us to move on from him. I disagreed vehemently and tried to change his mind, but I was wasting my time. His course was set. I was inconsolable. I couldn't imagine the SNP without him at the helm. I felt we had let him down; that he was paying the price for our collective under-performance, our failure to get to grips with devolution and take the new Parliament by storm.

He told me that I had earned the right to consider standing for leader myself if that's what I wanted. He was wrong about that – I hadn't earned the right – and he was only being polite. More pertinently, he advised me to throw my weight behind John Swinney.

He announced his resignation on 18 July, the day before my thirtieth birthday. Stuart and a couple of my friends had organized a surprise party for me in an Italian restaurant on Great Western Road in Glasgow's West End. Many MSP colleagues were there, including Roseanna, Mike Russell and Shona Robison. Not surprisingly, the only topic of conversation was Alex's resignation and the leadership election that now loomed.

Roseanna was my closest friend, and a potential candidate for the leadership. She had the right to ask for my support, to look to me to be her campaign manager even. But by then I had already given my support to John, someone who until then I hadn't been particularly close to at all, and I had agreed to spearhead his campaign. It wasn't just that I was following Alex's advice; I also believed that, for all Roseanna's strengths, John would make the better leader.

John and I developed a strong working relationship in the leadership election, which he went on to win. Although Roseanna was elected deputy leader, I became John's de facto deputy, assuming many of the responsibilities that might otherwise have been Roseanna's. I understand why she felt let down. In being so single-minded about my own career advancement, I didn't think about the consequences of my actions for our friendship, and I regret it. Roseanna and I have long since mended our differences and she was a key member of my government for much of my time as First Minister, but the events of that period undoubtedly robbed our friendship of a closeness it might otherwise have today.

It was behaviour all too typical of me at the time, caused in part by the self-doubt that chipped away at my confidence. That's not an attempt to excuse or absolve, merely to try to understand and explain. I had a burning ambition to succeed in politics but wasn't yet comfortable in my own skin. The ruthlessness I displayed was, to some extent, compensation for my insecurity.

On reflection, I should have spent more time on my personal development. I could have taken a step back from internal party machinations and built relationships; worked out my own views on different issues, rather than automatically adopting the party line; learned to think, and act, more independently; enjoyed life more; chilled out a bit.

Instead, I became a more intense version of the takes-herself-too-seriously, sound-bite politician I was increasingly seen as. When John became leader, he appointed me Shadow Health Minister. It was a steep learning curve. I threw myself into work, briefing myself to the eyeballs on every topic I spoke about, ensuring I was word perfect on every party policy and position. I must have sounded like a talking manifesto.

———

There's no doubt I made lots of mistakes, but it is also worth saying that they might not have had the same impact had I been male. Working hard, being driven and career-focused are desirable attributes in men. In women, the same traits are derided as unfeminine and unlikeable. The irony, of course, is that being feminine and likeable is also problematic for women as we are then criticized for not being serious enough.

I was unpopular among some of my colleagues, though I am sure there was some professional jealousy at play too. I was also the butt of jokes from the opposition, though I know it suited them politically to deride someone talked about as a possible future leader.

More seriously, I was subjected to some nasty bullying by a male MSP of another party. At some stage over this first term of Parliament, he started calling me 'Gnasher', both to other people and occasionally to my face. At first, I didn't understand it. Eventually, I discovered that it was a reference to a story being spread around that I had once injured a boyfriend during oral sex. Whether he was the instigator of the story or just enjoyed referencing it to make me feel uncomfortable, I don't know, and I'm not sure it makes much difference. It was untrue, and the fact I feel the need to say that is in itself horrible, but I was utterly mortified. On the day I found out about the story, I cried in one of the toilets in the Parliament office complex, wondering how I was ever going to face people.

His behaviour got steadily worse. He would often make 'jokes' about teeth or dentists when I was within earshot. I can still visualize the gleeful sneer on his face. He seemed to revel in my discomfort and I became quite scared of him. My heart would race whenever I saw him or heard his voice. His taunting of me abated eventually, but only after months of what felt like torture. Like bullies often do, maybe he just got bored. Every now and then, the 'story' would resurface. In 2004, when I briefly stood for party leader, Stuart, by that time my ex, was doorstepped by a tabloid asking if he had been the one. He sent the journalist packing, but the paper still printed a version of the story.

I thought it was just part and parcel of politics, something I had to endure. It wasn't until 2017, when I was filling out a survey conducted by the Scottish Parliament authorities in the wake of the #MeToo revelations, that I realized it had been bullying. It was bullying of an overtly sexual nature, designed to humiliate and intimidate, to cut a young woman down to size and put her in her place.

While I'd like to say that things are better now, I'm not sure it is true. Today, a story of this type would stalk a woman round social media, day and night. We have such a long way still to go to make the public sphere safe for women and girls. I just worry that by the time we get there, there will be too few women left in public life for it to matter.

Perhaps the fact that I have not named this man is another sign that things have not changed as much as I might have hoped. I have thought long and hard about whether I should reveal his identity. I worry that in deciding not to, I am being less brave than I should be. But the thought of his face all over the media, and of the backlash he might try to whip up against me, makes me feel sick. Even just thinking about it transports me back to the day I cried in the toilet all those years ago. It is for my own sake that

I am letting him off the hook. But he knows who he is. I can only hope that he has the decency to reflect on how his behaviour made me feel.

———

As this first session of the new Scottish Parliament drew to a close, I was miserable. Partly, it was personal. My relationship with Stuart was dead, though not yet buried. I was living a nomadic existence, staying as much as I could at a friend's place in Edinburgh to avoid going home. But it wasn't just that.

I had fallen out of love with politics. My expectations of the Parliament, like those of the country as a whole, had been high, probably unrealistically so – and the experience had fallen short. Tragically, towards the end of 2000, the First Minister, Donald Dewar, who had become a 'father of the nation' figure, died suddenly. It shocked the body politic, and the country, to the core. A year later, his successor Henry McLeish was forced to resign over an expenses 'scandal'. By today's standards, what he was accused of seems insignificant, but it all added to a sense that MSPs were not up to the task. I was starting to think it about myself too: was I good enough to make the difference that I wanted?

By the time of the 2003 election, I was going through the motions, with no real passion or enthusiasm. I was the candidate in Govan again, but this time I didn't I believe I had any chance of winning. At John's appointment, I was also the national campaign manager. We tried hard to apply the lessons of 1999 and, superficially at least, our campaign was more professional than four years previously. We had an advertising agency and PR professionals helping guide our message. But while our presentation may have been slicker, the politics were wrong. Our pitch was too negative. Our strapline was 'Time's Up' and most of our material focused on the failings of Labour in general and Jack McConnell, First Minister since late 2001, in particular. We still weren't giving people a clear reason to vote for us. Negative campaigns rarely win elections.

The public mood was difficult for us to navigate too. In 1999, many people were unwilling to vote for an independence-supporting party without first getting to experience devolution in action. In 2003, they were unwilling to do so because the devolved Parliament had been a disappointment and confidence in self-government had been undermined. Tony Blair was becoming ever more divisive, but although public opinion about the Iraq war was sceptical at that point, it hadn't yet turned as sour as it later became. Whatever doubts people had about Labour, they had deeper ones about us. The divisions and dysfunction that had bedevilled us over the past four years had made us look even less like a government in waiting than we had been in 1999.

The outcome was a disaster. We went backwards, losing seven of our thirty-five seats, with big names like Mike Russell amongst them. Our vote share dropped by five percentage points. For a third time running, I had failed to make the breakthrough in Govan. We entered the second session of the Scottish Parliament in a state of crisis, with John's leadership on shaky ground.

For me, it felt like the end of the road, the point at which my political story would be over. The only question was whether I would serve the term or stand down sooner. Either way, the girl who had lived and breathed politics for as long as she could remember was on the verge of quitting. She was done. Or so she thought.

CHAPTER SIX

Climbing the Mountain

A week after polling day, I moved out of the flat I had shared with Stuart for the previous few years. Our relationship had limped on for much longer than was good for either of us. In the end, he forced the pace, but it was me who moved out. Within forty-eight hours of biting the bullet, I had viewed, leased and moved into a swanky modern flat in Glasgow city centre. I have seen Stuart less than a handful of times since. Notwithstanding the upset of the break-up, the move proved to be really good for me. I went out more, saw friends I hadn't kept closely enough in touch with, and generally learnt to relax a bit more.

It was soon after that my relationship with Peter Murrell started. I had known Peter since I was a teenager. He had been recruited in 1987 to run Alex's constituency office in Peterhead and my activities with the Young Scottish Nationalists back then brought me into contact with him on a few occasions. However, it wasn't until he became the party's Chief Executive that I got to know him properly. During the 2003 campaign we worked together closely, seeing each other almost every day. It was when that was over and we no longer had to spend so much time together that I realized I still wanted to. And so did he. We tentatively started seeing each other outside of work as he, like me, was emerging from a long-term relationship. But as the year progressed, despite our intentions to take things slowly, we became a couple. I was happy.

I was still determined to get out of politics. I hadn't decided whether to do so quickly or wait until the end of the term, four years hence. As a regional MSP, I could have stood down with no by-election; the person behind me on the party list would simply have taken my place. My indecision on timing was perhaps a sign that deep down I wasn't as sure as I thought. But I felt certain at the time, and liberated. I started to think seriously about the different path I wanted to take. I knew going back to being a solicitor wasn't it, but something around human rights or international law appealed. I was also keen on seeing more of the world, maybe working overseas for a while.

I found that when I stopped obsessing about rungs on the political career ladder, I could think more deeply about the substance of politics. Suddenly I wasn't just swallowing the party line but was working out my own opinion. I was reading a lot of non-fiction about US politics, the Middle East, Ireland. I read a pile of books on the New Labour project – volumes by people like Philip Gould and Peter Mandelson. I tried to work out what the SNP should and should not learn from that example. I began to form strong views about what we had to do differently as a party. I told myself it was academic, that I was unlikely to fight another election, but, of course, it became highly relevant as we approached the 2007 contest.

It seemed suddenly obvious to me that any advance in the independence cause depended on the Scottish Parliament being a success. If confidence in it was destroyed, people's response wouldn't be to support independence; they would simply lose faith in Scotland's ability to govern itself. So, instead of opportunistically exploiting the growing pains of devolution, we had to become its champion and persuade people that we were the party to fulfil its potential. Only when the Scottish people could see and feel the benefits of self-government would they demand more.

Tied to that was the need to tell people what an SNP government would mean for their own lives. It's not that people don't care about the higher principles of politics. But, not unreasonably, they also want to understand how it translates to their day-to-day realities: their jobs and incomes, their children's education, the availability of healthcare when their family needs it. We hadn't yet given people confidence that we could make their lives better either in the clarity of our message or the credibility of our messengers. That needed to change.

The liberation was personal as well as political. I was also taking the time to indulge my passion for fiction in a way I hadn't for a while. I had loved reading novels as a child, but it was in this period that I realized just how important they were to me. Over the years, I have learned more from literature about people, places and periods in history than I have from the various non-fiction tomes I have ploughed through. Reading fiction is essential to my equilibrium, and during this period it helped me centre myself.

Over the summer of 2003, I went on a Margaret Atwood binge. *Oryx and Crake* had just been published and I went on to voraciously consume her back catalogue. It was over this summer that I also started reading the Scottish crime novelist Val McDermid. *The Distant Echo* – the first in what became her Karen Pirie series – was just out. Reading that then led me to everything else she had written. What I didn't know then – and couldn't have predicted – was that Val and her partner, Jo, would later become my best friends.

I was also having fun. I was a woman, in my early thirties, living alone in the centre of our biggest city. I was making the most of it, seeing Peter regularly, but also going out with pals – especially my longstanding friend, who would later become an MP, Anne McLaughlin. I even went on a health kick, becoming a committed disciple of the Carol Vorderman detox diet. Whatever people say about fad diets, it worked and I lost a lot of weight.

I was realizing more generally just how limited my thinking and experiences had been. It was no wonder that despite the raw talent I had for politics, I had wilted in the white light of scrutiny. While I had been focusing so exclusively on climbing the greasy political pole, even parliamentary trips overseas had seemed like an indulgence, as I was always worried about the intrigue and opportunities I might miss at home. It was incredibly short-sighted of me. In the year after the 2003 election, I went on cross-party trips to Croatia and Canada. I also spent a week on my own in Paris, at the invitation of the French government, meeting politicians and officials to learn more about governance and democracy.

I was, step by step, broadening my mind and my horizons. I wasn't doing it with an eye to my political advancement, quite the opposite in fact. Nevertheless, there is no doubt that when the moment came to recommit myself to politics, I was much better equipped for what lay ahead.

———

My own adventures took my mind off the ongoing – and deepening – troubles of the SNP. Far from being a wake-up call, the election setback turbocharged the internal bloodletting. The divisions were ostensibly about strategy and, unbelievably, we were still arguing about whether we were pro or anti the devolved Scottish Parliament. We were also split on whether the route to independence should be via a referendum or just a majority of seats in an election (at that point a laughably forlorn hope), and on how left wing or centre ground we should be.

Personality clashes and oversized egos also played a part. It always seemed to me that people like Alex Neil and Jim Sillars were serial malcontents who wanted to be in charge and couldn't reconcile themselves to the fact they weren't. In the autumn of 2003, a little-known MSP called Bill Wilson decided to challenge John for the leadership. Although they denied it, there is no doubt in my mind that Jim Sillars and Alex Neil were behind it. It spoke volumes that neither of them had the guts to stand themselves. I was strongly in support of John, but, as I considered myself to be in the exit lane from frontline politics, I didn't want to be as closely involved in the contest as I had been in 2000.

That position didn't hold for very long. A lengthy article that I wrote for a Sunday newspaper setting out what I thought the party had to do to get itself on track was interpreted as a thinly veiled pitch for a leadership bid of my own. Maybe I had been naive in not foreseeing that, but the upshot was that I threw myself into John's campaign. I wanted there to be no doubt that he had my full support. He won, but the contest was deeply unpleasant. It did nothing to broaden our appeal to the electorate; probably the opposite. At the time, SNP leaders were elected by just a few hundred delegates from branches across the country. These were the most active activists in our ranks, fantastic people, but not necessarily representative of the wider public. It was to John's credit that he set about trying to fix this.

In spring 2004, he drove through far-reaching reforms to our internal processes. The most important of these was the adoption of a 'one member, one vote' system for the election of the leader and deputy leader. This was more than just a technocratic change. It was instrumental in our journey to government in 2007. The wider membership of a party is still not perfectly representative of a country, but it is much more so than a narrow activist base and it forced us to look outwards.

Another of the proposed reforms was the adoption of positive action to boost the number of women elected to Parliament. It was a move I had long advocated, but the party had repeatedly rejected it. We had always had able, high-profile women in our ranks, including Winnie Ewing, Maggie Ewing and Roseanna. But quality was masking the lack of quantity, so I spoke out in favour of reform. 'Women are not a minority,' I argued, 'we form the majority of the Scottish population. If we can't get it right for the majority, what chance do we have of getting it right for the minorities we want to see represented in our parliament?'

For the first time, the SNP backed positive action. These reforms were vital, but they were not enough to save John's leadership. In the European election in June 2004, we polled less than 20% of the vote, going backwards, not forwards. Gil Paterson, an MSP who had lost his seat in 2003, was the first to call for John's resignation. That wasn't surprising. Much less expected was Mike Russell's public comment that it was time for the 'men in grey kilts' to step in. It was a move that hurt John deeply. Mike had been a long-time friend, and an MSP until 2003, when he lost his seat.

It was a horrible time. The party's difficulties were not solely John's fault, they were our collective responsibility. He did everything he could to turn things around, but on 22 June he announced that he was stepping down as leader.

_____

John Swinney's leadership ended on a sour note between the two of us. Given how close we had been, this made an already distressing situation even worse. My own naivety was partly to blame, but so too was a bit of foul play by Roseanna. In the days leading up to John's resignation, I had decided to reach out to her. I was upset by the continued deterioration in our relationship. My move was well intentioned but, in the circumstances, ill judged. We arranged to meet for lunch in a restaurant in Stirling. Referring to the possibility of a leadership election, I told her that I was worried about the potential in the weeks ahead of us being pitted against each other. I expressed the hope that we could avoid this.

Later that evening, I learned that the *Daily Record* was about to run a story to the effect that I had tried to persuade Roseanna to form a 'joint ticket' leadership bid with me, in what was essentially a plot to oust John. I was stunned and devastated. I felt stupid and more fearful than ever that there was no way back for our friendship. Worst of all, it quickly became clear that, though the story wasn't true, John believed it.

It seemed to me that the story could only have come from Roseanna or someone she had confided in. The motive? Perhaps it was revenge for the shoddy way she felt I had treated her, but it also gave her an advantage in the leadership election that was surely coming. It is a truism in politics that he, or she, who wields the knife rarely wears the crown. If she could make members believe that I had stabbed John in the back, any bid of mine to succeed him would be undermined from the outset.

Roseanna threw her hat in the ring almost immediately after John announced his resignation. She showed a lot of energy, guile and ruthlessness in those few days. Mike Russell would also soon declare, though his candidacy was never a serious proposition.

Suddenly I had a big decision to make too. I made the wrong call. Standing to be leader of the party, at that moment, was a stupid thing to do and, if I am being honest, I knew it. Although the debates around internal reforms had sucked me back in, I had only recently been contemplating giving up politics.

More to the point, I wasn't yet up to being leader. I was starting to mature in my thinking and approach to politics and I certainly wasn't lacking in ability or, relative to many others, political experience. However, my first difficult few years as an MSP should have told me that I needed to become a more rounded person, to build the experience and hone the skills I would require. I should have had the courage to recognize and acknowledge this. Instead, I succumbed to a dangerous duo of factors.

The first was the flattery of those encouraging me to stand. The second was my ambition. What if this moment never came around again? On 24 June, I announced my candidacy. I then formed a joint ticket with Kenny MacAskill as candidate for deputy leader. My long-time friend, Shona Robison, was my campaign manager, and on board my team were individuals with whom I would serve in government years later, such as Richard Lochhead, Angus Robertson and Kevin Stewart. Allison Hunter, the former full-time party organizer and latterly my election agent, played a key role too.

Shortly after, I flew to London to see Alex Salmond. He had encouraged me to stand and promised to endorse me at an appropriate moment in the campaign. However, I knew I had to strike a careful balance between the positive impact his support would have and being seen as his puppet. We spent a couple of hours chatting through pitfalls and possible tactics. Later that evening, just as I was going to bed, Alex called to tell me that Sean Connery was in Edinburgh and would like to meet me. Could I get myself there the next morning? It wasn't an invitation to be turned down, so I hastily rescheduled my flight home.

The next morning found me pressing the buzzer of Edinburgh's oldest and most prestigious private members' establishment. The New Club was founded in 1787 during the Scottish Enlightenment and is situated, unobtrusively, on Princes Street, Edinburgh's main thoroughfare. It is easy to miss, the front entrance nestled between shops on either side. The name I had been told to ask for, clearly Sean's pseudonym, did the trick and I was told to enter and come upstairs.

I was ushered into the library and told to make myself comfortable. A few minutes later, Sean appeared. I had met him before, but never just the two of us, one to one. Charisma is one of those attributes that it is almost impossible to describe in the abstract, but its presence, when encountered, is unmistakeable. Sean had it in spades. He was physically imposing and, even at seventy-four, as he was then, he was strikingly attractive. The famous voice with its highly distinctive timbre sounded exactly the same in person as it did on the screen.

We sat down and had tea. He asked me lots of questions about my leadership bid. Why I was standing, what did I think my chances were, where did I want to take the SNP? He was very complimentary, telling me he thought I was the best candidate for the job. His next comment, though, led to a very surreal experience. He said he had been watching me on TV and, while I communicated well, I would sound more authoritative if I deepened my voice.

He offered to show me how, using a simple technique taught to him when he was a young up-and-coming actor. Suddenly, there I was, under the instruction of 007 himself, pacing up and down the library of the New Club, with a folded piece of paper between my teeth, repeating sentences chosen, it seemed, for their particular combination of syllables, consonants and vowels. Over the next half hour or so, he made me do it again and again. At first, I felt really awkward, even wondering if it was a joke at my expense. But eventually I relaxed and it became fun. More to the point, it worked. My voice slowed and deepened. The trick, in future, he told me, was that whenever I wanted to project authority I had to speak as if I had a piece of paper between my teeth.

I'm not sure I remembered to apply the technique very often. It is probably better suited to filming movies than it is to the stress of a live political interview. Nevertheless, my lesson in voice projection from Sir Sean Connery, and the laughter we shared in the process, is an experience I won't forget.

The next couple of weeks were rocky. The consensus opinion was that I would be defeated, heavily, by Roseanna. My youth and relative inexperience, my perceived dourness, even my closeness to Alex, were all points against me. And yet I worked hard to develop my pitch. I put together a manifesto and a campaign plan and staged a successful media launch. By contrast, after the assertiveness of her opening gambit, Roseanna seemed to lack purpose, focus and organization. She also had a difficult outing on BBC *Question Time*. She was hesitant, unprepared, and struggled to offer any coherent response to a predictable question for someone on the verge of leading the SNP: why should Scotland be independent?

There was no doubt that the *Question Time* debacle was the catalyst that brought Alex into the race. The day after my launch, I met him for lunch in Valvona & Crolla, a favourite Italian restaurant of his in Edinburgh. He told me that several members had contacted him, convinced that a Roseanna leadership would be disastrous and that while they might support me, I wouldn't beat her. 'Some even think I should stand,' he joked (or so I thought).

I am certain that by this point he had already made up his mind to stand himself. I suspect he had also planned to tell me so that day, but I was so upbeat after my launch success that perhaps my optimism gave him pause for thought. More likely, he simply decided that my state of mind would make me less receptive to his proposal. Either way, I left that day with no real inkling of what was coming.

A couple of days later, he invited me to lunch again, this time at the Champany Inn, in his hometown of Linlithgow. We had steak and a bottle of red wine, which I drank most of since he was driving. This was the encounter that the media would come to describe as our Granita moment, the equivalent of the pact in which Gordon Brown stood aside to allow Tony Blair to become Labour leader.

He told me straight that it was far from guaranteed that I could win, and that even if I did, he thought the alternative plan he was about to propose was a better one. He proposed that I abandon my leadership bid and stand instead on a joint ticket with him. Although he would be standing for leader, with me as deputy, it would to all intents and purposes be a co-leadership. If we succeeded, I would be the leader in the Scottish Parliament. He, a Westminster MP at this point, would spearhead our campaign activities across Scotland. Our pitch to the party would be bold in its ambition – we would be offering nothing short of a team to win the next Scottish election. He would be standing not just to be leader of the SNP, but the next First Minister of Scotland.

I said very little. I was trying to weigh it all up. His argument wasn't lost on me. It was compelling. Having him back as leader would certainly create a stir and give the party an edge we had been lacking. But wouldn't it be a massive step backwards, proof that we were a one-man band after all, with our best days already behind us? Would I have any credibility as leader in Holyrood if I wasn't my own boss? And wouldn't the very fact that I was stepping aside from my leadership bid confirm all the doubts people had of me: that I wasn't up to the top job; that I was nothing without the guiding hand of Alex Salmond?

I told him that I needed to sleep on it, and that I'd give him my decision the following day. What he was proposing made a lot of sense, but the questions that had crowded into my mind posed genuine concerns.

In my heart, though, I knew I wasn't ready to be leader. I realized that what had ultimately convinced me to stand was a strange sense of duty. Whatever my shortcomings might have been, I believed myself a stronger candidate, more ready and able to do the job than those I was standing against.

With Alex now in the picture, that argument no longer held water. He was clearly a stronger candidate than I was. In putting himself forward, he was also letting me off the hook, offering me a lifeline, the chance to prove myself and prepare for a time when I would be ready to step up as leader.

So I said yes, and the Salmond–Sturgeon dream team was born.

———

Over six weeks or so in the summer of 2004, we toured the country together on the leadership campaign trail. We were driven from one end of Scotland to the other by Alex's election agent, a wonderfully gruff, north-east loon called Stuart Pratt. The days were long and tiring, hard work, but, largely thanks to Alex, good fun. In the car we would laugh and joke and play daft games. I discovered that he was a country music fan, so we also had the occasional singalong to Dolly Parton.

There was no doubt he was going to win the contest for leader and everyone knew the outcome was a foregone conclusion. It was much less certain that I would win the race for deputy. The main concern was that I would be too easily dismissed in the Scottish Parliament as Alex's mouthpiece, and that my election would be a gift to the opposition. The other candidates for deputy leader were Fergus Ewing, son of Winnie, and Christine Grahame, a feisty and independently minded MSP who I rated highly. Kenny MacAskill pulled out of the contest to support the Salmond–Sturgeon ticket.

Fergus and Christine each made the argument that, since their relationship with Alex was not as close as mine, it would be harder for the opposition to write them off as his puppet. It was an argument that was gaining traction with party members. The only question was how many. The election was being conducted by single transferable vote. There was a real risk that if I didn't win on the first ballot with more than 50% of the vote, a subsequent round would see the second preference votes of Christine push Fergus over the line, or vice versa.

Alex was kind and supportive to me throughout this period, although, of course, there was some self-interest at play. His grand plan depended on me winning, but even so there was a personal closeness between us then that I hadn't experienced before.

In the end, my concern was unfounded. We triumphed. Alex won by a landslide, with over 70% of the vote. In the event, I polled much better than anyone had predicted. I won comfortably on the first ballot, with 53% of the votes cast.

———

I wasn't just the deputy leader of the SNP. I was also now the leader of the principal opposition in the Scottish Parliament. The summer recess had ended and it felt like a fresh start. The leadership election had cleared the air and the internal sniping had calmed down. The new session was due to start the following week in the delayed and much derided Holyrood building. I had a front-bench team to appoint. And on 8 September, less than a week on from the leadership election result, I would take on Jack McConnell at First Minister's Questions.

I was already mulling over possible questions and tactics and thinking through how I would respond to what I thought (wrongly, as it turned out) would be the inevitable jibes about me being Salmond's lackey. In a theme that I would develop effectively over my time as opposition leader, I decided to ask the First Minister about the NHS, on this occasion about the centralization of hospital services. I opened, however, with a more left-field question. He had made a comment in the preceding days about the need for MSPs to take the opportunity of the new chamber to raise our game. So, I decided to ask him in what ways he thought he had personally fallen short and how he intended to raise his own game. It wasn't a question he had prepared for, and he waffled in response.

The session went well. I was judged to have given a strong performance. Afterwards, Jack McConnell sent me a lovely note saying, 'Well done. Great first question too.'

It was a nice gesture, but it symbolized a huge tactical error on his part, one that cost him dear and played a part in Labour losing the next election. Jack had decided that he was going to treat me with respect as opposition leader and eschew jibes about me not really being in charge. Maybe he was worried about sounding sexist and bullying if he was constantly taunting me about a man pulling my strings. Whatever the reason for it, his decision allowed me to establish myself, and then gradually get the better of him, in a way I might have struggled to do had I faced constant questions about legitimacy and credibility. It reflected well on him as a person, but it was naive politics.

There is an amusing postscript to my first outing at First Minister's Questions. Back in my office afterwards, the phone rang. It was an unknown number, but I answered anyway, and immediately thought I was being pranked by someone doing a Sean Connery impression. I wasn't. It was the man himself, still in Edinburgh, saying that he had just watched me on TV and thought the tone and depth of my voice had been perfect. I took that as a win.

———

I got to grips with my new role as opposition leader more quickly than I could have hoped. Alex pretty much left me to it.

I had taken on Noel Dolan as my senior adviser. Noel had worked for Alex a few years before, but appointing him had been entirely my own decision, and one of the best I made. He had worked in broadcasting before politics and had a keen sense of what made good TV and how to get maximum coverage. I had three main objectives as opposition leader and, at risk of blowing my own trumpet, I think I did a decent job on all of them.

First was to unite our group of MSPs. That was made easier by the fact everyone was fed up with the division that had dogged us since 1999. But I also made sure everyone had a task, something to focus on. It wasn't always sweetness and light, but, by and large, we rubbed along, and as the months passed a sense of cohesion and camaraderie that had been lacking started to emerge.

Second, I was determined not just to perform well at First Minister's Questions but to do so strategically. I knew that to have any chance of winning, we had to offer positive change. But we first had to make the country believe change was needed. It was my job to make Jack McConnell and his administration look less than average. I focused hard on perceived problems in public services, especially the NHS. I was also trying to make McConnell look weak. It was difficult for him to speak out against London Labour policies, even those that many in Scottish Labour disagreed with, so I focused a lot on these too: issues like the Iraq war, nuclear power and nuclear weapons. It slowly drained him of authority and created the conditions for us to pitch Alex as the positive alternative who would stand up for Scotland, not kowtow to Westminster.

The final strand was to build a policy platform. I had become obsessed with our past failure to offer people good enough reasons to vote for us that were directly relevant to their day-to-day lives. It was therefore in my Holyrood leader's office, comprised of a small team of staffers overseen by Noel, that we started to build a compelling offer. Policies like the council tax freeze; the small business bonus (rates relief for thousands of small enterprises across the country); abolishing tolls on the Forth, Erskine and Tay bridges; abolishing prescription charges; keeping NHS services local; smaller class sizes in primary schools and more police on the beat would all be central to our 2007 manifesto.

The mood in the ranks improved, but, at first, there was little change in public perceptions. The polls didn't really shift. While we did OK in the 2005 General Election, picking up two new seats from Labour to give us six overall, our national vote share fell slightly. It was a steady performance, but not one that suggested we were on the brink of a historic breakthrough. The muttering of the malcontents started to surface again.

But during 2006 things started to change. The catalyst was a moment of real sadness for the SNP. In March 2006, Margaret Ewing, one of the most popular and loved figures in the party, died suddenly after a long struggle with breast cancer. Her death meant a by-election in her Moray constituency in the north-east of

Scotland. Moray was a seat that the SNP had held in Westminster since 1987 and in the Scottish Parliament since its establishment in 1999. We were expected to win the by-election, but we did much better than anticipated. Our candidate, Richard Lochhead, increased both our number and share of votes. All of a sudden we had a sense of momentum and we never looked back.

In the summer of 2006, we pulled level with Labour in the polls, and by September we had crept ahead. The amount of work it took to achieve and maintain this position was huge. We were in constant campaign mode, throwing ourselves into local council by-elections, embedding our local teams in communities up and down the country, and developing a manifesto that would eventually answer the question 'What does voting SNP mean for me and my family?'

Our commitment to an independence referendum was also crucial, not so much as an encouragement to those who supported independence, but, more importantly at that time, as reassurance to those who didn't. Lots of people liked our policies and approach but were nervous about opening the door to independence. A referendum offered them the security of knowing there would be a separate process to decide that issue and an opportunity to vote against it if that's what they wanted. It enabled us to grow support for the SNP beyond our traditional independence-backing base.

———

We invested a great deal of time, effort and resource in voter research. It revealed that our biggest strength, even amongst people who had never voted SNP before, was relatability. People saw us as being 'more like them' than Labour or the Tories. It was a priceless asset, and we were determined not to squander it.

At the heart of our 2007 election campaign was a photograph of Alex and me. It was the visual representation of the strength of our joint leadership. Male and female. Older and younger. I softened the too aggressive, too alpha-male, hard edges of his persona. He strengthened the too young, too inexperienced, weaker aspects of mine. Our message was clear: no matter how strong we were individually, together we were stronger.

In 2003, our slogan had been the negative and downbeat 'Time's Up'. In 2007, we took essentially the same message, that it was time for change, and turned it into something positive, optimistic, aspirational and full of potential. 'It's Time' became the clarion call of our entire campaign. We were talking ourselves up and making a statement that we were ready to govern.

Added to our own growing appeal was deepening disillusionment with Labour. Scotland was angry about the Iraq war, cynical about Tony Blair, fed up with the constant psychodrama between him and Gordon Brown. They were also unimpressed with the mediocrity of Jack McConnell and his ministers. The only ingredient we lacked was belief. With the possible exception of Alex, we were so steeped in the psychology of defeat that winning was almost impossible to imagine. And so, then, to the final piece of the 2007 jigsaw: Claire Howell.

Claire was a London-based psychology coach and mentor. She was much more used to working with Premier League footballers than with politicians. We were introduced to her by Mark Shaw, who by then was an important figure in our campaign. Mark was a successful property developer and, in his spare time, a Formula 3 racing driver.

I had met Mark randomly one day in 2006. He chased after me as we were both disembarking the Edinburgh–Glasgow train and told me he was interested in getting to know more about the SNP.

We met up for a chat a couple of weeks later. Mark was small and wiry, with dark, closely cut hair and an infectious energy. I remember being quite guarded when we met, wondering whether the train station encounter really had been happenstance or was it some kind of sting? But as Mark became progressively more involved in our operations, my doubts eventually evaporated completely. He had an impressive range and depth of contacts which were hugely helpful to us in the campaigns to come.

Mark had worked with Claire in the past and persuaded us to meet her. We decided to invite her to Dundee for the strategy session we had scheduled over the first weekend of January 2007. I was hugely sceptical about the need for a psychology coach. I remember feeling irritated and resentful that valuable time would be wasted. I turned up on the first morning and sat alongside my Shadow Cabinet colleagues and party staffers with my arms folded, determined not to engage.

Claire was just a few years older than me and was blonde and glamorous. She hailed from the south of England and was fairly posh. She had clearly done her homework though and completely understood what we needed. Much to my surprise, and in spite of my best efforts, she won me over. Over the course of that weekend, through simple tricks of the mind and more complex exercises in visualization, she helped change our mindset. By the end of it, we believed we could win.

The campaign passed in a flash. We remained ahead in most polls, but the margin was narrow. There was also no guarantee that a win in votes would secure us the biggest number of seats. I knew it would be close in Govan too. I had given it my all and I knew that if I didn't win this time, I never would. My Labour opponent, and the incumbent MSP, Gordon Jackson had taken to joking that if he defeated me for a third time, he should get to keep me on his mantelpiece. Gordon and I got on well and he didn't mean it too unkindly, but it stung.

I arrived at the count in the Scottish Exhibition Centre, on the north bank of the Clyde, just after midnight. I was a nervous wreck. To make matters worse, for the first time the votes were being counted electronically. Instead of watching piles of paper mount up, which had always given a fairly accurate sense of how things were going, we were now watching lines on a bar chart on a big screen. My line was slightly ahead of Gordon's, but I had no idea whether the 'gap' represented ten votes or a thousand. It was excruciating.

Within a few hours, though, the anxiety had been replaced by joy. At only the fourth time of trying (if the 1997 Westminster attempt is included), I had won Govan. Nationally, my party was standing on the brink of power for the first time in history.

———

My majority of 744 was hardly a landslide, but it was enough. I would sit in Parliament, not as a top-up-list member but as a constituency representative. It is impossible to overstate how important the win was for me. It gave me a confidence in myself and in my ability to connect with the public that had been lacking until that moment.

I left the count in the Exhibition Centre to travel to Edinburgh, as results from across the country were suggesting that the SNP had polled very strongly. Dawn was breaking as we headed east and the commuter traffic was building up on the M8. My campaign car was emblazoned with SNP branding and, as we travelled through, the sun rising ahead of us, we were getting beeps of horns and thumbs-up gestures from other cars.

Party HQ, when I arrived, was buzzing with nervous tension.

The entire staff team was crammed into the boardroom, glued to the TVs that adorned the walls. Numbers were being crunched, press calls fielded.

As the results piled in over the course of the morning it became increasingly clear that the SNP would win more votes than Labour, in both the constituency and regional ballots. But whether us or Labour would be the largest party in terms of seats was still in the balance. I was nervously watching it all unfold and periodically talking to Alex on the phone. He was still up in the North East, having spectacularly, and very much against any conventional assessment of the odds, won the Gordon constituency from the Liberal Democrats.

We knew that Labour would find it easier than us to strike a coalition deal with the Lib Dems. So even if we 'won' numerically, we might yet lose out. We needed to shape the narrative of the election very quickly and that meant claiming victory, even while the votes were still being counted.

We decided to seize the initiative and with it the keys to Bute House. Alex flew by helicopter to Prestonfield House, a five-star hotel in central Edinburgh. I was there with a crowd of staffers and activists to await his arrival. We gathered on the lawn in front of the main hotel, a building steeped in Jacobite history, a place that had entertained the likes of David Hume, Benjamin Franklin and Samuel Johnson. A lectern bearing 'It's Time' had been situated next to the flagpole in the centre of the vast lawn. The saltire was fluttering in the breeze.

I remember watching the helicopter emerge from the clouds, feeling a swirl of emotions that I could barely process. Disbelief slowly gave way to pride. Above all, there was a sense of history in the making. Alex disembarked and strode purposefully to the lectern. It was like a scene from *The West Wing*. In a speech that was First Ministerial in both tone and content, he stated that it was our intention to form an administration. He pledged that we would govern with 'humility, but with verve and passion'.

Just like that, we had seized the moment, the narrative and the initiative. Labour was on the back foot, branded losers of the election and stripped of that vital but elusive quality, authority. For them to pull it back now, at a bare minimum they needed to end the day with the largest number of seats.

All we could do then was wait. Alex and I, together with his wife, Moira, and some key staffers, holed up in a room in the hotel to monitor the remaining results as they came in. I hadn't slept in almost thirty-six hours and was running on adrenalin and coffee. Labour was comfortably ahead in first-past-the-post constituency seats – 37 to 21 – but we were ahead in votes and the final regional places were still to be allocated. If the PR system did its job, these would take us over the line, but it was going to be tight.

Alex and I took it in turns to pace up and down. We distracted ourselves by speculating whether or not the Lib Dems, led by Nicol Stephen, might agree to form a coalition with us, or whether we should go it alone. During the conversation, Moira came out with a line that made us laugh but which would prove prophetic: 'If we don't have to put up with the Lib Dems, we can have a Nicola instead of a Nicol as Deputy First Minister. That'd be much better.'

By around 4 p.m., we were two seats ahead of Labour – 45 to 43 – with just one region, the Highlands & Islands, left to declare its seven 'top-up seats'. On the basis of what we knew of the vote shares, Mark Shaw, our number cruncher in the room, predicted that Labour would win three of the remaining seats, us two, with the Tories picking up the remainder. If he was right, we would be the largest party by one seat. We would win the election.

A strange silence descended on the room as we awaited confirm-ation. We were all lost in our own thoughts. At one point I caught Alex's eye. We were on the verge of a monumental political and personal achievement, for both of us. Moments of human emotion with Alex – for anyone – were rare. But the connection between us, in that instant, was electric.

And then, suddenly there was shock. News came through that we had won none of the seven top-up seats. Zero. Labour had four, the Tories two and the Greens one. It made no sense. Mark was adamant it couldn't be right. Our folk on the ground were stunned. Thankfully, one of them had the presence of mind to act. Dave Thompson, who would become an MSP that day, intercepted the Returning Officer as he made his way to the podium, and persuaded him that something was amiss. A check revealed that the votes had been tallied incorrectly. The actual result was just as predicted – Labour three, SNP two, Tories two. Dave's quick thinking had averted days of court action and confusion. Fate (or Dave) was on our side.

The final result, overall, was SNP 47 seats, Labour 46. For the first time ever, the SNP had won a national election in Scotland. It was truly historic.

I was buzzing with a feeling of pure elation. The girl who had stood on Kay Ullrich's doorstep twenty years earlier could not have comprehended this moment. A new chapter for the ancient nation of Scotland was about to be written.

———

The weekend after the week before was a blur of activity. On Saturday morning, our newly enlarged parliamentary group gath-ered in Edinburgh. We were a happy bunch, a mix of new and returning MSPs, all tired but excited for what lay ahead. One of the new intake was Bashir Ahmad. He and his family lived in my constituency. Bashir had been one of the founding members of Scots Asians for Independence. SAFI – as it was known – had been particularly important in my own victory in Govan, a constituency with a very sizeable Muslim population. Bashir had just been elected as a regional member for Glasgow, to become Scotland's first ever MSP of Asian origin. He was also one of the nicest, kindest, gentlest people I have ever known. He died suddenly in February 2009, but in his short time as an MSP he only ever enriched our public life. His presence at that first gathering added to the sense that we had achieved something special.

Hovering on the fringes that day was a senior civil servant. Andrew Goudie was at that time the Scottish Executive's Chief Economist and had been designated our civil service liaison for any coalition talks. While Alex and I had been leading the campaign across the country, John Swinney had been spearheading our pre-election discussions with the civil service. All parties who might conceivably be involved in coalition negotiations had been allocated a point person. It was still theoretically possible that Labour and the Lib Dems would lock us out of power, but it was looking unlikely. The stuffing had been knocked out of Labour, and it seemed clear that they were leaving the field to us.

We set about trying to put together a coalition with the Lib Dems and Greens, but to some extent we were going through the motions. We knew the Lib Dems were unlikely to play ball. And the Greens alone couldn't give us a majority. But, in any event, I think all of us, certainly the senior triumvirate of Alex, me and John Swinney, had decided that minority government was the better option. Those of us who would sit round the Cabinet table had worked together for years and were friends as well as colleagues. We trusted each other, so bringing others into the room, particularly politicians who opposed us on independence, would have

Baby Nicola. I got up to a lot of mischief in that baby walker.

My first 'official' portrait.

With my mum and dad – rocking the 1970s look.

A proud day – I was the first member of
my family to go to university.
I graduated LLB (Hons) from the
University of Glasgow in July 1992.

Just two months before my graduation I was
the SNP candidate for Glasgow Shettleston
in the 1992 General Election. The campaign
coincided with my final exams, so I sacrificed
any chance of a first-class degree, but the
experience – as the youngest candidate in the
UK at the time – was worth it.

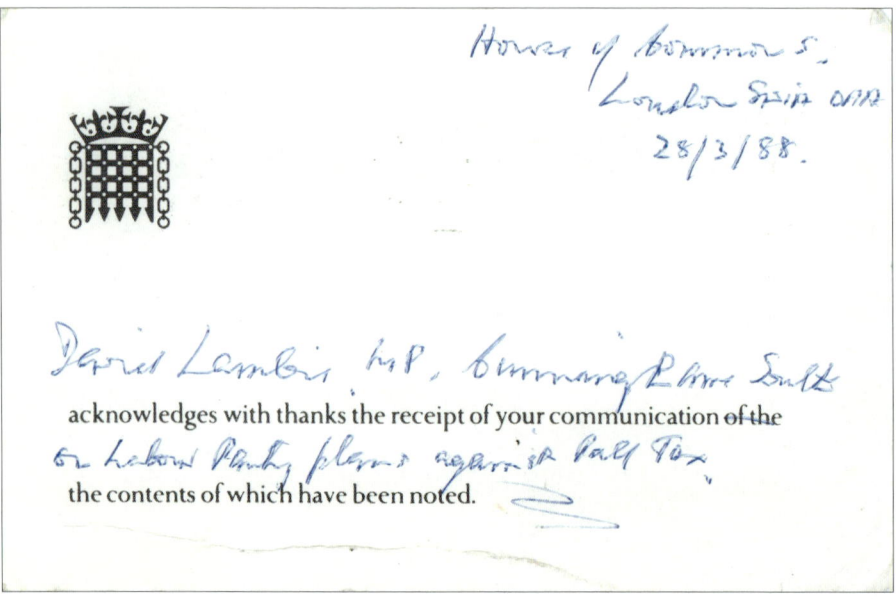

By 1988, I was immersed in political campaigning and full of righteous anger.
I wrote a long letter to my MP, urging Labour to stand more firmly against the poll
tax. I had spent hours crafting it, so felt very disillusioned by
the dismissiveness of the reply.

The Saturday after the Tories' unexpected win in the 1992 election, a 'Scotland United' rally in Glasgow's George Square sought to mobilize the campaign for a devolved Scottish Parliament. I was one of the speakers, and am pictured here with the lead singer of Hue & Cry, Pat Kane, and the then Labour MP for Glasgow Kelvin, George Galloway. I am looking every bit the public introvert that I am – capable of making a speech to thousands, but shy and surly with those around me.

Launching our manifesto for the first election to the new Scottish Parliament in 1999 – although it was a difficult election for the SNP, and me personally, we emerged from it as the main opposition in a devolved parliament and no longer just a fringe party at Westminster.

Outside Dynamic Earth in Edinburgh with Alex Salmond, kick-starting our campaign for the 2005 UK General Election – the first electoral test for the Salmond–Sturgeon leadership team, chosen by the party a few months earlier.

With Alex Salmond, launching the SNP manifesto for the 2007 Holyrood election, in front of the central image of our campaign.

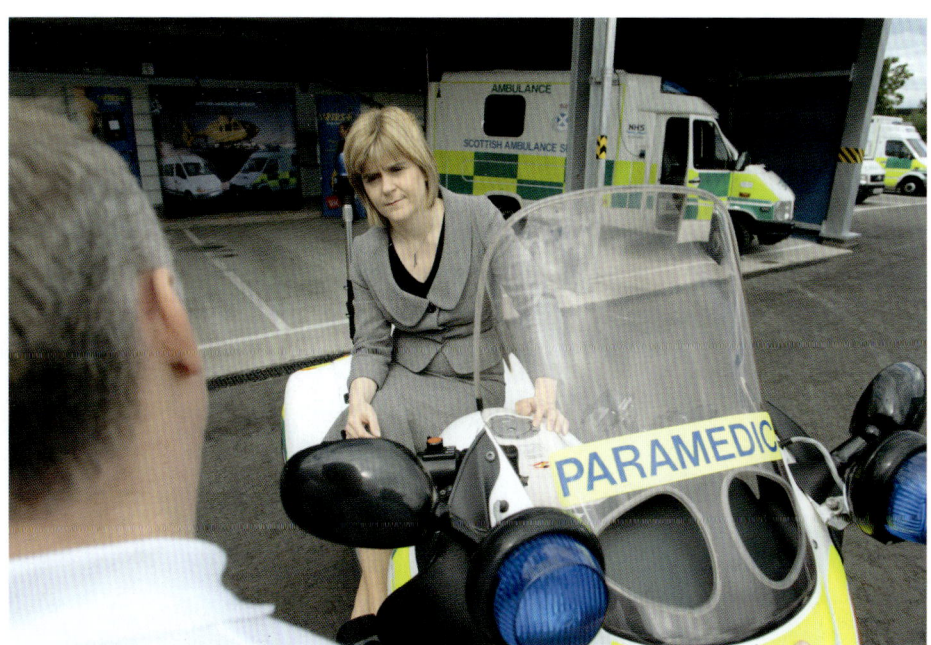

The SNP group on swearing-in day for MSPs after the 2007 Holyrood election, in which the SNP won power for the first time. Next to Alex is the now late Bashir Ahmad, Scotland's first Asian MSP and a very dear friend of mine.

Being Health Secretary was a tough but brilliant job. I loved getting out and about, talking to the wonderful people who work in the NHS. This is me in 2007, learning about the work of the Scottish Ambulance Service.

Attending the fortieth anniversary of the Ibrox Stadium disaster – a crush at an Old Firm game on 2 January 1971, which led to the loss of 66 lives and more than 200 injuries. It was a deeply moving occasion. However, what the rest of the world didn't know – though it seems written on my face – is that when this photograph was taken, I was suffering a miscarriage.

The Scottish Cabinet on the steps of Bute House, fresh from winning a landslide victory in the 2011 Holyrood election. I had just been reappointed Scottish Health Secretary, a job I would continue to do until September 2012.

Alex Salmond and me launching 'Scotland's Future', the independence White Paper. Getting it to print had been a tortuous process, but the launch was a success and it changed the dynamic of the referendum in favour of the Yes campaign.

Campaigning for a Yes vote in Bathgate. Over the course of the 2014 referendum campaign, I spoke at more than 200 public meetings in every corner of Scotland.

Campaigning for a Yes vote at Glasgow Central Mosque, highlighting a key principle of the independence campaign: that everyone who lives in Scotland, no matter where they come from, should have an equal say in the future of the country.

Addressing a mass rally at Perth Concert Hall on the eve of the independence referendum. I went home that night exhausted but exhilarated, and with hope in my heart. The next day, Scotland voted No to independence by 55% to 45% – a narrower margin than anyone would have predicted at the outset of the campaign. A day later, Alex Salmond resigned as First Minister.

created a difficult dynamic. We had come to believe that whatever we might gain in stability from a coalition, we would lose in our ability to deliver the responsive, fast-paced governance we aspired to. So when the Lib Dems made clear they were heading into opposition, we were relieved. We would go it alone.

The way forward, while not easier, was clearer. Getting anything done would mean building mini coalitions on an issue-by-issue basis. That would be difficult, but we would have a flexibility that a formal arrangement would deny us. We also knew that, in theory at least, the opposition could unite to bring us down at any time. Our administration might not last long, but that brought its own impetus. We were determined to achieve as much as possible as quickly as possible.

For all that we were set on minority government, we were still keen to reach some kind of understanding with the Greens. The numbers meant coalition was a non-starter as there wasn't enough benefit, for either of us, to make the sacrifices worthwhile. But we figured that even a loose confidence and supply arrangement – whereby, in return for certain concessions, they would vote for our choice of First Minister and, possibly, our budgets – would be advantageous. It would give us two more votes for key decisions and, less tangibly, it would give the sense that our reach was wider than it was.

So, over the course of the week following the election, and with no First Minister or government yet in place, a series of meetings was held between us and the Greens in St Andrews House, the HQ of the Scottish Executive (as it was still styled). These meetings consisted, on our side, of Alex, me and John, and, for the Greens, their two MSPs, Robin Harper and Patrick Harvie, as well as various staffers.

Robin, their leader, was pretty eccentric, and hard to take overly seriously. He always wore his trademark long, multi-coloured, Doctor Who-type scarf. Patrick was serious and focused, but, back then, still unprepared to contemplate any of the trade-offs that a substantive working agreement would have required. The discussions were slow and meandering. There was a constant flow of tea, coffee, sandwiches, cakes and biscuits. After the first couple of days, Alex, John and I started to joke that the free food was the reason the Greens were stringing things along.

Eventually, an agreement was struck. It didn't amount to much, but the Greens agreed to vote for Alex as First Minister, though they were not bound to vote with us in any future confidence votes, or for our budgets. In return, we agreed to nominate one of them as the chair of a parliamentary committee and introduce a climate change bill during our first term. The deal was announced by Alex and Robin on 11 May. With that out of the way, our path was clear to form a government.

———

The challenge for the SNP, in making the leap from decades of opposition into government, was as much psychological as it was psephological. It required an almost delusional self-belief and an ability to project it to others.

That first jump into government needed a big dose of Salmond chutzpah, and he delivered it at every turn. Betting on horses was Alex's pastime of choice, but the gambler's approach he brought to politics often had more of the poker player about it. He placed his political bets with such confidence, metaphorically eyeballing both journalists and political opponents as he did so, that they and many in our own ranks would wonder if he had some secret insight. He didn't, of course, but he presented what was often a bluff with such a strong poker face that people believed him.

Despite the growing disillusionment with Labour, they would likely still have limped over the line had it not been for Alex. In that campaign, he was like a man transformed. He was much more statesmanlike, less aggressively combative in the public eye, than he had ever managed to be before. He looked and sounded like a First Minister in waiting.

With Alex at the helm, me at his side and a united team behind us, we had pulled off a historic victory.

We were ready to govern.

CHAPTER SEVEN

The Invincibles

Alex Salmond became First Minister on 16 May 2007.

Safely ensconced in Bute House, his first task was to appoint a Cabinet. We had promised smaller, more joined-up government, and later that day a Cabinet of just six people was unveiled – Alex, me, John, Fiona Hyslop, Richard Lochhead and Kenny MacAskill. All Cabinet Secretaries would head up big, cross-cutting portfolios. I was appointed Deputy First Minister and Cabinet Secretary for Health & Wellbeing. The Cabinet was approved by Parliament the following day, after which we all headed to the Court of Session to be formally sworn in.

I had known all of these people since my teens. We had campaigned together for twenty years, united in a common cause. I doubt if there had ever been before, or anywhere, a closer group of people in government. It would not have entered our heads that the SNP would still be in government more than a decade and a half later. Given the arithmetic of the Parliament, we doubted we would last the year. What we didn't account for and would take some time to appreciate was the impact our election would have; the mood of renewal and optimism it created in the country.

We were a blast of fresh air blowing through Scotland. We were enthusiastic and energetic, almost to the point of hyper-activity. We were set on getting things done, righting wrongs and tackling challenges that the last government, tired and jaded, had said were intractable. During the campaign we had published a plan for the first 100 days of an SNP administration. It was full of important initiatives, albeit much of it low-hanging fruit, which allowed us to create a strong sense of momentum.

I remember in the early weeks of office getting a note to say that BBC Scotland's morning radio show *Good Morning Scotland* wanted me to appear the following day. The advice from my communications team was to decline. I said that of course I would do the interview. Why would I pass up the opportunity to talk about what the government was doing? It was an attitude reflected across government. Collectively, we were a team of ministers who wanted to rise to our responsibilities, not hide from them. We stamped our authority in another sense too. Since the establishment of the devolved Parliament in 1999, the term used to describe Scottish administrations had been Executive. No one really knew what an Executive was. We decided to dispense with the term and use 'government' instead.

Alex injected some theatre. Overnight, without any advance notice, the signage on all government buildings was changed to *The Scottish Government*. Quite literally, Scotland woke up to find that, for the first time, it officially had a government of its own. It both captured and created a mood. The country wanted more from its politicians in Edinburgh. It sent a subtle but unmistakeable message that the new SNP administration was different from what had gone before: more serious and grown up. A real government. It was a Salmond masterstroke.

We galvanized the civil service too. I had long internalized the assumption that civil servants were there to frustrate the ambitions of politicians. And I thought that, if this was true generally, it would be even more so in the case of a government seeking to break up the UK. As it turned out, my experience could not have been more different.

None of us had any experience of government but, actually, that was an advantage. We brought fresh perspective, unburdened by the cynicism and fatigue that beset our predecessors. And we were fearless. Or, at least in my case, that was the impression I wanted to give. Under the surface, I was anything but fearless. I was terrified.

After our swearing-in ceremony in the Court of Session, we were taken into a room in St Andrew's House where we were introduced to our Private Secretaries, in my case, a formidably clever, straight-talking woman from Northern Ireland called Clare Hicks. Clare would become indispensable to me over the next two years. So too would her successor, Beth Elliot, who hailed from Ayrshire, like me. The Permanent Secretary of the Scottish government at the time, Sir John Elvidge, popped in to give us a pep talk. He encouraged us to remember that, for the duration of our time in office, we would never not be government ministers. It was 24/7. Even on holiday, or on an evening off, we still carried the responsibilities of office. It was an obvious point, but it really brought home to me the enormity of what I was embarking on and it stayed with me through all my years in government.

———

My policy portfolio was massive. As well as the NHS, it put me in charge of issues like housing and sport, which are so often the determinants of good or poor health. Although I quickly came to love it, health hadn't been the job I initially wanted. I had shadowed a number of portfolios in opposition and education was my first choice. From personal experience, I understood the transformative power of education, and the prospect of having Cabinet responsibility for it excited me.

There was never any doubt that John would be the Finance Secretary. I had made my pitch for education, expecting Alex to agree. To my surprise and initial annoyance he had set about persuading me to do health instead. His argument, laced in some deliberate flattery, was that of any brief in government, health was the most politically treacherous and he wanted someone there who had the political nous, grip of detail and communication skills to handle it.

Had I insisted on education, would he have given in? Probably, but I'll never know. After some token resistance, I accepted his argument.

Being Health Secretary challenged me every single day. That said, I was fortunate to hold office during a period of relative calm for the NHS. After the era of Tory neglect, the years of above-inflation budget increases under the Blair governments had created a sense that the NHS was back on a firm and sustainable footing. Waiting times for treatment had fallen and they continued to fall during my time as Health Secretary. The length of time people stayed in hospital after operations for cataracts or replacement joints had also reduced significantly. More care was being delivered in the community. The population was getting healthier.

All of this was positive, but it led to what was, in my opinion, a mistaken view that the acute healthcare sector could be streamlined: fewer beds on fewer sites. I have always thought this to be flawed logic. A population living longer means more people needing care for longer. There was also an ever-expanding expectation of what, with new drugs and better technology, the NHS could do. Reform was and is needed in the NHS. The mistake, as I saw it, was to equate this with a reduction in capacity. The lengthening waiting lists we see today, with the system still struggling to recover from Covid and buckling under demographic pressures, demonstrates that the NHS, while it needs to be more efficient, cannot easily be shrunk.

The health pitch in our election manifesto had promised a reversal of the trend towards centralization. Our top pledge had been to halt the proposed closures of two major Accident & Emergency departments – one at Ayr Hospital in Ayrshire, the other at Monklands Hospital in Lanarkshire – which had been sanctioned by the Labour/Liberal administration. Hundreds of thousands of patients have been seen at these two units over the years since closure was prevented, and the idea that they could all have been cared for elsewhere now seems fanciful. But at the time, many NHS managers, civil servants and senior clinicians, as well as some politicians, thought it both possible and desirable.

As I embarked on my new role, I knew I had to be firm in what I wanted to do, at a time when my experience, knowledge and confidence were all seriously lacking. The health sector has a language of its own, acronyms and jargon abound, and despite my stint as opposition spokesperson, I didn't yet speak it fluently. But I knew that, for the first time, my decisions had real-life consequences.

My very first engagement was a meeting in St Andrew's House with directors from across the health department. These were people that I would quickly come to know well, and respect highly. But that day I detected a surliness. I was an unknown quantity. All they knew about me was that I was asking them to undo a key strand of the work they had been doing. I remember thinking that

I must sound utterly clueless. Much later, some of those present would tell me how impressed they had been with how much I appeared to know and understand. It hadn't felt that way.

I quickly saw just how easy it must be for a new minister to become the instrument of the 'experts'. I also realized how much I was going to have to read and learn, and how ferociously hard I was going to have to work, to avoid that being the case. As a relatively young woman in a room dominated by middle-aged men with specialist knowledge, I knew that I had a small window to establish authority and win respect. I had to show that I was willing to listen to their advice and learn from their expertise, but also that it was me who would take, and be accountable for, the decisions.

After my meeting with the directors, I had a one-to-one session with the head of the department, the Director General, Dr Kevin Woods. He was seen as a centralizer and the planned closure of the two A&Es we were pledged to rescue bore his fingerprints, so I expected stiff resistance. He set about probing and testing if I was really serious about reversing the closures. He suggested that I instruct an expert review instead. This would, so he argued, give us space and time to decide if our political promise had been a clinically sound one. His argument was not without merit, but I knew that going along with it would entail me breaking a flagship election promise. People in the communities served by these hospitals would feel betrayed and we would squander political capital. I also worried that if the civil service got an early sense that I was malleable, I would struggle to get anything difficult done in future. Most importantly, I strongly believed our policy to be the right one.

So, heart hammering, I stuck to my guns. I told Kevin that we had promised to reverse the closures and that is what we intended to do. To his credit, Kevin said that his job was to help me fulfil our promises safely and effectively. And that's what he did – not just on that decision, but generally for the next three years or so that we worked together. We went on to have an excellent working relationship, built on trust, mutual respect and a shared determination to always stand up and do our best for the NHS.

My decision sent the message to the rest of the civil service health team that I knew my own mind and was prepared to stand my ground.

By the end of our first week in government, my brain was frazzled. I spent Friday in my constituency, relieved to be out and about speaking to people again after a week in St Andrew's House. Later that evening, at home in Glasgow, I waited for my first ever ministerial box to be delivered. I didn't appreciate then that this would be my reality, almost every weekend, for the next sixteen years.

———

The next couple of weeks were full on. Much of my focus was on planning my first major announcement: saving the A&Es at Monklands and Ayr. I wanted to demonstrate that we had thought it through properly. Although it was massively popular, I needed to show that it wasn't blindly populist.

I made the announcement on 6 June 2007. As I did so, applause broke out in the public gallery. That kind of behaviour is frowned upon in Parliament, but it reflected a sense of jubilation in the communities affected – and a sense of relief across Scotland that the creeping centralization of the NHS was being turned on its head. By the end of that day, I had shown that I could deliver on my promises and established some early credibility. I would quickly learn that retaining credibility, for any Health Secretary, is a battle that is fought every day.

However, despite the sense of political triumph, I felt uneasy. It was the first time I had taken a decision with consequences beyond day-to-day politics. If it turned out that I was wrong, if those who argued that emergency services could not be safely delivered at these hospitals in the long term were right, the cost would be more than a few votes. It would be people's lives.

———

I worked harder as Health Secretary than ever before. The sheer magnitude of the job necessitated it. Add in the pressure I always put on myself – my fear of failing – and the result was a relentless and exhausting schedule of meetings, visits and briefing sessions. However, I was exhilarated as well as exhausted. The job tested me on multiple different levels. I had to absorb and make sense of huge amounts of information and be a master of detail, all the while trying to communicate clearly and with empathy. I also came to understand just how often governments are at the mercy of 'events'. This was especially true in health.

I had spent a lifetime thinking about how to shape or 'spin' events and had learned that the only antidote to being on the back foot some of the time was to be on the front foot as much as possible. I was also very aware of the importance in politics of telling a compelling story. So, I worked really hard to ensure that the different policies I was seeking to implement added up to more than the sum of their parts. I wanted people to see our wider vision, not just because I hoped it would provide some protection against troublesome events, but also because I really believed in it.

I developed an iron rule that, whenever possible, I would do a proactive media event on a Monday morning. The intention was to start the week on the front foot with a positive initiative. It would also allow me to respond directly to any issues that had emerged in the weekend media. I was determined to establish a sense of direction, momentum and authority which would shape the public's perception of our stewardship of the NHS. By doing this, we were less likely to be thrown off course by the mishaps and crises that are inevitable in a public service of such scale and complexity.

I set even tighter waiting-times targets for NHS treatment and reformed how performance against them was measured and reported. I established a process of independent scrutiny of major service change to make it harder for Health Boards to centralize services. I also started the process of scrapping prescription charges. This was a policy not without its critics – why shouldn't those with the means pay a small amount towards the cost of medicines? Wouldn't extending the categories of exemption be a better approach?

For me, the case for abolition weighed more strongly. There was no rhyme nor reason for the list of exemptions. Those with diabetes were exempt, but those with asthma, heart disease or Parkinson's were not. Exempting more people would have been possible, but the relative costs of administration would have increased. Scrapping charges altogether was the more sensible option. It also fitted with our overall vision of an NHS free at the point of use. I made a statement to Parliament on 5 December 2007 setting out gradual reductions in charges that would take effect over the next four years, culminating in complete abolition on 1 April 2011.

———

As is the fate of Health Secretaries everywhere, I quickly learned to expect the unexpected. In early summer 2008 there was an outbreak of the Clostridium difficile infection at the Vale of Leven hospital in Alexandria, West Dunbartonshire. The outbreak would have been bad enough in itself, but the way in which the facts emerged left me seriously exposed to claims of a cover-up, and I was initially very flat-footed in responding to it.

In late May 2008, Greater Glasgow & Clyde NHS Board reported that three cases of C-diff infection linked to the Vale had been identified and that one of the patients infected had died. At the time, it seemed that proper procedures were being followed and that the situation was under control. However, on 6 June, a local newspaper contacted my office to claim that as many as five people may have died. This triggered more detailed scrutiny by the Board. Although I was aware of the new claim, its potential significance didn't register strongly enough at first. I would have been dealing with many other issues at the same time. But it was no defence.

A couple of days after the newspaper tip-off, I did a TV interview and relied on the figures the Board had given in late May. They were the most up-to-date official figures available, but my antennae should have told me that they might be wrong. My failure to apply any caveat to the information I gave meant that, just two days later, when the Board confirmed the awful news that there had in fact been fifty-four cases of C-diff associated with the Vale, and that sixteen people had died, it appeared that I had been dissembling. I hadn't. I had just been very lax on the detail. On an issue of such gravity, that was hard to excuse.

The initial investigation carried out by the Board and later the findings of the independent review that I commissioned identified serious failings in infection control. Neither implicated any decisions taken by me in causing the tragedy. But it had happened on my watch and sixteen people had lost their lives. Until then, I didn't understand just how heavy the weight of responsibility could feel.

The families of those who had died launched a campaign for a public inquiry. They were assisted by the local MSP, Jackie Baillie, later the deputy leader of Scottish Labour. Her involvement coupled with the dignity and entirely justified perseverance of many of the bereaved families ensured that the matter remained in the news for some time, and rightly so.

After my initial ineptitude, I worked hard to make sure I had a grip on the situation. But privately, it affected me badly. The thought that the deaths might have been avoidable haunted me. For a few weeks, I struggled to sleep and was hardly eating. My confidence had taken a knock and I was questioning if I was up to the job. There was also a personal aspect that made it harder for me to cope. My gran's death in 2001 had been hastened when she contracted C-diff in Ayr Hospital. I knew how it felt to lose a loved one in this way and that made what happened at the Vale so much more difficult to deal with.

I focused on work with a renewed determination to prove that I was up to it, and to make sure that such an outbreak would not happen again. I became obsessed with actions to improve standards of cleanliness and infection control in hospitals. Over time, hospital infection rates were reduced to record low levels. The experience also kick-started broader work that made Scotland a global leader on patient safety.

The fact that the Vale tragedy led to tangible improvements doesn't make what happened any less terrible, but I hope it did bring some comfort to those who lost loved ones. I also hope that the scrutiny and recommendations of the public inquiry that I established in April 2009 delivered some closure.

As a minority government, we needed support from other parties to get anything through Parliament, especially when it came to passing our annual budget. For the budget vote in January 2009, we secured the support of Margo MacDonald, the former SNP MSP who was by then an independent. We also won the backing of the Tory group. Much was made over this term of Parliament about the support we relied on from the Tories for budgets and other key votes, the implication being that we were forced to move to the right, compromising our principles along the way.

In reality the 'concessions' we made to the Tories were things we wanted to do anyway, which in this budget were maintaining police numbers, freezing council tax, cutting rates for small businesses and supporting town centre regeneration.

Our problem was that support for the budget from Margo and the Tories wasn't enough to get it through. There was no way Labour or the Lib Dems, still seething over the election outcome, would vote with us. We needed the two Green votes too. There had been much haggling between them and John Swinney. They wanted more investment in home insulation and were adamant that the £22 million offered wasn't enough. Had it been left to John to reach agreement, it would probably have turned out fine. But twenty-four hours before the vote, Alex decided to get involved. The Greens found his 'charm' patronizing. Alex being Alex, though, he had convinced himself and the rest of us that his magic was working, and that they would vote with us. They didn't. They kept us guessing until the very last moment and then voted against, leaving the outcome tied at 64–64. The standing orders of the Parliament meant that the Presiding Officer had to use his casting vote against. Our budget fell.

There was shock in the parliamentary chamber. For all the hardball, we hadn't really expected the Greens to press the nuclear button. Back upstairs in the ministerial office block, John and I gathered with Alex and a few advisers. John was very distressed and offered to resign. He has a strong sense of honour and, as far as he was concerned, the responsibility to get the budget through had been his and he had failed. None of us agreed with that. It had been a collective responsibility. Nevertheless, the upshot was that the whole government might have to resign.

Only Alex was unflustered. Before John or I did, he had grasped the politics of the situation: it was us, not the opposition, who held the more powerful cards. We were popular and the public was in no mood for the kind of instability that would come from another election. If that happened, it would be the opposition parties, not us, who would shoulder the blame and pay the electoral price. Politically inept though they often were, Alex was prepared to bet that they would not be so stupid.

He hotfooted it from Parliament to St Andrew's House to do a press conference. He confirmed that we would present a revised budget and ask Parliament to vote for it as soon as possible. If it fell again, we would call an election and make clear that the opposition had created chaos and deprived public services of vital cash. He was throwing down the gauntlet, a typical Salmond gambit. It worked. The media narrative was scathing of the opposition parties, and, sensing the trap, they started to fall over themselves to find reasons to vote for the budget at the next time of asking.

The revised budget passed only a week later. Only the two Green MSPs voted against. To sweeten the deal for other parties, John diverted £7 million of the original £22 million he had offered for home insulation to other priorities. The Greens were humiliated. And it was deliberate. They had massively overplayed their hand and we were teaching them a lesson. A decade and a half later, however, as Scotland, in common with other countries, struggles to insulate homes fast enough to meet climate targets, it is hard to deny that the Greens were right.

The budget episode showed Alex as the 'big picture' politician he was. Had he left the detail to John, then a crisis might have been avoided, but once in crisis mode, he was a good person to have in the driving seat. In any emergency situation, for instance the terrorist attack on Glasgow Airport in June 2007 or the strike at the Grangemouth refinery which threatened fuel supplies in spring 2008, he would be omnipresent, trying to dictate every twist and turn. But when the immediate drama was over, any spadework that needed doing would usually be delegated. Even on the policy areas he was keenly interested in, such as the economy, energy, foreign affairs, his attention span was short. He would make a big commitment, such as promising Scotland will be the Saudi Arabia of renewable energy, for example, but then would leave the detail to others.

An exception to this came in the aftermath of the financial crash in 2008 as economies across the world teetered on the brink of recession. Although our government had no macro-economic powers, he was a man on a mission. He stuck with it, providing drive and leadership over many months. Capital spending plans were recast to stimulate the economy and a six-point plan, drawn up in late 2008, redirected the focus and resources of government to support those struggling with the impact of the global downturn.

As First Minister, Alex was more like the chair of a board than a chief executive. I was more of a micro-manager. There are strengths and weaknesses in both approaches. His way, things could drift. My way risked disempowering other ministers – and because, even with the best will in the world, I couldn't be across everything, this could sometimes mean less grip, not more. In some ways, the best possible First Minister would be a mash-up of me and Alex. And during those early years, that was sort of what the country had, with an added ingredient in the shape of John Swinney.

———

In one of the very first briefing sessions I had received as Health Secretary, I had been given the sobering news that the world was 'overdue' a flu pandemic and it was a just a matter of time before it happened. It was one of two moments during my years in government when I remember thinking, 'Yes, I know that will happen sometime, but almost certainly not during my time.' The other, shortly after becoming First Minister, was when I was briefed on Operation Unicorn, the arrangements to be triggered should Her Majesty the Queen die on Scottish soil. I turned out to be wrong on both. In the case of a pandemic, I was wrong twice over.

I was at home on the evening of Friday, 24 April 2009. It had been a long week. I'd been in the USA, visiting technology and life sciences companies on the West Coast, part of a drive to encourage investment in Scotland. Later, in New York, I had visited a busy emergency hospital in Queen's. I remember being shocked at how many people were crowded into A&E, not because they needed emergency care but because they couldn't afford planned care. Pitching up in the emergency room was their only way to access treatment. It was a stark reminder of how lucky we are to have the NHS.

I got home that Friday evening and sat in front of the TV with a glass of wine, half asleep, when my attention was caught by a report on the ten o'clock news. The World Health Organization had identified an outbreak of a novel flu virus, H1N1, in Mexico. With the warning from two years before still fresh in my mind, I fired off a couple of messages to my office asking if we had any more information. I was told that details were sketchy but the situation was being monitored by our health protection experts. I went to bed mildly, but not overly, concerned.

My level of anxiety shot up considerably the next day when I was advised that there were two suspected cases of H1N1 in Scotland. A couple recently returned from honeymoon in Mexico had developed symptoms of what quickly became known as swine flu. They were being admitted to Monklands Hospital, and samples were to be sent for testing to the Colindale laboratory in London. In an instant I sensed that I was about to face a big test.

I spent the rest of the weekend holed up in the 'bunker' – the nerve centre of the Scottish government's emergency and resilience operation, situated in the basement of St Andrew's House. I would spend hours and hours there over the next couple of months. And of course, I had no idea then that, just over a decade later, I would lead the country's response to Covid-19 from there too.

It would be Monday before we knew the test results for the honeymoon couple, but from the outset we acted on the precautionary principle that they would be positive. Even though it would take until early June for the WHO to decide that swine flu was a pandemic, it declared a public health emergency that weekend, on 26 April. We set about implementing the pandemic flu plan that the four UK nations had in place. Public health experts began tracing the contacts of the honeymoon couple. As this was a novel flu outbreak, rather than a virus of a different nature, we assumed that antiviral treatment would be effective, and we had good stocks of these, enough, initially, to treat half the population if necessary. We also released Personal Protective Equipment (PPE) from the stockpiles to the frontline and made sure that NHS Boards were on alert. Plans were made for ad campaigns to encourage good

153

hygiene to help stem any spread of the virus. Later, we procured and administered a vaccine.

It was important to avoid any sense of public panic. As the weekend progressed, I was increasingly worried about news of the honeymoon cases leaking out, which would have made it so much more difficult to keep things calm. I therefore decided to hold a press conference on Sunday afternoon to share the news of the two suspected cases and update the public on the steps we were taking. It was the first of many press conferences I would do alongside the then Chief Medical Officer, Harry Burns, to keep people informed about the developing situation.

That night, I was top of the news UK-wide and across much of Europe. It stayed that way for many days. On Monday, the two cases were confirmed as positive, putting Scotland very much at the centre of the global swine-flu storm. All eyes were on us. The other UK governments were learning from our experience, and other countries were watching closely too. The Director General of the World Health Organization, at that time a Hong Kongese woman called Margaret Chan, wanted to speak to me.

It wasn't important then, but looking back now, there's no doubt that this was my breakthrough moment in UK politics. From that point on, it wasn't just in Scotland that I was seen as a possible future leader. I was suddenly someone of note on the UK political and media scene too.

———

Throughout the crisis, we worked closely with the UK, Welsh and Northern Ireland governments. I attended COBRA meetings, which were chaired by the UK Health Secretary at the time, Alan Johnson. Alan was a class act, undoubtedly the best UK minister I dealt with in all my years in government. He was in command of the situation, but he also listened, both to his civil servants and to the devolved governments. A few weeks into the swine flu crisis, Alan was replaced as UK Health Secretary by Andy Burnham, now Mayor of Greater Manchester. I got on well enough with Andy, but he was nowhere near Alan's calibre. He didn't have his formidable grasp of detail, nor did he seem to wield quite the same authority with civil servants.

Tragically, sixty-nine people in Scotland lost their lives to swine flu. However, as the weeks passed, it became clear that for most people it resulted in fairly mild illness. I argued that we should adapt the flu plan to fit the reality of the situation we faced. By contrast, the UK government seemed intent on sticking rigidly to it. It created a degree of tension, with the then Welsh Health Minister Edwina Hart agreeing with me. Had Alan stayed in post, the tension might have been avoided, as I suspect he would have seen the sense of a more tailored response and had the confidence to shift the UK response accordingly.

Overall, though, the working relationships were good. The COBRA meetings of the time were certainly more purposeful than during Covid many years later. However, there was one quite bizarre moment along the way. Gordon Brown, Prime Minister at the time, had very little involvement in the swine flu response, leaving it instead to his Health Secretaries. Alex Salmond did the same. But ahead of one COBRA meeting, I was advised that the Prime Minister was likely to join that day's session.

Our discussions were well underway when the Number 10 switchboard broke into the call to advise that the Prime Minister was on the line. All of a sudden, with no introduction or apology for interrupting, Brown's disembodied voice told us we were all doing a great job and he hoped we would keep up the good work. And that was it. I wondered if he even knew what call he was on.

After a few seconds, a clearly somewhat embarrassed Alan Johnson thanked him for joining and gave him a precis of what we had been discussing. Shortly afterwards, Alan asked for his view on something, and there was silence. The Prime Minister had already left the call, after no more than about five minutes. It would have been better for him not to have turned up at all.

There were criticisms later that governments and the WHO had overreacted to swine flu. I disagree strongly with that. While I do think that the UK should have been quicker to adapt its approach when it became clear that the virus was mild for most, the early steps we took on antivirals, PPE and vaccine procurement were justified. The number of lives lost would almost certainly have been higher but for the precautionary action taken.

My experience of managing Scotland's swine flu outbreak undoubtedly shaped the way I handled the Covid response ten years later. Above all, it taught me about the importance of sharing information with the public in an open, frank and proactive manner, and about how strong the relationships between political decision-makers and the experts advising them needed to be. It was vital that they were built on trust, respect and mutual challenge.

———

A decision taken later in the summer of 2009 sent shockwaves across Scotland, the UK and much of the world, and for a brief period caused a crisis which rocked our government to the core. Had the political dynamic in Scotland been different, I have no doubt it would have brought us down.

The decision extended all the way back to one of the darkest, saddest dates of modern Scottish history, the dreadful night of 21 December 1988, when a bomb on Pan Am flight 103 exploded over Lockerbie, a small town in south-west Scotland. All 243 passengers and sixteen crew on board, and eleven people on the ground, were killed when the plane crashed.

I had been at home in Dreghorn that night, roughly eighty miles north-west of Lockerbie. At the speed of a jumbo jet, that is mere minutes away. I had just finished my first, rocky, term at Glasgow University and was looking forward to some respite over the Christmas break. My mum and dad were out, seeing my sister in her school Christmas concert. I was sprawled on the couch, watching TV. I vividly remember the sudden interruption of the newsflash.

It was all very confused to start with. An explosion in the south of Scotland, a suggestion that a plane had crashed into a petrol station. And then, over the minutes and hours that followed, the full reality of the horror became brutally apparent. The images of burning buildings against the dark night sky and, as dawn broke, of the enormous crater containing the plane's fuselage, bodies still strapped into seats, will never be erased from the collective consciousness.

After twelve years of investigation and seemingly interminable diplomatic wrangling, two men were finally brought to trial in a special sitting of a Scottish court at Camp Zeist in the Netherlands. In January 2001, one of those men was acquitted, but the other, Abdelbaset Ali Mohamed al-Megrahi, a Libyan intelligence officer, was convicted of 270 counts of murder and sentenced to life imprisonment.

It was a semblance of justice but no more than that. No one believed that Megrahi was the sole perpetrator or even the mastermind of the bombing. He was a cog in a much bigger machine. And in the opinion of many, including some of the victims' families, he wasn't even that. His guilt has always been contested. But it is an indisputable fact that he was convicted in a court of law, and despite several attempts his conviction has never been overturned. He is, so far at least, the only person to have been found guilty of the worst terrorist atrocity on UK soil.

In 2009, Megrahi was in Greenock prison, just eight years into his life sentence. He had also been diagnosed with prostate cancer. Two years earlier, the UK government had entered into discussions over a Prisoner Transfer Agreement with the then Libyan leader, Muammar Gaddafi, after a period of improving relations. We opposed the agreement and argued that if it was to be signed at all, Megrahi should be expressly excluded from it. These pleas fell on deaf ears. Political, diplomatic and commercial interests were a stronger motivation than justice for the Lockerbie victims.

In May 2009, the Libyan government made a formal application for Megrahi's transfer home. Criminal justice was devolved to the Scottish Parliament, so it fell to us, the Scottish ministers, to determine the application. In the following weeks, debate and speculation about his potential release was rife. And, as with everything associated with the Lockerbie case, it was intensely emotive and controversial. Opinions were deeply divided. Matters were further complicated when Megrahi also applied for early release on compassionate grounds, given his terminal cancer diagnosis.

I was firmly of the opinion that to send Megrahi back to Libya under the Prisoner Transfer Agreement would be wrong. He had been sentenced to life imprisonment in Scotland and had at that point served fewer than twenty days for each life taken. Whatever the technical niceties, it seemed to me that prisoner transfer would effectively overturn the sentence. The little bit of justice that had been delivered for the victims would be snatched away.

On compassionate release I was more undecided. There had been a process for such applications in place for many years in Scotland and it was far from unheard of for terminally ill prisoners to be released under it. And compassion surely must be one of the principles underpinning the justice system of any civilized society. Furthermore, compassionate release did not automatically and inevitably mean return to Libya. The practical and security implications of Megrahi leaving prison but staying in Scotland would have been significant, but it was still an option and would seem less like a free pass. Of course, Megrahi and his accomplices had shown a distinct lack of compassion to the 270 victims of the bombing. The feelings and views of their loved ones had to count too.

Earlier that year, two constituents – a married couple – had attended one of my weekly surgeries. The woman's brother, his wife and two children were among the eleven Lockerbie residents killed on the ground. They told me of the trauma and grief they carried every day. They told me of the heart-wrenching process to identify the bodies of their loved ones. They told me too of sitting through every day of the Camp Zeist trial and of their certainty that Megrahi was guilty. They left me in no doubt that they would see his transfer or early release as a betrayal of their loved ones' memories.

Had I been asked to take a decision based on my personal views, I would have decided against Megrahi's release or transfer. But I wasn't the minister charged with taking the decision and these were quasi-judicial matters, meaning that only relevant considerations, not political or personal opinions, could be taken into account. As Deputy First Minister, I was also well aware that the decision would be taken by the Justice Secretary, Kenny MacAskill.

However, given the magnitude of what was being decided, it was inconceivable to me that the Cabinet would not be consulted. At various points, I had asked Alex what stage the decision-making process was at. With hindsight, I should have pressed more firmly, but I was very much preoccupied with swine flu. On each occasion, I was told that the point of decision hadn't yet been reached, the implication being that I would know when it had. The last time I remember asking Alex was in early August when Kenny visited Megrahi in Greenock prison.

That move, frankly, astounded me. The explanation was rooted in the fact that the Prisoner Transfer Agreement with Libya was the first of its kind that did not require a prisoner to consent to transfer. As a result, Jack Straw, the UK Justice Secretary, had given a commitment that in any application not lodged by a prisoner personally, the prisoner would have the right to make representations. That was the justification Kenny gave for making the journey from Edinburgh to Greenock at the behest of a mass murderer. But it was wafer thin. Straw's commitment did not give Megrahi any right to meet with the Justice Secretary in person. Why he wasn't told to make representations in writing or, at most, offered a meeting with a government official was, and remains to this day, beyond me.

It also raised alarm bells that a decision was more imminent than I had believed it to be. I raised another query and again was reassured that the decision point had not been reached.

Then, on the evening of Wednesday, 12 August, I was in bed reading papers, with *Newsnight* on in the background, when the Scottish segment started at 11 p.m. and my attention was immediately grabbed. The BBC had a dramatic exclusive claiming that Megrahi was to be released the following week, that the arrangements for his transport from Greenock prison to Glasgow Airport were already in hand and that the Libyans had been told to prepare for his return in time for the start of Ramadan. I was stunned.

I phoned Alex. He was at home in Strichen. His response was

guarded, cagey. He implied that he was as surprised about the *Newsnight* story as I was and seemed to be suggesting that as Kenny was the decision maker in a quasi-judicial matter, he wasn't particularly in the loop either. I didn't believe him. Some issues did not merit First Ministerial attention, and there were also some that he himself had little interest in. This was neither. I did not think it credible that the civil service would have allowed a decision like this to be taken, or progressed to such a stage, without making sure that the First Minister knew and approved.

Besides, this was the kind of issue that Alex found irresistible. Matters of domestic policy rarely excited him. But on something of such high political intrigue and global significance, it would have been impossible to keep him away. Indeed, in the very first weeks of our new administration, he had made a dramatic emergency statement in the Scottish Parliament (rightly so) on the Prisoner Transfer Agreement and the failure of the Blair government to consult us or exclude Megrahi from its terms.

Despite my disbelief, this wasn't the time to argue that point. Nor was it advisable to discuss it on an unsecured phone line. We therefore agreed that he, I and Kenny would meet as soon as practicable. I came off the phone highly exercised, but with some remaining hope that it might still be possible to change course.

I was wrong again. The three of us met on the Friday evening in Bute House. I strongly made the case that we should pause and allow time for wider consideration. It wasn't that I couldn't see the case for compassionate release. However, ministers hadn't been given any opportunity to examine that case. Nor had we been able to consider the wider implications and unpredictable consequences of such a massive decision.

Kenny later told Parliament about all the 'groups and individuals' with whom he had consulted, including representatives of the Libyan government and Hillary Clinton, the then US Secretary of State. It was right that he did so. To me, it just makes it all the stranger that his colleagues within the Scottish government, who were expected to defend the decision, were afforded no such opportunity. During our discussion in Bute House, it became clear very quickly that the decision had already been taken, even if the formalities had yet to be completed, and that it was well past the point of no return. I left that night very upset and deeply unsure if our government would still be standing by the time Megrahi settled down for his first night of freedom.

Six days after our Bute House meeting, on 20 August, Kenny announced his decision. He rejected Libya's prisoner transfer application but granted Megrahi compassionate release. Underpinning the latter decision was medical opinion to the effect that three months was not an unreasonable life expectancy for Megrahi, given the stage of his cancer. He would live, not for three months, but for three more years. Kenny's intonation in making the statement made him sound like he was reading a bedtime story. The quasi-religious language he cloaked it in, saying that Megrahi would answer to a 'higher power', was also strange and made for uncomfortable listening.

Within an hour or so of the statement, there was footage of a police convoy leaving Greenock prison en route to the airport, followed by pictures of Megrahi, clad in a white shell suit, a scarf obscuring his face, climbing the steps of a plane. And then he was off, out of Scotland and on his way home. I remember the mood that afternoon being strangely calm. There was wall-to-wall coverage, but the debate about the rights and wrongs of release seemed quite rational, even though opinions were sharply divided and strongly expressed. I briefly wondered if I might have over-estimated the political reaction. And that might have been the case, had events in Libya later that night not developed as they did.

After Megrahi touched down in Tripoli, he appeared at the door of the plane, arm held aloft by one of Gaddafi's sons, like a conquering war hero returning from battle, greeted by a large crowd, many waving saltires and expressing their 'gratitude' to Scotland. It was grotesque. The reasoned debate of earlier in the day was understandably displaced by cold fury.

Would it have made any difference if the rest of the Cabinet, myself included, had been consulted? I doubt it. I suspect that the die had been cast. There was a view, and I believe it was one held by the UK government, that wider diplomatic and commercial interests were best served by him not dying on UK soil.

Would it have delivered any more justice to the Lockerbie victims had Megrahi stayed in Greenock prison for three more years? Yes, but perhaps only marginally. They would still face the hard reality that the key players who masterminded and executed the atrocity have not faced justice. We can only hope that they might yet do so.

———

My worst fears about the consequences for our government of the Megrahi debacle were not realized. The opposition could have united to bring us down, but they didn't.

I could have resigned, given my deep misgivings, and I did consider it. But I opted instead to accept collective responsibility. I rowed in behind Kenny and defended the decision. My justification was that my discomfort had been more about the process of the decision rather than the outcome. The issue of compassionate release had never been black and white in my mind.

But I do still feel a sense of guilt. It stems from a feeling I've never shaken: that the interests of those who lost their lives in

Lockerbie, and those they left behind, were incidental to the issues of politics, commerce and expediency. And that is wrong.

And my constituents, those who told me their harrowing story with such courage and dignity? They never spoke to me again and I understand why.

———

By the end of 2009, more than halfway through our first term, I think we had started to feel, if not invincible, then certainly that we were defying political gravity. We had weathered storms that according to conventional wisdom should have toppled a minority government. The defeat of a budget. A deadly hospital infection outbreak. The release of a man responsible, at least in part, for the deadliest terror attack on UK soil. But not only did we survive these storms, we seemed to emerge stronger from them.

Our magic ingredient was popularity. Even if people disagreed with us on certain issues, there was no mood in the country to replace us and the opposition knew this. This might sound like we got away with things we shouldn't have and to some extent maybe that was true. Perhaps some seeds of complacency were sown as a result, even if it would be several years before the shoots started to show.

There was a reason for our popularity though: we were proving ourselves as serious, substantial politicians. Alex had been sure-footed in the wake of the financial crash, making clever use of the limited powers and resources we had. I had handled the swine flu pandemic well. John was seen as a safe pair of hands in charge of the nation's finances. We could point to a list of policy achievements that were tangible for people, from scrapping university tuition fees and saving hospitals, to abolishing bridge tolls and freezing council tax.

It also helped that there was no impatience in our ranks, yet, on the independence question. There was a realism about the limitations of minority government, and an independence referendum was not considered to be an imminent prospect. It is just as well. Although it had enhanced Alex's reputation as First Minister, the financial crash had damaged the case for independence. We had long described the economic successes of Ireland, Iceland and Norway, three small, independent countries to our west, north and east, as an 'arc of prosperity' that an independent Scotland would join. With Ireland and Iceland both laid low by the crash, it was an argument that went from being a trump card to an albatross around our necks.

Another challenge served to demonstrate our strength more than our weakness. Fiona Hyslop had been under pressure as Education Secretary from day one. Our election promise to cut class sizes had run into the sand of local authority intransigence, or, as they would argue, a shortage of money. Rather than reducing the number of pupils in early-years classes, councils were reducing the number of teachers they employed. Figures showing a drop of 1,300 teachers over the past year prompted the opposition to finally table a vote of confidence in Fiona, and they had the numbers to make sure it passed.

It could have precipitated a crisis. Either we would have had to accept the humbling of Fiona's resignation, with the consequent damage to our authority, or threaten to resign as a government. The tactic had worked over the budget, but it would have rapidly diminishing returns if we tried it too often.

But, for neither the first nor the last time, we changed the rules. Alex refused to give the opposition a scalp, either by sacking Fiona or allowing her to be voted out. Instead, he replaced her with Mike Russell and made her Culture Minister instead. It was a demotion from Cabinet Secretary to junior minister, so the opposition couldn't claim there had been no accountability. To have pressed on with the vote of confidence would have seemed churlish.

We had once again outfoxed the opposition parties, with ease. They were left gurning on the sidelines while we headed for the festive break in fine fettle – the political masters and mistresses of all we surveyed.

CHAPTER EIGHT

The Wheels Fall Off

Over the Christmas holidays, Peter and I decided to get married. We had been a couple since 2003 and lived together since 2005. Of course, we shared a passion for the SNP and the independence cause. In its own way, Peter's contribution to the party's success was just as important as mine and Alex's. Our connection, though, was much deeper than that. We were in love and I had no doubt then that he was 'the one'. Our home life gave me stability amidst the madness of frontline politics. I enjoyed nothing more than closing the front door behind me at the end of a long week and relaxing at home with him. He could always make me laugh, no matter how anxious a problem at work might be making me feel. For all the pressures of his own job, he also looked after me, taking care of the domestic chores so that I could concentrate, without distraction, on the responsibilities of office. He cooked my tea, did my washing and kept the house clean, with rarely a word of complaint. Most importantly, he knew and understood the shy girl behind the powerful woman. With him, more than anyone, I felt that I could be myself.

Being with Peter had made me happier than I had ever been before and yet getting hitched was not something we had talked much about. I'd always been of the 'it's just a bit of paper' school of thought. But my fortieth birthday was looming, and the first inkling of life passing me by had started to gnaw. On Hogmanay 2009, in our kitchen, Peter asked if I would marry him. It suddenly felt like the most obvious thing in the world to do. I said yes. We were over the moon, and our families were delighted too.

We decided to go ahead fairly quickly, with a small, family ceremony and a big party afterwards. We booked Òran Mór, an old converted church in the West End of Glasgow, for 16 July, just three days before I turned forty. It was also our niece Harriet's fourth birthday. She would be a flower girl and our four nephews, Ethan, Cameron, Ross and Finlay, would be pageboys. We were excited and happy. Both politically and personally, life couldn't get much better.

However, I was about to find out that it could suddenly get much worse. The following weeks would be the toughest of my political career yet.

———

It all kicked off on the evening of 2 February 2010.

Alex and I were both in attendance at a fundraiser in Kabana, a restaurant in my constituency, for Osama Saeed, our candidate for the Glasgow Central seat in the looming General Election. The attendees were mainly wealthy members of Glasgow's Pakistani diaspora.

Labour was historically dominant in these communities. The incumbent MP for Glasgow Central was Mohammad Sarwar, whom I had lost out to in the 1997 election. Things were in flux though. While Scots Asians for Independence had been working hard since 1995 to change perceptions of the SNP for the better, Labour's reputation had been shattered by the Iraq war.

Mohammad Sarwar had decided to stand down in the May General Election. His son, Anas, had been selected to run in his place. The family's wealth and influence would be firmly behind the Labour campaign. It would be an important contest for us, tactically and strategically. Many in these communities had a visceral suspicion of 'nationalists' and worried that an independent Scotland would be a hostile place for them. From a global, historic perspective, this was an understandable view. But it couldn't have been further from our vision of a self-governing Scotland where everyone who chooses to live here, no matter where they come from, is a citizen with an equal say in the future of the country. Ours is a civic movement, not one based on any notion of ethnicity. It mattered to us that minority communities were reassured, first and foremost to allay the fears they had. But we also knew that their reassurance would strengthen the vision of the inclusive, progressive Scotland we wanted to portray.

So, the battle for Glasgow Central mattered. One of the organizers of the fundraiser was Humza Yousaf. He was not yet an elected politician, and he had worked variously for me, Alex and the late Bashir Ahmad. That night he took on the role of auctioneer, selling off assorted items of memorabilia to the highest bidders. The money was pouring in. Sensing that we could make more, Humza asked Alex and me if we would each auction a lunch in the Scottish Parliament restaurant. It was a spur-of-the-moment suggestion and we agreed. The lunches raised thousands of pounds, adding to the haul. The event was a roaring success.

Two days later, the feeling of optimism evaporated. Someone at the event in Kabana had videoed the auction and passed it to the *Herald* newspaper, which then published an exclusive front page story. Suddenly Alex and I were in the eye of a storm, accused of misusing parliamentary resources for party political gain, breaching the MSP code of conduct, taking cash for access and abusing our offices.

We pushed back hard. The parliamentary rules made no mention of the restaurant and it wasn't unusual for MSPs to auction lunches for charity. In any event, no lunches had yet taken place. If there was a problem, we would cancel them, and no money would be taken. But the opposition smelled blood. The parliamentary authorities were also making their displeasure known. By the end of the week, we were subject to investigation by the Standards Commissioner.

Given the decline of standards in politics in the years since, this episode might seem like small beer. But it was serious. Back then, quaint though it might sound now, a finding that we had breached the code of conduct would have meant resignation, and rightly so. And both of us had our neck on the line, First Minister and Deputy First Minister, leader and deputy leader of the SNP. If the Commissioner found against us, it would be catastrophic for government and party.

Alex was much more resilient than me in situations like this. Whereas he was bullish and determined, outraged that the accusations were even being made, I was distraught. I blamed myself for not having seen the danger. I felt that I had let myself and Alex down. Worst of all, I felt that the fear always gnawing away at me, that I just wasn't up to the job, was justified after all.

A week after the auction, Alex and I made a rare joint visit to officially open the New Victoria Hospital, which at that time was part of my constituency. As we departed the hospital, each of us getting in our own car to go on to our next engagement, Alex told me to stay positive and be careful not to show that the pressure was getting to me. As I travelled back to Edinburgh, I started to feel a bit better. Within just a few hours, though, 'auction-gate' was knocked from the top of my worry list by another 'scandal'. And this one was entirely about me.

A couple of years previously, a constituent, by the name of Abdul Rauf, had come to one of my surgeries. He was accused of benefit fraud. He came to see me a few times afterwards, on one occasion bringing his wife, who was extremely distressed by the situation. In early 2010, ahead of his case coming to court, he asked me to write a letter that he could give to his lawyer, setting out what he considered to be mitigating factors when it came to sentencing – his health, impact on family, the work he claimed to do in his community. I agreed; one of my case workers drafted the letter and I signed it. It was a decision that would now come close to killing my political career.

I was having one of my regular meetings with the various directors of the health department late that afternoon. My Private Secretary passed me a note saying that the press office needed to speak to me urgently. I left the meeting to be told that the Labour leader, Iain Gray, had just issued a news release demanding my resignation. Unbeknown to me, the Rauf case had been called in court that afternoon. His lawyer had read out my letter, and a court reporter had filed the story. Labour was describing it as a grotesque error of judgement that rendered me unfit for office. It didn't take long for the other opposition parties to weigh in too.

I was reeling. On the one hand, advocating for a constituent, even to a court, was not unheard of nor, in principle, wrong. But it was suddenly clear to me that the wording of the letter was a massive blunder. I had described Rauf's crime as a 'mistake', giving the impression that I was excusing it or downplaying its seriousness. This was particularly problematic as it turned out not to be his first conviction. Also, instead of just laying out the mitigating factors and letting the court make of them what it chose, I specifically asked for a non-custodial sentence to be considered. I had overstepped the mark. Why hadn't I seen that? Why had I been so careless?

I saw Alex later that evening and offered to resign. He was having none of it. He didn't disagree that the letter should have been written more carefully, but told me it wasn't a resigning matter. Even if he hadn't been of that view, I know he would have encouraged me to fight on. He was positively allergic to giving opposition parties a scalp. He would also have calculated that losing me from government would be a big setback. I was his deputy, widely viewed as his probable successor, and one of the triumvirate on whose shoulders the success of our administration depended.

The issue dominated the next day's session of First Minister's Questions. Alex came out swinging, relying on a section in the Parliament's code of conduct about an MSP's duty to represent their constituents. I appreciated his loyalty, but I knew his defence was disingenuous. The duty to represent constituents didn't oblige us to do absolutely anything they asked of us, no matter how morally or legally dubious. It didn't absolve us of the need to exercise judgement. I sensed that despite his best intentions, Alex had made my situation significantly worse. I was not going to be able to bludgeon my way through. In his office afterwards, I was in tears and again offered to resign. Again, he talked me out of it.

The opposition were demanding that I explain myself in the Chamber. We indicated that I was willing to do so when Parliament returned from the following week's recess. I needed time to review my files so that I could set out the facts properly. Labour and the Lib Dems said that wasn't good enough, that I needed to make a statement that afternoon, before Parliament rose for the recess.

However, the Tories agreed that the statement could be made on our return.

Had the opposition combined to force me to set out my position before I'd had time to properly process the situation and determine the right course of action, I'd almost certainly have pursued the same disingenuous line of defence that Alex had used on my behalf. It would have been fatal and I would have been forced out. Instead, I got time to draw breath. Already my instinct was telling me that I should admit I had made a mistake and apologize for the careless way the letter had been worded.

Our senior team spent that weekend at a pre-scheduled election-planning session in Dundee. I was there in body, but not in mind. I spent most of it holed up in a side room, bracing myself for the punishment beating I knew was coming from the Sunday papers, and trying to work out how to go forward. By my side throughout, listening to and supporting me – and, rather bizarrely, giving me jelly babies to eat – was Liz Lloyd, at that time an SNP press officer. Over that weekend, I learned a number of things about Liz that would be material when I chose her as my Chief of Staff in 2014. I knew from this experience that she was unflappable and exceptionally good at her job and that she was someone I could trust and rely on.

By the time I left Dundee, I had decided to throw myself at the mercy of Parliament, admit what I'd got wrong, apologize and resolve to learn lessons. I wasn't sure it would be enough to save my skin, but I knew that I would feel better for having done what I felt to be the right thing. I felt calmer, more at peace in my own mind.

Alex, though, was less than happy. In his alpha-male world view, admitting mistakes was a sign of weakness and saying sorry even more so. 'Never explain, never apologize' was his mantra. He told me in no uncertain terms that he thought my approach was misguided and that it would damage my standing. He urged me to think again. Normally his disapproval would have shaken my resolve, but not this time. I felt in my bones not only that my way was right in principle but that it was the only possible chance I had of saving my career.

On 24 February, I made a statement to Parliament, every word of which I had written myself. I set out what I believed I had got wrong, but also what I considered I hadn't. It was important to me that the apology I offered was genuine, not just a convenient device. That meant being clear about what I was, and was not, apologizing for.

As I sat down at the end of the statement, I could feel the change in atmosphere. The Chamber at the outset of the session had felt like a bear pit, the opposition baying for my blood. At the end, they were much more subdued and there even seemed to be some grudging respect. I saw David McLetchie, the former, now late, Tory leader, actually applauding. In that moment, I knew I had weathered the storm. The debate quickly became about whether politics would be better if politicians had more space to admit mistakes, as I had done.

I lived to fight another day, but I had learned some hard lessons, most importantly about the value of listening to my own conscience and trusting my own instincts. Had I followed Alex's advice, no matter how well intentioned, I would have been finished. He continued to assert that I'd been wrong to apologize. This moment changed our relationship, albeit subtly and imperceptibly at the time. Although I had been developing as a politician in my own right and out of his shadow, it was now that we shifted quite firmly from being mentor and mentee to something closer to equals. With that shift came a hint of tension that had not been there before.

On the same day that I made my apology, the Standards Commissioner ruled that Alex and I had not breached the code of conduct over 'auction-gate'. We were in the clear. Two controversies – entirely of our own making – which could have brought one or both of us down and caused deep damage to party and government, had not in fact done so. Our integrity had been called into question and our judgement shown to be fallible, but we were able to breathe a huge sigh of relief.

———

It is easy to forget now, given our landslides in more recent times, that back in 2010 the SNP had not even come close to winning a UK General Election in Scotland. Our high point had been winning eleven seats in 1974. Going into the 2010 contest, we held seven seats. One of these had been the result of a spectacular win in the Glasgow East by-election in 2008, which came at a time of momentum for us and deep unpopularity for UK Labour and Gordon Brown in particular.

David Cameron's Tories were widely expected to win the UK election. The situation in Scotland was different. Still scarred by the Thatcher years, the priority of the majority north of the border was to vote to defeat the Tories. Traditionally that had meant voting Labour, a tendency we had always struggled to overcome. It would be no easier this time round, but now expectations around us were much higher. We were on the up and Scottish Labour was very much in decline.

Our campaign centred on the notion that voting SNP was the best way to shield Scotland from the austerity cuts that everyone knew were coming. Alex came up with the strapline, which he thought very clever, of 'More Nats, Less Cuts'. I hated it. Not only was it grammatically offensive, but to my mind it was also weak.

Good slogans should be truisms, statements that leave voters nodding their heads. Those that have them scratching their heads and asking, 'But how?' rarely work. However, I didn't have a better idea, so I went along with it. We also decided to set a public target of winning twenty seats. The balance in politics between motivating your supporters with a stretch target and setting yourself up to fail, between ambition and realism, is always a tricky one to strike.

The context of the election, about who would enter 10 Downing Street, was not easy for us to navigate. We struggled just to be heard. Our demand for Alex to be included in the leaders' debates due to take place between David Cameron, Gordon Brown and Nick Clegg was rebuffed by the broadcasters. So, we decided to go to court. We didn't think that the Court of Session, Scotland's highest civil court, was likely to find in our favour (it didn't), but the publicity we got for trying was, to some extent, the objective of the exercise. It got us airtime that we would not otherwise have had.

It made little difference, though. We won the same six seats as in 2005, but lost our Glasgow East by-election gain. The perception was that we had gone backwards. Our vote share rose by 2.2 percentage points, but we fell just short of 20%. Labour's share went up by 2.5 percentage points, slightly more than ours. They polled 45% of the vote overall and won 41 seats. Given our recent ascendancy and the needlessly bold twenty-seat target, it was a massive setback. It gave the impression that our post-2007 momentum had halted, that Labour was on the up again and that we were heading for defeat the following year. We got on with governing, but the sense of invincibility had gone. Our unity also started to crack around the edges too.

———

In the aftermath of our election in 2007, we had promised that every penny generated by UK health spending through the Barnett formula (which determines how UK Treasury funding for the Scottish government is calculated) would be passed on to health in Scotland. I had taken every opportunity I could to reiterate and underline that commitment, so that it could not be easily reneged upon. However, as our 2011 budget talks progressed, it became clear that John wanted a way out of it. He argued that the NHS could only meet its objectives if the social care system was functioning well too, and that since social care was a local government responsibility, some of the so-called 'Barnett consequentials' should go to councils. His argument wasn't without merit, but the NHS needed all the money we could give it. Also, my political antennae told me that not honouring our commitment to the NHS would be deeply damaging – and, just months away from a re-election campaign that few gave us much chance of winning, that seemed to me a risk we should not take.

I also felt that my credibility as Health Secretary and my authority within the NHS would be shattered if I failed to deliver on such an important commitment. And there was probably some straightforward pique at play too. I didn't like not getting my own way. Consequently, I dug my heels in and, for the one and only time during my years in government, I threatened to resign in anger.

John and I had been with Alex in his office in Parliament, each of us making our case. It seemed to me that Alex was siding with John, and my arguments did not appear to be holding sway.

I lingered behind as John left the office and made my move with Alex. The word 'resign' didn't cross my lips but I simply looked him in the eye and told him not to underestimate how strongly I felt about this. My parting words were 'Do not push me, Alex.' I was confident he'd got the message, and the next twenty-four hours proved it. Suddenly, there was a shift in John's position. He proposed that £70 million of the almost £300 million Barnett health 'consequentials' should be invested in a Change Fund to encourage the NHS and councils to work together to improve social care. Crucially, however, the money would stay under the control of the health portfolio. Our promise to the NHS would be kept. It was a solution I could live with.

I may have won the budget battle, but our political fortunes didn't improve. A slow and flat-footed response to a spell of exceptionally bad weather in December made us look incompetent and led to the resignation of our Transport Minister, Stewart Stevenson. It was rough on Stewart – the weather was not his fault – but this was a scalp that even Alex couldn't or wouldn't save.

However bad the political climate, though, worse was to come in my personal life. For Peter and me, it was truly devastating.

———

Our wedding in July 2010 had been joyful. We had an intimate ceremony as planned, attended by close family only, in the gallery of Òran Mór, a small space above the main function room, with a stunning ceiling mural painted by the famous Glasgow writer and artist Alasdair Gray. In the evening, around two hundred friends and colleagues joined us for a party. Alex came late and left early – one of his aides told me later that his nose was out of joint because I hadn't asked him to make a speech. I had asked my sister, Gillian, to say a few words at the reception, and to say she did us proud would be an understatement. Her speech made Peter and me, and our guests, howl with laughter and cry tears of joy. It was perfect.

We didn't take much time off afterwards, with just a few days in Portugal. As always, the pressures of work, and the looming election, took priority. However, in the weeks after, we did make one very significant personal decision – to try for a baby.

Peter never put pressure on me, but I knew how much he wanted to be a dad. I was more ambivalent. I love kids. My niece and nephews are the greatest joys of my life. But I have never had a strong maternal yearning. All through my thirties, I waited for an uncontrollable biological urge to kick in, which as women we're conditioned to believe is inevitable. But it never happened. What kicked in, instead, was an awareness that I was reaching the 'now or never' stage of my life; a creeping anxiety that I would wake up one morning when it was too late to do anything about it and find myself full of regret.

For me, then, it was less a decision based on certainty about what I wanted and more a sense of seeing what happened. Of wanting to be able to tell myself that we had tried, even if it turned out that it wasn't meant to be. What happened is that I got pregnant very quickly. By mid-October, we found ourselves in an Edinburgh hotel room, looking at a positive pregnancy test. Peter was ecstatic. I wanted to be. I told him I was. But – and I still feel so guilty about this – I was deeply conflicted.

In truth, as a woman of forty, I had assumed that if I got pregnant at all, it would take much longer. In my stupid, work-obsessed mind the timing couldn't have been worse. By the Scottish election, I would be six months pregnant. It may seem hard to believe now, but even in 2010 it wasn't obvious how voters would react to a heavily pregnant candidate. Was I jeopardizing my personal chances of re-election? Worse, given my position as Deputy First Minister, was I risking the party's chances? I was riven by practical worries too. How would I cope? Elections are exhausting. It would be tough even if I sailed through the pregnancy. But what if I didn't? What if I had terrible morning sickness? Would I be able to do my job, never mind help lead an election campaign? I had become used to fielding constant questions from journalists about having children – if, when and, as I got older, why not? These are questions never asked of men, but they stalk women in politics. So I knew how much attention my pregnancy would attract.

These thoughts obliterated any sense of happiness that I might have felt. I was overwhelmed by guilt. I felt guilty about being pregnant, about not feeling happier about being pregnant, about not being as happy as Peter was, about hiding that from him. Later, what I would feel most guilty about were the days I had wished I wasn't pregnant. There's still a part of me that sees what happened as my punishment for that.

We decided we would tell our families on Christmas Day. It was a bit earlier than we might have done otherwise, but we felt it would be difficult to keep the news secret over the festive period, when we would be with them so much. Naturally, they were over the moon, and their excitement rubbed off on me too. I started to feel better, happier. The nausea that I had been feeling for the past few weeks also abated. I didn't realize then, of course, that this was because the pregnancy had already ended.

On the morning of 30 December, I noticed some spots of blood. I'd probably have ignored it but for an appointment I had that day with the GP for my flu jab. Since I was there anyway, I decided to mention it to her. I was expecting her to tell me it was nothing to worry about. Instead, she made an urgent appointment at the early pregnancy clinic at Glasgow Royal Infirmary, and that is where Peter and I spent the morning of Hogmanay 2010.

I think I'd known in my heart what the outcome would be, but I was still hoping for the best. It seemed that suddenly, belatedly,

I wanted to be pregnant after all. The nurse who did the scan was lovely. I didn't really know what I was looking for on the screen, but her face told me what I needed to know. The baby was gone.

The rest is a blur. We were taken into a side room and the nurse explained what we should expect. She said the pregnancy would probably pass naturally but, if not, they'd carry out a procedure after the New Year break. It was all very matter of fact. I don't know if it's because I wasn't told, or just that I was in too much of a daze to take it in, but I had absolutely no idea when I left the hospital that morning what an ordeal the next few days would be.

For four days I was in constant agony, the most excruciating pain I have ever experienced. At one point, when I naively thought the worst had passed, we went to visit Peter's sister. I ended up writhing in pain on the floor of her bathroom. Peter had to carry me to the car. And yet still, amidst it all, I went to work. On 3 January, I attended a memorial service at Rangers Football Club in my constituency, to mark the fortieth anniversary of the Ibrox disaster, and went from there to visit the NHS24 call centre to thank staff for their efforts over the festive period. There is a photo of me from that day at the memorial service that I find impossible to look at, the pain and anguish etched on my face.

Eventually, after four days, during the evening of 4 January 2011, the pregnancy 'passed'. I had the presence of mind to call Peter into the bathroom and, together, we flushed our 'baby' down the toilet. We later resolved to try again, but I knew then that we had lost our one chance of parenthood.

I was desolate and heartbroken for myself, but more so for Peter. I was consumed by guilt all over again, convinced that it was all my fault, that the stress of worrying about the impact on the election had caused the miscarriage; that I was being punished for not wanting the baby badly enough, for having even wished it away. These feelings have never quite left me.

I have always believed our baby would have been a girl. We would have called her Isla. Her middle name would have been Margaret, after my gran and Peter's mum. She would have had dark hair and dark eyes. She would be in her early teens now, possibly causing us all sorts of trouble. I don't want to give the impression that I am full of regret at not having children. I'm not. If I could turn the clock back and make it so, I would choose to have a child, but only if I could still do all the other things I've been able to do too. I don't feel that my life is worth less because I am not a mum.

But I do deeply regret not getting the chance to be Isla's mum. It might not make sense, but she feels real to me. And I know that I will mourn her for the rest of my life.

CHAPTER NINE

Majority Rules

The mood going into the 2011 Scottish election campaign was strange.

Since the spring of 2010 we had lagged behind Labour in the polls. It wasn't just the pundits who were writing us off. As the election loomed closer, there was a distinct sense that the civil service was preparing for a change of government too. It seemed that the election was Labour's to lose. I remember leaving my office in St Andrew's House on the day Parliament dissolved for the campaign with a heavy heart, feeling beaten, and thinking that I wouldn't be back.

And yet, somehow, the prospect of Labour winning the election didn't seem credible. They had no clear or compelling policy programme. Their leader, Iain Gray, was lacklustre and uninspiring. His campaign, disastrous by any objective standard, had moments of genuine absurdity. On one occasion, he fled into a sandwich shop to escape protestors and journalists and found himself trapped with no way out.

By contrast, our campaign purred. We produced one of our best-ever party election broadcasts. It was the brainchild of Peter and our marketing team, a brilliant parody of Monty Python's *Life of Brian*. To the refrain 'What has the Scottish Government ever done for us?' it listed all of the achievements of our first term. It caught people's attention and captured the mood. It was also our first campaign conducted to any great extent on social media. There is no doubt that we mastered social media earlier and better than Labour. During our New Year strategy weekend in January 2011, we decided that all of our key communicators would join Twitter. It quickly became a core part of the campaign.

The sense 'on the street' was that people liked the breath of fresh air that an SNP government had represented. They broadly supported what we had done and there was no discernible appetite for change. As soon as the campaign got underway and people began to focus on the decision at hand, the polls narrowed and then reversed. We would go through almost the entirety of the campaign in the lead.

I quickly realized that campaigning when expecting victory is more stressful than the opposite, not least because it can breed a dangerous risk-aversion – the fear of breaking something precious. It may have been the conditioning effect of losing so often in the past, or the old self-doubt gnawing away at me, but I kept expecting the polls to turn negative again.

The boundaries and name of my own constituency had changed since 2007. It was now called Glasgow Southside. Areas I had worked so hard in over years to build up support, including most of Govan itself, were no longer included, and much of the territory I was now campaigning in, like the Gorbals and Govanhill, was totally new to me. It felt like an unknown quantity, adding to my sense of unease.

Talking to members of the public, as I was doing every day, was an overwhelmingly positive experience. I lost count of the number of people who said they were thinking of voting for us for the very first time. More than a few, in typically blunt Glasgow style, claimed that assorted relatives would be turning in their graves. However, as the campaign wore on, a few of the conversations suggested potential voters might be scared away by the prospect of independence.

In 2007, we had successfully used the policy of a referendum on independence to 'de-risk' the issue. The promise of a referendum motivated independence supporters, but had been a reassuring safety valve for those not yet convinced. They could vote SNP on the strength of our other policies, knowing that it wouldn't automatically bring about independence. However, as the 2011 campaign entered its final stages, I thought I was detecting a shift. The more people started to think we might have the strength to deliver a referendum, the less reassuring it was. It was starting to seem more like a threat than an insurance policy.

To me, this was the biggest risk to our election prospects in 2011. I wanted us to address it directly and to be clear that we would allow ample time for debate and consideration before pressing ahead with a referendum. Alex didn't share my concern, blaming my usual campaign pessimism for my wobbles. During one of the leaders' debates, he did concede that any referendum would be in the second half of the next term, but I still wasn't sure we were being clear enough.

In the event, there was nothing to worry about. I won Glasgow Southside comfortably, polling 54% and increasing my majority from 744 to 4,349. My local success was more than replicated nationwide. In a PR parliament, elected under a system designed to prevent such an outcome, we won a majority, claiming sixty-nine out of the Parliament's 129 seats. To all intents and purposes, we had broken the system. It is quite likely that it will never happen again.

———

Winning a majority changed the tone, tenor and substance of our government, for both better and worse. It put the prospect of an independence referendum firmly on the agenda, although, privately, we knew we were nowhere near ready. It also meant we had more freedom to drive policy forward.

To my delight, we were able to get our world-leading alcohol minimum unit pricing legislation onto the statute book, having failed at our first attempt in 2010. This was a policy designed to tackle Scotland's problematic relationship with alcohol. By setting a minimum price per unit – initially 50p – it ensured that alcohol could not be sold too cheaply. For me, this was a personal as well as a political achievement. As Health Secretary, I had been the driving force behind the policy because I strongly believed in its power to reduce the burden of alcohol misuse that had afflicted Scotland for too long.

Unfortunately, the alcohol industry's disreputable campaign against the policy didn't end when Parliament passed the legislation. Led by the Scotch Whisky Association, it dragged the issue through the courts, losing at every stage but persisting all the way to the Supreme Court. It was an egregious example of private self-interest trumping the public good. It would take until 2018 for the policy to be finally introduced.

If minimum pricing was the upside of being able to impose our will on Parliament, the Offensive Behaviour at Football and Threatening Communications (Scotland) Act was definitely an illustration of the downside. Trouble at a match between Rangers and Celtic in March

2011, part of a pattern of rising tensions and sectarian incidents, had caused understandable outcry. Alex wanted a tough response, but we ended up producing one of the most unworkable pieces of legislation ever passed by the Scottish Parliament. Exactly what behaviour would be criminalized, and in what circumstances, was less than clear. There was uproar when the minister leading on the bill, Roseanna Cunningham, told a parliamentary committee that, in some circumstances, singing 'God Save the Queen' or making the sign of the cross could be offences under the new law. Instead of helping to heal sectarian divides, the bill made many law-abiding football fans feel stigmatized. Roseanna had made her concerns about the legislation known to Alex privately, but he was immoveable.

One of our biggest achievements in this term of Parliament initially sparked division within government as well as controversy across the country. In September 2011, the Scottish government published a consultation seeking views on the legalisation of equal marriage. I was the minister in charge of the issue and already a strong supporter. To me, it was such a fundamental human right that it didn't feel ethical to put it out to public consultation at all. However, I accepted that it was politically necessary to do so. My enthusiastic support wasn't shared by all of my Cabinet colleagues and I was braced for a strong backlash, especially from faith groups. Still ashamed about being pushed into a 'compromise' position on Section 28, I was determined not to let the same happen again.

I decided from the start to author a foreword to the consultation that was far from neutral:

'The Scottish government is choosing to make its initial views clear at the outset of this consultation. We tend towards the view . . . that same sex marriage should be introduced so that same sex couples have the option of getting married if that is how they wish to demonstrate their commitment to each other.'

I was seeking to frame the government's position in such a way that it would be difficult for Cabinet not to proceed with legislation. In effect, I was trying to bounce my colleagues. Looking back, I am glad I did, because, though I had expected some resistance, I had not anticipated quite how strong it would be.

The consultation ended in December 2011. It had attracted 77,000 responses, more than any previous Scottish government consultation. The majority were opposed to equal marriage, although when those from outside Scotland and the postcards prepared by lobby groups on either side were excluded, the balance shifted slightly in favour. Any time I commented on the consultation, though, I was careful to stress that it wasn't a referendum. Consultations were part of the process of reaching decisions; they were not determinative.

It took months for the issue to come to Cabinet. Partly this was down to the high number of responses, but it also reflected Alex's reluctance. I was never certain how much of his social conservatism came from genuine belief as opposed to political opportunism. Either way, he became increasingly hostile. This resulted in one of the most heated arguments we ever had.

We were in his study in Bute House on a Tuesday afternoon, just before a meeting of Cabinet. I had collared him to say I wanted the equal marriage decision on the agenda the following week. What started as a calm discussion very quickly descended into a shouting match. Alex very rarely raised his voice to me – or vice versa – so I knew that I had a real battle on my hands to get him to agree. He was implacably opposed. Couldn't I see that pushing gay marriage would lose us support in the referendum? I countered that not doing so would lose us support too: one of the concerns many people had about an independent Scotland was that the forces of social conservatism would hold too much sway. And anyway, surely it was a decision we should reach on principle, not from crude political calculation? Eventually, I realized that my approach wasn't working. Far from winning him over, my arguments were making him more obstinate, so I decided to beat a tactical retreat instead.

The consequent delay in us reaching a decision led to mounting speculation about which way the government would go. Would we strike a blow for equality or bow to the pressure of the churches and right-wing media? For a while, I wasn't at all confident of the answer. However, by the time it came to Cabinet for a decision, and after several more discussions, none of them as heated as the first one thankfully, I was sure I had persuaded Alex that we should proceed; that even if he personally wasn't convinced it was the right thing to do, at least he understood the political cost of abandoning the commitment.

I was wrong. A meeting of the Cabinet held on 17 July 2012 was meant to give the go-ahead. It didn't. The atmosphere around the table was grim as Alex dug his heels in. He claimed that the law would be a slippery slope and made arguments that seemed rooted in the prejudice which had put Section 28 on the statute book. He claimed that priests and ministers would be forced to conduct gay marriages despite the teachings of their faiths; that children would be taught about gay marriage against the wishes of their parents; that the freedom of speech of those who believed that marriage could only be between a man and a woman would be eroded; and that we would haemorrhage independence support if we went ahead.

Some others in Cabinet also had doubts but expressed them more moderately. I was instructed to go away and work out how the detail of the proposed legislation might address Alex's 'concerns'.

I was determined to get it over the line. I insisted to Alex that the proposed safeguards for freedom of speech and religion were already as strong as possible. I also emphasized that any chances we had of building a progressive coalition for independence would be fatally undermined if even David Cameron's Tories were seen as more liberal on gay rights than we were. He finally very reluctantly conceded and I was given the go-ahead to confirm our intention to legislate. I made the announcement on 25 July, before he had any chance to change his mind.

When my government responsibilities changed a few months later, my biggest worry was that Alex might kick our commitment to equal marriage into the long grass. To be fair to Alex Neil, who succeeded me as Health Secretary, he kept the legislation on track. The heat also went out of the issue when the Catholic Church in Scotland found itself engulfed by sexual misconduct allegations against its leader, Cardinal Keith O'Brien. Suddenly there was a strong reek of hypocrisy around its claim to be the defender of so-called traditional family values and it sensibly decided to lower the volume of its opposition.

The Marriage and Civil Partnership (Scotland) Act would eventually be passed by the Scottish Parliament on 4 February 2014 and the first same sex weddings took place eleven months later, on New Year's Eve. A country that just thirty-five years earlier still criminalized sex between men became the seventeenth nation in the world to legalize marriage for gay and lesbian couples, to recognize, and proclaim with pride, that love is love. It was a joyous moment.

———

Since winning the election in 2011, the prospect of a referendum loomed large. Speculation about its timing, followed by intense preparations and the heated disputes that would determine its outcome, soon began to crowd out most other issues in our national discourse. It was the culmination of a journey that had started centuries before I was born.

Scotland ceased to be an independent country when the Acts of Union came into force on 1 May 1707. It was a union imposed on the masses by an out-of-touch and unaccountable elite. The Scottish economy was in dire straits. An ill-fated venture to establish a trading colony in central America, known as the Darien Scheme, absorbed around a third of all money circulating in Scotland at the time. When the scheme failed, the country and its wealthiest investors faced bankruptcy. The unelected Parliament of the day found itself vulnerable to bribes of money, land and titles in exchange for passing the Treaty of Union. In the words of Robert Burns, they were 'bought and sold for English gold; sic a parcel of rogues in a nation'.

The population at the time was overwhelmingly opposed to union. As the Treaty passed through Parliament, objections were loud and widespread. Protests broke out across the country, and on the day it was signed in Edinburgh, the bells of St Giles Cathedral on the Royal Mile rang to the tune of 'Why should I be so sad on my wedding day?'

Scotland's independence was forfeited against the will of the people. That gave rise to a deep sense of injustice that has been passed from one generation to the next alongside an abiding conviction that Scotland is a nation in our own right. However, a significant caveat was that until recently, for most people, that sentiment manifested itself in a strong sense of patriotism and national identity, not necessarily in a desire to reverse the Act of Union and restore our independence.

What began to change in the 1980s, and then gathered pace in the lead-up to the 2014 referendum, was that the minority who thought that Scotland's distinct nationhood, in and of itself, justified independence was joined by another group: those who saw independence not as an end, but as a means of building a more democratic and successful country. It is this sentiment which came to define the modern independence movement.

The scale of our victory in 2011 meant we now had the numbers in Parliament to legislate for a referendum. This removed, at a stroke, the insurmountable obstacle of an opposition that could outvote us, which we had faced in the previous term of Parliament. For those of us who had spent our lives in the SNP, the chance to win independence as the means to building a better Scotland was what it had all been about. It is why I had stood on Kay's doorstep almost a quarter of a century before and dedicated myself to politics ever since. Knowing that the opportunity might now be close was tantalizing.

Yet the barriers still in our path were significant. The question of the Scottish Parliament's competence to legislate for a referendum without Westminster's agreement was unresolved. We had the numbers, but did we have the power? 'The Constitution' was a matter reserved to Westminster under the Scotland Act 1998, so could the Scottish Parliament, on its own initiative, pass legislation for an advisory referendum to consult the Scottish public on a possible change to the Constitution? Or was it the case that, for a referendum to be lawful, the UK government first had to transfer legislative power to Holyrood? Most experts thought the latter: that an Order in Council under Section 30 of the Scotland Act would be necessary.

Because the matter had never been judicially determined, it remained open for debate. This allowed us to assert publicly that Westminster's consent was not needed. However, the advice we got in our first term of government left us in little doubt that a credible and viable referendum would be nigh on impossible without Westminster's consent. In the immediate aftermath of the 2011 election, there was no guarantee it would be forthcoming.

There were a range of 'process' issues that were undecided too. For example, if we could set our ideal question, what would it be? Did we favour one binary question, for or against independence, or should we also offer the option of radically enhanced devolution? Should the franchise be limited to people resident in Scotland or extended to ex-pats? Would the referendum be governed by the Electoral Commission or some other body?

These were all important questions, but they were easy compared to big questions of substance. How long would it take, after a Yes vote, to make the transition to independence? What institutions would need to be established and at what cost? What would be the state of Scotland's public finances? How would the public services, pensions and social entitlements that people depended on be paid for? How would Scotland be defended? What currency would we use? Would we still be a member of the European Union?

We had rudimentary, top-line answers. But on very few big issues, arguably none, did we have positions that would withstand the full glare of scrutiny in a referendum campaign. It is hardly surprising, then, that while we were loudly and regularly asserting our intention to have a referendum, we weren't doing much to hasten its arrival. Instead, we were playing for time. It was our assumption that defeat would be catastrophic for the fortunes of the SNP and the cause of independence. We needed time to get ourselves ready, to build the case, give ourselves the best possible chance. However, the opposition, and David Cameron's government in particular, could smell fear.

In the first weekend of 2012, over 7 and 8 January, our 'political Cabinet' was gathered in Dundee for a routine strategy weekend.

We knew that David Cameron was due on the *Andrew Marr Show* on the Sunday morning, for his first big set-piece interview of the year. Late on Saturday night, we started to hear rumblings that he would say something very significant on independence. We spent much of that night over dinner and drinks speculating about what, precisely, that might be.

We didn't expect it to be this:

I think it's very unfair on the Scottish people themselves who don't really know when this question is going to be asked, what the question is going to be, who's responsible for asking it. And I think we owe the Scottish people something that is fair, legal and decisive.

So, in the coming days we'll be setting out clearly what the legal situation is, and I think we need to move forward and say, 'Right, let's settle this issue in a fair and decisive way.'

He had called our bluff and thrown down the gauntlet. It is fair to say we were stunned. On one level, we were pleased, as it removed the prospect of protracted wrangling over the legality of a referendum. But we were also worried.

The danger, as we saw it, was that the UK government would agree to a Section 30 Order that transferred to the Scottish Parliament the legal power to hold a referendum, but that, in the process, they would seek to dictate the terms: the question, the franchise and, perhaps of most concern to us back then, the timing of the vote. Would they seek to force a vote within months? Had we just lost the time we needed to get ourselves ready? Over the next few days, we managed to come up with a plan. It was vital that we didn't allow ourselves to be boxed in and held our nerve. It was in situations like this that Alex was often at his tactical best.

Firstly, we made clear that although we could see the benefit of a Section 30 Order, we didn't consider it absolutely necessary, holding to our public assertion that Holyrood had the power to hold a referendum without Westminster's consent if it so chose. Therefore, we would agree the Section 30 route to a referendum only if there were no strings attached. Secondly, we stressed that 'no strings' meant it must be left to the Scottish Parliament to set the terms of the referendum. We made the case that if these were imposed by a Tory government at Westminster, the referendum would be shorn of legitimacy from the outset.

Lastly, we announced our intention to publish a consultation on the terms of a referendum, which we then did on 25 January, Burns Day. It asked for views on the wording of the actual referendum question. The consultation also broached the design of the ballot paper, whether there should be a second question on enhanced devolution, the role of the Electoral Commission in overseeing the poll, the prospect of Saturday voting, extending the franchise to sixteen- and seventeen-year-olds, and campaign spending limits.

The purpose of the consultation, for us, was threefold. To give us public backing for our preferred terms and therefore strengthen our hand in negotiation. Second, we hoped it would give us some bargaining chips. We didn't expect to achieve an outcome with absolutely no strings attached; however, by including some conditions that, privately, we weren't wedded to, we would have ready-made 'concessions' for later in the process. Lastly, the consultation, due to run until May, helped to slow things down, as we couldn't be expected to conclude any negotiation with the UK government until the consultation had taken its course and the responses had been analysed.

Our plan forced the UK government into a negotiation, putting us back in the driving seat and with our foot firmly on the brake.

We had bought ourselves back the time we had feared was lost. Unfortunately, we didn't make the most of it. If I could pick any period of the run-in to the referendum and live it all over again, it would be late January 2012 through to the autumn of the same year. The responsibility for that rests with me as much as anyone else.

———

My own government responsibilities were keeping me more than fully occupied. The impact of austerity on the NHS was biting. Budgets were strained, staffing numbers were falling and waiting times were getting harder to meet. A scandal had blown up around allegations that NHS Lothian had been 'fiddling' the waiting times statistics. Suggestions that other Boards might be doing the same forced me to concede a review. For the first time since the Vale of Leven C-diff scandal in 2008, I was under significant pressure as Health Secretary.

Even so, I was the deputy leader of the independence-supporting government that was proposing a referendum. I should have been more on the ball. Would it have made a difference to the eventual outcome had we got our act together more in this period, sorted out those issues that would cause us problems later on? It is impossible to say, but it still gnaws away at me today.

The minister ostensibly leading the negotiation with the UK government was Bruce Crawford, the MSP for Stirling. Bruce is one of the loveliest human beings I know. He is also highly competent. In our first term of government, he was our Business Manager, responsible for making sure we got business through Parliament. He was a maestro in that job, at times a miracle worker.

But on the referendum preparations, Bruce did not have the seniority or the political autonomy to force the pace and make decisions. The negotiations with the UK government were going nowhere fast, and as spring turned to summer I started to feel intensely concerned.

This wasn't the only cause for alarm. I attended the official launch of the cross-party Yes Scotland campaign on 25 May 2012 at a cinema in the Fountainbridge area of Edinburgh. The venue was packed and there was tangible excitement in the air. However, as things got underway, the excitement started to feel more like misplaced triumphalism. The event was star-studded, featuring the actor Brian Cox, later of *Succession* fame; *Line of Duty*'s Martin Compston; Alan Cumming, the much-loved Scottish entertainer; and Liz Lochhead, Scotland's Makar (national poet). There were also recorded messages from Elaine C. Smith, who had played the legendary Mary Doll in *Rab C. Nesbitt*; George Mathewson, former chief executive and chairman of the Royal Bank of Scotland; and Sean Connery, without doubt the most famous celebrity backer of independence.

But the event wasn't our finest hour. We provided glitz, but not substance. It all ended with a bunch of celebrities dancing on stage with Alex, Patrick Harvie and Colin Fox, respectively the leaders of the SNP, the Scottish Greens and the Scottish Socialist Party. Anyone tuning in to find out what independence might mean for their mortgage, pension or living standards would have been bemused to find a display of questionable 'dad-dancing' instead.

The centrepiece of the event had been the launch of a 'Yes Declaration', with the aim of attracting one million signatures by autumn 2014, which was when the referendum was expected to be held. A few days after the event, we were forced to admit that the Yes campaign website had been counting anyone who followed the Twitter account as a supporter of the Declaration. It was a minor embarrassment in the scheme of things, but contributed to an impression that we were flying by the seat of our pants.

The launch event had gone ahead with no organization or infrastructure in place. At that point, Yes Scotland had no staff, no office, no money and no plan. It would be another month before former BBC journalist Blair Jenkins – one of the speakers on 25 May – would be named as the organization's chief executive, and three months until its advisory board, of which I would become a member, would take shape. The lack of proper thinking about exactly what role the umbrella organization should play, and how it should be structured, staffed and funded, hampered us for the duration of the campaign.

If that was one wake-up call, another came just two days later. BBC Scotland had decided to stage a set-piece TV discussion, *The Big Debate: Choosing Scotland's Future*, on the evening of Sunday, 27 May. I was one of the panel members. My mood going into the debate hadn't been great. It was a beautiful, warm sunny day and I had done most of my preparation that afternoon in the garden. I wasn't overjoyed at the prospect of spending the evening in a hot, sticky TV studio. It was more than that, though. As I read the briefings prepared by civil servants and special advisers, I became increasingly alarmed at how little development there had been in our positions on key issues, like currency, EU membership and defence. I am not trying to pass the buck. I was the Deputy First Minister – if our preparations weren't up to scratch, that was on me as much as anyone.

It all meant that my spirits were low as I put on my favourite red suit ahead of the debate. Red is always the colour I opt for when my confidence needs a boost.

On this occasion, my colour choice didn't help. I did not perform well and the debate was miserable from start to finish. It followed a *Question Time* type format, with a panel and a studio audience. So much of what we were arguing still rested on assertion, and the audience's scepticism quickly became obvious. Yes, we'd still be able to use the pound. Yes, the UK government would agree to a currency union. Of course, we'd still be in the EU. I am confident that all of these positions would have been borne out in the event of a Yes vote but, confronted by people of the opposite view with the status quo on their side, we needed more than assertion.

Our pitch was also based heavily on emphasizing what wouldn't change with independence. We'd keep the pound, the monarchy, we'd cooperate on defence, share a range of institutions. Our objective was reassurance, and in broad terms it wasn't wrong. But it was obvious in the debate that we couldn't yet articulate clearly enough what would change and how. The question lurking in the background was, if so much will stay the same, what is the point of independence? This balance between continuity and change remained tricky for us throughout the campaign, not least because Yes Scotland was so politically diverse.

The last worry I had swirling around my head as I left the BBC's Pacific Quay studio that evening was still only half formed, but it would later solidify and become a significant problem for us as the campaign progressed. There was a palpable imbalance in how the British media, the BBC in particular, covered the referendum. I am not claiming that journalists were biased. The problem was more subtle, structural, systemic. I can best describe it in two ways.

The referendum was a choice between two possible futures for Scotland: staying in the Union or choosing independence. There should have been examination and proper scrutiny of the consequences of both. But there wasn't. In a sign of what was to come, all of the set-piece audience questions in that BBC debate were, from the perspective of independence, loaded and pejorative. They weren't asking what would happen to standards of living if Scotland became independent compared to what would happen if we stayed in the Union; or what would happen to EU membership with independence compared to what would happen to EU membership if we remained in the UK. Instead, staying in the UK was presented as the benign, neutral option, with the questions framed entirely around what would happen if Scotland chose independence.

As we now know, staying in the UK turned out to be anything but neutral or benign in terms of our living standards and place in the EU, but there was very little media focus on these possible consequences. I accept that the advocates of change in any debate will inevitably bear more of the burden of proof than those arguing against change, but in the referendum the Yes campaign bore virtually all of it.

The second aspect of the imbalance, which became increasingly pronounced as the campaign developed, was in how different voices were reported. Whereas anything said by the Scottish government was treated as assertion, everything said by the UK government, or by other 'establishment' figures co-opted by them, from the President of the EU Commission to the President of the USA, was treated as fact, gospel. All in all, the playing field was far from level.

———

It took until the summer of 2012 for Alex and me to talk in earnest about picking up and forcing the pace in our negotiations with the UK government and with our preparations overall.

One recurrent issue was whether the referendum should be multi-option, with a question on what had become known in Scotland as devo-max. There is no universally accepted definition of devo-max, but broadly it means all powers being devolved to the Scottish Parliament, except macro-economic policy, defence and foreign affairs.

I had assumed that our talk of including a devo-max question was no more than a negotiating tactic, given that the UK government was adamantly opposed. I was slightly taken aback to learn that Alex still viewed it as a real option: something we might actually hold out for. I think he saw it as a possible insurance policy, that even if we didn't win independence, we could still secure significant progress towards it. I was certain a devo-max option would kill any chance we had of winning independence. If people were offered a 'safer' alternative, they would take it.

There were also massive practical challenges. Short of a two-stage referendum, with the least popular option dropping out after the first round, and the second being a run-off between the other two, it wasn't at all clear how a vote could be organized in such a way that majority support for the chosen option could be demonstrated. It would be a mess.

Alex's reluctance to give up on the devo-max option was symptomatic of a deeper issue. He was exuding a level of nervousness, fear even, that I had never encountered in him before. On one occasion, we were in his office on the fourth floor of the Scottish Parliament's ministerial suite. I was seated at the coffee table in the corner of the room and he was pacing up and down. All of a sudden, he sat down opposite me and said, 'Nicola, this is going to be so much tougher than we can imagine. Do you understand that?' I did, but in that moment I was more shocked by Alex's demeanour. It was so out of character for him to show doubt. It was virtually unknown for him to display anything short of total confidence.

We had all spent our lives campaigning for independence, and suddenly the moment of decision was looming. The stakes couldn't have been higher and most people thought we'd lose. It would have been odd if he hadn't been feeling the pressure. I was feeling it too. However, it felt to me at times that he was running from the fear rather than towards it, and that is what seemed so uncharacteristic.

Nerves aside, it was clear to both of us by this stage that the campaign urgently needed day-to-day oversight from a senior politician and that the leadership could only come from him or me. Alex had too many other responsibilities as First Minister, so he suggested reshuffling the Cabinet to put me in charge of referendum planning. He wanted me to drive the ongoing negotiation with the UK government to a satisfactory conclusion, get the necessary legislation through Parliament and steer the development of our much-heralded White Paper. He also wanted me to join the advisory board of Yes Scotland, to make sure we could exercise the necessary influence on the political and media direction of the campaign.

Someone needed to take a grip on things. For the girl who first started banging the independence drum at just sixteen years old, the prospect of playing such a prominent role in the campaign to secure it was hugely exciting. I had one big reservation though: giving up the health portfolio. I loved being Health Secretary. I was the longest-serving incumbent of that office since the establishment of the Scottish Parliament – a title I still hold today – and one of the longest serving of all time in the UK. I felt a huge responsibility to the NHS and to those who worked in it. I'd also been having one of my toughest periods in the job and I didn't want anyone to think I was cutting and running.

Ultimately, though, it was a move I had to make. And, in my heart, I wanted to make it. On 5 September 2012, I became the so-called 'Yes Minister'. The next phase of the referendum journey, and of my personal story, was underway.

CHAPTER TEN

Yes Minister

I was adrift for a couple of weeks after my change of job. I really missed being Health Secretary. It would take a few moments on waking up in the morning to recall that everything had changed, and I'd feel a sense of dislocation and loss all over again.

I was struggling again with confidence too. The media was full of stories about how historic my role was, the weight of the responsibility that now rested on my shoulders, and I felt small in the face of such a massive challenge. Alex hadn't wanted me to take on any specific portfolio responsibility in addition to the referendum preparations, but I had insisted, as I thought that my influence and authority with the civil service would be diminished if I didn't command a policy portfolio with a budget. So, I took on infrastructure too, the first time I'd had direct involvement in economic policy. I had plenty to keep me busy.

It was independence that dominated though. I had to strike a deal with the UK government on the terms of the referendum, and I was determined to do so swiftly. We had dilly-dallied for too long. Any longer and our credibility would be damaged. People would start to believe we weren't serious about the referendum. I had made it clear to Alex that I'd only take on the role if my remit was to get the job done, and I had the necessary free hand to do it. Part of that was finally putting to bed the multi-option referendum. While we might use it to leverage other concessions, we could not make it a red line.

Within a few days of my appointment, I met with David Mundell, the Tory Scotland Office Minister. David was second in command to the Liberal Democrats' Michael Moore, an MP from the Scottish Borders and Secretary of State for Scotland. David and I met in my office in St Andrew's House. There was a funny moment during the meeting when his mobile phone rang. It was his mum, phoning to check he was OK. Apparently, or so he told me, she had been worried that I might eat him alive. In that moment I realized that my reputation exceeded my self-confidence by a considerable margin! I made it clear that I wanted to strike a deal. We wouldn't do it on any terms, but I was confident we could reach agreement.

The discussion was amiable, the tone constructive, but it was Michael Moore who was ultimately responsible. Michael and I met a few days later in Melville Terrace, the labyrinth-like Edinburgh HQ of the Scotland Office. We agreed to talk in private first, before bringing our respective advisers into the room, a common trust-building exercise in inter-government meetings. Half an hour later, I think we were both confident we were on the right track.

By the end of that first meeting, we had established some important ground rules: there would be no game-playing, and nothing would be agreed or released until everything had concluded, one way or another. We had also developed a good rapport and a decent enough understanding of each other's positions that the outline of an agreement was already visible. We met again a week or so later to hammer out the detail, this time in Michael's palatial office in Dover House, the Whitehall base of the Secretary of State for Scotland. As we chatted, looking out over Horse Guards Parade, I joked that the size of his office seemed to be in inverse proportion to the weight of his responsibilities – in post-devolution Scotland, the duties of the Secretary of State for Scotland are not onerous. He took it in good humour.

It was in this meeting that we got down to brass tacks on red lines and tricky issues. From our side, the hard red line was that the key issues of date, question(s) and franchise must be for the Scottish Parliament to decide. For his part, the non-negotiables were a single-question referendum, a sunset clause guaranteeing the referendum would take place before the end of 2014, assurances around the 'fairness' of the question and Electoral Commission oversight of the poll. I made it clear that most of this posed no problem for us, but that the issue of a single question might still be a deal-breaker. I was bluffing.

Across these two meetings, the Edinburgh Agreement was crafted. I waited until I had secured everything I needed before agreeing that I would try to kill the devo-max demand with Alex. I had, of course, killed it already, but I still made great play of how difficult it would be. I'm not entirely convinced that Michael believed me, but he played along.

The deal was done on 10 October 2012. On a phone call, with me in Edinburgh and Michael on a family holiday in Florida, we shook hands, metaphorically speaking, agreeing that we had a package to recommend to our respective bosses, Alex Salmond and David Cameron. I was delighted with the end result. We had secured what mattered. We had control of the date, franchise, including extension to sixteen- and seventeen-year-olds, and the wording of the question.

A meeting between the First Minister and the Prime Minister, with Michael and me in attendance, where the Edinburgh Agreement would be formally concluded and signed, was scheduled for the morning of Monday, 15 October, in St Andrew's House. Ahead of the meeting, Alex insisted on having a large picture of the political map of Scotland hung on the wall immediately behind the seat he would sit in, so that David Cameron would have to spend the meeting looking at a big landmass of SNP yellow. It was typical Alex. I loved and loathed this side of him in equal measure.

The meeting itself was formulaic. The testosterone hanging in the air above Alex and David could have been cut with a knife. They were like two beasts, sizing each other up, staring each other out, one as determined as the other not to give an inch. We talked through the detail of the agreement and our hopes for the civilized conduct of the campaign. It was all very trite. And then we signed the agreement, each of us in turn adding our signatures to a document that was historic in its significance.

I am certain that David Cameron had no idea, when he picked up the pen that day, just how close he was to signing away the United Kingdom. Had there been even the merest inkling, I doubt that his pen would ever have touched paper. It is because we did come so close that the Prime Ministers who have succeeded him, so far at least, have refused point-blank to follow his example.

We went to the front door of St Andrew's House, where the photographers and broadcast camera crews recorded for posterity the moment that the referendum campaign started for real.

———

One of the questions the Yes side faced repeatedly during the campaign was about Scotland's membership of the European Union in the event of independence. Alongside what currency we would use, it was an issue that came to dominate debate. It centred on whether an independent Scotland would be expelled from the EU if we ceased to be part of the UK, given that it was the member state; or would we, instead, be treated as a successor state in international law, inheriting all of the UK's treaty obligations.

We tended towards the latter view and had some expert, academic opinion on our side. However, we knew that changing our status from being EU members as part of the UK to being a member in our own right as an independent nation would need negotiation. We argued that this could be done within the transition period between a Yes vote and Scotland actually becoming independent, meaning that there would be no break in our membership.

I am convinced that, had Scotland voted Yes, a pragmatic solution would have been found. Scotland had been in the EU for forty years, and we would have been a net financial contributor and an important strategic partner. I am certain there would also have been a reluctance on the part of the EU to punish Scotland for exercising, entirely constitutionally, our democratic right to self-determination. Even Spain, always talked up as the member state most likely to veto the membership of an independent Scotland because of the situation in Catalonia, never actually said it would do so.

But it was impossible for us to prove this in the abstract, especially when leading players at the time were happy to cast doubt on it. The President of the European Commission, José Manuel Barroso, went out of his way to help the UK government's cause. He always stressed that he did not want to interfere in the debate in Scotland, but these were weasel words. He implied that Scotland would have to apply afresh, and from outside the EU, for membership – and that we would lose the UK opt-outs on, for example, the euro, as well as any share of its financial rebate. In early 2014, he went further, stating that it would be 'extremely difficult, if not impossible' for Scotland to achieve unanimous support for independent membership.

Barroso's successor as Commission President, Jean-Claude Juncker, took a different view, as I later found out in private discussions I had with him in Brussels, during my years as First Minister, by which time the Brexit vote had happened. I got on well with Juncker and we were always able to speak frankly. He was clear with me that while there would be challenges for an independent Scotland in re-joining the EU, and always encouraged me not to downplay these, it was his view that a pragmatic solution could be found to make it happen.

The question we faced was partly political. Would the EU want to respect a democratic vote and keep part of its existing territory in the fold, or would it want to make an example of Scotland as a disincentive to independence movements in other member states? But it was also legal. What did the EU Treaties actually say, and what did they mean? It was this legal question which planted a timebomb I now had to defuse.

————

Back in May 2011, just after our landslide re-election, one of Scotland's Members of the European Parliament, Labour's Catherine Stihler, had submitted a Freedom of Information request to the Scottish government asking for any legal advice that we had received regarding Scotland's position within the EU in the event of independence. The Scottish government's response, in line with the Ministerial Code, was that we could not confirm or deny the existence of such legal advice.

Stihler then appealed to the Information Commissioner. The Commissioner's decision, issued in July 2012, was that on an issue of such importance to the independence debate, it was in the public interest for the government to say whether or not it had legal advice. She asked us then to confirm or deny its existence. Instead of immediately complying, the government indicated that it would appeal the decision to the Court of Session.

So far, so technical. The problem was that everyone assumed we did have legal advice from our law officers, and that we were only refusing to confirm it because we didn't want to come under pressure to publish it. Frankly, this was my initial assumption too. I should have been more engaged and, very soon after taking charge of the referendum preparations, I regretted that I hadn't been.

Within my first couple of weeks in the new job, it became clear that the reason for our coyness wasn't what I and everyone else was assuming. We didn't have law officer advice at all. That was bad enough, but by allowing people to think otherwise, we had compounded the problem. We were wide open to the charge that we had set out to deliberately mislead, to purposely create the impression that our position was backed by legal opinion when we knew fine well it was not.

I also had a distinct memory of Alex saying in an interview that we did have advice from our law officers. I checked, and in a BBC interview back in March, with veteran broadcaster Andrew Neil, he appeared to do exactly this. I was aghast. The exchange was a bit garbled, and it was certainly open to some interpretation, but the fact remained that in answer to the question 'Have you sought advice from your own law officers?' the first words out of Alex's mouth were 'We have, yes.' It was those words that turned the issue of whether or not we had legal advice into a much more serious crisis of integrity and trust.

I was in my office in the Scottish Parliament when I realized we had a major issue on our hands. I immediately went next door to speak to Alex. He was initially defensive, accusing me of seeing problems where none existed. Eventually, he agreed that we were in a hole and that if we went ahead with the court appeal against the Information Commissioner's ruling, we would be digging it deeper. Instead, we needed to come clean to Parliament as soon as possible. Even so, he still tried to play it down.

He thought there was a chance that the Andrew Neil interview wouldn't surface. I thought that was fanciful. More substantively, he was adamant that when the exchange was taken in the round, it was clear he wasn't claiming to have a formal 'law officer opinion'. He was referring instead to the less formal legal advice which is part and parcel of the normal process of government business. I agreed it was one possible interpretation and I believed too that it was what he had meant, that he hadn't intended to mislead. I still do. I know only too well how easy it is in the heat of a tough interview to garble your words.

Even so, this was an issue that could badly derail us and undermine trust in what we said in the future. So much of our proposition was essentially unproveable in advance and this made it all the more important that people had faith in what we were telling them. If we lost that, we would lose everything.

We agreed that I should set the record straight in Parliament after the October recess. By then, we hoped to have concluded the Edinburgh Agreement. That meant I could wrap the legal advice 'bombshell' into a wider statement and hope it didn't get too much attention. Waiting until after the recess also allowed us to get our party conference out of the way.

Our conference that autumn, held in Perth Concert Hall, was a bruising affair. The main debate was on a motion to overturn the SNP's long-standing opposition to an independent Scotland being a member of NATO. The new position was proposed by

Angus Robertson, then our chief spokesperson on defence. He was doing so with the support of Alex and me, though neither of us spoke in the debate.

My lifelong opposition to nuclear weapons made me feel slightly queasy about the notion of sheltering under a nuclear umbrella, even though most NATO countries don't have nuclear weapons. I was also worried about our independence prospectus striking the wrong balance between continuity and change.

However, I knew it was the right move. Given our geostrategic position, the suggestion that Scotland would not be in NATO was ludicrous. It would leave NATO with a significant gap in its territory, and Scotland extremely vulnerable. If that was obvious then, it is even more so now in the wake of Vladimir Putin's more recent aggressions and war crimes. We also knew defence would be a difficult issue for us in the referendum, and that it would be doubly so if we were opposed to NATO membership.

The conference debate turned out to be one of the most unpleasant and divisive in the SNP's history. The party was split down the middle and, from the vibe in the hall, it was not at all clear that the motion would pass. Alex and I were on the platform throughout, becoming increasingly nervous as the debate progressed, though trying not to show it.

The motion passed, after a recount, by the narrowest of margins. The crucial amendment which, if passed, would have retained our opposition to NATO, was defeated by just 29 votes, 394 to 365. It had been far too close for comfort, and though we had survived, victory came at a cost. The debate left many members feeling upset and wounded. It was not the best backdrop to the biggest campaign of our lives.

With the conference over, my attention very quickly turned back to the debacle over EU legal advice. My statement was scheduled for Tuesday, 23 October. On that morning, we were rocked by two of our MSPs resigning from the party over the NATO decision. John Finnie and Jean Urquhart were both list members for the Highlands region. I couldn't get hold of Jean, but I spent my journey into Parliament on the phone to John, trying to change his mind. He was unmoveable. While I understood his position, I felt angry and let down by the damage that would be inflicted on our campaign. Throwing a spanner in the works of Scotland becoming independent, just because he disagreed with a particular policy, missed the big picture spectacularly.

By the time I got to the Chamber to deliver my statement in the afternoon, I was frazzled. The statement, ostensibly, was to update Parliament on the signing of the Edinburgh Agreement. I tried to be as low-key and matter of fact as possible when it came to the revelation about legal advice, to make it sound entirely reasonable (as in fact it was) that we had waited until agreement had been reached on the process by which Scotland might become independent before seeking advice from law officers.

When I got to that part of the statement, there was a minor flurry of opposition excitement. Overall, though, the reaction in the Chamber was more muted than I had feared. Labour's hapless lead speaker, an MSP from Glasgow called Patricia Ferguson, seemed to miss the significance altogether. To her credit, Ruth Davidson for the Tories didn't miss a beat. Even so, I left the Chamber daring to hope that we might get through it without too much damage.

But by the time I had made the short journey back to my office on the fourth floor of Holyrood's ministerial block, all hell had broken loose. The Andrew Neil interview had gone viral on social media and Alex was being called a liar by all and sundry. It had become a crisis threatening to completely overwhelm us. The next morning's headlines were brutal.

'EU LIAR' screamed the *Sun*'s front page.

At First Minister's Questions, two days later, the Labour leader, Johann Lamont, normally pretty ineffective in these sessions, punched the bruise:

'How can this country have an honest debate about our future when we cannot trust a word that Alex Salmond says?'

This was the crux. Given the uncertainties that were inherent in our independence message, trust in the messengers was vital – and until that point it had been one of our strengths. The unionist parties knew that if they could destroy that, it would be game over. We were profoundly shaken and also faced very immediate jeopardy. Alex was forced to refer himself for investigation under the Ministerial Code. If he was found to have breached it, he would have to resign. Thankfully, although we had to wait until mid-January 2013 to get it, the verdict of the investigation was survivable. It found that, while Alex's answers had been confusing, muddled and incomplete, he hadn't intended to mislead, and consequently there had been no breach of the code.

It was a massive relief, but there is no doubt that the episode inflicted damage on us. The hard lesson for me was that we needed to be clearer about the evidence underpinning our assertions, and more open about how the uncertainties could be managed. We had to focus on building a credible, evidence-based case.

———

It was blindingly obvious – an inescapable fact of Scotland's electoral arithmetic in those days – that winning independence depended on a large number of Labour supporters voting for it. I knew that we had to park our tanks firmly, and quickly, on Labour's lawns.

To have any chance of doing this, we had to articulate more powerfully the 'why' of independence. This was an obsession stemming all the way back to my experience in the BBC debate in May. As long as the debate focused on 'how' questions, which is exactly where our opponents wanted to keep it, the 'obstacles' of the transition would seem too difficult. Of course, we had to answer these 'how' questions as clearly as we could, but we would never magic away all the challenge and difficulty. What we could seek to do, however, was persuade people that, even if the process was difficult, it would be worth the effort. As an independent nation we could turn our backs on austerity, inequality and creaking public services. With control of our own destiny, we could forge a new nation rooted firmly in the values of fairness, justice, equality.

With all of this in mind, I was scheduled to deliver my first major set-piece speech at Strathclyde University on 3 December. I put my heart and soul into this speech. I had asked Alex Bell, a former BBC journalist and by now one of our senior special advisers, to write a first draft based on early notes I had made. What he wrote was extremely good, but it needed work. Alex could be a bit too intellectual and on this occasion I felt it detracted from the solid, grounded arguments we needed to make. Between us, though, and it was most definitely a joint effort, we produced a speech that I am very proud of.

I was trying to do a number of things. I wanted to frame independence not as a rupture with the past, but the completion of a journey that had started with devolution. I referenced, disingenuously perhaps, Donald Dewar's words from the opening of the Scottish Parliament in 1999, about devolution being a process not an event.

I also sought to cast independence not as an end in itself, but as a means to better ends. It was not about flags or embassies, but the strength of the society we were all part of.

And I wanted to appeal to those who, no matter how Scottish

they felt, still valued their British identity. Many more independence supporters, myself included, were in this group than was usually assumed. So I argued that the risks to the NHS and welfare state, the institutions that so many of us considered intrinsic to British identity, now came from staying part of the UK; it was independence that would safeguard them from austerity cuts and privatization.

Lastly, to try to lift people's sights, I introduced Kirsty, the fictional child who would feature throughout the Yes campaign. She was a symbol of the future generations who would thrive in an independent Scotland if we won the referendum.

The speech was a success and the reporting of it largely positive. The *Guardian*'s take, under the headline 'Sturgeon Sharpens Independence Debate as a Battle for Centre-left', was typical:

'In her first major speech on independence on Monday, Scotland's deputy first minister has set out her case for independence, again marking out political territory which is a direct, open challenge to Scottish Labour.'

I felt we had started to claim the political territory we needed to win. We had started a conversation with people who would never describe themselves as nationalist, people who had probably never voted SNP, and people who were proudly British in their identity. Despite all of that, we had given them reasons to consider voting Yes.

It didn't go entirely to plan though. No sooner had I finished my speech than news broke that Prince William and Kate were expecting their first child. No one was going to keep them off the front page. At the time, it contributed to my sense that we just couldn't get a break.

———

As we moved into 2013, the No campaign's firepower stayed focused on the big issues of currency, public finances, EU membership and defence. But something was shifting. We started to get a sense that their messaging was backfiring, that people were beginning to feel bullied by the suggestion that Scotland would be forbidden from using the pound, or kicked out of the EU, if they voted Yes. The No side was also indulging in scare stories that bordered on the ridiculous. One of the more outlandish claims was that Scots would no longer be able to watch popular BBC programmes like *EastEnders* and *Doctor Who* if the country opted for independence, despite these programmes being viewable in dozens of countries around the globe. This wasn't an assertion from the fringes but came straight from the mouth of Gordon Brown.

This tactic developed into a significant problem for the anti-independence forces. The more they insulted the country's collective intelligence, the less likely people were to believe them on matters of substance. There was even worse to come for them. In summer 2013 it was revealed in a leak to the *Sunday Herald* newspaper that the leaders of the No campaign privately referred to themselves as 'Project Fear'.

On the day that story broke, I could scarcely believe our luck. It was a spectacular own goal by the No side and a precious gift to the Yes campaign, all the more welcome because not much had been going our way until then. It gave us the moral high ground: whereas we were trying to inform and persuade, they were trying to scare. From then on, the Project Fear tag was a powerful antidote to anything they said.

While we rubbished the credibility of the No campaign's attacks, we worked to strengthen the detail of the independence prospectus and broaden the appeal of our message. Social media became ever more important, given the heavy one-sidedness of the so-called mainstream media. Slowly but surely, the Yes message was becoming one of hope and aspiration, a vivid contrast to the negativity of Project Fear.

In May 2013, I took part in the first head-to-head debate of the campaign, on STV's *Scotland Tonight* programme. Over the course of the next year, I would do three more of these STV debates, in addition to countless other TV and radio interviews. The debates allowed me to road-test arguments and hone our attack lines. In this first one, I was up against Michael Moore. I started to paint a less than flattering picture of what a No vote would mean for Scotland. I argued that independence was a means to reduce poverty levels, which would only rise if we stayed as part of the Union. The post-debate consensus was that I had bested Michael.

However, the most important strand of our work to strengthen the independence case was the development of a White Paper. I was convinced that publication of what, in effect, would be the manifesto of the Yes campaign could be a game-changer if we got it right. But getting it right was a monumental challenge. It had to tick an almost impossible combination of boxes. It needed to convincingly set out the case for change, both the disadvantages of staying in the Union and the inherent advantages of independence. It needed to explain exactly how we would make the transition from a Yes vote to being an independent country. It needed to be convincing on the big issues of currency, public finances, pensions and EU membership. It had to be exciting and inspiring about the potential of independence to make Scotland a better country, while also recognizing that the policies pursued in an independent Scotland couldn't be guaranteed in advance; they would depend on the colour of the governments elected. And, above all, it needed to provide answers to the myriad of questions people were asking. Was all this even possible in a single document?

What we ultimately published wasn't perfect; however, I firmly believe that its publication contributed significantly to the momentum the Yes campaign generated into 2014. To this day, I am immensely proud of it.

We called it 'Scotland's Future – Your Guide to an Independent Scotland'. It ran to 649 pages and concluded with a list of almost every conceivable question people might ask and provided an answer to each of them. There were 650 in total, ranging from what the currency would be to whether we'd have our own Olympics team and every imaginable subject in between.

The Q&A section was, in my view, the most important part of the project. It allowed us to say, even to people who would never read it, that the answers to their questions were there. Until then, our alleged lack of answers had been a big problem. Now it was no longer so easy for the No campaign to claim the answers didn't exist, even if the credibility of them would continue to be a matter of intense debate.

While the White Paper did the job we needed it to do, getting it to the point of publication was tortuously difficult. The civil servants who worked on it, headed by Ken Thomson and David Rogers, were exceptional. Stephen Noon, a former SNP staffer and at that time a Yes Scotland strategist, also gave me invaluable input. However, at times, it felt like we were trying to push a boulder up a hill. On one Sunday evening in late October, I was at home in Glasgow, reviewing the latest draft (the document was so long that even reading it from start to finish took several hours) and feeling utter despair at how much work still remained. I remember very suddenly being overcome by a feeling of sheer impossibility. I ended up on the floor of my home office, crying and struggling to breathe. It was definitely some kind of panic attack. I had never experienced anything like it before, nor have

I since. I was freaked out by it, as was Peter, who came upstairs to find me in that state.

Adding to my stress at that point was that despite my repeated efforts, Alex hardly engaged with the White Paper at all. The one exception was the estimates for future oil revenues that we were intending to include. We'd already had a foretaste of how tough the scrutiny over finances would be in March 2013 when a paper prepared for the Cabinet by John Swinney a year earlier had been leaked, sparking lurid headlines. The paper had discussed the heavy financial responsibilities an independent Scotland would assume, such as servicing a share of the UK's debt, not to mention the fiscal challenges in paying the bills for pensions, welfare and public services.

The leak rocked us badly for a while. It allowed the No campaign to claim that the NHS and pensions would be at risk if Scotland was independent. Just as with the EU legal advice debacle, it also gave them an opportunity to question our integrity: to claim that what we were discussing in private was different from what we were saying in public. It was also the first major leak we had suffered from within the Scottish government since 2007, so it made us highly paranoid.

To me, the very terms of the discussion were misleading. The opening balance sheet we faced would not be static. The point of independence was not simply to replicate the status quo, it was to make different choices and build a more prosperous country. The success of independence would depend on our ability to increase tax revenues through a more dynamic economy. Nevertheless, the leak made us determined to cast the opening finances of an independent Scotland in as positive a light as possible. Crucial to that were the projections we would make for future oil revenues. Back then, oil prices were high, but, even so, Alex spent a lot of time persuading the government economists to push their projections higher, taking them to the outer edges of credibility.

Other than that, he showed little interest in the detail of the White Paper. By late October, I was becoming increasingly worried about how I was even going to get him to read it before the sign-off date. When I found out he was planning a week-long trip to China in early November, I was incandescent. How on earth would I get him to read it amidst all the distractions of an overseas visit? And then there were the security concerns about him taking a copy of it to a country where he would almost certainly be subject to covert surveillance.

I made my views clear to him, but he was immoveable. He promised he would read it on the plane. I knew his good intention would not survive contact with the first glass of in-flight champagne.

He did send some comments back when he arrived in China, most of them trivial and all of them related to the early pages.

The final straw that week came on the Thursday morning. I was about to stand in for him at First Minister's Questions. The Ministry of Defence, with one eye firmly on the referendum, had made an announcement about the future of shipbuilding and I was anticipating that this would dominate FMQs. Given my long interest in the subject, I was confident in what I was going to say, but I knew it would be tough.

I was doing my final preparations before heading to the Chamber when I got a call from Alex, who was in Hong Kong. It was early evening there, and he was calling to tell me what a great afternoon he'd just had watching horse-racing, and to give me some 'tips' for FMQs. He was far from sober and not a word he said was of any use to me. I was so angry with him that I hung up.

I eventually focused on getting him to just read the bits of the White Paper I thought were most important or controversial, and gave up on him for the rest. I first held a printed copy of the independence White Paper in my hands on the evening of 22 November. It felt weighty and looked like the serious document it was. I felt a sense of achievement, but, moreover, of relief. We had got there. But would it make a difference?

———

On the morning of 26 November, Alex and I launched the White Paper at the Glasgow Science Centre before an invited audience and the world's media. It was a huge event, in both size and significance. I had been persuaded to showcase a Scottish designer and chose a jacket by Judy R. Clark, who had just won the Scottish Womenswear Designer of the Year. It was more flamboyant than anything I would usually have worn, black Harris tweed with cuffs made from Ayrshire lace. I loved wearing it, and the sense of occasion and confidence it gave me helped me through one of the biggest news conferences I had ever done.

Alex, that day, was at both his worst and his very best. He had insisted on having a Cabinet meeting in the Science Centre boardroom ahead of the launch. He was like a bear with a sore head, barking questions at ministers and advisers alike. Everyone was on edge. After the meeting, we ran through the questions that would likely come our way. I gave him the page and paragraph references for the key issues we would be asked about and he flagged his copy of the White Paper accordingly. I knew, however, that his familiarity with the text was limited at best and I was terrified it would show.

We then faced the media in what was, undoubtedly, one of the biggest moments of our lives. To my relief, he smashed it. He was at his brilliant best, absolutely winging it for sure, but with the panache and confidence that made him seem on top of his brief.

He quoted the page and paragraph numbers with an authority that made everyone think he knew the document inside out.

The event went as well as we could have hoped. The media coverage afterwards was largely as expected – a mix of scepticism and scorn, though there was also a sprinkling of grudging respect that what we had published was weightier and more detailed than many had anticipated. But the most important thing was that it was out there, offering answers to the many questions that people were asking. We had promised to make copies available free of charge to anyone who wanted one, and, in the days that followed, the number of orders and downloads told us that there was a significant level of interest.

We now had to defend and promote the White Paper at every opportunity, and much of the heaviest lifting again fell to me. Over the following two nights, I was scheduled to do the final STV debate and then to appear on BBC *Question Time*. In the STV debate, I was up against Alistair Carmichael, who had replaced Michael Moore as Secretary of State. The MP for Orkney & Shetland, Alistair was considered to be a more pugnacious and combative figure than Michael, and more capable of taking me on.

My debating style has always been assertive, sometimes counterproductively so. It used to be how I overcame my shyness. But it isn't everyone's cup of tea and I was always aware of the fine line I was treading between persuading and irritating my audience. On this occasion, I needled away at Alistair, getting under his skin so much that he kept asking the debate moderator, STV's Rona Dougall, to intervene. This led to him being dubbed Alistair 'help me Rona' Carmichael on social media. It wasn't a good look.

On the substance, I used the same approach on child poverty as I had with Michael a few months earlier. It was an obvious issue for us, so I had assumed Alistair would be much better prepared than he was. Also, his lines of attack on currency and monetary policy were easier to rebut now that they could be labelled as Project Fear. It was on EU membership that the most telling exchange took place. I put it to Alastair that the biggest risk to Scotland's place in the EU was the in/out referendum promised by the Tories. He accused me of baseless scaremongering. History proved me right, much to my regret. BBC *Question Time* the following evening continued the momentum.

All in all, by the time I collapsed on the sofa with a glass of wine on Friday evening, I was feeling more upbeat than I had in a long time. It was a feeling that didn't last the night.

I was just about to go to bed when social media started to buzz with reports of a helicopter crashing onto a pub in central Glasgow. I put a call into my office and a few minutes later received the tragic confirmation that a police helicopter had crashed into the Clutha, a popular bar on the north bank of the Clyde that I had frequented in my student days. It was horrifying. The following day, I visited the site of the crash alongside the Chief Constable. The structural instability of the building caused by the crash meant that it would be three days before the bodies of those who died could be retrieved. The suffering and anguish of the bereaved families was almost unimaginable. Ten people in total lost their lives – the pilot and two police officers on board the helicopter and seven members of the public who had been enjoying live music in the bar as tragedy struck. It was an unspeakably sad end to 2013.

CHAPTER ELEVEN

The Final Straight

Just a day or so before Christmas 2013, I was in a greetings card shop in the Buchanan Galleries shopping mall in Glasgow, choosing cards for my family. I became aware of two shop assistants behind me, restocking the shelves opposite. They were in a passionate discussion about whether an independent Scotland should keep the pound or establish its own currency. I was struck by how detailed and informed the discussion was. I took longer over the choice of my family's Christmas cards than I ever had before.

As 2014 dawned, Scotland was buzzing with debate. It was an exciting, energizing time. Most Scots wanted to know what independence would mean for them, their families and the country as a whole. The appetite for information was insatiable. There was a real sense of possibility in the air, a feeling that the choice we were facing could fundamentally reshape our country, that we had an opportunity to create a brighter future for generations to come.

People quickly became experts on the big issues at the heart of the debate. I would bet that during 2014, the Scottish population was the most politically engaged and educated anywhere in the world. There was, at one and the same time, both a giddiness and a heavy burden of responsibility. The mood was hopeful but also deeply serious.

Just a few weeks on from the card shop, I was on Pollokshaws Road on the Southside of Glasgow, just down the street from my constituency office, when I was stopped by a man, probably in his seventies, who wanted to ask me what the lender of last resort arrangements would be for the banks in an independent Scotland. Again, I was struck by how knowledgeable he was on such a highly technical issue.

In my long experience in politics, I've always found the public much more switched on than they are given credit for. But what was fundamentally different about early 2014 was the extent to which people were going beyond what they read in the media. They were asking sharp questions, doing their own research and thinking deeply about the choice they were being asked to make. This was also reflected in the many public meetings I was hosting across the country.

I did around two hundred of these Q&A-type events over the course of the campaign, in packed town halls and community centres across the length and breadth of Scotland. By the final few weeks, I was doing at least one a day.

At first, I assumed it was mainly diehard Yes supporters turning up, and, initially, it probably was. But it soon became obvious that more and more of those coming along were genuinely undecided. The attendances were sometimes so big that people had to be turned away – so we developed a practice, at the start of every meeting, of asking those who had already decided to vote Yes to give up their seats for those still swithering. On some occasions we opened windows and encouraged those who couldn't get a seat to listen from outside.

I developed a stump speech for these meetings, structured around three arguments – why and how Scotland *could* be independent, why we *should* be independent and why we *must* be independent. I didn't try to pretend there wouldn't be difficulties. Instead, I argued that the hurdles would be worth it and pointed out that staying in the UK carried its own risks. I honed the pitch over time and by the final few months of the campaign I had it exactly as I wanted and delivered it word for word, night after night. I would round off by urging people not to pass up what might be a once in a lifetime opportunity to transform Scotland for the better.

Later, when I was First Minister and pushing for a second referendum, this 'once in a lifetime' or 'once in a generation' line came back to haunt me. Our opponents claimed it meant that I was going back on my word. In their shoes, I might have done the same, but it was a gross misrepresentation. 'Once in a lifetime/ generation' was a warning, not a promise. I hadn't said that I would never argue for another referendum. Instead, I pointed out that there was no guarantee that we would get another chance in our lifetimes, which is why I was urging everyone to seize this one with both hands.

By this time, I had been making speeches for more than twenty years, but these experiences turned me into a very different type of public performer. I felt that I had discovered how to communicate in a way that engaged both heart and head – not by elevating emotion over facts and figures, but, for the first time, and very intuitively, understanding the deep connections between them. I mastered the art of addressing an audience of hundreds while, simultaneously, connecting directly and intimately with each individual in it. The person who emerged on the other side of the referendum was a very different politician to the one who started out on that campaign.

Much has been written since the referendum about how unpleasant and divisive it was. My experience, exemplified by these public meetings, was the opposite of that characterization. However, I know I didn't make enough effort at the time to appreciate what it was like for those on the other side. It wasn't until the Brexit vote that I fully understood how it felt to face the prospect of having part of my identity, in this case my European citizenship, taken away. Even so, I view it as an achievement of Yes and No supporters alike that the contest was, in the main, positive and good-natured.

———

In early 2014, it seemed that almost everyone who was changing their mind on the independence question was going from No to Yes. Clearly worried, the No campaign decided it was time to bring out the big guns.

On 13 February, the Chancellor, George Osborne, flanked by Ed Balls for Labour and Danny Alexander for the Lib Dems, pitched up in Edinburgh to emphatically rule out a currency union. It was a clever move on the face of it, as it meant that all three potential parties of government were singing from the same hymn sheet. It was a flat no. I happened to be in London that day and ended up fronting the media coverage for the SNP. Alex stayed out of view at home in Strichen, attracting some media criticism in the process.

My most bruising encounter of the day was an interview with Andrew Neil on the lunchtime BBC *Daily Politics* show. Armed with the Osborne / Balls / Alexander currency veto, he skewered me. I clung to the argument that since a currency union would be in the interests of the rest of the UK as well as an independent Scotland (a proposition that was arguable either way), minds at Westminster would change in the event of Scotland voting Yes. The fact that I genuinely believed this to be likely didn't make it sound any less fanciful in the moment.

One of the other meetings I had in London that day was with BBC network editors. As I sat around a boardroom table in Broadcasting House, I remember feeling shocked by how ill-informed they were about the nuances of a debate which by this point had been underway in Scotland for two years. They genuinely seemed to think that their entry into the fray marked the start of the campaign. I was showered in condescension about currency in particular. When I asked if they had read the Scottish government's Fiscal Commission report on our proposals, I got the sense that most of them weren't even aware of its existence. This metropolitan arrogance on the part of some London-based journalists, especially in the BBC, and the shoddy reporting it often gave rise to, posed problems for the Yes side throughout the campaign.

I am certain that the No side saw the currency veto as a killer blow. I worried that they might be right, but, a week later, a poll in the *Daily Mail* showed a six-point leap in Yes support. It led John Curtice, the doyen of political polling, to say:

'The poll's headline findings suggest that, if anything, the "no" side's stratagem has not only failed to deliver any immediate boost to the Unionist cause but has actually backfired.'

It was the Project Fear effect writ large. The tactics of the No campaign were being increasingly seen in Scotland as bullying. People felt that the country was being insulted. If there was no respect for Scotland within the Union, no recognition of our contribution to the UK's success, no acknowledgement of shared assets, then surely that bolstered, rather than undermined, the case for independence?

There was another unanticipated boost for the Yes campaign in late March, when the *Guardian* broke an explosive story, with quotes from a senior UK government source saying that in the event of a Yes vote, a Westminster government would of course agree to a currency union. This gave credence and credibility to our assertion that UK ministers were bluffing on currency.

As 2014 progressed, it was the Yes campaign with the spring in its step. The mood over that summer was electric. The staging of the Commonwealth Games in Glasgow, a triumph for both city and nation, added to the festival atmosphere. There was a growing belief in our camp (delusion, perhaps) that victory was possible. The flipside of this was an even greater sense of responsibility, and perhaps it was because of this that there were simmering tensions in the hierarchy of the SNP over the final weeks. I found it all a bit bewildering. For reasons that I found hard to fathom, it was also me who seemed to bear the brunt of it. It felt unjustified and unfair.

Despite the early creation of a centralized, top-heavy organization in Yes Scotland, the campaign had grown organically, and slightly chaotically, from the ground up. The grassroots dynamic was a strength, but it posed challenges for those of us schooled in more traditional methods of campaigning. Perhaps because I was so immersed in the community effort, through the public meetings and other events, I found myself embracing it reasonably easily. Others weren't so sanguine.

Angus Robertson, who was the SNP campaign director (and a friend, both then and now), started complaining that there wasn't enough 'science' behind the campaign. By this he meant that we weren't conducting focus groups regularly enough so that we could then tailor messages in a more granular way. The clear implication was that this was my fault. It is certainly one of the things I have reflected back on. Would more 'science' have made a difference? Back then, though, I felt aggrieved at the backbiting. I was giving the campaign every ounce of physical and emotional energy I had and it felt unfair to be on the receiving end of so much snash.

It all came to a head in mid-July when Angus and I had a spat about the scheduling and agenda of a campaign meeting. Alex sided with Angus. It was probably a sign of exhaustion, but I had a childish strop, telling Alex that I wasn't prepared to play silly games and that if he was going to undermine me, he could take charge of the national campaign and I'd just concentrate on touring the country, speaking at meetings.

He dropped in to see me at home on 18 July, on his way back from a Commonwealth Games oversight meeting. We had a good chat and cleared the air between us. Or so I thought. This was also when he told me that if we lost the referendum, he would stand down as First Minister. To be frank, I didn't take him seriously. By this time, I was starting to believe we would win. And even if we didn't, I assumed he would change his mind. He loved being First Minister. I couldn't see him giving it up easily.

The chat with him didn't resolve the strange dynamic that existed between us in the final stretch, something I never really got my head around. Sometimes I thought he felt guilty about not engaging sooner and was trying to make up for lost time. We certainly had to listen to plenty of pontification from him about what we had got wrong while he had been missing in action. At other times, I detected a resentment on his part towards me. Did he think I was getting too much attention, hogging the limelight? I felt I was only doing the job he had asked of me and filling a vacuum he had created.

It might have been possible to dismiss all of this as a figment of my increasingly tired imagination, had it not been for the circumstances around the first televised leaders' debate. Two debates had been scheduled to take place between Alex and Alistair Darling, the 'leader' of the No campaign. The first would be hosted by STV on 5 August and the second by the BBC on 25 August. These debates were hugely important for us. We had momentum but we were still behind in the polls, and the debates were amongst the final opportunities we would have to change the game.

I had assumed I would be involved in Alex's preparations. Given the number of debates and key interviews I had already done, my sense of the most potent lines of attack from the No side, how best to rebut them and what arguments worked best to promote our own case was probably more honed that anyone else's. It didn't occur to me that this insight would not be fully utilized. But that is precisely what happened.

Alex froze me out completely ahead of the first debate. I wasn't in the room for a single one of his prep sessions. The message was clear: he didn't want me there. I was a bit hurt and also confused, but more than anything I was angry.

On the evening of the first debate in the Royal Conservatoire in Glasgow, I was in the spin room. It was packed and the atmosphere was tense. I had no idea what Alex's strategy or pitch was going to be. I told myself that he was an experienced debater and that he would do just fine.

It was a disaster. Darling was sharp and incisive. Within a few minutes it was obvious that he had prepared well and intended to strike hard at the weaknesses of the independence case. Alex on the other hand looked tired and uneasy, and it quickly became clear that whatever preparation he had done had been inadequate. He waffled. He floundered on currency. Most bizarrely, when he had the chance to put Darling on the spot, he missed the mark spectacularly.

Instead of pointing out the consequences of continued Westminster governance compared to the opportunities of independence, for example on pensions, levels of poverty or EU membership, he indulged in obscure debating points. He had obviously decided to try to puncture the absurdity of the Project Fear attacks. This was not a terrible idea, and had he picked his examples more wisely, it might have worked. Instead, he started talking about aliens. Some peripheral figure on the No side had made the claim that Scotland, with independence, would be more vulnerable to attack from outer space. It was so ludicrous that it had passed most people by, and yet here was the First Minister of Scotland, the leader of the movement for independence, majoring on it on live TV. It sounded ridiculous and deeply unserious.

I have never had a more excruciating experience in a spin room, ever. I had to keep a poker face and comment positively to the media about his performance, all the while crying inside. The snap poll afterwards recorded a win for Darling. It felt, in that moment, that our campaign might be over. Surely there was no surviving a performance as poor as the one I had just witnessed.

The debate debacle did not actually lead to a haemorrhaging of Yes support, but it did cost us. We knew that the onslaught on issues like currency, and our inability to get decisively off the ropes on them, was acting as a brake on our momentum. Too many of the people we still needed to convert from No to Yes were being held back. The debate had been one of our last remaining chances to build confidence and increase the flow of support to our cause. It was an opportunity squandered.

Stung by his mauling on currency, Alex flirted with dumping our commitment to a currency union. He called John Swinney and me into Bute House one Sunday evening. We were in the Cabinet room when he dropped the bombshell. He wanted to shift to a position of 'sterlingization', using the pound but not as part of any formal arrangement. John and I looked at each other in horror and told him in no uncertain terms he could not do that. This was no longer about the pros and cons of a currency union versus an alternative position. We were past the point of no return. To have changed now, weeks out from the vote, would have made us look utterly unhinged. It was classic Alex, though. A gambler to his fingertips, he was always ready to risk disaster for the chance of winning big. It had served us well on many occasions, but it would have proven calamitous this time. Thankfully, he didn't pursue it.

I was brought into the final prep session for the next debate, giving me the opportunity to try to influence Alex's approach to the encounter. The second debate was hosted by the BBC in Kelvingrove Museum on 25 August. In my view, Alex still wasn't at his best, but he performed much better than first time round. He was livelier and much more focused on making the points we needed to hammer home. He also articulated the currency position much more effectively. Crucially, the post-match polls gave him the win.

There was more of a swagger in his step afterwards and, whilst we knew we still had a mountain to climb, we entered the final four weeks in good heart. Our thoughts were turning to what would happen if we pulled it off. We had assembled a full civil service transition team. It was situated in St Andrew's House and was ready to get to work immediately if Scotland voted Yes. The prospect was both thrilling and terrifying.

––––

On Saturday, 6 September, I was in the campaign hub in my constituency when Kevin Pringle, our head of communications, called to tell me that the next day, the *Sun on Sunday* would publish a poll showing Yes 2 points ahead. I was ecstatic. The poll was embargoed so I had to be careful about who else I told. There was no way I was ever going to contain myself though, so I pulled my trusted election agent, Mhairi Hunter, into the back office and shared the secret with her. We did a wee jig around the room.

By the time I got home later that afternoon, the euphoria had started to give way to the reality of the likely consequences. The onslaught this would trigger from the No side would be more ferocious than anything that had gone before. We were still almost two weeks out from the vote. Could we withstand the pressure? We quickly came to believe that it would have been much better if the poll lead had come a week later. By then, it might have been too late for No to turn back the tide.

As it was, our opponents immediately mobilized. David Cameron, Nick Clegg and Ed Miliband took the joint decision to cancel Prime Minister's Questions on 10 September and hit the campaign trail in Scotland instead. We staged our own show of unity as a counterpoint. All of the various political strands that made up the Yes coalition came together for a photocall in Edinburgh. Alex and I even linked arms with Jim Sillars, the long-time armchair nemesis of SNP leaders.

Perhaps we also made a blunder that day. We characterized ourselves as Scotland United against the might of the London establishment. The description implied that anyone who wasn't an independence supporter was somehow not part of Scotland. I doubt it made much difference to the final result, but, from the perspective of trying to persuade those who were still nervous about our proposition, it wasn't the best tone to strike.

The pressure continued to build as the week progressed. First, our hopes of a Yes endorsement from the *Sun* newspaper evaporated. Alex had been courting Rupert Murdoch assiduously for months and we thought the efforts were paying off. Ironically, it was over the weekend of the bombshell poll, when Murdoch was actually in Scotland, that the mood music started to change.

Then, late on the evening of Wednesday, 10 September, news filtered out that the Royal Bank of Scotland and Lloyds Banking Group were about to confirm plans to relocate their HQ operations to London in the event of a Yes vote. There was little doubt this was the result of political pressure. It was not as dramatic as it sounded. It would be a 'brass plate' move, not one that would affect jobs or the banks' physical presence in Scotland. Alex actually managed to get the head of RBS, Ross McEwan, to say as much. The damage, though, was done, solidifying the fear in the minds of those already nervous that independence would lead to an exodus of jobs and investment. It also came hot on the heels of warnings about the costs and availability of mortgages should Scotland choose independence.

This, then, was the backdrop to our 'one week to go' press conference in the Edinburgh International Conference Centre on the morning of 11 September, which also happened to be the anniversary of the 1997 devolution referendum. On the stage were Alex, me and Anum Qaisar, a young Labour activist who had joined Yes and the SNP during the campaign and would later serve as the SNP MP for Airdrie & Shotts.

What unfolded at the press conference would later demonstrate Alex's capacity to bear a grudge, long after most people would have let it go. His rage was still burning years later. The then political editor of the BBC, Nick Robinson, asked a question about the banks, to which Alex gave a lengthy and detailed answer. Different people would come to different conclusions about the quality of the answer, depending on their perspective, but Nick claimed in his news package later that day that Alex hadn't answered the question at all.

There is no doubt that Nick was in the wrong, and to be fair he later conceded that he had made a mistake. It added to concerns we had harboured throughout the campaign about aspects of the BBC's coverage. Alex was right to feel aggrieved but his reaction went beyond what was sensible. He gave tacit approval to Yes demonstrations outside the BBC HQ at Pacific Quay in Glasgow. In my view, attacking the BBC was a distraction and wrong in principle. I also feared that it would be counterproductive. Amongst the middle group of voters we had to persuade was a fear that an independent Scotland would be a one-party state, controlled for eternity by an over-powerful SNP. I was intensely worried that intimidatory protests outside the BBC would serve to exacerbate those fears.

On the evening of 11 September, I took part in the final big TV debate of the campaign. The BBC had brought 10,000 sixteen- and seventeen-year-olds to the Hydro Arena to hear me and Patrick Harvie make the case for Yes, and Ruth Davidson and George Galloway fly the flag for No. I had been really nervous about this encounter, as my memories of a younger George Galloway, as the MP for Glasgow Kelvin, made me think he might be a hit with the young demographic. I couldn't have been more wrong. He pitched up wearing a hat, and came across as a weird, and deeply unpleasant, crank who understood little about modern Scotland. I have no idea why Ruth Davidson agreed to be his sidekick that evening.

The young people already committed to Yes were informed, passionate, enthusiastic. As the debate progressed, it was also clear that many of those who had come along as No supporters were swinging the other way, and it wasn't me or Patrick swaying them but their peers.

The event filled me with hope, not just about the possible result of the referendum, but the future of Scotland more generally. To this day, I am convinced that it will be this generation, teenagers in 2014, now approaching their thirties, who will propel Scotland to independence and make a success of it.

———

My tour of the country drew to a close and I spent most of the last few days in Glasgow. My constituency was awash with Yes window posters. It seemed that almost everyone I passed in the street was wearing a Yes badge.

The mistake I made in that final stretch was to assume that the mood in Glasgow was reflective of the whole country. It sent me into polling day with an inflated and, for me, totally uncharacteristic sense of optimism. We had a final rally in Perth Concert Hall the night before the poll. It was a highly charged affair. As we were leaving at the end, Alex and I had one of our rare emotional moments. We hugged and wished each other luck. We knew that by the time we were next together, for better or worse, the world would have changed.

When I got home to Glasgow that night, I had a glass of wine and cried. I wasn't sad, just utterly drained. I was proud of the campaign; of those who had led Yes Scotland and of the armies of volunteers who had brought us to the brink of a possible victory. I knew that there were many things we could, maybe should, have done better. I felt in my gut that if we didn't win, it would be down to fears over currency and economic sustainability. Had we been convincing enough to give people the reassurance they needed? I feared that the answer to that was no. As such a key figure in the campaign, the lion's share of responsibility rested on my shoulders. However, I knew that I had devoted every ounce of energy I had to the cause.

I also knew that whatever the outcome, we had pulled off

something extraordinary. Even just six months previously, I could not have comprehended going to bed the night before polling day feeling that victory was within grasp. I had just fallen asleep when my phone buzzed with news that Andy Murray had tweeted support for Yes. We had been trying, indirectly through a friend of his, to get him over the line for ages and had all but given up hope. It was probably too late now for it to make any difference, but, still, I was delighted.

I went to sleep happy, excited and more nervous than I had ever been before.

———

Finally, 18 September 2014 dawned. Scotland's date with destiny.

I voted early at my local polling station in Broomhouse Community Hall in the East End of Glasgow. Marking my cross in the box that said Yes to the question 'Should Scotland be an independent country?' felt like the culmination of a long journey.

I spent the rest of polling day in my constituency. It was the most emotional day at the polls I have ever known. I had people literally crying on my shoulder. Young people excited at the prospect of building a new nation. Older voters who had spent decades campaigning for independence with little hope or expectation that they would ever see it happen.

I also witnessed the entirely understandable resentment of some No voters, angry at having to defend something they had thought could be taken for granted. I saw the strain etched on the faces of those who still hadn't made up their minds as they entered the polling station. I assume most of these people ultimately voted No, but I spoke to one or two who had gone in expecting to do so but couldn't. 'How could I say no to my own country?' was how one woman put it.

The interaction that sticks most strongly in my mind from that day was with a man at a polling station in the Gorbals, at St Francis Primary School. He was fifty-five and told me he had never voted before in his life. He said that this was the first time he had ever felt any point to voting, the first time he had ever felt any hope in politics.

As he was leaving, he handed me a box of Lees Chocolate Teacakes, a sugar boost for me and the team, he said. A few days later, when I was helping clear out the Yes hub in my constituency, I found the empty box. I sat on the floor, holding it in my hands, thinking about that man, about the hope that had been lit within him, and which would now be extinguished. I cried my eyes out.

I got home around 9 p.m. on polling day and almost immediately began to feel really unwell. It was the start of one of the worst colds I have ever had. It was as if my body was telling me that enough was enough.

I felt so bad that I lay down on my bed and fell asleep. I woke with a start around midnight. I watched the first declarations, with an open line to party HQ. We were losing, but there was still some hope. It didn't last long. By about 1.30 a.m., it was all over. The result in Clackmannanshire, very much a bellwether, was decisive: 56% to 44%. We had lost. The sense of deflation was instant and absolute.

I had to gather myself to go to the Glasgow count. Victory in Glasgow was bittersweet. The mammoth round of interviews I did with all the main UK and international channels was the rawest I had ever been on live TV. My heart was breaking. It was around 5 a.m. by the time I got in the car to go to Edinburgh. The hoped-for victory party was now a wake. On the journey there, I spoke to Alex. I had all but forgotten our 18 July conversation, so it was like a bolt from the blue when he told me he intended to resign later that morning. I tried to talk him out of it, an effort that would continue over bacon rolls in Bute House a few hours later, but his mind was made up.

When I arrived, there were lots of tears. John Swinney, Geoff Aberdein, Alex and his wife, Moira, and I all gathered in a meeting room, with others coming and going sporadically. At some point, Alex took a call from David Cameron. This turned out to be the only ray of sunshine in an otherwise dark night. It was obvious that Cameron was making a massive miscalculation and, instead of acknowledging the closeness of the result, and promising positive change for Scotland, he used the moment to pledge English votes for English laws. It sounded like punishment for Scotland, and we immediately saw it would give us something to work with in the throes of defeat.

Alex announced his resignation later the same day. No one had really seen it coming, but no one was all that surprised either. I spent the day wandering around like a zombie. I went to St Andrew's House to thank the transition team. They were, metaphorically speaking, all dressed up with nowhere to go. We couldn't have wished for a more professional and dedicated team of civil servants. They were there ready and willing to serve their country in line with the popular will.

Everyone assumed that I would succeed Alex. In that moment, though, it felt overwhelming. I felt drained and depleted. How could I possibly step up to lead a country in this state? I decided to take the weekend to make up my mind. Deep down, however, I knew that there was little, if any, serious chance of me opting not to stand. Apart from anything else, at a moment of great vulnerability, I could not leave my country or my party in the lurch. But it was more than that. Often without knowing it, I had been preparing for this moment for much of my life.

Peter and I spent Friday evening and much of Saturday at Prestonfield House Hotel with a few close friends. It was while there that we learned of the surge in SNP membership. What started as a trickle on Friday afternoon was, by Saturday lunchtime, a torrent. It became obvious that, though we had lost the referendum, a fire had been sparked in Scotland that was not ready to be extinguished. I might have been hoarse from the cold, but the country had found its voice and was not about to be silenced.

CHAPTER TWELVE

First Lady

On 24 September 2014, I announced my intention to stand for leader of the SNP and First Minister of Scotland. I was the only contender in the race to succeed Alex Salmond, but, even so, the two-month period between him announcing his resignation and stepping down seemed interminable. On 14 November 2014, the interregnum finally drew to a close, and I became the first woman in the eighty-year history of the SNP to take the helm.

As I stood at the podium at our annual conference in Perth Concert Hall, taking the applause of the delegates, I felt a mix of pride, incredulity and fear. Taking charge of the party I had joined at sixteen was a massive moment for me. I had worked incredibly hard over two decades to put myself in this position, often to the detriment of my private life and personal happiness. I felt I was entitled to feel a sense of achievement, and I did.

But I felt something else too, something much harder to express, and much less comfortable. I was about to take on one of the highest-profile and most difficult jobs in the country. I was also stepping into the shoes of a man considered to be, by friend and foe alike, a political colossus. Nerves were only to be expected, but I was also feeling a sort of dissociation; in more clichéd terms, a sort of out-of-body experience. The shy, dour, always self-doubting, frumpy girl was standing in the wings watching a confident, articulate, almost stylish version of herself bestride the stage, and wondering, 'Who is that woman? Is she real?' The gulf between the inner me and the version on the stage that day had never felt so wide. I think I was scared that my public persona was now so far removed from my private self that I wouldn't be able to live up to her.

It was all mixed up in a wider worry that what had unfolded since the referendum was upside down, and back to front. The losers had become the winners and vice versa. Our opponents in the No campaign might have saved the Union, for now, but they were in the doldrums. By contrast, we were soaring. SNP membership had jumped from 25,000 on referendum day to more than 100,000 by the time I became leader. Later, the unwieldiness of this – the almost impossibly broad church that it created – would become a challenge, but in the immediate aftermath of the referendum, it felt like riding a wave. I had spent the weeks since the referendum fuelling the phenomenon, speaking to packed-out venues across the country, in a tour that would reach its dizzying peak just a week later at the Hydro, Glasgow's biggest music arena. In the preceding few months, the Hydro had hosted megastars like Beyoncé, Lady Gaga, Kylie, Ed Sheeran, Prince and Robbie Williams. Soon I would be looking out at a capacity crowd of twelve thousand people, all there to hear me speak.

It was exhilarating but also surreal. Was it the political equivalent of a dot.com bubble that would burst as quickly as it had inflated, an intoxication that would soon give way to the mother of all hangovers? I had a concern that it was unsustainable, and this doubt would only grow as the 2015 General Election drew closer. I had the sense that I was carrying something fragile, and it never went away completely.

———

On 19 November 2014, I was formally elected as Scotland's fifth First Minister, the first woman to hold the office. Being the first woman to occupy Bute House was undoubtedly significant, but, by the time of my election, Holyrood had been in existence for less than two decades. Perhaps of more significance in the grand sweep of history was the accompanying function of Keeper of the Great Seal of Scotland. The Seal is one of the principal symbols of Scotland, used by the monarch to authorize official documents. The continuation of a Scottish Seal was one of the guarantees for Scotland in the 1707 Treaty of Union. The first recorded Keeper of the Seal in the fourteenth century, pre-union days, was Sir Alexander de Cockburn. The first, post-union, was Hugh Campbell, the 3rd Earl of Loudon. For more than six hundred years, every Keeper of the Great Seal had been a man. In November 2014, I became the first woman to bear the title. Notwithstanding the largely symbolic nature of the role, it is a piece of history I take pride in.

The process of election in the Scottish Parliament that after-noon was relatively short. At its conclusion, Tricia Marwick, a close friend since my teenage years, and the first woman Presiding Officer of the Scottish Parliament, declared that I had been duly selected and that in line with the requirements of the Scotland Act she would recommend my appointment to the Queen.

The other party leaders then made short speeches of congratu-lations. Reading these now, I am struck by how gracious they were.

Political markers were laid down in each of them, but there was none of the spite and rancour that so often characterizes discourse today. There was respect for the occasion and for the office of First Minister.

After the other leaders had spoken, I gave my acceptance speech. I pledged to be a First Minister for all of Scotland and to:

> build a Scotland that all those who live and work here can be proud of – a nation both socially democratic and socially just; a Scotland confident in itself, proud of its successes and honest about its weaknesses; a Scotland of good government and civic empowerment; a Scotland vigorous and determined in its resolution to address poverty, support business, promote growth and tackle inequality.

I was acutely conscious of the significance of my gender and I expressed the hope that my election would send a 'strong, positive message to girls and young women – indeed, to all women across our land.'

My then eight-year-old niece, Harriet, was watching, probably a bit bemused, with the rest of my family in the public gallery. Her brother, Ethan, and my other nephews, Cameron, Ross and Finlay, were alongside her. I said this about Harriet:

> She does not yet know about the gender pay gap, underrepresentation or the barriers such as high childcare costs that make it so hard for so many women to work and pursue careers. My fervent hope is that she never will, and that by the time she is a young woman, she will have no need to know about any of those issues, because they will have been consigned to history.

To have a woman leading the country seemed to have touched something in the consciousness of many, as in the following days I was inundated with emails and letters from women and girls, telling me that, regardless of who I was and what my politics were, my presence as First Minister signified something important – the hope of a more equal future for them and their daughters. The weight of responsibility that I already felt became heavier. I knew there were some who, however subtly and implicitly, would try to lay any mistakes and missteps that I made at the door of women generally, proof in their eyes that we are not up to the top jobs after all.

Living up to the honour of being the first female incumbent of my office was almost an obsession, and I don't use that word lightly. One of my early priorities was helping to achieve gender equality on public and company boards. Progress on this had been glacial throughout my time in politics. When I took office, companies were just starting to take it seriously, and only as a result of mounting evidence that those with more women on their boards were more profitable. Who could possibly have guessed that, when the top talent from half the population was no longer excluded or grossly under-represented, performance and productivity might improve?

The obsession came partly from the sense that I would inevitably be held to higher standards – or, at least, different standards – than a man in my position would be. The journalist Mary Ann Sieghart describes, in her brilliant book on the topic, a concept called 'the authority gap'. I know it to be true not from a textbook but, like women everywhere, from the everyday experiences I have had over my lifetime.

It is unarguably the case that women have to work twice as hard to be considered half as good as men. Whereas men are presumed to be competent, to know what they are talking about, as undisputed experts in their field, unless and until it is proven otherwise, for women, it is usually the opposite: no matter the expertise or experience we have, the onus is always on us to prove our worth and it is always a work in progress.

It is a daily fact of life for women, almost regardless of our expertise or seniority, that we will be interrupted and talked over by men. Ideas and suggestions that are dismissed or ignored when we express them will be treated as epiphanies when they come out of the mouths of men.

We are judged, usually unkindly, on our appearance and the tone and timbre of our voices, in ways that men never are. The more feminine we look and sound, the less seriously we are taken. But, if we go the other way, as I tended to do in my younger years, emulating the men around us, dressing more soberly, lowering the tone of our voices, being more assertive, we will be written off as aggressive and unlikeable. Not feminine enough.

Shortly after I became First Minister, I was at an event attended by a fairly prominent Scottish businessman. He will remain name-less, partly to spare his blushes but also because I suspect the behaviour I am about to describe wasn't even conscious on his part, though that doesn't excuse it. On the occasion in question, he didn't shake my hand or greet me as First Minister, as I had seen him do countless times with Alex. Instead, he stroked my upper arm and said, 'How are you, Nicola?'

This is not me being precious because he didn't address me as First Minister. It was being treated so differently from my male predecessor that annoyed me. As is so often the case, an anecdote that seems almost trivial in fact tells a bigger story, one that is familiar to women in every walk of life.

———

The days following my election as First Minister were non-stop. On the morning of 20 November, after the Royal Warrant had been signed by the Queen, I was sworn in at the Court of Session – a short but solemn occasion before a full bench of judges. It was then straight back to Parliament for my first session of First Minister's Questions, which ranged over a wide variety of topics, such as access to cancer drugs, education and criminal justice. It was an early reminder of the weight of responsibilities I now carried.

In the afternoon I met with a group of unpaid carers in Bute House, a deliberate signal of my desire to amplify the voices of those traditionally ignored in the corridors of power. This became a source of tension throughout my time in office, as vested interests, used to having a virtual monopoly on the time and attention of political leaders, felt squeezed out. One of the constant refrains of my time as First Minister was that I was anti-business. I was not. I just happened to think that the voice of the business community was not the only one that should be heard by decision-makers. A vibrant economy generating the wealth a country needs is dependent on having thriving, successful businesses. However, it does not follow that the views businesses express on, for example, taxation and regulation, will always be right – or selfless and altruistic. Nor are they the only views that should be taken account of.

I later put the final touches to my first Cabinet, which I unveiled the following day. I had decided that Mike Russell and Kenny MacAskill should leave government. They had both been good ministers, though it seemed to me that Kenny's Justice portfolio had become mired in problems that he was struggling to get to grips with. Moreover, I wanted to freshen things up and put my own stamp on the Cabinet, so I called them both into Bute House early Thursday evening to break the news. It was horrible. Kenny appeared to take it well, expressing the view that he felt it was time for him to take a break from government. However, I also suspect that he is one of those men who would not have enjoyed having a woman as his boss. Mike, who was Education Secretary, took it much less well. He and I had been close for years and I was and am extremely fond of him, so it took all of my resolve not to crumble in the face of his protestations.

With the deeply unpleasant part of the reshuffle done, I turned my attention the following morning to ministerial appointments. I had asked John Swinney to be my Deputy First Minister in addition to his role as Finance Secretary. It was one of the best decisions I made. His counsel, wisdom, experience and work ethic were indispensable to me throughout my time as First Minister.

I appointed Michael Matheson as Justice Secretary in place of Kenny, and Angela Constance as Education Secretary in place of Mike. I also promoted Roseanna to Cabinet for the first time. The other big change was to appoint Shona Robison as Health Secretary. I moved Alex Neil, who had succeeded me in the Health job, to Social Justice. I had been hearing disquiet for some time, from within the civil service and across the NHS, about Alex's lack of focus as Health Secretary. There was admiration for his energy and innovative thinking but a concern that many of his ideas were madcap and unworkable – that his officials would be sent on wild goose chases, only to find some time later that he had lost interest in whatever he had tasked them to do.

The most striking aspect of the new Cabinet was that, for the first time ever, it was gender-balanced. This was deliberate, not happenstance. At that time, just three Cabinets in the world included as many women as men. It was important to me to have balance in my team. I got many letters questioning whether all the women in my Cabinet were really there on merit (they were!). No one asked the same question of the men, as their abilities were just taken for granted. The lack of gender balance in our society isn't because women are less able, it's because ingrained bias and centuries-old stereotyping make us less likely to be promoted into senior positions.

———

The whirlwind didn't ease up over the coming weeks. Getting to grips with the day-to-day realities of the job seemed to involve a different challenge every hour. I also had a fair amount of business outside of Scotland in the final few weeks of the year.

At the end of November I travelled to the Isle of Man for the biannual summit of the British–Irish Council. The British–Irish Council is one of the institutions created by the Good Friday Agreement, bringing together governments from across the whole of the British Isles. It is an important body, but its potential is curtailed by the lack of respect and priority shown to it by successive UK governments. The Taoiseach – Prime Minister of Ireland – attends these summits as a matter of course. But, until Keir Starmer attended in Edinburgh in December 2024, the last UK Prime Minister to do so was Gordon Brown in 2007. Rishi Sunak's decision in 2022 to show up for the official dinner before hotfooting it back to London ahead of the start of the summit doesn't count.

For me, over and above the formal business, these gatherings were an opportunity to lay the foundations of relationships with other leaders. I drew a lot of personal strength from these interactions. It didn't take me long to find out how lonely leadership is. I had naively assumed that my proximity to Alex through his years as First Minister had given me a good understanding of the pressures involved. I quickly realized that this was only true up to a point. Being a leader is qualitatively different from being second-in-command. It comes with a constant, ever-present sense of responsibility and anxiety, of always expecting the unexpected and never being able to switch off or breathe entirely easily. The decisions that land on a leader's desk are the most complex and difficult, those that no one else has been able or willing to take. By the time they arrive there, there is nowhere else for them to go, no one else to pass them to. The buck always stops with you.

Leaders of devolved governments don't attend international summits – the COP climate change conferences being an exception – so the British–Irish Council is a rare opportunity to talk to people who live with the same pressures. I formed a good relationship with the Taoiseach of the time, Enda Kenny. He was a wily character, with the gift of the gab. He would routinely arrive late and then have us all eating from the palm of his hand as he regaled us with his latest take on the political issues of the day. Much as I liked Enda, though, I came to know his successors, Leo Varadkar and Micheál Martin, better. From time to time during the tortuous process leading up to the UK actually leaving the EU, they were able to give me helpful steers about the progress, or otherwise, of the negotiations.

By far my closest relationships, however, were with the Welsh First Ministers. Carwyn Jones was in office when I became First Minister. There had been some frostiness between Alex and Carwyn. During the referendum campaign, Carwyn had said he would veto any attempt to set up a currency union if Scotland voted for independence. It is doubtful if he would have had the power to do so, but the intervention infuriated Alex. He thought Carwyn should have kept quiet. I didn't want to continue the grievance, so I made a real effort to get on with Carwyn, and he reciprocated. We developed an extremely good personal rapport and formed an effective strategic alliance which allowed us to exercise more influence with the UK government than we could have done individually. My relationship with Carwyn's successor, Mark Drakeford, especially during the Covid pandemic, was even stronger. The determination of the devolved administrations, often including Northern Ireland, to present a united front in disagreements with the UK government was significant. However, because of the fundamental imbalance in current UK constitutional arrangements, UK governments can, and often do, simply impose their will, regardless of the united objections of the Scottish, Welsh and Northern Irish governments.

Perhaps the most unexpected bond of affection I formed through the British–Irish Council, however, was with Martin McGuinness, then deputy First Minister of Northern Ireland. He and I hit it off from the first moment we met. Obviously, we had a shared political outlook in the sense that neither of us wanted our countries to be governed by Westminster, but it ran deeper than that. I think he detected how naturally shy I was and, especially in my early days as First Minister, he seemed to make it his business at events we both attended to put me at ease. He would always make a beeline for me and give me a massive bear hug. I am acutely aware that for many people Martin will always be viewed through the lens of his IRA past, and, of course, I often thought about this too. And yet, it was hard to reconcile that with the kind, gentle man I got to know. He had risked a great deal to help bring the violence to an end and, as far as I could tell, his commitment to peace was absolute.

In previous BIC summits as Deputy First Minister, I had seen up close the remarkable relationship Martin had with the then First Minister, Ian Paisley. There was something deeply inspiring, humbling in fact, in watching two individuals, from opposite sides of a bloody and protracted civil war, put enmity aside and focus on what they had in common. They were famously nicknamed the 'Chuckle Brothers' and in one sense it could not have been more apt – they were always making each other laugh. But the personal dynamic was more filial than brotherly. Martin displayed a tender solicitousness towards Ian Paisley that was absent when Peter Robinson took over, but, otherwise, the new relationship seemed equally strong.

———

On 10 December, I had my first private audience with the Queen. Of the many audiences I had with her during my time as First Minister, this was the only one to take place in Buckingham Palace. I was there to be formally admitted to the Privy Council. I was really nervous as my car pulled into the Palace courtyard. My door was opened by the Queen's equerry and I was ushered inside and down a corridor I had only ever seen in pictures, grand portraits adorning its walls. My heart was hammering as I was taken into the anteroom for the official ceremony. An air of mystery surrounds the Privy Council, so I had no concrete sense of what to expect. Thankfully, it was not as strange as I had feared, though it did involve kneeling before the monarch and kissing her hand.

Even more nerve-wracking than the Privy Council induction was the prospect of being in a room alone with the Queen. Would it be awkward? What would we talk about? Would I be able to sustain the conversation? I needn't have worried. As befitting someone who had been hosting audiences like this one for her entire life, she made it easy. She was interested and informed. And utterly fascinating. She shared stories of past audiences with Winston Churchill, meetings with Nelson Mandela, and the Kennedys' visit to London, shortly after JFK's election. I am not a monarchist by instinct, but the private time I spent with the Queen ranks as one of the great privileges of my life. It was clear from our first meeting that she was an extraordinary woman.

———

The final 'first' in my early weeks in the job was in Downing Street, on 15 December, when I had a meeting with David Cameron, the twelfth Prime Minister of the Queen's reign. I had been inside Number 10 before, but this was my first meeting in the Prime Minister's study. The room had a strangely informal feel to it, more like a place to 'hang-out' than to conduct important matters of state. It would have a very different feel under Theresa May.

The discussion with Cameron was cordial. Even so, he tried to snare me in a political trap. He wanted to talk about how our two governments could cooperate more closely on security matters, in light of the growing threat from ISIS. I was fully on board and we reached an agreement that the UK government would share intelligence more routinely with the devolved administrations. However, he tried to use the focus on security to extract my unconditional support for the Investigatory Powers Bill, a highly contentious piece of legislation that his government was seeking to enact. I might have been new in the job, but I wasn't as naive as he hoped and I swerved the trap.

David Cameron was the first of five Prime Ministers I interacted with during my time in office. In terms of background and political outlook, he and I had little in common. Perhaps I am being unfair, but it seemed to me that politics for him was just one of several potential career choices that his whole life had been preparing him for. It didn't seem to be a vocation driven by pursuit of any great cause. He always appeared to bear the burdens of office quite lightly.

However, by some margin, he was the Prime Minister I found easiest to deal with. He had an effortless charm, burnished at Eton no doubt, and, despite our differences, I liked him. Also, while this is definitely relative, he had a level of respect for devolution that, however inadequate I might have thought it at the time, far exceeded that displayed by any of his successors. Indeed, given some of the characters who came after, I would later feel quite nostalgic about my interactions with Cameron.

———

As 2015 got underway, my focus was very much on the policy agenda I wanted to pursue. In February, I made a visit to a London primary school called Blue Gate Fields in Tower Hamlets. I had targeted closing the poverty-related attainment gap in education as a priority and had been impressed by the so-called London Challenge, a school improvement programme established by the Blair government to raise standards in some of the poorest areas of the city. A visit to an inner-city school was a chance to see first-hand the kind of initiatives that had been delivering results. My main take-away was the need to target extra resources to areas of highest deprivation and then allow schools the flexibility to invest in the kinds of intervention most likely to improve the educational experience of children whose life chances were being blighted by poverty.

This visit was instrumental in the launch shortly afterwards of the Scottish Attainment Challenge. The £100 million that we invested supported a wide range of initiatives, from extra staff to breakfast clubs and programmes to get parents more involved in school life.

My record on education as First Minister has been much traduced. It is certainly the case that I didn't achieve nearly as much as I wanted to, but programmes like the Attainment Challenge made a difference. I also came to understand that closing the poverty-related attainment gap is only possible if we do more to tackle poverty itself. Kids who turn up in class hungry, or who don't have space to study at home, or whose parents can't afford extra-curricular activities are obviously less likely to do well than their better-off counterparts.

We need to focus not just on what happens in the classroom, but on improving children's lives outside of school, and long before they get there. That's why I put such an emphasis on expanding early years education and childcare. It doesn't just help children's development; it also makes it more affordable for parents to go to work. The need to tackle the root cause of the attainment gap is also why, much later in my tenure, when the Scottish Parliament had gained the necessary powers, I established the Scottish Child Payment, money that low-income families get every week for each child in the household. At the time of writing, it has lifted tens of thousands of children in Scotland out of poverty.

The numbers we had used in the referendum White Paper to illustrate an independent Scotland's fiscal position had been heavily dependent on oil revenues. And, of course, we had based these on the optimistic estimates that Alex had insisted on. I didn't know then that a total collapse in the oil price was just around the corner.

In early 2015, this caused significant political and practical problems. The practical came from the impact on the economy of Aberdeen and the north-east, which is heavily reliant on the oil and gas supply chain. As the major companies started to shed jobs and curtail activity, the effects were quickly felt across the region. Given the significance of the north-east to Scotland as a whole, the impact wasn't limited to that region. In January, the then Governor of the Bank of England, Mark Carney, warned of a serious negative shock to the Scottish economy. The prospect of a Scotland-only recession was all too real.

The UK government held the powers to give the industry the tax breaks it was calling for. The levers I could use were very limited. Nevertheless, I established an Energy Jobs taskforce. Its focus was on the issues that the Scottish government actually had responsibility for, such as helping apprentices complete training, supporting those facing redundancy with re-skilling programmes and providing assistance for companies seeking to maintain employment through innovation.

The taskforce, well led by the then chief executive of Scottish Enterprise, Lena Wilson, did a good job, but the opposition parties still sensed a political opportunity. To have the price of a barrel of crude fall to around $40 when we had relied on a figure of well over $100 in the referendum blew a massive hole in the credibility of our argument. I resolved then that in any future referendum, we must not allow the strength of the independence prospectus to stand or fall on the volatile value of oil, especially as it is a finite commodity. We needed to show how Scotland's economy would be sustainable in the long term without it.

Looking back, I find it astonishing how little climate change featured in the debate at that time. As recently as ten years ago, apart from the Greens, all parties were committed to maximum exploitation of North Sea resources, even with abundant evidence of the environmental impact of fossil fuels. I wish now that the price shock of 2015 had prompted us to do more, sooner, to prepare for the challenges involved in making a just transition away from oil and gas to renewable sources of energy.

———

As 2015 dawned, we were flying high in the polls. It's quite extra-ordinary, and at least in part a sign of our deeply unsettled times, that in eight and half years in the top job I steered my party to victory in no fewer than eight elections – three UK General Elections, two Scottish Parliament contests, two Scotland-wide local council polls and a European Parliament election. Then there was also the small matter of the Brexit referendum in 2016.

In my time in charge, there were only two full calendar years – 2018 and 2020 – with no election, and in one of those we faced a global pandemic. Never having a clear period without an election or the possibility of one on the horizon made my job much more challenging. It meant I had no extended run at governing, no time when I could make tough but necessary changes without worrying about the impact on my party's poll rating. Indeed, it's no coincidence that the boldest of my annual Programmes for Government came in 2017, when I thought our next electoral challenge would be in 2021. Two unscheduled contests in 2019 – for the European and UK Parliaments – and the arrival of Covid in early 2020 changed all of that.

At the end of 2014, Jim Murphy, formerly Secretary of State for Scotland in the Gordon Brown government, had been elected leader of Scottish Labour following Johann Lamont's sudden resignation. On her way out, in what was a huge gift to the SNP, she had described Scottish Labour as nothing more than a 'branch office' of the UK party. Murphy was a typical alpha-male politician: boorish and cocky, full of his own brilliance. In the closing stages of the referendum, he had made great play of touring Scotland with two Irn-Bru crates, which he would stand on to make speeches in town centres across the country. The almost entirely male Scottish press corps thought he walked on water. And, looking forward to the UK General Election in May 2015, I began to worry they might be right.

The campaign was gruelling and intense. Our opponents, and parts of the media, were desperate to see me fall flat on my face (and it was a perennial worry for me too that I would do so). The establishment was worried that the UK-wide polls, coupled with our ratings in Scotland, raised the very real prospect that we would hold the balance of power in a hung parliament.

I had already made crystal clear that we wouldn't do any kind of deal with the Tories in that scenario. Instead, we would seek to be part of a progressive alliance with Labour to lock the Tories out. This position was sincere, but also tactically important. Anti-Tory sentiment in large swathes of Scotland is still ingrained. The alliance Labour had struck with the Tories in the referendum was deeply offensive to many people and was partly the reason they struggled so badly in its wake. It was therefore essential to confirm that SNP MPs would be in the same anti-Tory column as Labour MPs to neutralize the familiar mantra we had always faced in General Elections, that people had to vote Labour to keep the Tories out.

The prospect of us being kingmakers meant that there was intense debate, especially in UK-wide media, about what we would exact from Labour for our support. Even though I had reduced our bargaining power somewhat by ruling out any deals with the Tories, our position would nevertheless have been strong. This was still the brief era of the Fixed Term Parliaments Act. Prime Ministers couldn't simply threaten a General Election to pull people into line. If they were unable to marshal enough votes to pass budgets or key legislation, they'd be in limbo. A minority Labour government would need our votes, and we would drive a hard bargain.

This narrative suited us down to the ground north of the

border, where the post-referendum mood was all about giving Scotland more clout and a much stronger voice. However, in England, it suited the Tories. We became, for them, a convenient bogeyman. Their claim, reinforced in the right-wing media, was that the SNP would be the strong tail wagging the weak Labour dog. In pursuing our 'separatist' agenda, we would supposedly wreak havoc on the stability of the UK, and Ed Miliband would be powerless to stop us.

The Tory campaign caused me some unease. The idea that I might, however inadvertently, help them win an election was anathema to me and my 1980s Ayrshire upbringing. I was able to rationalize it, though, and make sure it didn't inhibit my arguments or performance in the campaign. My job was to maximize the SNP vote and I firmly believed that a big cadre of SNP MPs would give Scotland greater clout at Westminster than ever before and also make a minority Labour government bolder and more radical than it would be otherwise.

If the prospect of the SNP giving Scotland a stronger voice at Westminster was hurting Labour in England, the solution wasn't for me to soft-pedal, it was for Labour to be more confident in rebutting the Tory attack. Their response, bullishly expressed, should have been that while they hoped Scotland would vote Labour, Scottish votes should be respected whatever the outcome; by suggesting that Scotland's democratic choice if it turned out to be the SNP was illegitimate, the Tories were the ones threatening the Union, not Labour. To this day, I firmly believe that if Labour had summoned the courage to articulate that argument with confidence, instead of cowering in the face of Tory tabloid attacks, the outcome of the election might have been different.

———

Scotland has always had televised leaders' debates, and I participated in these in 2015. However, the two UK debates I was included in were far more significant.

Until 2015, the SNP had always struggled for relevance and, therefore, airtime in UK elections. Now we were being included in the UK-wide broadcast coverage as of right. This gave us parity for the first time ever, but it gave us so much more than that. Whereas the other Scottish parties were covered in Scottish news, and their UK counterparts in the UK news, I straddled both. It elevated and amplified me and contributed to the sense that we played in a different league.

The first of the debates took place in ITV's Salford studio on Thursday, 2 April. My stomach churned all day. I did FMQs at lunchtime, almost on autopilot, before hotfooting it down to Manchester in the afternoon.

A couple of my aides had gone ahead of me. Liz Lloyd had wanted to establish contact with the debate producers to make sure she knew the process for raising complaints during the debate if I wasn't given a fair amount of time to speak. All of the other parties would have been doing likewise. Ria Robertson, who looked after my logistics, had travelled down with the clothes I was planning to wear, to make sure that if anything untoward happened to my outfit in transit, there would be plenty of time for an emergency dash to the shops.

Ever since I had run for deputy leader of the SNP a decade earlier, there had been periodic media talk of me getting 'makeovers', softening my image, and being deliberately more feminine in what I wore and how I styled my hair. It was rubbish. I've never had a 'makeover' in my life. Colouring my hair was just a feature of getting older. Similarly, wearing dresses and more flattering suits was just a sign of the enhanced confidence that often comes with age. I felt more comfortable in my own skin than I had in my younger years, no longer so compelled to fit in with the men around me in dull trouser suits.

That said, when I became First Minister, I knew that my appearance would be under even more scrutiny than before. This is when a group of truly wonderful women came into my life. First and foremost, there was hairdresser and make-up artist Julie McGuire. Often at short notice, and almost always out of hours, I'd visit Julie's salon in Leith, or she would come to me in Bute House to cut and colour my hair. I'd get to enjoy a couple of hours of peace and tranquillity amidst the madness of my daily life. Julie still does my hair and, even now, never fails to calm me down and cheer me up.

Personal shopper and stylist Zoe Radcliffe was on hand to pick up any outfits I needed at the last minute. She was also able, at what seemed like lightning speed, to do the necessary alterations to make clothes fit me. Then there were Holly Mitchell and Lynsey Byrne of Edinburgh dress designers Totty Rocks. I wore off-the-peg clothes most of the time, but when I was First Minister I would sometimes commission Totty Rocks to design outfits for special occasions. The dress that I'd worn the day I became First Minister was a Holly and Lynsey creation. So too was the suit I wore in the first leaders' debate.

I made a quick visit to the studio to familiarize myself with the layout, a couple of hours from going on air, which calmed me down a bit. I told myself that it was just a TV studio, a natural habitat for me by then, and that as long as I took deep breaths, engaged my brain and spoke from the heart, I'd be fine.

Just before 8 p.m. we were all backstage, waiting to be introduced to the studio audience. The 'we' were David Cameron, Ed Miliband, Nick Clegg, Leanne Wood of Plaid Cymru, Natalie

Bennett of the Greens, Nigel Farage and me. ITV's Julie Etching-ham was the debate moderator. With one exception, we were all quiet, lost in our own thoughts. The exception was Nigel Farage, who I recall telling someone, quite loudly, how much alcohol he had consumed. I have met him in the flesh only a handful of times, and while I found him every bit as odious in person as he appears on TV, it also seemed to me that underneath the bombast is a brittle, fragile ego. He seems very insecure, especially around women.

The wait was over. We were on air, live, and into our opening statements. I was determined to try to appeal to centre-left voters across the UK, and not just in Scotland. I needed to show I didn't have two heads, that our priorities chimed with those of many people in England. So, while I didn't hide the fact that I wanted Scotland to be independent, I stressed that for as long as we were part of the Westminster system, the SNP would be a partner for progressive change across the whole UK.

Despite my nerves, I settled in quickly and got some early applause from the audience. But it was only during the midway commercial break that I got any sense of how it was really going. We had been told we had four minutes to go to the toilet during the break. I knew that wasn't long enough for me to extricate myself from the microphone battery pack which, because I was wearing a dress and didn't have a waistband, was attached to my underwear. So, as the others went to the bathroom, I stayed back and chatted to some audience members from England. They were effusive, saying that they wished they could vote for me. Some Scottish people sitting behind them butted in to say they were glad they could actually vote for me. It was a massive boost to my confidence, and I felt like I flew through the second half. The most positive audience reaction came when I spoke about being the first member of my family to go to university and the importance of free tuition to making that possible, and how, as a leader now, I had no right to take it away from future generations.

In the green room at the end of the show, I could tell from my team that it had been a success. They were ecstatic. When the snap polls came out, we had reason to be even cheerier. I had scored well in all of them, but YouGov had me as the clear winner. We couldn't have hoped for a better night and we made our way back to Scotland on a high.

Success came at a cost though. If I'd been seen as a threat to the establishment before the debate, the target on my back now was even bigger. While we didn't know it then, trouble was just a day away.

———

The following evening, a Friday, I was slumped on the sofa, barely able to keep my eyes open, when a press officer sent me the front page of the next day's *Daily Mail*. The banner headline, next to a photo of me, was 'The Most Dangerous Woman in Britain'. This kind of rhetoric worried my security team, but I was delighted. It burnished my credentials and showed just how potent our electoral strength was. It might also be the nicest thing the *Daily Mail* has ever said about me.

However, as I was idly scrolling through social media, enjoying the various reactions to the *Mail*'s hysterical hyperbole, I started seeing references from journalists to rumours that the *Telegraph* was about to break an explosive story about me. There was no detail, just breathless excitement. One said that if what he was hearing was true, the SNP campaign would implode.

It's hard to explain exactly how I felt in that moment. I couldn't begin to imagine what the story might be. Oddly, the *Telegraph* had made no approach for reaction or comment. I would later have a press complaint upheld on this point. Before publishing such a potentially damaging and, as it turned out, wholly inaccurate story about me, the *Telegraph* should have offered a right of reply. It didn't, no doubt because they feared that my flat denial would have destroyed the story. It was atrociously bad journalism.

The rational part of my brain was telling me that as I hadn't done anything terrible, the story couldn't be anything terrible. And yet I knew that even something made up, or twisted out of all recognition, could do real damage. As the old saying goes, a lie will be halfway round the world before the truth gets its boots on.

Finally, the story dropped. 'Sturgeon's Secret Backing for Cameron' screamed the next day's front page. In summary, the *Telegraph* had been leaked a copy of a Foreign Office memo about a meeting I'd had back in February, in Edinburgh, with the French ambassador to the UK, Sylvie Bermann. It was claimed that I had told her that I wanted David Cameron to win the election and that I thought Ed Miliband was not prime ministerial material. The author of the memo hadn't been in the room but had been given an account from the French consul-general in Edinburgh, Pierre-Alain Coffinier, who had been there. The memo expressed scepticism that I would ever have voiced such a view and contained a caveat that there might have been an error in translation. None of that mattered to the *Telegraph* though. It didn't let the truth get in the way of the story.

It was obvious to me that there had been a mistranslation. I had the highest regard for Pierre-Alain and did not believe he had intended to misrepresent me. I had no reason to think that the Foreign Office official who wrote the memo did either. I recalled exactly what I'd said to the ambassador. I had told her that Cameron might well win the election, as Miliband was seen by many as weak. It was a prediction of what I thought could happen, not an expression of what I wanted to happen.

Although it had taken me a matter of seconds to know that the story was rubbish, I wasn't at all sure that I'd be able to convince the wider world. I was painfully aware of how damaging it would be to me and our campaign if people believed it. Most of Scotland wanted to see the back of the Tories. I feared that if there was now a suspicion that secretly we really wanted them to win, the trust people had in us would disappear. The effect on my personal reputation would be devastating too. The word that had been used repeatedly about me since the TV debate was 'authentic'. If people now bought into the *Telegraph* story, I'd be written off as just another mendacious politician saying one thing in public and another in private.

'Frenchgate', as it had already been dubbed, was leading the BBC news coverage. It would dominate the next day's papers too. I issued a furious denial. We then activated the considerable SNP social media network to make sure my response was shared far and wide. Thankfully, the French Embassy also issued a strong rebuttal, making it clear that I had not said what the memo and the *Telegraph* were claiming. I was immensely grateful. It would have been all too easy for it to sit tight and say nothing, for fear of being seen to interfere in a UK election.

The next day I spoke at an anti-Trident rally in Glasgow's George Square. As I fought my path through the crowd on my way in and out of the square, it became clear that, far from hurting us, the story was working in our favour. For many of our core supporters, it was evidence that the 'establishment' was trying to stitch us up. The UK government ordered a leak inquiry the day after the *Telegraph* published the story, and, a few weeks after the election, the Liberal Democrat MP for Orkney and Shetland, and former Secretary of State for Scotland, Alistair Carmichael, was forced to come clean as the culprit. Despite his denials at the time, he had authorized his special adviser, Euan Roddin, to give the Foreign Office memo to the *Telegraph*. He paid a heavy price when a group of his constituents later tried to get his election overturned in court on the basis that he had lied to voters. The bid was unsuccessful, but it must have cost him a lot of stress and money.

In the moment, though, a story that could have been fatal to our campaign ended up giving it a boost. It all added to the sense that I had the Midas touch.

———

The second UK leaders' debate took place at the Methodist Central Hall in Westminster on 16 April. It was different from the first in that only opposition leaders took part. David Cameron was absent. So too was his coalition partner, Nick Clegg, though rumour was that he had wanted to be included. David Dimbleby was the moderator. This debate covered much of the same ground as the first, but, absent government voices, the dynamic was different. The snap poll afterwards declared Ed Miliband the winner, with me a close second. To his fury, Farage came third, prompting allegations from him that the BBC had been biased in its audience selection.

Although Miliband won on the night, the debate was in my view a disaster for Labour. His very presence there, standing alongside me, Leanne and Natalie, was from the Tory perspective a perfect illustration of their central attack line: he would be a weak Prime Minister, presiding over a 'coalition of chaos', with me pulling his strings. He should have been debating, head-to-head, with the other candidate for Prime Minister, not perched in a line-up of 'minor' parties. Why Labour agreed to him taking part is beyond me. It allowed me, through stronger commitments than his on standing up for public services, tackling poverty and strengthening the Scottish Parliament, to paint a vivid picture of how much bolder a Labour government would have to be under the might of SNP pressure.

As the credits rolled at the end of the show, the optics got even worse for Ed. Leanne, Natalie and I were pictured in a group hug, with him looking forlornly on from the side. I have always felt a bit guilty about that moment. Farage had already stormed off in a huff, so we should have given Ed a hug too. Although an image of him and me hugging might have been a thousand times worse for him than the one of him looking like a little boy lost.

———

I wish I'd had the inner confidence to enjoy the 2015 campaign more. All year, our poll lead over Labour never fell below ten percentage points and was usually closer to twenty. In terms of our percentage share of the vote, we were polling, consistently, in the high forties or low fifties. The experience was of a kind I don't think any other Scottish politician – possibly no other UK politician – has ever had.

I simply couldn't bring myself to believe what the evidence was telling me: that the SNP was riding an unstoppable wave. Far from being the weak link, I was seemingly the star attraction. In the latter stages of the campaign, every visit I made attracted crowds of hundreds, sometimes thousands. I was mobbed everywhere I went by people wanting to hug me, take a photograph, thrust a child into my arms, or press a card or letter into my hand.

Every campaign stop overran, even though I was rarely able to walk more than a few yards from my car. People jostled each other to get to the front. On countless occasions I witnessed grown men push small children aside to get to me first (I always tried to stop this if I could). I am not very tall, so I couldn't see over the heads of those closest to me, but I was aware of being at the centre of a mass of people, all pressing in on me. It was crazy and, once or twice, frightening. I have an aerial photograph, taken in Inverness on the Saturday before polling day, where I am just a small speck in the centre of an enormous crowd – it illustrates my perspective on the campaign rather perfectly.

A private security team, working alongside my police protection officers, had the task of keeping me safe on these visits. It was led by a truly lovely man called Billy Kirkwood. Billy attended so many public meetings with me during the referendum that we often joked about how he could have delivered my speech word for word. No matter how big the crowd, or intimidating the situation, a glimpse of Billy Kirkwood out of the corner of my eye always made me feel safer.

I spent the final few days on a whistlestop tour of the country, in a helicopter emblazoned with a larger than life-size picture of me, alongside our campaign slogan 'Stronger for Scotland'. I'd never flown in a helicopter before and took quite a lot of persuading that I should do so now. It was an experience that I have repeated only once since, in the 2017 General Election, and I have no desire to do it again.

On May bank holiday Monday, it reached fever pitch. With lots of people off work, the crowds were even bigger than before. The helicopter was surrounded as soon as it landed in Battery Park in Greenock. Ahead of our arrival in Largs, one of Scotland's douce seaside towns, there was gridlock. Every street was packed with people trying to get to where the action was, to where I was going to be. The Largs police were so worried about crowd control (possibly the first and last time that sentence has ever been used) that there was a brief discussion about skipping it and heading straight to the next stop. I would have hated to do that and was relieved when the decision was taken to stay on plan. I even made it to the world-famous Nardini's cafe for an ice cream. The Ed Miliband bacon-sandwich episode of the same campaign had turned the public consumption of food by politicians into a risky business. I could see how relieved my team were when I managed to eat the ice-cream cone without smearing it all over my face.

The last stop of the day, and of the helicopter tour overall, was Dumfries, where I spoke at a public meeting before heading by car back to Edinburgh. By the time I got into the car that evening, I was exhausted, hoarse, sore. It felt like every muscle in my body was aching. I spent the next couple of days close to Edinburgh. This being a UK election, the Scottish Parliament was still sitting. On top of the exhausting campaign schedule, I still had all the day-to-day responsibilities of being First Minister. That included First Minister's Questions each week, and most nights when I arrived back in Bute House after campaigning, I had to wade through the papers in my ministerial box before I could collapse into bed.

———

By the time polling day dawned, two things were clear in Scotland. First, the polls were predicting that the other parties faced virtual wipeout from an oncoming SNP juggernaut. Second, no one – including us – really believed it would be quite that seismic. Even accounting for the 2011 earthquake, what the polls were suggesting now was beyond our collective comprehension.

I spent the day in and around my constituency, accompanied by Matt Bendoris of the *Scottish Sun*. The *Sun* had endorsed us in this election, as it had done in 2011 and would again in 2016. I'm a bit ashamed of this, to be honest, which is no reflection on Matt, a journalist I really rate. However, even in 2015, the power of the tabloid media was waning and it was no longer clear that the benefit of a *Sun* endorsement outweighed the inevitable criticism it provoked. There wasn't much in the *Sun*'s view of the world that aligned with mine and it made me feel slightly grubby. Certainly by 2016, I think I might have won more support for turning down its backing than I got from welcoming it, but I just wasn't brave enough to do it.

Despite always telling myself on election days that I should get a couple of hours' sleep ahead of the usual twenty-four-hour media marathon from the point polls closed, I almost never did. I was always scared that I might miss a final few conversations that would somehow tip the balance. It was almost 8 p.m., then, when I eventually made it back home, accompanied by Liz and another close adviser, John McFarlane.

I distracted myself for a while with the unlikeliest of activities – trying on the hats which my Private Office had sent through from Edinburgh with John. I was flying to London early the next morning to attend a service to commemorate the seventieth anniversary of VE Day and, since headwear doesn't sit easily on my thick hair, this would be the first time I had worn a hat in public. I also took some time to pack. If the outcome of the election was a hung parliament, it was likely that I'd need to stay on in London over the weekend to be on hand for any coalition discussions.

We ordered pizzas and waited for the exit poll. I really was bracing myself to hear that, despite all the hype, we were projected to win our usual six or so seats. There was silence in my living room as Big Ben struck ten and the exit poll numbers flashed onto the screen. I think my heart actually stopped for a few seconds.

The poll was predicting that the SNP would win 58 of Scotland's 59 constituencies. It was preposterous . . . surely? Even at my most optimistic I couldn't believe for a second that our victory would be on anything like that scale. My instinct was to dampen down expectations. I immediately fired off a tweet asking people to treat the poll with huge caution. However, as the initial intelligence trickled in from counts across the country, we started to think that the prediction might not be too far off.

It took me a few minutes to process the other news from the exit poll. The Tories were projected to be the largest party, with a slightly increased seat tally. Labour looked to be down by a few seats. The Liberals had taken a hammering after their coalition with the Tories, and especially their tuition fee betrayal, having infuriated swathes of their core supporters. A progressive coalition, with us as major participants, looked like it just might be in play, but it was going to be tight and, with Labour losing ground, it would struggle for moral authority even if the numbers stacked up.

We ended up with fifty-six seats in Scotland, leaving Labour, the Tories and the Lib Dems with just one apiece. Big-name politicians, including Jim Murphy, had fallen like ninepins. We polled just a fraction shy of 50% of the total votes cast. Not all of the news was good, though. The prospect of a hung parliament evaporated. The Tories, against all expectations, had pulled off a majority. There would be no coalition haggling, no kingmaker status.

I made a quick visit to the Glasgow count, where the SNP won all seven constituencies in a city steeped in generations of Labour folklore. It was obvious from some of the questions in the media interviews I did that there would be an attempt to pin the blame for Labour's UK-wide failure on me and the SNP. I made the point that even if Labour had been handed all fifty-nine Scottish seats on a plate, they'd still be trailing the Tories. Labour's problem wasn't being beaten by the SNP in Scotland, it was failing to beat the Tories in England, and that was on them, not me.

———

As soon as I entered the airport the next morning, surrounded by TV cameras and photographers, all hell broke loose. Only then did the scale of our victory properly sink in. All along my route from the entrance, through security, to the departure gate, people were breaking into spontaneous applause. The airport shops emptied as passengers and staff alike poured out to watch, clap, shout congratulations. People were coming up to hug me, cry happy tears on my shoulder, get selfies, tell me how ecstatic they were at the result. As I passed the Wetherspoons pub, a number of stag and hen parties abandoned their cooked breakfasts and early morning pints to come out for photos.

As I finally boarded the plane to London City, I thought I could at last relax a bit, but as soon as I appeared at the front of the aircraft, passengers started to clap. I found out only much later that one of the Labour MPs we had just defeated had been on the same plane that morning. For Tom Harris, until a few hours earlier the MP for Glasgow Cathcart, my presence must have made an already miserable morning feel even worse.

I was accompanied on the trip by Liz Lloyd and Katy Bowman. At that time, Katy was one of my Private Secretaries, but she would later become a special adviser and one of the most valued members of my support team. I dozed a bit on the flight, but the madness kicked off again as soon as we landed. There were live aerial pictures on TV of our plane taxiing to the gate, and the media helicopter hovered over our car all the way into central

London. We got into London in good time for me to divert to my hotel on Westminster Bridge, where I took a call from an understandably very bullish David Cameron. He congratulated me and I likewise congratulated him, and we agreed to meet properly soon. We had lots to talk about, not just delivery of the promised new powers for Holyrood on income tax and welfare, but also a referendum on EU membership that he had rashly committed to, no doubt on the assumption that he wouldn't have the majority needed to actually get it through the Commons. Suddenly, though, he did.

It was then on to the Foreign Office, where we assembled ahead of the service at the Cenotaph. Nick Clegg looked shell-shocked and Ed Miliband utterly broken. I didn't really know what to say to them, especially to Ed. I wanted to commiserate, but knew that whatever I said would sound hollow, condescending even. To his great credit, Ed was lovely. With a wry joke about hoping I appreciated his sacrifice in making our victory possible, he congratulated me. I like to think I would have mustered as much grace had the roles been reversed but, in truth, I doubt it.

The service was sombre and moving, a moment of peace in the midst of the tumult. And then, to be honest, I don't remember much about the rest of the day. I know I caught up with Angus Robertson, the leader of our MP group, and did a string of interviews at the makeshift media village on St Stephen's Green outside the Houses of Parliament. It was there, early evening, while speaking to Jackie Bird on *Reporting Scotland*, that I realized tiredness had finally stripped me of the ability to string a sentence together. I told Liz not to let me speak to another journalist until I'd had a sleep.

––––

Back in Scotland the next day, I did a photocall with all fifty-six of our new MPs at South Queensferry, with the iconic Forth railway bridge as the backdrop. They were a diverse and eclectic bunch. Only a few had been in the House of Commons previously – veterans like Mike Weir, Stewart Hosie, Pete Wishart had all been re-elected. Alex Salmond was back too. Amongst the newbies was Mhairi Black, precociously talented and, at just twenty years old, the youngest person ever elected to the Commons. Tommy Sheppard was a former deputy general secretary of the Scottish Labour Party. John Nicolson had been a BBC presenter. Anne McLaughlin was one of my oldest friends. Alison Thewliss was a Glasgow councillor. Philippa Whitford was a breast cancer surgeon. Deidre Brock was a former actress from Australia, who had briefly starred in *Home and Away*. They and many others would make their names in the months that followed.

I didn't linger long. I had to catch another flight back to London. Peter came with me this time and we were able to have a quiet dinner together that evening. It was only now that we were finally able to absorb the enormity of what we had just achieved.

The main event the next morning was another VE Day service, this time in Westminster Abbey. Leaving the Abbey after the service, I found myself, for the first time ever, in conversation with Boris Johnson, who, though still Mayor of London, had just been re-elected to the Commons. As we walked together to the post-service reception, we seemed to be drawing more attention than anyone else from the crowds lining the streets. Shouts of 'Boris' and 'Nicola' were ringing out periodically as we chatted away to each other. Part of the conversation I had with Boris that day stuck with me so strongly that my account of it is almost verbatim. He asked me what would it take 'to buy you lot in the SNP off? Would full fiscal autonomy shut you up?' I replied that, on the right terms, full fiscal autonomy would certainly be welcome, a step in the right direction, but that it wouldn't 'buy us off' because we believed in independence. I could sense him struggling to process this strange notion of politicians who actually believed in something!

Later that day, Peter and I decided to go for a walk through central London. As my profile in Scotland had risen over the years, I had always enjoyed the relative anonymity of visits to London. That afternoon left me in no doubt that anonymity, even in London, was a thing of the past.

I was, by now, desperate to get home to Scotland and back to normal, whatever that was. I was the First Minister of Scotland, I had a country to run. I would find out, in the days, weeks and months that followed, however, that getting back to 'normal' was easier said than done.

CHAPTER THIRTEEN

A Mandate of My Own

I was never entirely comfortable with the 'rockstar' mania. Even my practice of never turning anyone down for a photo, which was often mocked by opponents, was in part a coping mechanism. They might have called me 'Selfie Queen', but in those fleeting moments when I was being photographed with someone, sharing a quick hug or a few words, I was able to connect just as me: the slightly awkward, shy girl from Ayrshire. I wasn't having to step outside myself and project the image that appeared on the TV.

However, it is impossible, in the kind of bubble I was caught up in back then, not to get carried away occasionally. Even run of the mill activities had a tinge of the surreal about them. My first full day back at the coalface after the General Election was a case in point. I had scheduled a visit to Edinburgh Royal Infirmary to hear about the work being done by doctors and nurses in the accident & emergency department to hit our target of 95% of patients seen, admitted, discharged or transferred within four hours.

The visit was important in its own right, but also a welcome antidote to the craziness of recent weeks. As I left the hospital at the end of the visit, however, instead of the expected handful of onlookers, word had got round and the atrium was heaving with staff and patients who had nipped out of shifts or away from appointments to catch a glimpse or get a photo. I was visiting one of our busiest hospitals for a serious purpose but causing chaos and disruption in the process.

It seemed, for a while, that everything I did inflated the bubble that bit more.

———

A few weeks after the election, I made my first overseas trip as First Minister, to New York and Washington DC. The prospect of a Brexit referendum was a hot topic of conversation and prompted a lot of questions in the political and business meetings I attended, which gave me the opportunity to stress Scotland's commitment to Europe. When I met in DC with Anthony Blinken, later President Biden's Secretary of State, but at that time deputy to John Kerry, it was clear that the Obama administration was already concerned about the possibility of a UK withdrawal from the EU. The notion of the UK as a diplomatic lynchpin in the relationship between the USA and continental Europe was seen as important.

During the trip, I also made a speech to the Council on Foreign Relations and answered questions afterwards about Syria and Ukraine. My backing for sanctions against Russia in the wake of Putin's aggression in Crimea actually attracted some criticism in Scotland at the time. However, if the international community had been tougher back then, Ukraine might not have faced Russian invasion in 2022.

Other than diplomatic engagements, the trip, as all such trips tend to be, was about encouraging investment. I met with a range of US companies investing in Scotland and Scottish companies exporting to the US. I was also trying to build alliances on some of the policies I was passionate about pursuing at home. Our initiatives on tackling climate change and boosting inclusive economic growth as part of a well-being economy were high on the agenda. There was keen interest in the latter from the International Monetary Fund, and a session with its then Managing Director, Christine Lagarde, gave us a lot of encouragement.

I consider it an achievement that Scotland's international presence and profile increased significantly while I was First Minister. We expanded the Scottish government's physical presence beyond existing bases in Brussels, North America and Beijing, opening new offices – proto embassies, really – in Dublin, Berlin, Paris and Copenhagen. It is not an accident that in every year of my tenure in Bute House, Scotland was the most successful part of the UK, outside London, in attracting foreign direct investment. It was helped by concerted efforts from my government, supported by Scottish Development International and our diaspora network, Global Scots, to project a positive vision of the country to decision-makers across the globe.

Building Scotland's reputation on the international stage wasn't all about self-interest, though. I also believed that a nation of Scotland's size, experiences and outlook could make a positive contribution to solving some of the problems the world was grappling with. Around the time of this trip, I was asked by the United Nations' Special Envoy to Syria, Staffan de Mistura, to establish a programme in support of UN Security Council resolution 1325. The outcome was the 1325 Women in Conflict Fellowship. With funding from the Scottish government, it helps build the capacity of women from conflict zones to contribute more effectively to peace processes. To date, with the help of the brilliant non-governmental organization Beyond Borders Scotland, it has supported almost 400 women from more than thirty countries across the Middle East, Africa, South Asia and Latin America. I am very proud of it.

Besides all the important and purposeful activity of the trip, I also found time for a little 'soft power'. I had been invited on *The Daily Show*, hosted in those days by legendary comedian Jon Stewart. If I accepted the invite, I would become the most senior serving UK leader at that time to have appeared on the show. Tony Blair and Gordon Brown had both waited until they left office. I figured that the opportunity to project Scotland on such a platform was worth any criticism that might come my way, so I agreed. I was no doubt succumbing to flattery too.

As the day of the appearance drew closer, I became more and more terrified. My friends kindly tell me I am funnier in private than I am in public. Not a high bar. I know that comedy is not my forte. There was every chance I would be humiliated, with the entire trip ending up a casualty of my over-inflated ego. By the time I arrived at the New York studio, late in the afternoon of 8 June, I was a nervous wreck. The show producer talked me through the broad outline of the script, which helped, but then he told me Jon never stuck to the script, so I should just be ready for anything. I thought I was going to be sick.

Just before we started recording, Jon himself popped into the green room to say hello. He was much smaller than I had expected, not much taller than me, in fact. He was also lovely, and seemed quite shy, which helped me relax. Before I knew it, we were on set and it was showtime. Against all my fears, I survived. Much to my relief, the crowd laughed, and I actually enjoyed the experience. When I arrived back in the green room, the relief of my team was palpable.

Leaders always risk criticism for doing things that seem

frivolous and my *Daily Show* appearance could have gone horribly wrong, but finding ways to project the less tangible aspects of a country's character is hugely important. Promoting culture, which is intrinsic to Scotland's health and well-being, as well as our economic success, was a responsibility I took seriously. Early in my tenure, I was asked by Nick Barley, then head of the Edinburgh International Book Festival, if I would continue what had become an annual tradition: the First Minister interviewing a leading author on the festival's main stage. I enthusiastically agreed, but knew I wanted to do it differently. My predecessors had all opted for authors of non-fiction works, often journalists and other politicians who had written books. I decided, instead, that I would always pick a writer of fiction. In my debut year, I chose Val McDermid, Scotland's 'Queen of Crime', a novelist who was at the very top of her game. In the years to follow, I had the thrill of interviewing some of Scotland's most loved writers, such as Ali Smith, Jackie Kay, Louise Welsh and Douglas Stuart, as well as some 'rock stars' of international literature, like Chimamanda Ngozi Adichie, Arundhati Roy and Bernardine Evaristo.

I also established the First Minister's Reading Challenge, a school initiative to encourage children to read for pleasure. Reading novels has enriched my life in so many ways – emotionally, intellectually, educationally. I will always be evangelical about it.

My heartfelt advice to leaders who come after me is that no matter how much your critics deride it, don't neglect what makes you happy. It will be the things that bring joy into your life that will help sustain you in tough times. For me, that was always reading. And as much as your job is to worry, every day, about the economy, schools and the NHS, don't overlook culture and sport, history and heritage, landscape and the natural environment.

These all touch people at a deeper, more profound level than day-to-day politics ever will. They also shape how the rest of the world sees us.

———

Just after the 2015 General Election, David Cameron's government had announced plans to relax the fox hunting ban in England. It was an issue that divided opinion across England and in the Tory party itself, and there was serious doubt that he'd be able to get it through the House of Commons. If the fifty-six SNP MPs decided to abstain, however, his chances would be massively increased. Given that the decision didn't affect Scotland (indeed, the change would simply have brought the law in England into line with what it had always been in Scotland), that's what most people assumed we would do.

We had different ideas. On 14 July 2015, I met with our group of MPs in a room just off the central lobby of the House of Commons, where we decided not to abstain, but to vote against any relaxation of the ban. Our justification was that since there was a possibility of the law in Scotland being tightened, it would be hypocritical for us, by sitting on our hands, to enable a relaxation in England. It was tissue-thin, and we knew it. The decision was pure politics. We stood to lose a lot of political capital from environmentalists and animal rights advocates if we were seen to let Cameron get his way, and conversely to win a lot of credit if we didn't.

Mainly, though, I wanted us to flex our muscle. Even with fifty-six MPs, the arithmetic of the Commons was against us. It would be difficult for us to score many wins, so I knew we had to take the opportunity to make our presence felt whenever we could. There was also a smidgeon of revenge in the mix. Cameron and his government had shown precious little respect for our landslide win.

When I emerged from the meeting to tell the waiting media that our MPs would vote against the proposed change, all hell broke loose. Suddenly, just a couple of months after his own election victory, Cameron was facing a Commons defeat, and within a matter of hours he had cancelled the vote. We had given him a bloody nose and gained some kudos in the process.

I am not surprised Cameron was furious; in his shoes, I would have been too. What I didn't expect was that six months later he'd still be nursing his wrath. On 15 December 2015, I was in his study again in Downing Street. Aside from the PM and me, the only people in the room were my Chief of Staff, Liz Lloyd, and a member of Cameron's Private Office team. The main topic of discussion was the ongoing negotiation on the new fiscal framework to support the recommendations of the Smith Commission, which had been established post-referendum to consider new tax and welfare powers for the Scottish Parliament. The negotiation was highly technical and crucially important to get right. There was a risk that the Treasury would try to railroad us into an agreement disadvantageous to the Scottish budget, so we were taking a very hardline approach.

I was also determined to use the meeting to push back against the Tories' proposed changes to trade union laws. I saw them as a direct attack on fundamental civil rights and pressed for Scotland to be excluded from the bill. It was on this point that the Prime Minister suddenly erupted and went on a rant about the fox hunting bill. No, he would not exempt Scotland, he said, and even if he had been minded to, which he wasn't, why should he show me any flexibility when I had allowed my MPs to derail a proposal that applied only to England?

Unwilling to be spoken to like a misbehaving schoolgirl, I returned fire, telling him that, if he would occasionally show Scotland some respect and stop trying to impose right-wing policies on us, we might not be in this situation. From there, and with Liz and his Private Secretary shifting uncomfortably in their seats, the exchange degenerated into what can only be described as a playground spat; our voices were raised as we slugged it out for a good few minutes. Even as it was happening, I wasn't proud of it. Afterwards Liz told me, bluntly but fairly, that the episode hadn't reflected well on him or me, and she was right.

———

I barely had time to draw breath after the 2015 election before I was fighting my second election campaign as leader, the 2016 Scottish Parliament election, where I would be seeking my own mandate as First Minister. The manifesto we campaigned on was a strong one. It included commitments that would later rank amongst the achievements I am proudest of – the doubling of the provision of state-funded early years education and the establishment of Social Security Scotland, for example. We also promised to freeze the basic rate of income tax for the duration of the next Parliament. This was a promise that, arguably, we did not keep. Although we did freeze the basic rate, we would later use our expanded tax powers to create a new 'intermediate' tax band between the basic and higher bands. This meant that some people who had been basic rate taxpayers found themselves in this new band and subject to a higher rate. The commitment to freeze the basic rate points to the tendency I had in the early days of leadership to seek a middle path that would keep everyone happy, especially on contentious issues. I figured that our decision not to follow the UK government in raising the threshold at which people started to pay the higher rate of tax would cause consternation enough, and that we should balance it with the commitment to freeze the basic rate. I judged that any future reform to the band structure could be introduced in a way that would maintain the spirit of the commitment. I was trying to be too clever by half.

I came to realize that in government, the end result of trying to please everyone is usually pleasing no one. Of course it is important to seek compromise and consensus, but, ultimately, leaders have to lead; to pick a side and then set out the reasons for the choice we have made.

In 2016, however, I was still learning.

———

The 2016 manifesto was also my first attempt at navigating the thorny issue of a second independence referendum. Much as I would have loved an early opportunity to make good the failure of 2014, I knew that the desire of independence supporters alone wasn't sufficient reason to immediately re-run a decision that Scotland had so recently, and so deeply, searched its soul over. That said, I was under no illusion about the pressure I would face from within the SNP and the wider independence movement to set a faster pace.

I tried to find a rational way through. Instead of ruling out a second referendum for a defined period of time, or embarking, gung-ho, on a bid to secure one at the earliest possible opportunity, I set out the conditions under which another vote might be objectively justified. I sought to be guided by reason rather than sentiment. Our manifesto said as follows: 'The Scottish Parliament should have the right to hold another referendum if there is clear and sustained evidence that independence has become the preferred option of a majority of the Scottish people, or if there is a significant and material change in the circumstances that prevailed in 2014, such as Scotland being taken out of the EU against its will.'

I wasn't expecting these conditions to be quickly met. It still seemed inconceivable, even just a couple of months before the Brexit referendum, that the UK would vote to leave the EU. I also thought that the work of building sustained majority support for independence would take considerable time. In fact, when I started out as First Minister, I had no real expectation that a second referendum would be secured at all during my time as leader. This makes it somewhat ironic that my failure to secure one is now judged by many, including me, as one of my biggest failures.

With the manifesto off to print, all that remained was for me to hit the campaign trail and win the mandate I craved. I was never overly confident about any election, but this time I felt genuinely upbeat. Unfortunately, less than a week in, I already had reason to doubt myself. Out of nowhere, I was engulfed in a 'scandal' entirely of my own making.

I was about to set sail on the overnight ferry to Shetland on 3 April when the media queries started to come in about a story that would rumble on for the duration of the campaign. My immediate panic was heightened by the fact I was about to lose mobile phone reception. The crossing from Aberdeen to Shetland takes about thirteen hours and, once out on the North Sea, the signal goes. I would have no idea how bad the story was until we docked in Lerwick at 8 a.m. the next day. I had plenty of time to brood and to kick myself hard about the sequence of events that had brought us to this point.

On 21 March 2016, just before Parliament dissolved for the election, I had signed a memorandum of understanding with two state-backed Chinese companies, SinoFortone and China Railway No.3 Engineering Group, to explore up to £10 billion of investment in transport, clean energy and housing projects in Scotland. The agreement was brokered, in part, by a British businessman and adviser to the Chinese companies, Sir Richard Heygate. The Scottish government hadn't formally announced the deal. Journalists in Scotland got wind of it from reports in the Chinese media, which only added to my embarrassment. The opposition smelled blood.

The parent company of China Railway No.3 Engineering Group stood accused of gross corruption, with claims that it had been blacklisted by Norway's oil fund as a result. The opposition claimed that this meant one of two things: either we had failed to do the proper due diligence that would have brought these issues to light, or we had known about the accusations but chosen to turn a blind eye. We were also criticized for our lack of transparency.

In some ways, it was much ado about nothing. The purpose of the deal had been to create jobs in Scotland – surely not a hanging offence. The memorandum of understanding did not legally bind us to either company or oblige us to accept any actual investment, so the time for due diligence and formal announcements would have been if and when specific investment deals were being concluded. Privately, though, I was worried. I knew that we had blundered. Our – my – handling of the whole affair had left us open to charges of hypocrisy and secrecy that were not entirely unreasonable.

Our desperation to win investment had blinded us to the possible reputational risks. In normal circumstances, I'd have been shouting from the rooftops about an agreement with the potential to lever in £10 billion to the Scottish economy. My silence on this occasion was uncharacteristic and it spoke volumes.

As I pondered all of this in the dead of night on a ferry in the middle of the North Sea, I felt despondent. The story had so many juicy ingredients – China, corruption, secrecy. It would be easy for the opposition to scream 'scandal'. What if it started to cut through with the public? Could our election prospects be seriously wounded?

The story dogged me periodically throughout the campaign, and beyond, but it didn't have any impact on the outcome. However, as I look back now, the whole episode seems symptomatic of a misguided attitude to China. Scotland was far from alone in this, but nor were we immune. In our clamour for investment, we were too often blind to China's appalling human rights record and disdain for democracy. I visited China twice as First Minister – in July 2015 and again in April 2018 – and, while I went through the motions of raising concerns about human rights, it was far too *sotto voce*. I told myself that speaking up more loudly would have been all pain for no gain. It wasn't as if China was going to mend its ways because the First Minister of Scotland expressed her disapproval. It would, however, be highly likely to find ways to punish Scotland if she did so. New investment would have been harder to come by and existing interests, for example, Grangemouth, Scotland's only oil refinery, co-owned by PetroChina, might have been at risk (it now faces closure anyway).

It is long past time for the balance of these judgements to change. As concerns about China and the threats it poses to global stability continue to grow, governments everywhere need to be much more alive to the dangers. With Donald Trump back in the White House, upending the rules of trade, commerce and democracy, and with the world order in a state of flux, it might be tempting for some countries to move closer to China. Compared to Trump's America, there will even be a sense that China is the saner, more reliable trading partner. The world is likely to be uncertain for some time to come. Even so, we must still be wary of allowing China to become ever more enmeshed in huge swathes of our lives, from critical national infrastructure to technology to universities, and much more besides.

————

The front cover of our 2016 manifesto consisted of my face and the single word, 'Re-elect'. 'Nicola Sturgeon for First Minister' became the strapline of the campaign and it appeared on our billboard posters alongside a big picture of me. Within a few days of the campaign kicking off, the country was awash with party merchandise bearing the slogan '#ImWithNicola'.

Even if it didn't ultimately do us any harm, this relentless focus on me, to the virtual exclusion of everyone and everything else, was overdone. It emerged from a strange mix of insecurity, electoral expedience and arrogance. No one other than me thought I lacked legitimacy as First Minister. However, I was obsessed with getting my own mandate. As far as I was concerned, until I had put myself on the line and been elected First Minister in my own right, I wouldn't be taken seriously. Making myself such a dominant figurehead of the campaign reflected this concern. But it made political sense too. According to the polls, I was hugely popular. My personal approval ratings routinely exceeded the party's. There is no doubt that I was a massive electoral asset, and we would have been crazy not to capitalize on that. Even so, it all ended up a bit over the top and that was down to my ego. I had started to believe, politically speaking, that I really did walk on water. Indeed, if there was any period in my time as leader when I succumbed to hubris, this was it.

The '#ImWithNicola' merchandise made me the most uncomfortable. The implicit suggestion was that voters were expected to pledge loyalty to me rather than the other way round and I hated it. I wasn't micro-managing the leaflets and marketing materials, but I should have put a stop to it.

Even so, we won the election handsomely. In Glasgow Southside, I polled 61.4% of the vote. My majority rocketed to 9,593. Nationally, we increased our share of the constituency vote from 2011 and became the first party since the re-establishment of the Scottish Parliament to poll more than one million votes. The number of constituencies we won first-past-the-post increased too. However, the swings and roundabouts of the PR system, and the fact that our share of the regional vote slipped slightly, meant that our total number of seats dropped to sixty-three, below the 2011 tally. We were slightly short of an outright majority, enabling some commentators to deride our victory as disappointing, a failure even. It was a sign of our success – and my first experience of being a victim of it – that a supposedly impossible feat had become the benchmark against which we were judged. It was frustrating, but that, I suppose, is politics.

Probably the biggest story of the election was that the Tories beat Labour into second place. Ruth Davidson was a strong leader of the Scottish Tories, with many of the same qualities that people saw in me. She was straight-talking, authentic and down to earth. She deserves credit for leading the Tories, for so long the pariahs of Scottish politics, to a position of standing and credibility. However, the switch in their positions was as much a reflection of Labour's weakness as it was Tory strength.

For me, though, I was now First Minister with a mandate of my own. What I didn't yet know was that the next year or so, a period dominated by Brexit and culminating in two more elections, would be the most politically difficult of my Bute House tenure.

CHAPTER FOURTEEN

Europe No More

'Sordid SNP love triangle' was the headline I woke up to on 17 May 2016, the day I was due to be formally reinstalled as First Minister in the Scottish Parliament. Stewart Hosie, the deputy leader of the SNP, and one of our most senior MPs, had been caught cheating on his wife, Shona Robison, the Health Secretary and one of my best friends. However, that wasn't the full extent of the story. The details were even more salacious. It turned out that the Westminster-based journalist Stewart was seeing had previously been involved in an extra-marital affair with Angus MacNeil, the SNP MP for the Western Isles.

I am ultra-liberal on matters of sex and relationships. What consenting adults get up to is their business, no one else's. But I was furious on behalf of Shona. She felt humiliated. When the revelations emerged, she spent much of the day tearfully holed up with me in my office in Parliament. In that moment, I needed to be a friend as well as the First Minister. The political and the personal were hard to separate. I didn't speak to Stewart for days, even though he was my deputy. I didn't trust myself not to lose my temper with him. The first, and only, contact came when he called to tell me he intended to resign as deputy leader.

In some ways, Angus's involvement was no surprise. Back in 2007, it had emerged that a couple of years earlier, while at a music festival in Shetland, he had taken two teenage girls back to his hotel bedroom. His pregnant wife was at home in Barra. When the *Sunday Mail* broke the story, Alex had, unwisely in my view, backed him to the hilt – no doubt part of the reason Angus was so slavishly loyal to Alex when allegations were levelled at him more than a decade later.

The drama died down reasonably quickly and, thankfully, hearts were healed. Shona and Stewart separated. Shona is happy. Stewart got married to Serena, the woman he had the affair with. She later became an SNP councillor. Angus continued to be a colourful character.

However, this was not how I had expected to spend the first few days of our third term in government.

―――

Just a month later, UK politics was shaken to its core. It was Thursday, 17 June, and I was hosting a lunch in the Scottish Parliament restaurant when one of my Private Secretaries appeared. He handed me a note with the awful news that an MP in England had been attacked at a constituency surgery and was in a critical condition. Later that afternoon, it was confirmed that Jo Cox MP, the mother of two small children, had died from her injuries. I was in SNP HQ recording a pro-EU campaign message for the Brexit referendum, by now just a week away, when the news came through. Everyone in the room was crying.

I never met Jo, but for me and for every politician who, week in and week out, sits in community centres and church halls, with doors open to any constituent who chooses to walk through them, her murder felt personal. It also profoundly elevated my sense of unease, brewing for some time, that politics was now so toxic that it had become, at its most extreme, an unsafe environment.

Obviously, what happened to Jo was not because she was a woman. The dreadful murder, in similar circumstances, of the Conservative MP David Amess just a few years later proved that. But there is no doubt that women and minorities bear the biggest brunt of the nastier side of politics. At its most 'mild', it takes the form of horrible online abuse, which is bad enough. But Jo's murder was a reality check that the impact on politicians can be much more terrifying. Of course, it is easier to identify the causes of the problem, principally the radicalizing and polarizing impact of social media, than it is the solutions. However, unless we find a way of reversing the trend, I fear that it will become increasingly difficult to entice women into politics at all.

The day after Jo Cox was killed, I hosted the British–Irish Council summit in Glasgow. This was the first time Arlene Foster of the Democratic Unionist Party (DUP) had attended, as First Minister of Northern Ireland. The deputy First Minister, Martin McGuinness, was also there. There was, understandably, a sombre atmosphere surrounding our discussions that day. However, I remember being very conscious of two things about the Northern Ireland delegation. First, that while Martin and Arlene were as appalled and upset by Jo's murder as the rest of us, there didn't seem to be the same sense of utter shock, bewilderment, numbness – an absence that was perhaps derived from living, for as long as they had, with political violence as a daily reality.

Secondly, having witnessed Martin's interactions with Ian Paisley and Peter Robinson, I was struck by the lack of any warmth between him and Arlene. In its place was a simmering tension. I was reluctant to automatically assume that Arlene was to blame. Northern Ireland society is just as macho as Scotland's, so I entertained the possibility that there was a gender issue at play. But, still, Martin had managed to build and maintain solid relationships with two Unionist First Ministers in the past. Arlene was the factor that had changed. I would later learn from my own experience how difficult it was to establish any rapport with her.

I remember leaving the summit fearing that the Northern Irish Executive was on shaky ground. And this was before the disaster of Brexit made matters significantly worse.

———

Back in February, David Cameron had named the date for the vote as 23 June 2016. The following day, Boris Johnson declared his support for Leave. It seemed that he was picking the side he thought would serve his interests best. The stage was set for an almighty battle over the UK's place in the world.

I wasn't worried about the likely outcome in Scotland. I had no doubt in my mind that we would vote to stay in the EU. There was certainly a strand of Euroscepticism in the country, mainly in fishing and farming communities, where frustration with the Common Fisheries and Common Agricultural policies was both acute and understandable. There was also a minority of people whose hostility to immigration fuelled an antipathy to the EU, and to free movement in particular. For some others, support for continued membership was based on a functional assessment of benefits outweighing downsides, more than it was on any strong affection for the EU itself. However, it was also true that many Scottish people did, and do, have a deeply emotional commitment to European identity. It is telling that UKIP never established any significant foothold in Scotland.

I was much less certain about the outcome south of the border, though still reasonably confident that it would turn out OK. Even when I became much more anxious, with a couple of weeks to go, I thought, on balance, that Remain would prevail. However, for all that I was, both emotionally and intellectually, very strongly in favour of staying in the EU, I found the campaign difficult and, at times, deeply uncomfortable.

Even though I swung both the SNP and the Scottish government firmly behind the case for continued membership, I felt a tension with the wider UK Remain campaign. There seemed to be a suspicion that I secretly wanted Leave to win on the strength of English votes, as this would satisfy one of my 'conditions' for a second independence referendum. I resented this, as it was not remotely true. The idea of losing EU membership horrified me. Also, at that time, I was more worried than enthusiastic about the prospect of a hasty re-run of the independence vote. Much as I wanted Scotland to be independent, I did not believe that a headlong rush to another vote would be good for either the country or the independence cause.

While I resented the doubts about my motives, there was one issue on which I stupidly gave them credence. I was becoming increasingly worried about the negative, fear-mongering tone of the Remain campaign. It reminded me of Project Fear in the independence campaign and I did not want to see Remain make the same mistake now. But instead of just communicating these concerns privately as I should have done, I spoke out publicly in a speech to the Resolution Foundation in late February and then again, in May, when the Treasury published a report on the dire economic impact of Brexit. It wasn't that I didn't share the Treasury concern, but I had seen in 2014 how badly these 'establishment' warnings could backfire. However, the coverage of both these interventions made it seem that I was attacking the pro-EU side. I don't blame the Remain campaign for being aggrieved with me.

Less fair, though, were the low-level mutterings that I wasn't pulling my weight in the campaign. There seemed to be a view that I should be doing more to influence the vote in England. The fact that I wasn't was taken as evidence that I secretly wanted Leave to win. In fact, it was the opposite. If I was keeping a low profile, it was because I feared I would be a liability to the pro-EU side. I thought it would suit Leave down to the ground if I appeared to be lecturing voters in England. I know I am a Marmite figure south of the border. I also knew that to some ears my arguments against Brexit sounded illogical and hypocritical when set against my arguments for independence.

There is nothing intrinsically inconsistent between support for Scottish independence and support for EU membership. The EU is comprised of independent countries. I was perfectly comfortable making the positive case for international and supranational co-operation, for the pooling of sovereignty for the greater good and in our national interest. I am certain that an independent Scotland would work on that basis with the other countries of the UK, as well as in the EU, NATO and a range of other international forums.

My problem was that to many people, it simply didn't sound credible for the person who claimed that Scotland could easily extricate herself from a 300-year-old union, to argue that the UK couldn't do likewise from a much looser partnership of just forty years. Likewise, if I started banging on about the risks and costs of Brexit, however much I believed them to be true, it would sound as if I was indulging in Project Fear tactics.

My concerns came to a head when I was asked by ITV to be part of the three-person Remain team for its big debate on 9 June, two weeks before the poll. The Leave team was to be headlined by Boris Johnson. I could see why ITV wanted a showdown between Boris and me, but I wasn't sure it was a good idea. There was heavy pressure for me to do it, from both ITV and the Remain campaign. My own advisers wanted me to do it too. But I was genuinely worried that I would do more harm than good. Even after agreeing in principle to take part, I was still mulling the possibility of pulling out. Perhaps unexpectedly, it was the Prime Minister who finally persuaded me to take part.

David Cameron and I were both in Orkney on 31 May for a service to mark the centenary of the First World War Battle of Jutland. As we waited in a council building corridor before moving across the road to Kirkwall's magnificent St Magnus Cathedral, we had a quick private chat about Brexit. He said he was pleased to hear I was doing the ITV debate. When I told him I had reservations, he encouraged me to put them aside, saying that he thought it was important to have political diversity in the Remain campaign. He also thought my debating skills and experience would be valuable. He said he was growing more confident, though not complacent, that Remain would win. After our conversation, I felt that pulling out wasn't an option. I had to step up and play my part.

And so I travelled down to London after First Minister's Questions on 9 June. There was behind the scenes sniping about my failure to go down earlier for a rehearsal with the other team members, Amber Rudd of the Tories and Labour's Angela Eagle. The suggestion seemed to be that it showed a lack of commitment. It really didn't. It was simply that I was the First Minister, with responsibilities in Parliament.

It was clear when I arrived at the studios that some in the Remain camp were nervous about what I might say. Would I repeat my Project Fear attack or bang on too much about independence? I tried to put minds at rest, to reassure that I was there to help the pro-EU cause not hinder it. However, I was irritated and wondered why they had been so keen for me to take part if they were worried about what I might say. I had agreed to meet Craig Oliver, David Cameron's Number 10 head of communications, an hour or so before going on air, so that we could talk through the format. It was obvious that he didn't share his boss's enthusiasm about me taking part. By this stage of my career, I had done more TV debates than Mr Oliver had enjoyed hot dinners, but that didn't stop him tediously mansplaining it all to me.

By the time I was gathering my thoughts in the green room before going on air, my confidence was low. The people who had persuaded me to take part, against my own better judgement, were now exuding the same anxiety that had made me reluctant in the first place. I had a terrible sense of foreboding that it was going to be a disaster.

In the end, it wasn't a disaster, but it wasn't my best debate performance either. I tried to concentrate as much as I could on the positive arguments for staying in the EU. I pressed the point, which I thought hadn't been made nearly strongly enough so far, about the EU's role in maintaining peace on the continent for the past sixty years. I had a go at Boris for the lie on the side of the bus. And I tried to steer clear of the arguments I feared would make me sound like a hypocrite. Amber and Angela performed well. Angela skewered Boris on the NHS funding deceit. Amber came up with the best line of all, describing Boris as the kind of guy women were all too familiar with – the life and soul of the party, but not someone we'd want driving us home at the end of the night. It struck, pretty effectively I thought, at the issue of trust and integrity.

Boris was his usual bluff and bluster, which is not to write off his performance. On the contrary, it was clear that his style and approach had plenty of admirers. It is worth noting, though, just for the record, that a woman would never get away with his chaotic approach to politics. The lack of detail, stuttering incoherence and dishevelled appearance would herald any woman's downfall, as it should have done for him.

The others on the Leave side were the Tories' Andrea Leadsom and Labour's Gisela Stuart. Of the two, I thought Andrea was the stronger performer. Actually, she was the best of the three, in my view – solid, quite down to earth, though rabidly right-wing. Gisela suffered, albeit for different reasons, from what had worried me. She sounded disingenuous. She was supposedly a lifelong socialist, but here she was enthusiastically sharing a platform with politicians whose support for Brexit, however much they tried to deny it, was all about a de-regulatory race to the bottom on workers' and environmental rights.

What struck me most, though, and worried me greatly, wasn't any of the individual performances. It was the contrast in demeanour between the two sides. There was a lot of nervous tension on our side, but only swagger and confidence on theirs. It might just have been arrogance, or the fact that their simplistic, dishonest arguments were easier to make than our more complex, serious ones, but I remember thinking, for the first time, that they might just be winning.

———

The result was a body-blow. Scotland, as I had expected, voted overwhelmingly to remain – 63% versus 37% in favour of leaving, with every local authority area recording a pro-EU vote. It didn't matter, though. The 52%/48% leave vote UK-wide meant we would be ripped out of the EU against our will.

I spent most of the night in SNP HQ, tracking the results,

before heading back to Bute House around 6 a.m. A team of tired and shell-shocked officials and advisers was waiting on me. We gathered in the Cabinet room to discuss the content of the speech that I would make later that morning. Breakfast consisted of coffee and Tunnocks caramel wafers.

My team made various suggestions which I noted down, but then I locked myself away in my study on the top floor of Bute House to craft what I wanted to say. At such an enormously significant moment, there was never any question of me asking someone else to draft a speech on my behalf. It had to come from my own head and heart.

The speech flowed more easily than it should have done, given I'd had no sleep and kept being interrupted by my Private Office patching calls through to me. Over the early part of the morning, I spoke to the Governor of the Bank of England, Mark Carney, about the steps he was taking to try to calm the markets, and to the Mayor of London, Sadiq Khan, about how we might join forces to make sure the voices of Scotland and London, which had also voted to remain, would be heard in the negotiations to come.

I also spoke with the Scottish Labour leader, Kezia Dugdale. In the course of a call that would later feature in a 2017 General Election TV debate (thanks to a stupid split-second decision of mine), she seemed to indicate that her view on independence might be open to change in the wake of the Brexit vote; that it might be time for Scottish Labour to drop its opposition to a second referendum. I spoke to the leaders of the other parties later that day too, but none of them stunned me like Kez had.

Kezia's curveball aside, my most significant conversation of the morning was with David Cameron. He called me just minutes before stepping out onto Downing Street to announce his resignation. He seemed emotional, which was hardly surprising given the circumstances. He said that the referendum had been his call and, since he had failed to deliver the right outcome, the only honourable course for him was to step down; and that, in any event, he wasn't the right person to lead the UK through the exit negotiation as his heart wouldn't be in it. He was gracious about the contribution he thought I had made to the Remain campaign, saying that the vote in Scotland showed the SNP had done our job in a way he hadn't managed in England. He promised that for his remaining time in Downing Street, which at that point he assumed would be a few months, he would do all he could to make sure Scotland was properly represented in the negotiation process.

I told him that my job now, as far as I was concerned, was to do everything possible to ensure that Scotland's democratic choice was respected. I also wished him well. Although he and I agreed on little, and vehemently disagreed on a great deal, the relationship I had with him was cordial and constructive. The last conversation we had during his premiership would be on 10 July, in the Royal Box at Wimbledon. We were both there as guests of the All England Club for the men's singles final, me with Peter, David with his mum, and got to enjoy the privilege of watching Andy Murray lift the trophy for the second time.

David and I had a brief chat after the match, taking care to stay out of earshot of Prince William and Kate. He was expecting to be Prime Minister until around September, when the Tory leadership contest between Theresa May and Andrea Leadsom was due to conclude. He was talking about the things he still wanted to do. We had no idea that Leadsom would pull out of the race the following day, and that in less than a week he would be out of Downing Street and Theresa May would have his job. Politics can be brutal.

Back, though, to 24 June, the day after the calamity of the

Brexit vote. I made my speech sometime late morning. Amid the sense of turmoil and panic that was gripping the country, and what seemed to be a complete lack of any visible leadership at UK level, I knew it was important to strike a note of reassurance. The prospect of serious economic instability was real, and while I had limited ability to do anything concrete about it, I tried to sound a note of calm, to communicate a sense that, in Scotland at least, there was a steady hand on the tiller.

It was also important to reach out to citizens of other EU countries living in Scotland. At our early morning discussion, Ken Thomson, a senior civil servant, had been the first to make the point that many people who had come to live in Scotland from elsewhere in Europe would also be feeling deeply insecure, possibly even unwelcome. Again, frustratingly, there was little I could do to change the reality for them. As things stood, it would be the UK government that decided the immigration rules to replace free movement, but I desperately wanted to offer some empathy, find words that might make them, on a bleak day, feel a bit better. What I said was short and to the point, but heartfelt and, I hoped, comforting:

'I want to take the opportunity this morning to speak directly to citizens of other EU countries living here in Scotland – you remain welcome here, Scotland is your home, and your contribution is valued.'

When I remember this speech, I often think about one of Maya Angelou's best-known quotes: '. . . people will forget what you said, people will forget what you did, but people will never forget how you made them feel.'

I always tried to be guided by the spirit of these words, but it is only now, looking back, that I understand how true they are. Even today, almost ten years on, I am told by some continental

Europeans living in Scotland that my words that morning saved them from total despair.

Perhaps they also offer a lesson to all politicians about the importance of connecting with people at an instinctual level. Emotional intelligence is much talked about, but very few politicians ever take the time to develop or demonstrate it. In my view, it is the single most important quality for a leader to possess.

My toughest task that morning was to try to get the balance right on independence. On the one hand, it was hard to imagine a more egregious illustration of Scotland's democratic deficit than being dragged out of the EU against our will. Personally, I felt distraught and enraged by the prospect of Brexit and what it said about Scotland's powerlessness within the UK. I had a strong sense of 'if not now, when?' However, I was still worried that a headlong rush to another referendum in the midst of such an upheaval would be a mistake. If we looked unduly hasty or as if we were trying to exploit the outcome for our own ends, it might repel rather than attract the cohort of voters we needed to win over.

There was another reason for caution, even though it didn't feature too much in my thinking that morning. Amongst the million or so Leave voters in Scotland, there had to be a number of people who had voted Yes in 2014. How would they react to a push for a second independence referendum predicated on re-entering the EU? This was something of a blind spot for me. Indeed, my failure to understand the sentiments of this section of the population helps explain the electoral difficulty I got myself into over the next year.

I tried to steer a course that was firm but also careful. I deliberately described the Brexit vote as 'a significant and material change of circumstances', which had been the language used in our manifesto. In so doing, I was acknowledging that one of the conditions we had set for a second referendum had been met. However, I was also cautioning against a rush to judgement.

In short, I was trying to keep all options open, to buy some time, to see how opinions shaped up as the dust settled. However, having tried so hard to craft words that would maximize my room for manoeuvre, I then managed in the Q&A session that followed to achieve the opposite. In response to a specific question about the likelihood of another referendum, which I think came from Glenn Campbell of the BBC, I answered that it was 'highly likely'. I don't know whether it was a lack of sleep, or a fear of sounding weak to the independence supporters who would be listening avidly, or a bit of both. However, by moving away from the careful formulation I had articulated in my prepared speech, and pointing much more firmly in a set direction, I boxed myself in much more than I intended. I was kicking myself hard as I went back upstairs to my study.

I doubt it made much difference to how things worked out. The pressure from my support base and also my own instinct of what was in Scotland's long-term interest would always have led me down the referendum path. However, it is a reminder of how difficult it is for politicians to express nuance and find balance. The pressure is always on to be absolute, black or white, and, if that was true then, it is even more so now, when the world is more polarized than ever.

———

In the days immediately following the vote, I spoke to a number of different voices across the EU. It gave me a sense of how Scotland's predicament was being viewed. However, what emerged was a paradox.

At the start of the new week, I welcomed the President of

Ireland, Michael D. Higgins, and his wife, Sabina, to Glasgow. President Higgins is a delightful man. He is deeply cultured and scholarly. He exudes humanity and compassion and has an infectious sense of humour. On the evening of the first day of his visit, we attended a celebration of Celtic music in the Glasgow Royal Concert Hall. As we were leaving, news reached us that Iceland had just beaten England in the European Championships. It is fair to say we enjoyed a moment of Celtic solidarity, and mild gloating, at England's football misfortune.

Even though his visit to Glasgow had been long in the planning, and in no way related to Brexit, it was still a timely opportunity to assess Ireland's reaction to the tumultuous events of the past few days. A sense of shock and genuine fear about what it could mean for peace in the north of Ireland was palpable.

I was able to get even more of a sense of European reactions on a hastily planned visit to Brussels a couple of days later. As well as seeing most of Scotland's MEPs, I met with the various political groupings, some member state ambassadors and, most significantly, in what was my first one-to-one session with him, the President of the Commission, Jean-Claude Juncker. It was on this visit that I came face to face with the glaring paradox. On the one hand, the support for Scotland and the warmth towards us was overwhelming. I think I was late to almost every meeting that day as I was stopped so often in the Parliament and Commission buildings by people wanting to wish Scotland well. If I could sum up the sentiment expressed, beyond simple good wishes, it was that the loyalty Scotland had just shown to the EU must somehow be repaid.

On the other hand, no one seemed to know *how*, in practice, it could be repaid. There were no easy answers. I came away clear on two points. Although neither were in any way surprising, it was nevertheless sobering to hear them articulated so firmly. The first was that if a credible proposal for a bespoke Scottish solution came forward, continued membership of the single market, for example, the EU would listen and engage. However, any such proposal would have to come from the UK government. There could be no parallel negotiation with the Scottish government. Secondly, I was left with very little doubt that if Scotland voted for independence, the EU would do all it could to ease our path to membership in our own right. Indeed, all my post-Brexit discussions, whether in Brussels or member state capitals, convinced me on that point. The sting in the tail was that neither the EU, nor any of its member countries, not even Ireland, would ever say so in advance of a vote. Nor would they enter into any upfront discussions about the nature and timing of the process, or any conditions that Scotland might be subject to.

Across Europe, sympathy for the independence cause was higher than it had ever been, but the practical hurdles remained significant. All of this reinforced my belief that care was needed. If there was to be another referendum, the ground must be well prepared. From the perspective of demonstrating to 2014 No voters that independence was the best, possibly the only, way of protecting Scotland's interests, we also needed to show that all other options had been exhausted.

The established narrative now, though, is that I went hell for leather for a second referendum immediately after the Brexit vote. It isn't true. On the contrary, I spent the next nine months doing the precise opposite. I tried hard to persuade the UK government to pursue a compromise option, to work up a proposal which would allow Scotland not to stay in the EU, but to retain a closer relationship to it than England and Wales wanted, and to include this as part of the Brexit negotiation.

I tasked Scottish government officials with doing the work to show how such an option might work in practice. Theresa May had said on becoming Prime Minister that she wouldn't trigger the process of leaving the EU until 2017. She had also promised to listen to any proposals that the Scottish government brought forward. It was in good faith, therefore, that we published 'Scotland's Place in Europe' in December 2016, mapping out what a different outcome for Scotland might look like and how it could be achieved. In my foreword to the paper, I was explicit that this was a solution for Scotland within the UK; in other words, an alternative to independence.

The solution we were proposing would have been complex, but not impossible. The outcome ultimately achieved for Northern Ireland is broadly similar. Of course, the circumstances in Northern Ireland with the sensitivity of the border with the Republic, and the potential for the peace process to be fatally destabilized, were unique. The EU might not have had the willingness, or patience, to negotiate a similar outcome for Scotland. However, we will never know because the UK refused point-blank to ask.

A smarter UK government, and a more flexible Prime Minister, would have tried. Even the effort would have made the UK seem more like a Union in which Scotland's voice was heard. Success would have demonstrated that it was one in which our interests might be protected, even if only up to a point. It would have been a much more effective and sustainable riposte to independence than the democracy-blocking tactics UK governments have resorted to since. However, despite my best efforts, Theresa May refused to give our proposals even cursory consideration. There was a brittle inflexibility about her that seemed to derive as much from her personality as from her political convictions.

I had sympathy for the difficulty of her task. Indeed, if David Cameron was the UK Prime Minister I found it easiest to get along with, Theresa May was the one I had most respect for. She was ferociously hard-working and always on top of her brief. I also believed that, albeit from the perspective of a Conservative Party leader, she was trying to achieve the least damaging Brexit deal possible for the UK. Even before the 2017 UK election humbled her (as it did me, to be fair), she probably figured that the job of selling a deal to her own party was tough enough without having to worry about finding one acceptable to mine. While I can understand this, I still think it was short-sighted.

We were both walking something of a tightrope with our respective support bases – her on defining exactly what Brexit would mean for the UK's relationship with the EU, and me on working out what it meant for independence and Scotland's relationship with the UK. It always struck me that we might have found a way of helping each other. Arguably, she would have had more to gain than me. If a deal along the lines we were proposing could have been struck for Scotland, it would have made it harder for our MPs to vote against the overall agreement she struck with the EU, and also, at least in the short term, for me to make the case for another independence referendum. Indeed, that's why some on my own side were so nervous about it. As it turned out, they had no need for nerves. Compromise wasn't to be.

I might have found it easier to find common ground with May on politics, if we had managed to establish better personal chemistry. But it was impossible to build any genuine rapport with her, and I really did try. I recall one occasion when we were meeting in her office in the House of Commons. As we sat down, I made a point of admiring the very stylish shoes she was wearing. Instead of the few moments of ice-breaking chat about shoes I had hoped for, a look of horror crossed her face. For what seemed like an eternity, she said absolutely nothing, staring down at the briefing folder on her lap as if looking for the appropriate 'line to take'. The civil servants and advisers in the room were shifting uncomfortably in their seats. Eventually, she mumbled something that I couldn't really make out, before launching into her script for the meeting. It was so awkward that I vowed then and there never to repeat the exercise.

It was all so frustrating; I felt that instinctively we should have been able to forge a closer relationship. For all our many and deep political disagreements, we actually had a fair amount in common. Like me, she is shy and introverted, a bit awkward at times. We shared an obsessive attention to detail. No doubt she, just like me, had learned the hard way that a woman will never get away with anything remotely resembling the Boris Johnson approach to preparation.

We were also both women leaders in a world which was still predominantly male. We understood only too well the kind of treatment and commentary this can entail. The famous *Daily Mail* front page the day after we met in Glasgow in early 2017 is a case in point. Beside a picture of the two of us sitting side by side, facing the cameras, both wearing skirts, was the banner headline 'NEVER MIND BREXIT, WHO WON LEGS-IT?' On the inside pages, a female columnist, while declaring May the winner overall, described my legs as 'altogether more flirty' and suggested that they were 'tantalisingly crossed' in a 'direct attempt at seduction'. Quite who she thought I was trying to seduce will forever be a mystery to me.

I did get one insight to Theresa from this episode, which I found interesting. While most women, myself included, were raging about the blatant sexism, she opted to defend the *Daily Mail*. It seems we were destined to have no meeting of minds.

Ultimately, though, her political inflexibility was my real

problem. We met in person on several occasions and had countless phone calls, but these conversations were, for her, no more than a tick-box exercise. They allowed her to stand up in the House of Commons and claim that she had engaged with the Scottish government, but I doubt she could have pointed to a single detail of her policy approach that changed as a result.

She simply wasn't willing to even try to find a way of accommodating Scotland's democratic choice. She was clearly frustrated with what she saw as Remainer intransigence in England, a refusal to accept defeat, as she might have described it, and I think she viewed me as an extension of that. She couldn't seem to grasp that for Scotland, where the Remain cause had triumphed, this characterization was deeply unfair. She couldn't or wouldn't see that, for us, Brexit wasn't just the loss of EU membership, it was also a fundamental denial of democracy.

If I am trying to be fair to UK governments, and see things from their perspective, I can understand why there was a caginess towards me. They believed that I was always trying to game things to suit the independence agenda, even when I claimed to be playing with a straight bat. Of course, I took opportunities to make the case for independence when I could, but more often than not I was simply trying to get Scotland's voice heard: to protect my nation's interests. The frequency with which I was joined in these endeavours by unionist First Ministers of Wales underlines this point. Time and again, it was the UK government's indifference to these pleas that ended up reinforcing the arguments for independence.

This, then, was the context for my decision, in March 2017, to fire the starting gun on the process for a second independence referendum. I felt I had exhausted all other options.

CHAPTER FIFTEEN

To Win or Lose It All

On 13 March 2017, I made another speech in Bute House. Theresa May had said she intended to invoke Article 50 of the EU Treaty before the end of the month, starting a two-year countdown to UK exit. I considered this to be the moment I had to set out the path I was proposing for Scotland.

In the speech, I lamented the position the country was now in and described the 'brick wall of intransigence' that our efforts to reach a compromise agreement with the UK government had run into. I expressed fear that the UK was headed down the road of a hard Brexit and that Scotland deserved a choice. Did it want to follow the UK or opt instead for independence? The expectation at that point was that the Brexit deal would be done by autumn 2018, with the UK finally leaving the EU in March 2019. I therefore set the window between autumn 2018 and spring 2019 as the optimum time to have a referendum.

If it's possible for a decision to be both absolutely right and catastrophically wrong, that's what this was. I recognized that it would divide opinion. I felt a massive weight of responsibility. I had lost sleep for weeks before making up my mind. Even though I talked through the arguments for and against with colleagues and advisers, I knew the final call had to be mine, and it felt lonely. That was probably why I reached out to Alex. We had always talked through big political decisions together and, just as it had in the past, I thought doing so now would help me. That it might make me feel less alone.

A week or so before I announced the decision, I had invited him to Bute House for dinner, just the two of us. It was the only time I hosted him there, rather than the other way around. I knew it would have been hard for him to come back as a guest, rather than the incumbent, so I felt grateful to him for making the effort.

It didn't take long for me to regret it, though. I had hoped for a sounding board, some wise counsel from someone I trusted. He was my friend as well as my mentor. To my dismay, he showed no interest in talking things through properly. Instead, he boiled my dilemma down to a single question – did I have the guts? Alex always had a bank of go-to quotes, which his photographic memory allowed him to pull out at will. One of his favourites was from James Graham, the seventeenth-century Marquis of Montrose:

> He either fears his Fate too much,
> Or his Deserts are small,
> That puts it not unto the Touch,
> To win or lose it all.

This was the sum total of his advice to me that night. It was time to gamble, to go all-in. He quoted James Graham at me another two or three times over dinner, as if it was really that simple. At least he had the good grace to change the pronouns. I felt very dispirited. Over my years of trying and failing to secure a referendum, it would be suggested periodically that my lack of courage, or excess of caution, was the problem. For some, including Alex in later years, this was mischief-making, a way of undermining me. For others, believing this to be the case was probably just easier than engaging with the very real legal and practical hurdles we faced. Whether or not I had the courage to go for a referendum wasn't the issue I was wrestling with. I was trying to decide if it was the right, or wrong, thing to do at that moment in time. Of course I wanted another chance to win independence, but Scotland's future wasn't a casino chip. I went to bed that night feeling lonelier than ever.

It would be false to say that my lifelong desire for independence or the pressure I felt from sections of my own support base played no part at all in my considerations. It's also possible that these factors held more sway in my subconscious than they did in my front-of-mind decision-making. However, I genuinely tried to base my decision on what I thought was best for the country overall. Ultimately, my decision to press ahead was based on my certainty that at such a fork-in-the-road moment, people in Scotland deserved a choice.

Did we want to accept a Brexit we hadn't voted for, with all its damaging consequences, especially if the Tories opted for the hardest possible version? Or did we want to take a different course, to forge our own future as an independent country? In this moment, if I decided against a referendum, I would effectively be making that choice for the country. That couldn't be right. If a collective decision was not merited in this moment, when would it ever be? This conclusion seemed then, and now, to be entirely reasonable.

However, my attempt at reason collided with a febrile public mood. I thought I understood the different strands of opinion, and at a rational level I did. About a third of the country was unshakeably pro-independence and impatient for a referendum. At the other end of the spectrum, there was another third which was unreachable, implacably opposed to both independence and a referendum. The rest, the middle ground, were open to persuasion, or so I thought, by the kind of reasoned arguments I was trying to make. But this didn't tell the whole story. I was under-appreciating just how viscerally many people felt.

The independence-ultras were frustrated with what they saw as my overly ponderous approach. But those implacably opposed to independence were becoming angrier at what they saw as my refusal to accept the 2014 result. In the minds of some of them, I was now doing the same with the Brexit vote.

However, my biggest misjudgement, or blind spot perhaps, was in reading the mood of the middle. Anger about Brexit was certainly opening minds to independence, but it was still more tentative than I allowed myself to acknowledge. I had expected soft Yes voters to harden their views and soft No voters to finally make the jump. What I encountered instead was a sense that this was a time for divisions to heal and the dust to settle. There was a suspicion on the part of some that I was motivated by partisan rather than national interests and that my decision was piling upheaval on top of chaos. There were also some independence supporters who were pro-Brexit, and my decision alienated many of them too.

It was this mood which emboldened Theresa May to do what I had thought, on balance, she wouldn't: to issue a flat 'no' to any negotiations about transferring legal competence to Holyrood so that it could legislate for a referendum. This, then, was the bind I found myself in. Not only was public opinion sceptical at best and, at worst, hostile, but there was also a massive legal roadblock in my path.

Even so, while I was certainly discomfited, I was not yet overly worried. I figured that I had time on my side. I wasn't proposing an immediate referendum; it would be at least eighteen months in the future. As the dire consequences of Brexit became real rather than hypothetical, it seemed plausible that more and more people would come to see independence as a lifeline. The strength of public opinion would then allow us to overcome Theresa May's Westminster veto. That was my thinking. Events, however, took a different turn. The chaos of Brexit was only just getting started.

———

At the start of April 2017, I travelled to the United States to undertake a range of trade and political visits. There was an immense amount of interest stateside about the prospect of another independence vote and the fallout from the Brexit referendum.

In the UK, most of the attention ahead of the trip was on whether I would meet Donald Trump, who, by then, was three months into his presidency. There was never any intention for me to do so. I have never met him, a fact I am not unhappy about. When he visited Scotland in 2018, there was a brief flurry of interest from his people about a possible brush-by, but thankfully I avoided it. On the morning he played golf at Turnberry, one of his two golf courses in Scotland, I opted to lead the annual Pride march through Glasgow, the first head of government in the UK to do so. I considered this to be a more appropriate way to 'welcome' Donald Trump to my country.

I did have some interactions with him, though. On at least one occasion when I was first in Bute House, and before he became President, I received what can loosely be described as a 'green ink' letter from him. When building his golf course in Aberdeenshire, he had taken great umbrage to a proposed offshore wind farm which he claimed would spoil the view from his property. He took the Scottish government to court, and even though he lost at every stage, up to and including our ultimate victory in the UK Supreme Court, he sent me cuttings of newspaper articles about the evils of wind power. He underlined passages and scrawled single words followed by multiple exclamation marks in the margins – 'CRAZY!!!!' for example – all in thick black Sharpie. Of course, later on during his White House years, his use of a Sharpie became something of a talking point.

My only other interaction with him was a phone call in the period between his first election and the inauguration in January 2017. Martin Gilbert, at that time the CEO of investment company Aberdeen Asset Management and a good friend to the SNP, had taken it upon himself to broker the call. Martin and Trump knew each other through golf and were sufficiently close for Martin to be invited to the inauguration a few weeks later.

Martin acted with the best of intentions. His view, not unreasonably, was that, regardless of who was in the White House, it was important for Scotland to maintain a constructive relationship with the US. I concurred, which is why I agreed. The call came on a Friday afternoon. I was in my constituency office in Govanhill and was told that he was aboard his Trump-branded aircraft, waiting to take off from somewhere.

The ten minutes or so that followed must rank amongst the most absurd of my entire time in office. I accorded him due courtesy, greeting him as Mr President-elect, and tried to keep the conversation as high level as possible. I had rightly suspected that if I didn't say my piece straight away, I might not get the chance. So, I jumped in quickly. I said that notwithstanding our political disagreements, something of an understatement, I wanted to see the long-standing relationship between Scotland and the US go from strength to strength. I also expressed the hope that some of the rhetoric of the campaign (I was thinking Muslim bans, for example) would find no place in the actions of his administration. Lastly, I enquired about the management of his Scottish businesses and whether his sons would take the reins.

I doubt he heard a single word. He must have sensed that I had finished speaking, though, because he launched into his monologue. It was hard to keep track – and obviously I am paraphrasing – but this was the gist. Did I know he was Scottish? On his mother's side? She was the best mother anyone had ever had. Scotland was a great country. Apart from our mad obsession with wind power, which was a danger to the future of humanity, didn't I realize? I should bring my family to stay at the White House as soon as he had moved in, at which point he asked the person next to him when that would be and said I was just to let him know dates. Had I noticed what had happened to the US economy since his election? The stock-market had reached an all-time high. No President had ever created such a strong economy and he wasn't even in office yet. His popularity ratings were soaring too. It was unprecedented. And his sons? Did I know he had the smartest sons any father had ever had? And so it went on. When the call ended, I wondered if I had just woken from a very bad acid dream.

There was more to come. A few minutes after the call concluded, Liz Lloyd, my Chief of Staff, took a call from his National Security Adviser, General Mike Flynn. Flynn was phoning to ask Liz if it was true that the President-elect had just spoken to the First Minister, and, if so, could she tell him what had been discussed? It seemed that he had known nothing about it.

Meeting Trump on my US trip might not have been a priority, even if it had been remotely likely, which it wasn't, but I was looking forward to seeing his defeated rival, Hillary Clinton.

I was due to be interviewed at the Women in the World summit in New York by the legendary Tina Brown, former editor of *Vanity Fair* and *The New Yorker*. I was relishing the interview, but I knew that the highlight would be a private meeting with Hillary Clinton. Hillary is someone I had looked up to for a long time. She is a trailblazer on the frontline of all the battles that women of my generation in politics have had to fight, the battles we are still fighting in many ways. Her fortitude, dignity and sheer resilience in the face of everything that has been thrown at her, mainly by men not fit to lace her boots, inspires and energizes me. When the US finally does elect its first female President – which at the time of writing feels further away than ever – she will owe an enormous debt of gratitude to Hillary Clinton. I am just sorry it couldn't have been her.

Unfortunately, I woke up that morning with the hangover from hell. I was utterly mortified, thinking that Hillary, my heroine, would never have got herself into such a state. I had taken my team out for dinner the night before. It was the mid-point of the trip, and everyone had been working hard. We had a lovely meal and ended the night in an amazing bar overlooking the Empire State Building. I always manage to somehow 'forget' that in the US, spirits are free-pouring, not served by the measure, which meant that the three gins I thought I'd drunk, on top of wine with dinner, were more like nine. I tried to blame John Somers, my Principal Private Secretary (and my rock for four years of my tenure as First Minister), but I knew it was all my own fault.

Thankfully my meeting with Hillary wasn't until late afternoon, so I was feeling a bit better by the time I arrived at Women in the World. We met in her dressing room, just the two of us. I had been slightly worried that she wouldn't live up to my expectations, but I couldn't have been more wrong. Much later, in 2022, I spent a couple of days with her at a women leaders' summit in Italy. My conclusion there was the same. She would have been an outstanding President, and it is the USA's great loss that she never got the chance.

We spoke for about twenty minutes in New York. She was smart, funny, informed, on top of everything that was happening in the UK and Scotland. She also gave me some words of encouragement about keeping going when things seem impossible. These words have been a source of strength to me on many occasions over the years. Unfortunately, they couldn't save me from the deep despondency that would engulf me on my return to Scotland.

———

It was a Tuesday morning, 18 April 2017. I had just kicked off the weekly meeting of the Scottish Cabinet in Bute House when I was passed a note from one of my Private Secretaries. She apologized for the interruption, but said she thought I'd want to know that the Prime Minister would shortly make an unscheduled statement from Downing Street. There was heavy speculation that she was about to call an election.

My heart sank. Rather than press on distracted, I decided to suspend the meeting so that we could watch the statement. A short time later, Theresa May emerged onto Downing Street to a lectern shorn of the official Prime Ministerial crest, a give-away that what she was about to say was political not governmental. She announced a General Election on 8 June.

I had been due to travel south later that day for the official opening of Scotland House, the new Scottish government office in London. A meeting with our MPs and a round of media interviews were hastily added to my schedule. I struck a confident and defiant note in London, both to my MP colleagues, who were clearly and understandably nervous, and to the massed ranks of journalists, who were all predicting losses for the SNP. My outward demeanour belied a deep sense of foreboding. My gut told me that, for us, this was the wrong election at the wrong time. I still believed my referendum call would turn out to be the right one, but in that moment I knew it was unpopular and I feared that Scotland might be about to give me a bloody nose: that I would bear the brunt of all the frustration people were feeling about politics in general and Brexit in particular.

I was also concerned that Jeremy Corbyn might prove to be more popular, especially in Scotland, than anyone was anticipating. I never warmed to Corbyn. I met him a few times during his leadership of the Labour Party, and he exuded the same aura of aloofness and sneering superiority that I have detected in many men on the far left over the years, particularly around women. I was no different from everyone else, in that I initially expected May to win a thumping majority in 2017. Nevertheless, I had a niggling feeling that Corbyn's ability to tap into a mood might be underpriced.

The next few weeks were amongst the most miserable of my political career. It wasn't just that the circumstances were tough, I also underperformed. I was woefully below par, not firing on any cylinders. I was unwell throughout the campaign. I had come back from the States with a mystery bug that just wouldn't lift. I was struggling to breathe properly and coughing all the time with an excruciating pain in my chest. It was horribly debilitating and got so bad at one point, around mid-April, that I ended up in Edinburgh's Western Infirmary having my chest and lungs scanned. The scans showed nothing untoward, but the symptoms wouldn't budge. I badly needed rest, to go to bed for a few days, but I had to keep going, pumped full of antibiotics and painkillers. I didn't feel properly better until well after the election.

The first leaders' debate of the campaign was on 18 May, in

Manchester. It was hosted by ITV and chaired by Julie Etchingham. The experience could not have been more different from my 2015 triumph. First of all, May had refused to do any leaders' debates and, for this one at least, Corbyn had decided not to show up either. The absence of the two main players sucked any real drama out of the occasion. I was under pressure on Brexit, my referendum position, the performance of the Scottish government on education, health and a whole host of other issues. The feisty upstart of 2015 was nowhere to be seen. I was defensive and unconvincing, and I felt physically awful. My breathing difficulties kicked in halfway through my opening statement, and for the rest of the debate I felt on the verge of collapse.

A second UK leaders' debate was hosted by the BBC, in Cambridge, on 31 May. Again, neither May nor Corbyn was scheduled to attend and, because I was feeling so bad, I decided that I wouldn't do this one either. Angus Robertson would do it in my place. Not pitching up to a debate, taking the risk that I'd be accused of being frit, ran counter to every political instinct I had. However, I knew I needed to conserve energy, and so a combination of my own common sense and the pleas of my team persuaded me to sit it out.

But then Corbyn changed his mind at the last minute and decided to participate. This, in turn, piled pressure on May. Had she bowed to that pressure, I'd have been marooned as the only leader not taking part. It would have been a dreadful look. There was a window of a couple of hours when I could, just about, have rejigged my schedule and got to Cambridge on time, but I didn't. I spent the rest of the day terrified that May would turn up and, in the process, make me look as weak as I was feeling. I was also consumed by guilt that I had exposed my party to such a risk. Yes, I was unwell, but if I am being honest there had also been an element of avoidance. It wasn't just my illness weighing me down in the campaign. I knew I was getting the politics wrong too. Convinced that I'd perform badly, I had decided it might be better to just not be there.

In the event, Theresa May, probably the only person in the country having a more miserable election than I was, missed the opportunity to humiliate me, and Angus performed well, but it was an episode that summed up our entire, ill-fated campaign.

We got a sense of which way the wind was blowing in Scotland with local council elections on 4 May, my third electoral test as SNP leader in less than three years. We won handsomely with 431 seats, compared to the 276 won by the Tories, who had, yet again, beaten Labour to second place. The hype around the Tories at this stage was ridiculous. An alien watching from outer space would have been forgiven for thinking they had won the election hands down.

Although we were the victors, I was disappointed and worried. We should have done better. It felt like an ominous straw in the wind for what would come a month later. Already pessimistic about the General Election, my mood slumped further. I had to work hard to overcome a sense of inevitability and focus on what I could do to turn things round. It wasn't easy. The Tories had crudely, but very effectively, turned the election into a referendum on a second independence referendum. Their campaign was based on opposition to a new vote in principle, but also on the notion that our 'obsession' with one was distracting us from the 'day job'. It wasn't true, but it was striking a chord. Obviously, shifting course and ditching the referendum wasn't possible. Those who opposed it wouldn't have believed me, and those who desperately wanted it would have deserted me in droves. Moreover, I still strongly believed that giving Scotland a choice in the face of Brexit was the right thing to do.

In retrospect, I should have gone the opposite way. I should have devoted my energies to explaining why a referendum was necessary and outlining the better future for Scotland that I believed it could usher in. In the mood which prevailed at the time, I wouldn't have won over many doubters, but I might have given my own supporters more motivation to vote. Instead, I opted for, or, perhaps more accurately, stumbled onto, an uneasy middle ground. I sounded as if I was apologizing for the referendum commitment. I constantly pointed out that it had been a last resort, made necessary by May's intransigence, and emphasized that it wasn't happening immediately, that it was almost two years away.

There is always a danger in politics that standing in the middle of the road gets you mowed down from both directions. And so it proved. By the time polling day rolled around, I was fearing the worst. Our private polling and campaign intelligence was suggesting that our own vote was demoralized. More worrying, there was evidence of likely tactical voting, of people who opposed independence voting for the candidate best placed to defeat us. Our big strength since 2014 had been that the pro-independence support largely coalesced behind us, while the unionist support was divided. If that changed, we would be in trouble. I remained sceptical, though. While I could see the potential for natural Tory supporters to vote Labour on that basis, I grossly underestimated the potential for the reverse.

Going into the final few days, I was also completely exhausted. I am not sure how I made it through that campaign. The effort it took to keep going every day in spite of whatever it was ailing me had drained me of energy. There were days I could barely stay upright. I couldn't wait to get the election over and collapse in a heap, whatever the result.

Unfortunately, I had one more TV debate to get through,

between the Scottish leaders, hosted by STV in Glasgow and chaired by veteran broadcaster Bernard Ponsonby. I'd been feeling particularly ill that day, but while I would love to offer that as an excuse for what can only be described as a moment of madness, I won't. It would be a pathetic attempt to let myself off the hook for an error of judgement that someone with my years of experience should never have made. The debate had been going reasonably well. I scored some early applause from the audience and had started to feel the return of the confidence which had been absent for most of the campaign.

During the section when we had to cross-examine each other, when it was Kezia Dugdale's turn to question me, she went for the jugular. She asked me how it felt to be as unpopular in Scotland as Thatcher had once been; to hear people talk about 'that bloody woman' and know it was now me they were referring to, not her.

I should have risen above it. Kezia was only doing her job, and doing it well. It was also a patently ridiculous assertion; 2017 was undoubtedly the low point of my popularity as First Minister, but to suggest it was anywhere near the depths that Thatcher's had plumbed was nonsense. It was beyond hyperbole. Nevertheless, after the positivity that had surrounded me in 2015 and 2016, the instances of open hostility I had encountered in this campaign had been tough to deal with. I felt hurt and Kezia's jibe was salt in my wounds.

Instead of letting it wash over me, the red mist descended and I revealed the content of the call we'd had the morning after the Brexit vote, when she had told me she thought Labour should shift position on a referendum. The justification in my head in that split second was that she was being hypocritical in arguing that a referendum was unthinkable, beyond the pale, when I had reason to believe she thought otherwise.

It was stupid and wrong. It had been a private conversation, and I should not have breached the confidence. The error was on me. It had been no part of my debate preparation. On the contrary, whenever I had even joked about revealing the secret, my team had told me it was a terrible idea. So terrible that it wasn't even funny. As soon as the words were out of my mouth, I wanted to take them back. It was one of those horrible slow-motion moments. At first, no one seemed to register what I had said. And then, suddenly, Ruth Davidson did, and all hell broke loose. It was, not surprisingly, the only news story out of the debate.

Despite Kez's sort-of denial, no one doubted I was telling the truth. However, I got flak from the media for the breach of confidence. Indeed, had it happened earlier in the campaign, it would have done me much more damage. It might also have cost us even more seats.

The Tories' entire pitch for tactical voting was built on the premise that Labour couldn't be trusted to defend the Union and that only they could. My moment of madness, suggesting Kezia was a secret referendum supporter, played straight into their hands.

———

Watching the exit poll at 10 p.m. on 8 June brought none of the jubilation of 2015. I was at home after a long day touring polling stations in my constituency. When Big Ben chimed, and the numbers flashed up on screen, I felt sick. Thirty-four seats was the projection for us. If that came to pass, it would be a loss of twenty-two seats: twenty-two friends and colleagues. It was worse than I had feared. There was just one glimmer of hope when the BBC reported that due to an issue with methodology, the Scottish number had to be treated with caution.

There was a bigger story out of the poll, though, with it

projecting that the Tories would lose their majority across the UK. An unnecessary election called by a seemingly unconquerable Theresa May had exposed the full extent of her weakness. If the exit poll was correct, it would be one of the biggest own goals in modern electoral history.

The next few hours were awful as we waited for results from across the country. There were some nail-biting photo finishes in our favour. Pete Wishart held on in the SNP heartland of Perth & North Perthshire by twenty-one votes. In North East Fife, the margin was even tighter when Stephen Gethins won by just two votes. Overall, though, there was more gloom than joy. The exit poll turned out to be almost exactly spot on. We finished the night with thirty-five seats, a loss of twenty-one. Our vote share was down from 50% to 37%. Even Alex Salmond lost in Gordon. The man who had, until then, won every seat he had ever contested had been defeated in a campaign led by me. I was distraught.

Tactical voting had definitely played its part. The Tories went from one seat to twelve, Labour from one to seven, and the Lib Dems from one to three. UK-wide, May had indeed lost her majority. In the blink of an eye, she had gone from iron lady reborn to lame duck, and it was all her own doing. We might have been the only two people in the country that night who knew how the other was feeling.

The deep irony, of course, was that this was the second-best Westminster election result in the history of the SNP, by several country miles. We had won by a massive margin. And yet it was also an abject failure. Having set the bar so high, in my fourth election as SNP leader in less than three years, I was now a victim of my own success. It was no comfort. I had got the politics wrong, performed badly and felt that I had let my party down. I did some serious soul searching. I also learned a lot about the loneliness of leadership.

The mood in Scotland post-referendum was electric. A speaking tour of Scotland to mark my election as SNP leader and First Minister – dubbed the 'rockstar' tour – culminated in a capacity crowd at Glasgow's Hydro Arena, where I spoke on a stage that in previous weeks had hosted Lady Gaga, Robbie Williams, Prince, Beyoncé and Katy Perry.

Taking the oath of office in the Court of Session to become Scotland's fifth – and first female – First Minister.

My first Cabinet on the steps of Bute House – at the time, one of only three gender-balanced Cabinets in the world.

The second of two leaders' debates in the 2015 General Election, in which the SNP won 56 out of Scotland's 59 constituencies. At the end of this one in London on 16 April, Leanne Wood of Plaid Cymru, Natalie Bennett of the Greens and I hugged. It hadn't been planned this way, but Ed Miliband ended up marooned.
Nigel Farage had already stormed off in a huff.

Taking to the skies. Over the final weekend of the 2015 campaign, I travelled the length and breadth of Scotland in a helicopter. It's not the most relaxing mode of travel, but I reached places I'd never have got to otherwise and was able to pack in lots of on-board interviews between stops.

During the 2015 campaign, the *Daily Mail* dubbed me 'the most dangerous woman in Britain'– possibly the nicest thing it has ever said about me. My team presented me with this souvenir.

At a campaign stop in Inverness on the final Saturday of the 2015 campaign – part of the helicopter tour. This image sums up my view of the campaign – everywhere I went I was surrounded by crowds of people, and often couldn't move more than a few steps.

The 2015 exit poll predicting that the SNP would win 58 seats (in the event, we won 56). I was at home, holding my breath, when the image appeared on the screen at 10 p.m. I couldn't believe it.

The 56. Our newly elected MPs in front of the iconic Forth railway bridge.

On the 2016 Scottish election campaign trail. This was my chance to win a mandate of my own as First Minister.

Launching Scotland's 'Baby Box'. The policies I am proudest of from my time as First Minister are those that help give children the best start in life.

Behind the scenes at Women in the World, New York, April 2017. Meeting Hillary Rodham Clinton, a woman I have long admired, was a highlight of the trip.

Adding my voice to the campaign for a second Brexit referendum at a mass rally in London on 22 March 2019.

Welcoming the new Prime Minister, Boris Johnson, to Bute House on 29 July 2019, after the tawdry campaign to oust Theresa May had succeeded. Johnson was the third of five occupants of 10 Downing Street during my tenure as First Minister.

One of my early Covid briefings, accompanied by Chief Medical Officer,
Catherine Calderwood *(left)*, and Health Secretary, Jeane Freeman *(right)*. I
would do more than 200 of these over the course of the pandemic.

Leading Scotland through a global pandemic took its toll on me,
mentally and physically, and occasionally it showed – such as here,
during an update to the Scottish Parliament on
1 December 2020.

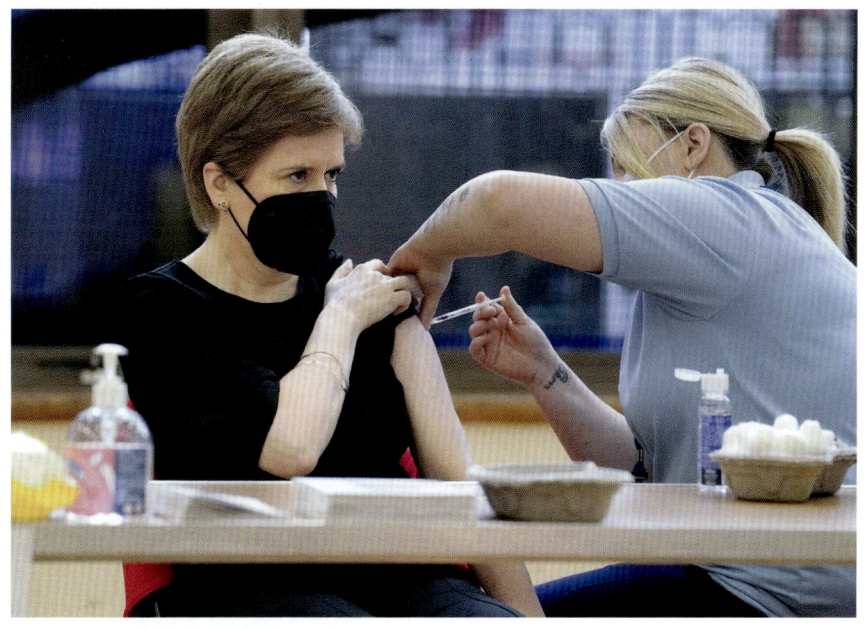

Light at the end of the tunnel – receiving my Covid vaccine.
The rapid development of vaccines for Covid was the greatest scientific
achievement of our generation.

An audience with Her Majesty, Queen Elizabeth at Holyrood Palace on 29 June 2021, the
first time I had seen her in person since before Covid. Over the course of my tenure as First
Minister, I spent hours of private time with this extraordinary woman. Our conversations
ranged far and wide, and were always fascinating.

The 'family' photo at the British–Irish Council in Blackpool in November 2022. It was the first attended by a British Prime Minister since the days of Gordon Brown – although Rishi Sunak stayed only for dinner and left before the summit. It was my last as First Minister.

Meeting President Joe Biden at the COP26 climate summit in Glasgow. Boris Johnson's government had briefed the press in advance that one of their objectives for the summit was to stop me being pictured with the President.

Leaving Bute House for the last time on 28 March 2023, my 3,05 and final day as First Minister.

Having lost his seat, Alex refused to take my calls for two weeks. I told myself I deserved it, that I had let him down. I knew how massive a psychological blow the defeat would be for him. But his rejection really hurt me. For a long time we had been equals more than teacher/pupil, but this was a reminder that, deep in my psyche, his approval still mattered to me. Conversely, his disapproval sapped my confidence. It was tough. It felt like the lowest depth our relationship could sink to. I would soon discover that it wasn't even near.

CHAPTER SIXTEEN

Alex Salmond

I have talked about Alex a lot already. I have tried not to rewrite history; not to allow the events which unfolded in the period after 2017 to distort my portrayal of our past relationship. The impact he had earlier in my life was overwhelmingly positive.

However, what happened in the wake of sexual allegations made against him forced me to reassess all manner of things. I came to question whether the man I once thought I knew had ever really existed. And, of course, I could not have comprehended when I started writing this book that, by the time I finished it, he would be dead.

When news of his death reached me, in a phone call from my friend, the SNP's former Westminster leader, Ian Blackford, I was hit by a wave of emotion much stronger than I would have anticipated. I thought I had already done my 'grieving' for him and the relationship we once had. I was wrong. It wasn't that the anger and hurt I felt about his behaviour in the preceding few years dissipated. It didn't and hasn't. However, in that moment, and for some time afterwards, I felt an overwhelming sense of sadness and loss.

In the days after he passed away, I also agonized about whether I should even write about the events which shattered our relationship. What purpose would it serve, now that he was no longer here? Would I just be stirring up pain for his wife and family (which I truly don't want to do)? However, I knew that I owed it to myself and to many others who bear the scars of these events to write my account. Right up to the moment he died, Alex was accusing me, and others, of being part of a conspiracy against him. He was trying to rewrite history; to supplant the truth with an alternative reality. I cannot let that stand unchallenged.

What follows has been more difficult to write than I would have imagined. Nothing about this chapter of my life has been, or ever will be, easy. All I can do, just as I have done in my accounts of our earlier relationship, is strive to be fair and, above all, true to myself.

————

My relationship with Alex started to deteriorate the moment I became leader. I should have been more prepared for it. I had seen it all before, during John Swinney's leadership. Shortly after Alex stood down from his first stint as leader in 2000, it became obvious that he still expected to call the shots. When he wasn't able to, he became huffy and difficult. He acted in ways that, deliberate or otherwise, served only to undermine John.

Fast forward to 2014 and I assumed things would be different. He had been First Minister for seven years and achieved a great deal. I thought he was ready to occupy a different role: less frontline, more elder statesman. It became clear quite quickly that he wasn't. Even so, I viewed any tension between us as no more than a symptom of our changed positions. At no point did I feel that our underlying friendship was in doubt, and I could certainly never have imagined that we would one day be political enemies.

There was one particular note of sourness between us in the last days of his time in office. He told me that I should sack Peter as the party's Chief Executive when I became leader. To be fair, there are many people, particularly in light of more recent events, who will think he was right. I saw it differently. There is no formal line management of the Chief Executive by the leader. SNP staff are overseen by the party's Business Manager and accountable to its governing body, the National Executive Committee.

By the time I became leader, Peter had been in post for many years. He was also exceptionally good at the job. His role in turning the SNP into a modern, effective, election-winning machine cannot be overstated. It seemed to me wrong that my election as leader should deprive him of a job he loved and the SNP of a highly successful Chief Executive. I also suspected a smidgeon of vindictiveness on Alex's part. His and Peter's relationship was often strained. When Alex first became an MP in 1987, he had recruited Peter to run his constituency office, a job he did well for many years. As a result, Peter had become somewhat impervious to the Salmond 'charm'. I think this annoyed Alex. In fact, had Peter not already been in post when Alex returned as leader in 2004, I doubt he would ever have been appointed Chief Executive – he simply wasn't fawning enough. I thought Alex might have been seizing a belated opportunity to get one over on him.

For better or worse, this was my thinking at the time. In later years, for obvious reasons, Alex would take great pleasure in saying 'I told her so'. However, back in 2014, although the conversation had been awkward, it wasn't a source of tension between us.

Not long after I entered Bute House, I started hearing that he was complaining about me on other grounds. He was reportedly furious that I hadn't found an important role for him. I was so busy at the time that I didn't pay it much attention. In retrospect, I should have been more sensitive to how difficult the transition out of office is and handled him with more care. Now that I understand it first-hand, I regret that I wasn't. However, the idea that this should have been top of my priorities while I was trying to get to grips with being First Minister has always seemed a bit unreasonable.

There were also attempts to force me to do things his way. On one occasion, ahead of the 2015 election, he told me that I should set three possible conditions for another independence referendum, any one of which we could then use to trigger a poll: Scotland being forced into a Brexit we hadn't voted for; the Tories continuing with austerity; or a UK government deciding to renew the Trident nuclear weapons system. I agreed with the first, but told him that I thought the other two would be lunacy. These policy developments were virtually guaranteed. We would be shutting down any room for manoeuvre. There was also no basis for saying that these represented a material change of circumstances in the way that Brexit would. We had quite a tetchy discussion about it before he left my Scottish Parliament office, telling me he had an interview to do. Later that afternoon, I saw the clip of his interview online. He said that as someone who knew my mind well, he was fairly certain that I would set three conditions for a referendum – Brexit, austerity or Trident renewal. I was not amused.

Given this attempt to box me in on a referendum, and his taunting of me in early 2017 about whether I was brave enough, it is ironic that towards the end of the 2017 campaign, stung by the negative response he was getting in his constituency, he called me to suggest I find a way of ditching the referendum commitment before polling day.

The first alarm bell about potential sex allegations rang on the evening of Saturday, 4 November 2017. Sky News submitted a media query about the alleged harassment of staff at Edinburgh Airport whose jobs it had been to usher him through security and look after him until he boarded his flight. I spoke to him on the phone about it on the Sunday morning. Though he vehemently denied the allegation, he seemed pretty shaken. I remember feeling uneasy. By the following day, he had 'lawyered up' and seemed much more characteristically bullish. When Sky didn't run the story, I just assumed there had been nothing to it.

In any event, a few days later, he generated another story that I had to respond to. He had told me he was in negotiations with a broadcaster about hosting a chat show but refused to tell me which one, citing commercial confidentiality. He promised to tell me as soon as the deal was done, which he didn't. To be fair, I wasn't giving it much, if any, thought, as I had too much else on my mind.

On the evening of 9 November, I was en route to a British–Irish Council summit in Jersey. Just before my flight took off, I got wind that he had signed up with Russia Today. I was with Mike Russell, a former close confidant of Alex and by then my Brexit minister. We were stunned. By the time we landed in Jersey, the deal with Russia Today had been announced at a glitzy party in London. His caginess with me should have been a giveaway, but, still, I was incredulous. Signing up with the state broadcaster of the brutish, anti-democratic, autocratic regime of Vladimir Putin was an appalling misjudgement, even from someone who had always seemed drawn to the strongman breed of politics. I was asked about it at the post-BIC press conference. There was a sense of bemusement amongst the other leaders there, and no wonder. I remember Leo Varadkar asking me what on earth Alex was thinking and me having to concede that I had no idea.

I didn't try to defend him. It would have called my own judgement into serious question had I done so. In a statement of the
obvious, I said that Russia Today would not have been my choice
and, had Alex asked me about it in advance, which he hadn't, I'd
have advised against it. I got a caustic text from him while I was
travelling home. My comments had clearly displeased him. But I'm
not entirely sure what he had expected. A commercial tie-up of
this kind with the Russian regime was wrong in principle and
potentially disastrous for the SNP's reputation. There was no
shortage of voices keen to claim that independence would be an
opportunity for bad faith actors to use Scotland to undermine UK
stability, and here he was, helping them make that case.

After his text, we had no contact at all until April the following
year. What came then was devastating.

_____

It is important here to recap the background. Two women made
complaints to the Scottish government about Alex's conduct towards
them while he was First Minister. These complaints were investigated during 2018. Alex told me about them in April 2018 and they
became a matter of public knowledge in August that year through
a leak to the *Daily Record* newspaper. At this point, Alex announced
that he would challenge the Scottish government in court, claiming
that its investigation of him was unfair. Due to a procedural error,
which came to light in late 2018, and which I will explain later, the
Scottish government abandoned its defence against his court action
in January 2019. The following month, he was criminally charged
with multiple alleged sex offences. He was tried in the High Court
in March 2020 and acquitted on all charges, being found 'not guilty'
on all except one, which was found 'not proven'. In Scots law, 'not
proven' has the same effect as 'not guilty' – acquittal.

I was cleared by an independent process of the allegation he made against me that I had breached the Ministerial Code by misleading Parliament over the detail of what I knew and when. The investigation was conducted by a senior Irish lawyer, James Hamilton, and his verdict eventually came on 22 March 2021. I was certain that I hadn't breached the code, but I had obviously been deeply anxious that James Hamilton might take a different view. Had he done so, I would have had to resign. If that had happened, it would have left my party leaderless just two days before the start of an election campaign. It was unthinkable and yet it might have happened. In the days leading up to the publication of the Hamilton report, when I was already worn down by the strain of dealing with Covid, I hardly slept. The relief when I was finally cleared on all points was overwhelming. Even now, it strikes me as deeply ironic that though this whole episode arose out of allegations against Alex, I felt for a while as if it was me on trial. This isn't the only time during my career that I've had to answer for and found myself embroiled in 'scandal' over the alleged conduct of men. I'm not trying to let myself off the hook, as no doubt there has been misplaced trust and poor judgement on my part along the way too. Even so, it has often felt to me, and never more so than during the Alex Salmond affair, that when a man is alleged to have done wrong, some people's first instinct is to find a woman to blame. I know I wasn't just any woman but the leader of my party and my country, but I think the point still stands.

This feeling of being on trial was most intense when it came to the work of the Scottish Parliament committee set up to investigate the Scottish government's handling of the original complaints against Alex. From day one, it seemed clear that some of the opposition members of the committee were much less interested in establishing facts, or making sure lessons were learned, than they were in finding some way to blame it all on me. If it sometimes felt to me like a 'witch-hunt', it is probably because for some of them that is exactly what it was. I was told, and I believe it to be true, that some of the opposition MSPs were taking direction from Alex himself – though possibly through an intermediary – on the points to pursue and the questions to ask.

The Committee Inquiry came to a head on 3 March 2021, when I appeared before it and gave eight hours of sworn evidence. It was a gruelling experience, not least as I was still trying to steer the country through a global pandemic at the time, but it was also a cathartic one. It also gave the significant number of people who tuned in to watch the chance to see for themselves just how partisan some of the committee members were being. Not surprisingly, the opposition majority on the Committee managed to find some way of asserting in their report that I had breached the Ministerial Code. However, it was the verdict of the independent Hamilton report that mattered.

I don't intend to rehearse in greater depth here all the sordid detail of what happened during this bruising episode of my life. It is all on the public record, not least in the transcript of those eight hours of sworn evidence.

However, it is important to challenge, robustly, the claim Alex made, right up until his death, that he had been the victim of a conspiracy. He wasn't. He was never able to produce a shred of hard evidence that he was. All of which begs the question: how did he manage to persuade some people that he was the wronged party, and lead others to at least entertain the possibility?

In short, he used all of his considerable political and media skills to divert attention from what was, for him, the inconvenient fact of the whole business. He sought to establish his conspiracy narrative by weaving together a number of incidents and developments, all of which had rational explanations, into something that, with his powers of persuasion, he was able to cast as sinister.

In the course of his trial, and in what he told me face-to-face, Alex admitted that he had acted towards women in ways that weren't always acceptable. It is clear that what unfolded was firmly rooted in his own conduct, not in a conspiracy. That was the inconvenient fact. The conspiracy narrative was hatched when he realized there might be no way to avoid being confronted with the consequences of that conduct. It leads back to the fateful occasion on 4 April 2018 when he came to my house to tell me that the Scottish government was investigating complaints of sexual harassment against him.

Even though there had been a lingering unease at the back of my mind, ever since the Sky News approach in 2017, what I heard on 4 April knocked me for six.

In the dining room of my house on 4 April, with just him and me across a table, Alex showed me a copy of the letter he had received from the Scottish government's Permanent Secretary, Leslie Evans, informing him of the complaints against him. The investigation was being conducted under a process adopted by the Scottish government in the wake of the MeToo furore a few months earlier to allow complaints of a historic nature to be considered.

The substance of the complaints, one in particular, shocked me. I felt sick. After appearing to be upset and mortified by the allegations, Alex became cold. He effectively admitted the substance of one of the complaints, but claimed that it had been a 'misunderstanding', for which he had apologized at the time. According to him, the woman concerned had no right to bring it up again. He made it obvious that he considered the whole process to be illegitimate. He would later claim differently, of course, but it was evident that he wanted me to intervene and to stop the investigation in its tracks or divert it into some kind of siding.

I knew that I shouldn't do that. It would have been a betrayal of the women concerned and, in some ways, of all women. It would be proof – yet again – that powerful men with powerful connections can get away with anything. I wouldn't have been able to live with myself.

I didn't realize it then, but this decision made the break-up of one of the most successful partnerships in modern British politics all but inevitable. More than half a decade later, and even after his death, the aftershocks from it are still reverberating.

I am convinced it was when Alex realized I wasn't going to give him a route out of the situation that he resolved to find another path. What he should have done was acknowledge that his behaviour had fallen short. He should have shown contrition and resolved to learn lessons. I can't know for sure, obviously, but had he done so, I think it at least possible that the heartache which followed might have been avoided.

However, it was not in his DNA to admit fault. So, instead, he launched a bid, simultaneously outrageous and, to anyone who knew him, utterly in character, to turn himself into a 'victim'.

Looking back, it seems clear that, as far back as April 2018, he was gearing up to claim that the new policy was designed specifically to 'catch' him. It was a ludicrous notion. In the wake of MeToo, organizations across the whole world had been reviewing their procedures with a view to ensuring that complaints about harassment could no longer just be swept under the carpet. However, it was what came after that gave him the rocket fuel he needed. There were three strands, strokes of 'luck' for him, if you like, that allowed him to weave his conspiracy theory.

First, on the day before the Scottish government was due to

publish the fact and outcome of the investigation into the complaints against him, the story was leaked to the *Daily Record*. I do not know who leaked it, but it was not me or anyone acting with my authority or knowledge. It crossed my mind many times that it might have been Alex himself, or, more likely, someone acting on his behalf. To those with no experience of the dark arts of media manipulation, I know this will sound preposterous. Why would he leak such a damaging story about himself? However, in many ways it would have been classic Alex. I had known him to make these kinds of calculations about political stories in the past. It takes a lot of gumption and a gambler's instinct to behave in such a way, but the basic thinking is not complicated. If there is damaging information certain to emerge about you and there is nothing you can do to stop it, get it out in a way that gives you the best chance of controlling the narrative.

I have no evidence to substantiate any allegation that it was him. I am merely speculating. Regardless of who was responsible, though, there is no doubt that it was Alex who benefitted. At a stroke, he was able to cast himself as the victim of underhand dealing.

His second strand arose out of an error by the Scottish government. As soon as the fact of the complaints had become public, Alex launched a Judicial Review of the process. As the government's defence was being prepared, it came to light that the Investigating Officer, whose role it had been to consider the basis of the complaints and prepare a report for the Permanent Secretary, had engaged in conversations with the complainants prior to her appointment. This, and the fact she had not initially been open about the prior contact, created the perception that her investigation and report might have been biased.

There was no evidence that the Investigating Officer had

actually been biased, but in a case like this even the perception is fatal. In these circumstances, the Scottish government had no option but to abandon the case. The end result was that the investigation, and its conclusion, was rendered null and void. Alex was able to take a narrow and technical flaw and spin it as evidence that the whole process had been an unlawful attempt to snare and convict him. In his narrative, he wasn't just a victim any more, he was now a vindicated victim.

It was also at this point that his animus towards me was cemented. He was reportedly furious that I hadn't demanded the resignation of the Permanent Secretary, Leslie Evans, treating it as further 'evidence' that I was against him.

There is an argument that I should have asked Leslie to resign. I know more than a few fair-minded people who think I made a mistake not to. Even though I had satisfied myself that the error was inadvertent and in no way malicious, it had massive consequences. The women who had made the complaints were badly let down. They had every right to feel that the stress of giving their accounts had been for nothing. And, although the error hadn't been her fault, Leslie was the head of the civil service that had 'botched' the process. It was not unreasonable to say that the buck stopped with her.

I also think it likely that had I asked Leslie to resign, my own life would have been easier. If I had given Alex the scalp he wanted, he might not have come after me with the venom he later displayed. So why didn't I?

Bluntly, I knew that, for him, Leslie's resignation was not about accountability. It was about vengeance. He wanted her punished for allowing him to be investigated in the first place. He would then have used her quitting as further 'proof' that he had been a victim all along. It felt to me, then and now, that this would have been wrong. Leslie had been right to make sure that the complaints were investigated. The error in the process was deeply regrettable, but the initial decision to treat the complaints seriously, and not to brush them under the carpet because of who they pertained to, was correct.

For a man accused of sexual misconduct to be able to bully the woman responsible for investigating him out of her job would have sent a signal that nothing had changed – that powerful men always win in the end, no matter how they behave. I did not want that to be the take-away. That was my judgement then and I stand by it, even now.

The third of his strands emerged from the disclosure of evidence in both the aborted Judicial Review action and his criminal trial. A number of text and WhatsApp messages were revealed to him, some between women complainers and others involving SNP staff members. He spun these as evidence of people conspiring to bring him down, rather than simply what they were – messages between individuals who had loyally supported him over many years expressing deep upset at the nature of the allegations against him. In addition, women who considered themselves victims of his behaviour were seeking support and comfort from each other. That he tried to distort and weaponize genuine expressions of shock, in some cases trauma, was truly disgraceful, and it strikes at the heart of why I found it so hard to forgive him.

These three strands, then, were the basis for his conspiracy theory.

It is worth reflecting on exactly what a conspiracy against him would have entailed. It would have needed a number of women deciding to concoct false allegations, without any obvious motive for doing so. It would then have required criminal collusion between them, senior ministers and civil servants, the police and the Crown

Office. That is what he was alleging, and his evidence for it boiled down to a leak that served his interests more than it did those of the alleged conspirators, a procedural error, and some out-of-context text and WhatsApp messages. The 'conspiracy' was a fabrication, the invention of a man who wasn't prepared to reflect honestly on his own conduct. When all's said and done, this is what I found hardest to come to terms with.

He was acquitted of criminal behaviour. But, in the course of his defence, a picture emerged of behaviour towards women that, on occasion, had been inappropriate. He seemed content during his trial to concede this, to persuade a jury that while he could have been a 'better man', he wasn't guilty of actual offences. What he never did was show any contrition.

In his efforts to turn himself into the wronged person, he demonstrated that nothing and no one was sacrosanct for him. There was never the merest hint of concern about the damage he did to the party he previously led. Indeed, it felt to me that he would have rather destroyed the SNP than see it succeed without him.

He impugned the integrity of the institutions at the heart of Scottish democracy – government, police, Crown Office. The fact that he never produced a shred of credible evidence that a conspiracy existed, because it didn't, wasn't enough to stop him seeking to damage the reputation of these institutions and shatter the morale of those who worked in them.

He was prepared to traumatize, time and again, the women at the centre of it all. A jury concluded that what they experienced wasn't criminal, but that does not mean those experiences didn't happen. Even if he never said so explicitly, he was accusing them of being liars, of making it all up. I obviously know some of the women involved. After James Hamilton and the Scottish Parliament Committee had published their reports, I also spoke personally to the two original complainants. I was the First Minister during a Scottish government process that had let them down. It was important to me to say sorry to them directly. It also let me hear first-hand the impact on them of the claims of conspiracy, and the scars they bear as a consequence.

As for those of us who had been his friends and colleagues over decades, those of us who had supported him, campaigned with him, celebrated and commiserated with him, we were suddenly his mortal enemies, accused of trying to bring him down and all for reasons that he was never able to explain.

In that regard, I was clearly public enemy number one. For a while, I told myself that the bonds between us would be stronger than his thirst for revenge. Eventually, though, I had to face the fact that he was determined to destroy me. I was now engaged in mortal political combat with someone I knew to be both ruthless and highly effective. It was a difficult reality to reconcile myself to.

So too was losing him as a friend. I went through what I can only describe as a grieving process. For a time after we stopped speaking, I would have conversations with him in my head about politics and the issues of the day. I had occasional, but always vivid, dreams in which we were still on good terms. I would wake up from these feeling utterly bereft.

And now? How do I feel about him now? Before he died, I thought I had reached the point of feeling nothing and that I had come to terms with it, wholly and completely. The emotions I felt on hearing of his death suggested otherwise. Yes, I have made peace with how things are, but it is an uneasy peace. On the one hand, I no longer expend energy wishing things had been different, that he had been different, that our relationship had still been intact. But, on the other hand, part of me still misses him, or at least misses the man I thought he was and the relationship we once had. I know I will never quite escape the shadow he casts, even in death.

The other reason my peace feels uneasy is that it's impossible, no matter how hard I try, not to feel regret about the breakdown of our relationship. It is not regret about a lost future, as that would have gone anyway with his passing. It is about the tainting of our past achievements. The fact that he was so integral to so many of the best moments of my life makes it hard for my memories of them to be as happy and uncomplicated as I would want. In time, I hope this is something I will get over.

There is one sense in which my peace is absolute and not uneasy in the slightest, and that is my certainty that none of what happened to him was my fault. He was the master of his own fate.

Alex's claims of conspiracy and betrayal were the cries of a man who was not prepared to look honestly at himself in the mirror, and that is why, ultimately, my greatest regret might be for him. He died without reckoning with himself.

CHAPTER SEVENTEEN

Back on Track

In the immediate aftermath of the 2017 election, I was physically and mentally exhausted, lacking motivation, and full of doubt about whether I was the right person for the job. There was no suggestion in the SNP that I should quit as leader in the wake of the result, but it was definitely a question in my mind. I asked John Swinney if he thought I should go, and he told me in no uncertain terms not to consider it.

So I set about trying to pull myself out of the hole I had fallen into, and to work on getting the party back on track. Before Parliament broke for the summer recess, I attempted to reset our position on a second referendum. It felt like walking a tightrope. In a statement to the Scottish Parliament on 27 June, I reaffirmed my belief that there should be another independence vote. However, I backed away from taking any immediate steps to try to bring it about, saying instead that I would wait until the terms of the UK's exit from the EU were clearer. As was so often the case with my efforts to navigate the issue of independence, I didn't really satisfy anyone. Those who desperately wanted another vote thought I had reneged, while those bitterly opposed to the very suggestion were angry that I hadn't reneged more firmly.

Over the summer, I took a few days holiday with Peter in Portugal, where I tried to do nothing but read, sleep, drink wine and enjoy the sunshine. I read two books over that holiday which rank amongst my all-time favourites: *Pachinko* by Min Jin Lee and *The Bastard of Istanbul* by Elif Shafak. Losing myself in a good book did more to lift my spirits than almost anything else I could imagine.

When I came home, working with my Cabinet colleagues and advisers, I set about crafting a direction that I hoped would propel my government and the country through to the next election and beyond.

The Programme for Government that I delivered to the Scottish Parliament on 5 September 2017 was, in my view, the strongest of my period in office. I was determined to be bold, to set the bar high. There was a view at the time, held by some of my Cabinet colleagues and civil servants, that it might be too ambitious. Was it affordable? Could we deliver it? We certainly did not succeed in delivering everything we set our minds to. For example, the commitment to an education bill was later shelved in favour of a non-statutory approach to achieving its main aim: greater autonomy for head-teachers over the curriculum, budgets and staff recruitment. We judged that this would deliver change more quickly and deny the opposition the chance to frustrate the legislation.

For all the criticism I got on education, the other parties invariably sought to block our attempts at reform. The introduction of standardized assessments to monitor the progress of children at primaries 1, 4 and 7, intended to inject more rigour into the curriculum, was a case in point. The policy was undermined and frustrated at every turn. Many in the opposition ranks wanted me to fail and were prepared to do everything possible to ensure I did.

Moreover, while I could set education policy, delivery was in the hands of local authorities, who didn't always want to play ball. Of course, none of this alters the fact that I did not succeed in all that I set out to do on school education – and that is on me.

My underlying problem, I think, was one of diagnosis. The children I met on my many visits to schools were curious, engaged, smart and knowledgeable. Their teachers were dedicated and determined. School leaver destinations suggested that most young people transitioned from secondary education into successful futures. The Scottish education system is not the failure that many claim. And yet, it was undeniable that our performance in international league tables was falling. Why was this?

Scotland's school curriculum, devised before the SNP entered government, prioritizes rounded education over rote learning. Some, particularly in the teaching profession, argued that these international assessments were ill-suited to the Scottish system and shouldn't be used as a benchmark at all. Others argued that the 'decline' was happening precisely because we had moved away from a rote approach to literacy and numeracy. I had some sympathy with the latter view, hence my introduction of standardized assessments. But the questions were more fundamental. Was the comprehensive model itself the enemy of excellence? And, if so, how should that be addressed without compromising the principle of inclusion that it is based on? Did we have a teaching profession that had become too complacent and, therefore, resistant to challenge and innovation?

I established a Council of Education Advisers, made up of internationally renowned experts, to help shape the answers to these questions, and the work it did was extremely helpful. Even so, it often felt that I was grasping at 'solutions' that I hoped, rather than knew, would make a difference.

In reality, it is the policies I introduced to tackle child poverty, enhanced by the Scottish Child Payment which came later, that I believe will have the biggest long-term impact on educational attainment. So much of what a child achieves in school is influenced by the quality of the life they lead outside the classroom. Good education should be and often is life's great leveller. But no school can ever completely eradicate the impact on a child's life of growing up in material poverty. Tackling the underlying causes of educational under-attainment is therefore as vital as anything done inside the classroom.

Overall, the programme that I unveiled in September 2017 was a success. It was also the foundation of many of the policy achievements I am proudest of.

From the summer of 2017, the parents of every newborn in Scotland had started to receive the 'Baby Box', which provides a range of essentials for the early months of a child's life. It is a simple and not very expensive policy, originating in Finland, which brings to life a principle close to my heart: that every child, no matter their background, should get the same basic start in life. In the Programme for Government, I pledged that by the time the 'baby box generation' reached primary school, we would have doubled the provision of state-funded early years education and childcare – and we did. The commitment was delivered in full in 2021.

I also committed to a programme of work to ensure that by 2030 young people from poorer backgrounds would have just as much chance of going to university as their wealthier peers. Scotland is now well on track to achieve this, and I believe it matters. University is not the be-all and end-all, and it is certainly not for everyone. Vocational education matters just as much, and, indeed, in this Programme for Government I also committed to a significant expansion of apprenticeships. However, access to university should not be dictated by background or family wealth. As the first in my family to go into higher education, I feel that very personally.

There were important economic developments too. I signalled our intention to expand our network of overseas 'embassies', which have helped make Scotland a magnet for inward investment. I committed to the establishment of a new National Manufacturing Institute, which is now open and operational, providing young people with skills for the future and driving innovation in one of our key industries. I also pledged the establishment of a state-owned National Investment Bank. The Scottish National Investment Bank opened for business in 2020 and is already helping power the Scottish economy to a net zero future. It is one of the most important economic initiatives so far of the SNP's time in government.

Significantly, this was also the programme which paved the way for our reform of income tax. The detail was yet to be hammered out and wouldn't come until the budget later that year, but, without it, we wouldn't have been able to provide our public services with even partial protection from austerity. Furthermore, my proudest policy achievement of all, the Scottish Child Payment, would not have been possible.

When I look back at the 2017 programme now, in light of more recent developments, something else strikes me too. Policies which today are hotly contested were, back then, uncontroversial. It later became fashionable to blame environmental policies that caused the SNP political headaches – such as a deposit return scheme, for example – on the 2021 Bute House Agreement with the Greens. In fact, I announced this policy in the 2017 Programme for Government, alongside a proposal for Low Emission Zones for our major cities, four years before the Bute House Agreement was even conceived.

Policies like these became difficult, but not because they are innately problematic. Indeed, I would argue that they are necessary, which is presumably why many other countries have implemented them without controversy. But when an unholy alliance of forces in Scotland decided to co-opt them into the wider culture war discourse and use them to undermine the SNP, then progress was derailed.

Advancing the policy programme I set out in September 2017 occupied me and my government through 2018 and much of 2019. In almost a decade as First Minister, 2018 was the only year that came anywhere close to being free of extraneous distraction, a time when I could concentrate on normal governance.

However, even 2018 couldn't be described as 'normal'. Notably, it was the year that Scotland departed, for the first time, from the UK structure of income tax. From April, the three-band system which had, until then, applied across the UK – basic, higher and additional – was replaced with a new five-band structure.

We froze the basic rate at 20% and introduced a lower, starter band of 19% for the first £2,000 of taxable income. This meant that the majority of taxpayers would pay slightly less than their counterparts elsewhere in the UK. Some people who had previously been in the basic-rate band now found themselves in what we called the intermediate category, paying a rate of 21%. For them, our promise at the 2016 election not to increase their tax rate had been broken. We also increased the higher and additional rates by 1p each, to 41% and 46% respectively.

I remain certain that reforming the system was the right thing to do. It became fairer and more progressive, and millions of pounds of badly needed additional revenue was raised. The suggestion put about by big business and some rich individuals that it would drive wealth out of Scotland proved to be unfounded. We also smashed the conventional wisdom that it was electorally impossible for governments in the UK to raise income tax, proving that politicians with the courage to pick a side and make reasoned, evidenced-based arguments can win support even on the most contentious of issues.

———

Domestic politics aside, it was the interminable Brexit negotiation which dominated 2018. As we moved into 2019, Theresa May's inability to get a deal through Parliament raised real fears of a no-deal exit from the EU, a potential development for which the Scottish government had to do a very significant amount of preparation. The opportunity cost was huge. The time and energy expended by me, my ministers and countless civil servants, not to mention the money spent, could have been much more productively invested elsewhere.

It might not have been obvious publicly, but I felt a fair amount of sympathy for Theresa May during this period. In the early months of 2019, as she suffered no fewer than three humiliating defeats in the House of Commons, I spoke to her reasonably often. I am not claiming that she opened up to me in any way. This was not her style, and, even if it had been, I would not have been her chosen confidante. However, I heard the strain and emotion in her voice on many occasions. It was to her credit that she kept going for as long as she did, in the face of treacherous behaviour from the many charlatans in her own ranks, Boris Johnson chief amongst them.

It was when she went too far in seeking to appease them that my sympathy evaporated. The disgraceful speech she made in Downing Street in March 2019, in which she sought to pitch Parliament against the people, is a case in point. It was a brand of populism that Jacob Rees-Mogg would have been comfortable espousing, and, indeed, it was meant to appeal to MPs like him.

In the early part of 2019, I came under heavy pressure to throw my weight behind a second Brexit referendum, not one on the terms of a deal, but an in/out vote on the principle of Brexit. The pressure was coming mainly from those in the People's Vote campaign in England, chief amongst them Alastair Campbell, Tony Blair's former spin doctor, who was relentless in his efforts to get me on board. I would have loved to see the Brexit decision over-turned, but I had grave doubts about supporting a second vote. I worried about cementing the reputation I had in the minds of some as a politician unable to accept the outcome of referendums. I was also wary of creating a precedent that could be used against us if Scotland ever did vote for independence, with the expectation that the terms of a negotiated independence settlement should be put back to the people for approval.

I held out for a while, convinced that giving my support would be a mistake, not just for me and the SNP, but for the People's Vote campaign too. My belief in independence, and desire for a second referendum on that issue, made it too easy for Brexiteers to dismiss me or, worse still, weaponize me against the pro-EU forces. It was an echo of the concern I'd had back in the 2016 Brexit campaign.

However, as the negotiations became utterly deadlocked and it started to seem that putting the issue back to the people might actually be a possibility, albeit a very slim one, it became harder for me to withhold support. If I was as opposed to Brexit as I claimed to be, why wouldn't I get behind any opportunity to reverse it?

Somewhat against my better judgement then, I put my support behind the second vote campaign. I was a keynote speaker at the huge People's Vote march and rally in London on 22 March 2019 and got a rapturous response. For all the reservations I'd had, it turned out to be the right decision, electorally at least. It helped alleviate the suspicion some harboured that I secretly wanted Brexit to happen so that I could leverage it for independence. Given that Labour under Corbyn was anaemic in its opposition to Brexit, it also allowed me to position the SNP as the only mainstream party in Scotland that was full-throated in our support for EU membership, which served us well in both of the unscheduled elections of 2019.

The first of these was the European Parliament election which took place on 23 May. It was an election that wasn't meant to happen, but the UK's delayed exit from the EU rendered it necessary. It was without doubt the moment of greatest humiliation for Theresa May. For the SNP, it was a triumph. We won 38%, our highest ever vote share in an EU election, and took three of Scotland's six seats. When the results were being declared, I was in Dublin, the only time I have ever watched an election unfold in Scotland from the shores of another country. It was striking just how many people there were in Ireland at that time, politicians and citizens alike, who assumed that Scotland was on the cusp of independence and expressed genuine enthusiasm about the prospect.

The European elections were the final straw for Theresa May. Elections to a Parliament that the UK should have been out of already, and, according to her critics, would have been out of but for her failure to do a deal, made her position untenable. By the time she delivered her emotional speech in Downing Street on 24 May, confirming that she would resign as Tory leader on 7 June, there was little doubt that Boris Johnson, who had done everything possible to undermine her, would be the next Prime Minister. He entered Downing Street on 24 July and visited me in Bute House five days later.

———

Johnson was the third Prime Minister I had hosted in Bute House. These meetings always involved a lot of careful choreography. The details mattered to all of us. For example, when Theresa May visited, there were two saltires in the shot behind us, one behind each of our chairs. I got a lot of online abuse for this, from people accusing me of disrespecting the Union flag. In fact, it was the Number 10 team who vetoed the Union flag, as they hadn't wanted it and the saltire on an equal footing, side by side, giving the impression of two independent countries. Ahead of the Johnson meeting, I told my team to suggest no flags at all, which is what happened.

The planning for such meetings is never straightforward either. However, the sense of chaos which surrounded the Johnson visit was on a different level to anything that had gone before. It is normal on these occasions for the 'principals', the heads of government, to have some private, one-to-one time, before being joined by the armies of civil servants and advisers who are in attendance for the main event. It is in these private sessions that, for better or for worse, relationships are forged and the basis for any concrete outcomes established.

It had been agreed that the PM and I would do media shots in the Bute House drawing room on his arrival and then go through to the Cabinet room for the meeting. My team suggested to his that as everyone else moved through for the meeting, he and I should stay behind for a few minutes alone together. The response from his Chief of Staff, Sir Ed Lister, was adamant. There would be no one-to-one time at all. The subtext appeared to be that they couldn't trust what he might say or agree to with no one else in the room.

It was preposterous, as was the plan I then devised with my team to secure the private meeting we wanted. Essentially, we hatched a plot to kidnap the Prime Minister. We agreed that at the end of the photocall, I would distract Boris while everyone else moved through to the Cabinet room. When all of his team were out of the drawing room, one of my Private Secretaries would close and guard the door, leaving the two of us alone.

The plan worked, and, to be fair to Boris, he seemed unperturbed when he realized what had happened. We ended up chatting for almost half an hour, mainly about Brexit and independence. It was in one sense a breath of fresh air being able to converse so easily with a Prime Minister after the stilted interactions with Theresa May. On the other hand, I was taken aback by how deeply unserious he seemed about everything. It was as if we were in a student debating competition. He appeared much less interested in the substance of what we were discussing than he was in making clever wisecracks and winning debating points. It was dispiriting, but also, at a certain level, fascinating.

What I didn't know at the time was that on the other side of the door his Chief of Staff was, almost literally, trying to wrestle my Private Secretary to the ground in an effort to get back in the room. Eventually, after valiantly seeing him off for almost half an hour, she agreed to interrupt us, and we moved through for the meeting proper.

The formal session was tame and scripted compared to our private conversation. The only moment of drama came when I was pressing him to give the necessary UK government agreement to the establishment of safe consumption rooms for drug users. Scotland suffers a shamefully high number of deaths from drugs misuse every year – the highest in Europe, in fact. The reasons are complex, but it is one of my deepest regrets that I wasn't able to turn the situation around more decisively while First Minister.

One of the steps we had long wanted to take, which experience from other countries suggested would be effective, was to establish a facility in Glasgow where addicts would be supervised by health professionals when taking drugs. The objective was to reduce the risk of overdose or use of infected needles, and to help link drug users with support services. It is about treating the problem from a public health, rather than a criminal justice, perspective.

Drugs law, however, is reserved to Westminster and so we needed the UK government's agreement to progress such an initiative quickly. When I raised the matter with the Prime Minister, he laughed and made a gag about me wanting to establish 'shooting-up galleries'. I was furious and told him so. It was another example of what I quickly came to believe about him, that in his mind, nothing was beyond a joke, no matter the issue.

At the end of the meeting, his protection officers told him they wanted to take him out by the back door of Bute House. He had been loudly booed on the way in. To be fair to him again, he said he'd rather leave by the front door. When his team dug their heels in, however, he turned to me and asked if going out the back door would look OK. To paint a picture, the back door of Bute House is in the basement, two floors below the Cabinet room. It is accessible via a narrow corridor that runs past the kitchen and laundry room and leads out, through a high metal security gate, onto a dingy car park. I told him not to worry, it would look just fine.

From the moment Johnson became Prime Minister, it felt that another General Election was only a matter of time, and so it proved. My sixth electoral test in five years as First Minister came on 12 December 2019. As well as the political challenge of the election, I felt a deeply personal obligation to make up for what I considered to be my failure of 2017. I am not sure anyone else saw it this way, but, in my head, it was an opportunity for redemption.

The campaign felt a world removed from 2017. Our basic message was pretty much the same as it had been then, with opposition to Brexit and a commitment to offer Scotland an alternative future through an independence referendum, but it chimed with the public mood in a way it hadn't two years earlier. The chaos around the Brexit negotiations had turned people even more strongly against it, and as a result we were able to emphasize the anti-Brexit part of our message much more than the independence part, allowing us to maximize our support. We were now, courtesy of Corbyn's political ineptness, the only mainstream voice in Scotland that was unequivocally pro-EU. Just as in the EU election a few months earlier, we were able to sweep up the votes of those who wanted to see Brexit overturned.

We ended up winning 45% of the vote and 48 seats. It wasn't quite the 50% and 56 seats of 2015, but it was much better than the 37% and 35 seats of 2017. Many of my colleagues who had lost their seats in 2017 were re-elected. Politically, I was delighted, but also personally. I had slayed my demons of 2017.

The joy of the election was tempered with personal sadness. On the day we launched the campaign, Peter's dad, my beloved father-in-law, Harry, passed away. Harry and I always got on so well. We shared a taste for gin and tonic and red wine and, at family gatherings, would put the world to rights over a few drinks. I felt his loss very deeply and, though he is not always the most emotionally demonstrative person, I know that it hit Peter really hard.

As 2019 drew to a close, I felt I had got the party back on track. That said, I was well aware that 2020 would bring its share of challenges. We still faced an uphill struggle in securing an independence referendum. More immediately, the Alex Salmond High Court trial on sexual assault charges was looming large. I felt sick in the pit of my stomach every time I thought of it. And though I didn't know it then, I was about to face another scandal relating to inappropriate behaviour, this time at the heart of my government.

———

It was 5 February 2020, early evening, the day before we were due to present our annual budget to the Scottish Parliament. I arrived back in my office after voting in the Chamber to find a couple of very anxious-looking advisers waiting to speak to me. They told me that the *Sun* had been in touch, alleging that Derek Mackay, my Finance Secretary, had sent what they described as inappropriate messages to a sixteen-year-old boy.

Derek had long been a rising star of the SNP. Many thought him my most likely successor as SNP leader and a future First Minister. He was a supremely talented politician. I was also personally very fond of him, having known him since university days. Derek had come out as gay relatively late in life, when he was already a government minister, which meant that his wife (now ex-wife) and two young sons had to deal with the revelation in the full glare of the public eye. It was tough for all of them and I knew it had taken a toll on Derek, but it was obvious that it had made him happier too. I admired his courage.

These allegations came out of the blue. I went into a bit of denial initially, thinking it couldn't possibly be true. Could it? Normally, if a minister got into bother, they'd be summoned to my office, but on this occasion, with some misplaced empathy perhaps, I felt I didn't want to put Derek through the ordeal of walking through my outer office, past staff who already had wind of what was afoot. So I went to find him instead. He was in his office, a copy of the budget speech he would never deliver sitting on the desk in front of him. He was chalk-white and almost totally uncommunicative.

Eventually, he told me that he had been in contact with a young man some time ago, but he didn't think he was as young as sixteen, and he couldn't recall anything in the messages being inappropriate. His responses, which seemed vague to me, combined with his demeanour, shook me out of my denial. Immediately, I felt in my gut that we were dealing with something serious which, politically, Derek would not survive. Even so, I still felt I needed to see the detail of the allegation before telling him to resign. However cagily and unconvincingly, Derek was, after all, denying the pertinent points. It was still possible that the *Sun* was embellishing the story.

In the meantime, I had to make contingency plans for the budget. I asked my team to bring another rapidly rising star, Kate Forbes, the Public Finance Minister, to my office. I told her she had to be ready to step up and deliver the budget the following day. She looked shell-shocked. She was close to Derek, who was her immediate boss, and she was clearly concerned about him. But she remained admirably calm. Even though the budget was ready to go and she had been closely involved in shaping it, the responsibility I was putting on her shoulders was massive.

I was back at Bute House when the *Sun* story went online, late that evening. I felt sick as I read it. The messages were published in full and were not open to benign interpretation. They would be seen by any objective reader as Derek trying to engineer reasons to meet with the boy and to strike up a relationship with him. Given the age difference and the power imbalance, it was impossible to describe the exchanges as anything other than inappropriate. I had received and accepted Derek's resignation within the hour.

The next couple of days were incredibly tough. Derek's resignation had been unavoidable. However, even if the public doesn't always want to acknowledge it, politicians are human beings. The feelings of shock and upset were palpable. For me and my ministerial team, Derek had been a friend as well as a colleague. However, he had made a serious mistake and, rightly, paid the price. He eventually got his life back on track and, though it would be a few years before I spoke to him again, I still count him as a friend.

The episode was also a reminder of the misogyny that is still rife in our society, and the hypocrisy that lurks not far beneath the surface of our media discourse. For neither the first nor the last time, I was hounded by journalists determined to find a way of making me responsible for the sexual behaviour of a man. How could I not have known what he was doing? When had I known? Why hadn't I acted more quickly? Why did I allow him to resign instead of sacking him? It was an interrogation that I do not think I would have been subjected to, in quite the same way, had I been a male leader.

And the hypocrisy? Among the almost exclusively male journalists, all of them with their dictaphones thrust aggressively in my face, spitting morally indignant questions at me, there was at least one who had a reputation for acting inappropriately towards women, and I am pretty certain that his fellow hacks knew it. When it came to suggestions of covering up the sexual misconduct of colleagues, the assembled journalists would have been better advised to look in the mirror.

A shock ministerial resignation aside, the first few months of 2020 were marked by rising concern over a virus. However, there were other matters to be attended to as well.

In the world of any government, normal business is never quiet and rarely calm. In February, Storm Dennis battered the UK and brought serious flooding to parts of the south of Scotland. A day or so later, I donned my wellies to view the damage and commiserate with those whose lives had been turned upside down. Politicians are often criticized for visits like this, but one of the lessons I learned in the job is that when people are suffering, they want political leaders to feel their pain, to show that they care, and often the only way that you can get a sense of that, and a true sense of what they might need from you, is by listening to them directly.

The event which stands out most in my recollection of this twilight period, before we all discovered the brutal reality of living through a pandemic, is one which engaged my heart as much as my head, and which was the culmination of many years' work. In 2016, the organization Who Cares? Scotland had launched a campaign to draw attention to the life-long disadvantages suffered by those who spend some or all of their childhood in care. As part of the campaign, they had asked me to engage with 1,000 young people to hear first-hand their experiences of the care system. These encounters, which happened over many months, affected me profoundly. It is not an exaggeration to say that they changed how I see the world, even my own future. If my life ever calms down enough to make it a healthy environment for a vulnerable child, fostering is something I would love to consider in years to come.

As I listened to these 1,000 voices, I became familiar with statistics that made me feel ashamed of the country I led. At that time, only around four per cent of young people with experience of care went to university. Nearly half suffered mental health issues. A third had experienced homelessness. Around a quarter of all adults in prison had lived in care when they were growing up. I had listened as, time and again, young people told me that the 'system' dehumanized them, that it reinforced rather than healed the trauma they had suffered, that they had been separated from their siblings for no reason other than it was easier for the 'system' than accommodating them together. That they felt stigmatized and unloved.

I had been determined to try to fix it. In October 2016, I had announced a root and branch review of the care system. I had pledged that we would rebuild it from the ground up if necessary, and that its foundation stone, in future, would be love. Any 'system' charged with looking after children and young people must, as its most important duty, make them feel loved and secure.

Back in 2016, I had appointed a brilliant woman, Fiona Duncan – herself care-experienced – to lead the review. She did an outstanding job, and in February 2020, in Bute House, Fiona and some of the young people who had shared their personal experiences with me presented their final report. It gave rise to The Promise, a ten-year programme of work to ensure that all public agencies in Scotland are focused on supporting families better so that fewer young people need care at all; and, for those who do, on making sure we have a system which loves, protects and supports them so that their life chances are as good as anyone else's.

The Promise is still a work in progress. Covid, as it did in so many ways, stalled momentum, which we all have a duty now to recover. But there have still been important steps forward. For example, a dedicated bursary is now helping many more care-experienced young people go to college or university, and there is now a legal presumption against sibling separation. For me, the First Minister who looked those young people in the eye as I made it, The Promise is as personal as it gets, and it always will be.

———

In these early weeks of 2020, there was another issue gnawing away in the background. I hadn't given it much attention at first, but it was starting to get under my skin. For some time, social media had been awash with 'rumours' that I was having a secret relationship with a woman. There were slightly different versions of the story in circulation, but the consistent theme seemed to be that I was having a torrid lesbian affair with the woman who was at that time the French ambassador to the UK, and who would later become the French Foreign Minister, Catherine Colonna. In one of the variants of the story, there had been a violent encounter between us, involving an iron, in Edinburgh's Balmoral Hotel. We had also supposedly set up a love nest, in a house in Bridge of Allan, that I had bought from Andy Murray's mum, Judy.

Normally, I wouldn't have known nor cared about wild stories from the darker recesses of social media, and, if this one had stayed there, it would have been easy to ignore. But by late 2019 it was being openly talked about. My family and friends were being asked about it by people who'd heard it in their local pub or cafe. Colleagues were being asked about it on doorsteps. One of our neighbours in Glasgow mentioned it, obliquely, to Peter, presumably thinking he had a right to know that his wife was having an affair. I was told by a journalist that it was the talk of the London dinner-party circuit (whatever that is!). It seemed it was only a matter of time until the mainstream media found a way of reporting it. They obviously couldn't have covered it as fact (given it wasn't), but if a journalist had asked me about it and I had denied it, they could have reported the denial. This denial, of course, would have required them to disclose the detail of what I was denying.

It all reached a head one Saturday night in February 2020, when the social media site Guido Fawkes tweeted to the effect that a salacious story about my private life was only still secret because I had a superinjunction in place to stop it being reported. I was furious. It was a blatant lie. Not only was there no superinjunction in place, but such a legal remedy isn't even available in Scots law. I asked Liz, my Chief of Staff, to phone the author of the tweet and, after some stalling on his part, it was deleted.

Shortly after, the all-consuming focus on Covid put a stop to the rumour, but only for a while. It would resurface a few months later. I had little option but to shrug it off, however irritating it might have been. Catherine, the French ambassador, helped. She was aware of the rumours too and, the first time I saw her after lockdown, at a meeting of EU ambassadors in the Scottish government's London office, we laughed about it. We were photographed together a couple of times after that, at COP27 in Egypt, for example, and the online frenzy which ensued suggested that we had successfully trolled the trolls.

Although the French ambassador and I could laugh about it, a saga like this does throw up serious issues. How do fake stories like this take root in social media? I have often wondered if this one had its origins in the 2015 Frenchgate saga, the real-life incident involving me and a French ambassador. Did that give some Russian bot factory the raw ingredients to concoct and seed a made-up story? Who knows? But, regardless, having taken root in social media, how do these falsehoods suddenly break out into real life? What instinct makes otherwise reasonable people peddle them with glee, with no consideration of the impact they might have on those whose lives are being gossiped about? These are not trivial questions. From scores of conversations I've had, with young women in particular, I know it is a fear of this kind of phenomenon that makes many of them want to run a million miles from public life.

Then, of course, there is the blatant homophobia at the heart of the 'story'. For many of those peddling it, 'lesbian' and 'gay' are meant as insults. There was naked bigotry behind the attempted smearing of me that deeply disturbs me, because of what it says about the prejudice still prevalent in our society. However, while the fact I was being lied about got under my skin, the nature of the insult itself was water off a duck's back. Long-term relationships with men have accounted for more than thirty years of my life, but I have never considered sexuality, my own included, to be binary. Moreover, sexual relationships should be private matters. One of the things I look forward to as I leave politics is being able to reclaim a private life, to no longer feel that who I am in a relationship with is anyone's business other than my own.

CHAPTER EIGHTEEN

Covid

I can't recall exactly when I first heard news of the mystery illness circulating in the Chinese city of Wuhan, but it must have been sometime in early January, when reports started to appear in UK media. My first official government briefing came on 17 January. It advised me of a cluster of pneumonia cases associated with a novel coronavirus, explained what was known about the virus, which at that stage was very little, and outlined the actions being taken to monitor developments. Although my swine flu experience from 2009 told me that it would take time to understand exactly how serious the situation was, I felt immediately concerned. Indeed, I chaired a meeting of our Resilience Committee to discuss Covid as early as 29 January.

It is hard to know how to write about Covid here. All of us lived through it. Far too many lost loved ones to it. Some of us, in a myriad of different ways, will be living with its legacy for a long time to come. A simple chronology of events with which everyone is painfully familiar, and which most just want to forget, doesn't seem enough and it won't add much to the collective understanding. I am also acutely conscious that, at the time of writing, public inquiries are still underway – one UK-wide and another focusing specifically on Scotland's response. It would be wrong of me to write this account in a way which appears to prejudge, or which could be seen as trying to influence, the conclusions that will be reached.

All I think I can do is give a sense of how it felt from my perspective, as the First Minister who happened to be in office when a global pandemic struck. What guided me through the most impossible decisions I have ever had to take? How did I keep myself upright in the most difficult moments? What are my reflections and regrets?

Before I get to any of that, it is important for me to say my job over this period was tough, but it wasn't the toughest in the country. Nowhere near it. I wasn't caring for desperately sick people in hospital. I wasn't comforting the elderly residents of care homes deprived of visits from their loved ones or watching on as they took their last breaths. I wasn't one of the many people whose jobs were vital to keeping the rest of us supplied with food, fuel and medicines. It is simply not possible to come up with words to convey the depth of my gratitude and admiration for those who, in various different ways, cared for and kept the country going in those dark days. This includes the Scottish government officials who helped me do my job. However inadequate it feels, I want to say thank you to each and every one.

My life also wasn't impacted in the way that many others' were. I didn't lose a loved one to the virus. I didn't even catch it myself until spring 2022, and, although it was an unpleasant experience, I recovered quickly and fully. Nor was I stuck at home during lockdown, trying to hold down a job while home-schooling children.

All of that context makes me feel uncomfortable – guilty, even –

in saying that leading Scotland through Covid was extremely hard, almost indescribably so. At the time, I just did my job, but I know now that it took a heavy toll, physically and mentally. In the weeks leading up to and over the first lockdown, I barely slept more than three or four hours a night. When I look back at photographs of myself from that time, I am shocked at how thin I was. Indeed, if it hadn't been for the flasks of home-made soup sent into St Andrew's House every day by Susan Stewart, my long-time friend and the partner of my then Health Secretary, Jeane Freeman, I doubt I'd have eaten at all during those long days in the office. It was only Susan's insistence that Jeane take the empty flask home to her each evening, as proof that I'd eaten the soup, which made me stop long enough to get it down. For most of 2020, I existed in a permanent state of nervous tension. It took a grip of me in late January and didn't let go for months after.

When I think back to early 2020, what I remember most is how frightened I felt. I was scared of the toll that would be taken on the country and I had a deep dread about the number of lives that might be lost. I was also overwhelmed by the weight of responsibility. I have spoken before about the imposter syndrome that has stalked me throughout my life, but the voice in my head telling me I might not be up to the job had never been louder than it was then.

On one day, I was shown the latest version of what is known as the Reasonable Worst-Case Scenario, an estimate of what might happen if preventative action wasn't taken. I remember it vividly. It painted a horrifying picture. It estimated that the death toll in Scotland alone could be as high as 68,000. I didn't sleep a wink that night. I lay awake thinking that before long we would all know someone in our circle of family and friends who was seriously ill or dead.

The necessity of lockdown is questioned much more now than it was at the time. Of course the decisions taken back then must be rigorously scrutinized, but the passage of time and the benefit of hindsight mustn't distort the brutal reality we were facing in those early months of 2020. Far too many lives were lost in the pandemic, but lockdown averted the worst-case scenario. Without it, the death toll would have been much higher. At the time, there were no vaccines or effective treatments and, in short, we had no other 'tools in the box'. Thanks to lockdown and, crucially, the public's compliance with it, tens of thousands of lives were saved. The doubt and regret I carry is that it took too long for us to arrive at it.

In the face of the intense fear I was feeling, I kept telling myself that all I could do was my level best. That might sound unremarkable. Leaders should always do their best. I like to think I always have. But, in this context, it meant stripping out any consideration of what might make me or my party popular, or the reverse. I resolved to take the soundest decisions I could, based on the best information and advice I had, regardless of what it might mean for me politically. I knew that everything I did would have consequences. Every decision designed to mitigate one harm would inevitably cause another. That was the nature of the situation we faced. My duty, in the face of it, was to try to keep the country as safe as possible.

I knew that I wouldn't be able to take every decision personally, and those I did take would depend on the advice of many others. The Health Secretary, Jeane Freeman, in particular, was steadfast, shouldering huge responsibility herself, but also giving me great support. However, given the unprecedented nature of what those decisions would entail, I knew I needed to bear more than my fair share of the burden. I was the First Minister. The buck had to stop with me. It could be no other way. This realization created a strange paradox. I was the most fearful I had ever been in my life, but I felt greater focus and clarity of purpose than ever before too.

By early March 2020, I was frantically worried that we weren't doing enough, quickly enough, to slow the virus down. The scenes we were seeing from northern Italy of people struggling to breathe and hospitals buckling under pressure were terrifying. The public, several steps ahead of their politicians it seemed, were demanding action. I was being advised that the timing of interventions was critical. If we acted too soon to impose restrictions on daily life, public compliance would erode too quickly. I understood, but was concerned that we were running out of time to take ourselves out of the path of the avalanche heading our way.

We were working closely at this time with the UK government, as well as the Welsh and Northern Irish administrations. I knew we were dependent on Westminster for financial support, and I also didn't want it to seem as if I was trying to score political points, so I didn't voice my concerns publicly. But I did try to force the pace. In mid-March, we moved more quickly than the other governments to ban mass gatherings and close schools. I hoped this would prompt the others to follow suit, and it did, though the pace was already picking up because of the exponential rise in cases.

Even so, by the time of the weekend before lockdown, there was still a sense of dither and prevarication. A meeting of the UK government's emergency response unit, COBRA, late on the afternoon of Friday, 20 March 2020, illustrates the point. I was in the bunker in St Andrew's House, accompanied by the Health Secretary Jeane Freeman, the Chief Medical Officer and various other officials on the call. Also on call with their respective teams were Boris Johnson and the leaders of Wales and Northern Ireland.

The meeting had been called to discuss the urgent advice the four governments had received from clinical advisers to close pubs and other hospitality businesses. I was clear in my mind that it was advice we had to follow, but it was obvious that Johnson was reluctant. Eventually, he conceded that closure was unavoidable, but insisted that he didn't want it taking effect until the following day.

There was a kind of stunned silence on the call for a few seconds before many of us piled in to point out how calamitous that would be. The risk of people crowding into the pubs later that night for one last hurrah, thinking that it must be safe because their governments were allowing it, and therefore turbo-charging the spread of infection, was enormous. After some discussion, agreement was eventually reached that closure should take effect immediately. I was relieved, but the episode was an early indication of just how much resistance there was, even at that stage, and especially on the part of Boris Johnson, to taking firm and decisive action. It was also a portent of some of the disagreements that would arise between me and Johnson later in the pandemic.

I didn't have the financial powers to support a Scotland-only lockdown. However, even though I probably wouldn't have succeeded, I wish now that I had used my voice to press harder to get the UK into lockdown sooner. I don't believe that an earlier lockdown would have saved us from the impact of Covid, but might it have reduced the toll? I can't know for certain, but my gut says yes, and I suspect the public inquiries will conclude likewise. Either way, the doubt will haunt me for ever.

By the time the lockdown decision was taken by COBRA, late on the afternoon of Monday, 23 March, I felt huge relief. By sheer coincidence, it came on the same day Alex Salmond was acquitted of the charges against him. A trial I had dreaded for months ended up almost passing me by, such was the enormity of what we were dealing with.

On lockdown, the four UK governments were in agreement, but there was a further hint of tension to come. In announcing the decision, Boris Johnson refused point-blank to use the term 'lockdown'. Bluntly, I thought that was stupid. 'Lockdown' was the phrase already being used by the public for what we were now asking them to do – stay at home. Given how important public understanding and compliance was, it made no sense not to use terminology that was already widely understood. I was reluctant to break ranks completely, so I came up with the compromise of describing our decision as 'effective lockdown'. Even that seemed to annoy Johnson and his allies.

Much later, they would accuse me of always trying to steal a march, of vying to be the first to announce UK-wide decisions, the suggestion being that I was doing so for political reasons. It was nonsense and deeply insulting. Despite our political disagreements, I genuinely tried hard throughout the pandemic to foster a good working relationship with the UK government. In fact, the lockdown announcement was the only occasion on which the sequencing of public statements was even discussed and I agreed that the Prime Minister should speak first, with my Scottish press conference following only when he had finished. More generally, in these early days, the air of chaos around UK government decision-making was such that the likely timing of Johnson's pronouncements was rarely clear. Had I sat around waiting for him to go first, I would have been neglecting to do my own job. Our task was to slow down the rapid spread of an infectious virus, which meant that, once taken, our decisions had to be communicated quickly and clearly. That is what I sought to do. The scheduling of my media briefings quickly became fixed at 12.15 p.m., and it was Boris Johnson's decision to schedule those from the UK government for late afternoon.

——

In the days following lockdown, amidst the mountain of work that had to be done across the entirety of government, we managed to establish a good rhythm of decision-making and reporting. My daily briefings were critical to this. I did more than 250 of these over the course of the pandemic. Given the enormity of the sacrifices people were being asked to make, I felt instinctively that explaining exactly what was being asked of the public, and why, was vital. I also felt that people needed to know that governments didn't have all the answers, that we were dealing with huge uncertainty and very limited knowledge, so missteps were inevitable. I didn't want to be defensive about the things we got wrong. I was determined to be up front and learn from any mistakes we made. The briefings were my attempt to bring the public into the room where the decisions were being taken. I figured that high compliance with our decisions depended on a good understanding of why we were making them.

What I didn't realize at the outset is how important the briefings would become for my own ability to cope. Knowing that I had to stand in front of the nation every day to explain the government's decisions meant there was no hiding place. I had to make absolutely sure that I fully understood the advice and rationale underpinning our decisions. Having to exude to the public a sense of calm amidst the chaos, but also openly sharing some of the impossible choices and uncertainties we were grappling with, helped me achieve a level of composure and focus that wasn't always present when I woke up in the morning.

Most importantly, it became clear quite quickly that the

briefings were a crucial source of support for the public. I started to receive emails from people across the country, and more than a few from south of the border, telling me how much they valued and relied upon the information provided. They made it clear that it was helping them understand how to keep themselves and their loved ones as safe as possible. As the weeks passed, I realized that there was a strong emotional element at play too. A lot of people told me that understanding the data and scientific advice was mitigating their sense of powerlessness. Some told me that scheduling their lunchbreaks around the briefings was helping give structure to days stuck at home. Others, especially those living alone, told me that tuning in every day was making them feel less isolated. It wasn't uncommon, especially on the most stressful days, for messages like these to make me cry. However, knowing that what I was doing was helping others cope made me feel stronger too.

The impact of these briefings wasn't just down to me and the Scottish government team. A Scottish comedian called Janey Godley started posting satirical videos online, in which she would apply her own voice-overs to my briefings. Her sign-off to these videos, me supposedly saying, 'Frank, get the door,' to a mythical aide as I exited the stage, became a viral catch-phrase of the time. These voice-overs were hysterically funny and the importance of making people laugh during that dark period should not be underestimated. However, they had a more serious function too. Through humour, Janey communicated vital public health messages to people who would never normally have listened to a politician speaking from a government podium. Janey died at the end of 2024. Her legacy is a rich one and part of it was helping save lives during the pandemic.

Beside me in the briefings was the Chief Medical Officer, Catherine Calderwood. She was a good communicator and became the trusted clinical voice of our early public health messages. As

Health Secretary, I had developed a close working relationship with Catherine's predecessor, Harry Burns, but, at the outset of the pandemic, I didn't know her particularly well at all. We quickly established a good rapport and a high degree of mutual respect. She became the principal conduit of clinical advice to me and helped me make sense of the vast amount of information I was having to process on a daily basis. She also provided a constructive challenge to my thinking, and me to hers. We made a good team.

It was the strength and centrality of that relationship which made what happened next so difficult to handle. On the evening of Saturday, 4 April, I took a call from one of my special advisers, Ross Ingebrigtsen, to tell me that the *Sun* had photos of Catherine visiting her holiday home in Fife and intended to publish them in the next day's paper. If true, this would have been a blatant breach of the guidance she was asking others to follow.

I was stunned and, initially, disbelieving. There must be a rational explanation. I called Catherine immediately to get her side of the story. She was shaken and apologetic, but there was no getting round the fact that the essence of the *Sun*'s claim was accurate. She had gone with her family over that weekend to her second home. It later transpired, after some initial confusion, that she had gone there the previous weekend too. She had interacted with no one other than her family unit. No one had been at any risk as a result of her actions. But there was no doubt she had broken the rules.

With hindsight, I should have told her immediately that resignation was necessary and inevitable. Not only would it have avoided hours of mounting public anger, but it would also have been kinder to her. She would have been spared the excruciating press conference that she endured the following day. Had I asked her to resign straight away, I doubt she would have resisted. Having made a serious error of judgement, she never tried to evade responsibility. On the contrary, she displayed genuine concern for the impact her actions might have had on public health and the integrity of our messaging. So, why didn't I ask her to resign straight away?

I knew that protecting trust in the public health messages was paramount. But Catherine had been playing such a central role in our pandemic response that I feared it would be severely disrupted if we lost her from the team. As a result, I tried to square the circle. Catherine would profusely apologize, as she wanted to do anyway, and I would make clear there was no excuse for her breaching the rules. However, I would appeal to the public to see the bigger picture. Losing an experienced Chief Medical Officer at this juncture was in no one's best interests.

I don't think any of this was unreasonable. However, as I quickly came to realize, to a country in which emotions were raw and running high, it must have seemed like the worst kind of politician response: detached and tone-deaf. People were furious that someone in her position had acted as if the rules didn't apply, at a time when they were making enormous sacrifices to do the right thing.

In an hour-long press conference on Sunday, 5 April, I tried to take as much of the heat as I could. This was my decision and not something she had asked me to do. Unsurprisingly, I was pummelled by journalist after journalist. I had no sooner arrived back in my office, when I took a call from John Swinney asking if I was sure that resisting her resignation was the right thing to do. My Chief of Staff, Liz Lloyd, was also worried that I was making the wrong call. As I mulled it all over on my journey home later that evening, feeling increasingly uneasy, I knew in my gut that I was in the wrong place. I also knew that if I stayed in that place, it wasn't just Catherine's credibility that would be shot. My own would be fatally undermined too. And, if that happened, if people stopped listening to me at a time when compliance with our decisions was literally the difference between life and death, the entire country would be in deep trouble and it would be my fault.

By the time I got home, I knew Catherine had to resign. The call I then made to her was incredibly difficult. She had been a fantastic Chief Medical Officer – dedicated, committed and innovative. She had made a very bad error of judgement, but at no point have I thought it was motivated by a reckless disdain for the public. We were all working under extreme stress. She figured that taking her family bubble to their home in Fife, seeing no one else along the way, would give her space to think for a few hours and bolster her mental resilience for the challenges to come. She was absolutely wrong in that judgement, but that's what it was: a misjudgement, for which she paid a very heavy price. When I spoke to her, she had reached the same conclusion as me. She could have dug her heels in, as I had no actual power to sack her, but she didn't. She accepted responsibility and did the right thing, in a way that other senior figures caught breaking the rules did not. This is to her credit.

Losing Catherine was a massive blow, and it took me a few days to settle into a new way of working. Her deputy, Gregor Smith, stepped up to fill the role and, alongside the National Clinical Director, Jason Leitch, provided excellent advice and support. It was a really tough episode, but, thankfully, for the country, there was no lasting damage.

In the days and weeks after Catherine's resignation, I periodically checked in to see how she was. I knew she had taken it hard, and I was worried about her. After the Covid restrictions lifted, we would catch up occasionally for coffee or a drink, and gradually became pals.

The day after her resignation, there was another dramatic

development. On Monday, 6 April, Boris Johnson, who had tested positive for Covid, was admitted to intensive care in London. It was a moment in which the existential peril of the pandemic truly hit people. Whatever the science said, if it could fell even a Prime Minister, no one was safe. I remember feeling profoundly shaken by it and also fearing the worst. As I got dressed for work early on Tuesday morning, I wondered if I should wear black. It was horrible. When I sent Boris good wishes from my lunchtime briefing, I felt myself welling up.

Learning to allow the raw emotion of those early days to sit alongside the need to be professional and rational, to take good decisions, was hard. It was also necessary. I knew I couldn't allow emotion to overwhelm me or drive my decisions. On the other hand, I didn't want to suppress it. I was feeling just as disorientated as everyone else was. I was missing my family and my sense of normality. I thought it important for the public to know that I wasn't detached from what they were feeling; that I understood, and felt, the impact of the decisions I was taking. Getting the balance right wasn't easy.

As the weeks passed, over the spring and into the summer of 2020, the nature of the challenge changed. For one thing, the political consensus that had held firm over the initial period of the pandemic started to fracture. The compliance of the public, underpinned by a strong sense of responsibility and solidarity, held firm. Lockdown only worked because people the length and breadth of Scotland abided by it. Indeed, the early advice that interventions had to be carefully timed because the public's patience wouldn't hold for long turned out to be wide of the mark. The Scottish people were the heroes of our Covid response.

However, with me dominating the airwaves and a Scottish Parliament election less than a year away, opposition politicians quickly reverted to type. Of course, in certain respects, it was important that they did so. Robust scrutiny of the decisions we were taking was crucial. This was especially so given their impact on everyday life, not to mention that they were being made, by and large, under emergency legislation. Mistakes and misjudgements were inevitable in the unprecedented situation we faced. The opposition had a vital role to play in making sure lessons were learned.

Tiredness sometimes made me tetchy when I was being questioned by journalists at the daily briefings or by other politicians in Parliament, but I didn't resent the scrutiny. On the contrary, I welcomed it, even when it was uncomfortable. What bothered me were the claims that our mistakes were rooted in bad faith, and the repeated attempts to manufacture 'scandals' out of situations with perfectly rational explanations. Rightly or wrongly, I know that in normal times this is the stuff of politics, but deliberately manipulating events to erode the trust of the public in their government during a deadly pandemic was irresponsible. It often felt like the motive was to undermine rather than enhance the effectiveness of our response.

Nothing exemplified this better than the furore around an international Nike conference that had taken place in Edinburgh in late February. The second person in Scotland who tested positive for Covid had attended this conference. The case was publicly reported on 2 March and contact tracing was done in the normal way. Public Health Scotland established an Incident Management Team to oversee efforts to contain spread of the virus from cases associated with the conference. A genomics study conducted a few months later confirmed that these efforts had been successful. There had been a total of thirty-nine cases directly or indirectly linked to the conference, only eight of them in Scotland, but infection control measures had curtailed onward transmission.

The 'scandal' arose from the decision, which I take full responsibility for, not to disclose the link between some of the early Covid positive cases in Scotland and the Nike conference. When the connection came to light a few weeks later, claims of a deliberate 'cover-up' ensued. It was no such thing. The advice that I had received from the Chief Medical Officer not to disclose details of the conference was grounded in patient confidentiality. Only seventy-one people had attended the conference and just ten of them lived in Scotland, with the others hailing from England, Ireland and the Netherlands. Given the low number of cases at this time, there was a concern that labelling any of them as Nike conference delegates would risk patient identification. I wasn't entirely comfortable with it, but, on balance, I accepted this advice. With hindsight, I think it was the wrong call. Openness and transparency were vital to building and maintaining public trust. It was a mistake not to be explicit about the Nike link at the outset. But it was an error of judgement in a complicated situation, and one which had, as the genomic study had shown, no impact whatsoever on the overall spread of the virus. That didn't stop the opposition, for months afterwards, claiming that it had all been a sinister and malicious cover-up, though for what purpose they could never quite explain.

The public didn't buy it. People were able to listen to my daily briefings and make their own minds up, which helped build an exceptionally high level of trust in me and the Scottish government. This trust was priceless. As I tried to get the country out of lockdown and back to a semblance of normality, I needed every ounce of it.

———

Taking a country into lockdown, instructing the public to stay in their own homes, for all but the most exceptional of reasons, is one of the most momentous decisions any leader can be faced with. I quickly discovered that decisions about the pace and sequencing of bringing a country back out of lockdown are, if anything, even more difficult. I had access to excellent advice from the Scottish government's in-house experts, and from external academics and public health doctors who sat on an advisory council that I had asked the Chief Medical Officer to establish in the early weeks of the pandemic. From my point of view, I had quickly become frustrated by the limitations of the UK-wide Scientific Advisory Group on Emergencies (SAGE). It wasn't that I doubted the quality of its advice, but I had no direct access to those providing it, to ask questions or challenge anything I was unsure about. SAGE advice was also geared towards UK government decisions; it understandably didn't give much consideration to the differing approaches of the devolved governments or the variations in demography or health systems in the four UK countries. Our own advisory council was chaired by eminent scientist Professor Andrew Morris and included experts like Professor Devi Sridhar, whose media appearances throughout the pandemic were also vital in helping the public understand what was happening.

There was enormous concern that, as we lifted restrictions, the virus would wreak its revenge. Contained so effectively by lockdown, would it rage through the population? Would our worst-case estimates about illness and deaths rematerialize? The overwhelming clinical advice was to be careful and cautious, an approach which aligned with my own instincts. I wanted to get the country back to normal as quickly as possible, but I was convinced that slow and steady was the surer way to do it. Letting the virus run amok would only set us back and make a return to normal life even more difficult. This cautious approach did create more complexity. Being told to stay at home was easy to understand, even if it was very difficult to do. When that straightforward advice was replaced with a complex, and frequently changing, set of rules, it was hardly surprising that tolerance started to wane. There were places that we could go and those we couldn't; rules on how many people we were allowed to gather with, indoors and out, and stipulations on the precise distance we had to maintain. What was truly remarkable is how patient people were and how hard they tried to still do the right thing.

Over the summer, the Scottish government followed a policy of maximum suppression. This was sometimes wrongly equated with the 'zero Covid' approach that a few countries, such as New Zealand, had been pursuing. It was a controversial approach in some quarters. Many in the business community thought they were being subjected to trading restrictions for longer than necessary and in pursuit of a goal that was unattainable. Of course, I knew that achieving and sustaining zero cases of Covid was impossible in a country as integrated to the wider world as Scotland is, and that wasn't what we were seeking to do.

We were instead trying to keep transmission as controlled as possible. Ahead of a vaccine being available, it was the only way to minimize the damage of Covid. In blunt terms, it was about trying to save lives. But it also seemed obvious to me that if the virus ran out of control again, public panic and a need to protect the NHS from being overwhelmed would push us back into another tight lockdown.

I believe it is an approach which ultimately saved lives. The number of lives lost to Covid in Scotland was far too high, but our age-standardized mortality over the course of the pandemic was lower, by a not insignificant margin, than in other parts of the UK.

I understood the stresses and frustrations of men and women across the country who were running businesses and desperately trying to stay afloat in the grimmest of conditions. I knew the almost impossible balancing acts they had to perform every day to protect lives and livelihoods, and I had massive respect for them as a result.

Our maximum suppression approach also contributed to growing tension with the UK government over the summer of 2020, as it started to pull in a different direction. Boris Johnson was keen to lift restrictions much more quickly than Scotland, Wales or Northern Ireland were comfortable with, even if it meant living with a higher level of transmission. With an unvaccinated population, this seemed reckless to me.

The first flashpoint came in early May when, without any consultation whatsoever with the devolved administrations, the UK government dropped the 'Stay at Home, Protect the NHS, Save Lives' advice that we had all used since the start of lockdown, replacing it with the much vaguer 'Stay Alert'. All three of the devolved administrations declined to follow suit, sticking instead with the original messaging. Indeed, this underlines a point that was often lost. Although the Scottish government was regularly accused of pursuing a different course through the pandemic for the sake of it, or perhaps for political effect, it was almost always the case that the positions of the devolved administrations were aligned. The outlier, invariably, was the UK government.

This tension continued, to a greater or lesser extent, throughout the summer. By this time, Johnson wasn't engaging directly with the devolved administrations very much at all, leaving that largely to Michael Gove. Whenever he did grace us with his presence, I would be taken aback all over again by how unserious he was. The fact that this was a virus that had come close to taking his own life made his attitude all the more inexplicable. The peak of my frustration came with Rishi Sunak's 'Eat Out to Help Out' scheme in summer 2020. Again, it was a policy that the Scottish government was not consulted on, nor did we have any ability to opt out of it. We just had to sit back and watch the UK government hand people a financial incentive to, effectively, fuel a second wave of a potentially deadly virus. It was infuriating, and I was powerless to do anything about it. I don't think anyone could ever convince me that lives weren't lost as a result of that initiative.

These frustrations were real, and they had consequences. The root cause was the unwillingness of the UK government both to respect the autonomy and parity of esteem of Scottish, Welsh and Northern Irish ministers and to understand the impact of their decisions on our areas of responsibility.

Despite the tensions and disagreements, the four governments did manage to work together effectively on many occasions, a fact that is often overlooked. Indeed, one of our most difficult moments arose from a collective decision to ease restrictions for a few days in the run-up to Christmas 2020. After months of family separation, we were all keen to allow some respite over the festive period. Even so, I was very anxious about its potential to fuel a new wave of infection. On the other hand, I was acutely aware that if I tried to deny people in Scotland the same freedom to see loved ones over Christmas as those in other parts of the UK were being given, I might lose their trust and forbearance, and the risk associated with that going into 2021 was also significant.

Despite all my reservations, I signed up to the four-nation agreement and told myself it was the right decision. However, the ink had barely dried when the Kent (later named Alpha) variant hit us like a truck. The speed of transmission and the initial uncertainty about whether the new variant would lead to more severe illness left all four governments in an impossible position. We had no choice but to take away many of the proposed Christmas 'freedoms'. Plans that families had been given the go-ahead to make, celebrations that children had been allowed to get excited about, were about to be snatched away. After all the sacrifices that people had made, it was the cruellest of blows.

I broke the news at a media briefing late on the afternoon of Saturday, 19 December. Without doubt, this was my lowest moment in nine miserable months of dealing with the virus. I knew how hard it would be for people to handle the news. I had been looking forward to time with my own family too, so I shared the distress. I struggled to get through the briefing without breaking down. When I eventually got home later that evening, the floodgates opened. My inbox was heaving with howls of anguish and a fair bit of understandable anger too. Most people weren't blaming me, but I felt responsible. I knew it wasn't rational – after all, the arrival of a new variant wasn't my fault – but I couldn't help it. I spent the evening, well into the early hours, sitting on my sofa, drinking far too much wine and crying. In that moment, I wasn't sure I could cope for much longer.

———

I did cope, obviously. And, while 2021 was still very tough, with lots of ups and downs on the Covid rollercoaster, the arrival of the vaccines made everything progressively easier to handle. The speed with which effective vaccines were developed and manufactured after Covid struck must be one of the most impressive scientific achievements of our generation. Those who worked round the clock to make it possible, including the Oxford University / AstraZeneca team in the UK, deserve all of the plaudits that came their way. The first doses of vaccine were administered in Scotland on 8 December 2020. It was an emotional moment. For the first time in what felt like for ever, there was light at the end of the tunnel. I recall sitting down after my daily briefing that day feeling less anxious about Covid than at any time since February.

There were still challenges and setbacks to come, of course. The emergence of the Delta and Omicron variants would throw us off course in the spring and then the winter of 2021. Campaigning in the Scottish Parliament election in May was a strange experience, given the restrictions still in place. The dining room of my house became a makeshift TV studio. It was from there – just me speaking to a camera – that I launched our election manifesto. During the campaign, an outbreak took hold in the South Asian communities of my Glasgow Southside constituency and the situation across the city remained difficult for weeks after, as it did in other parts of Scotland, most notably Aberdeen and the north-east. In the summer, the delayed Euro football championship was staged, with matches played in Glasgow, albeit in front of limited crowds, and a huge fan zone in Glasgow Green. I was beside myself with anxiety about the possible impact of the fan zone, but, thankfully, it passed without incident. I was similarly worried about the COP climate change conference in Glasgow in November. Here, though, we struck lucky, as the summit ended before Omicron took hold. Had it not, COP might have become the mother of all super-spreader events. Omicron would pose enough of a challenge without that being added to the mix.

Very slowly but surely, an increasingly vaccinated Scotland found its way back to normal, or what, in the post-Covid world, now passed for normal.

I find it hard, even today, to look back on Covid without a torrent of emotion. It was the hardest period of my career, possibly my life. I have found myself pausing as I write this, wondering if

I am expressing it too strongly, but I don't think I am. I am still haunted by the impact of the decisions I took and those I didn't take. I still agonize over what I might have done differently. I think part of me always will. Should – could – I have taken the country into lockdown sooner? Given constraints on testing, and our imperfect understanding of asymptomatic transmission, could we have protected older people in care homes better than we did? Did we worry too much about hospitals being overrun? Could we have mitigated more of the impacts on those most vulnerable to infection, or on those who were always destined to bear the deepest and longest-term consequences of lockdown?

Based on what we know now, the answers to some of these questions might be yes. But based on what we knew then? I really don't know. It will be for others – history – to judge. The UK and Scottish Covid Inquiries are crucial to our collective understanding. They also matter for accountability and the learning of lessons. Nothing I say here is intended to question the vital work they are doing.

However, this is a personal account, and it wouldn't be complete if I didn't talk about my appearance at the UK Covid Inquiry in January 2024.

———

The period between standing down as First Minister and stepping into the Inquiry witness box in the Edinburgh International Conference Centre on 31 January 2024 had not been stress-free. Far from it. Somehow, though, I had coped.

However, in the days and weeks after my appearance at the Inquiry, I came perilously close to a breakdown. Without everything else I'd faced over the preceding year, I suspect that the impact on me wouldn't have been anywhere near as bad as it was. But, in the event, the Inquiry became the straw that almost broke the camel's back. For a while afterwards, I could barely function. I cried, on and off, for days on end. On some mornings, getting out of bed was difficult, and leaving my house even more so. I lost any sense of perspective. I told myself I was personally responsible for every life lost to the virus. I was impervious to reason.

The support of my close friends helped, though I did my best to hide how I was feeling from my family. I had also received an avalanche of positive messages from members of the public in the days after my appearance. These really helped. However, for the first time in my life, I sought professional help. It took several counselling sessions before I was able to pull myself back from the brink. I want to stress again that I am not criticizing the Inquiry. It had the right to examine whatever it considered necessary. I am simply explaining how the experience made me feel.

I had painstakingly prepared. However, as I discovered when I found myself crying on the witness stand, I hadn't properly considered the emotional impact of being confronted with everything my worst critics wanted people to believe of me. That in managing Covid, I was politically motivated. That I had acted in bad faith. That I hadn't been transparent. That I was a control freak. I had expected tough questioning on the substance and quality of the decisions I had reached. I know that, even in trying to do right, I got many things wrong, and I feel as strongly as anyone that lessons must be learned from the mistakes we made – from the mistakes I made.

However, the thought that people might doubt my motives devastates me. It must be the worst charge that can be made against a leader – that in the face of a deadly crisis, they acted in a manner that was selfish or self-serving. I know, in my heart and soul, that I did not. I know that whatever mistakes I made, I made them in good faith. I know that I kept the promise I made to myself to do the best I could. In the period after my appearance at the Inquiry, however, I completely lost touch with that and allowed the very worst caricatures of myself to take root in my mind.

It was a dark time. Thankfully, it passed. But while it lasted, it frightened me. I have never felt so utterly adrift from any rational sense of who I am, or so completely unable to find any lightness in life.

CHAPTER NINETEEN

The Final Phase

It seems obvious to me now that my days as First Minister were numbered as soon as Covid was behind us. It had exhausted me. I had taken almost no time off at all during the first year of the pandemic, not a single day, in fact, not even at weekends, from around February 2020 until the end of that year. The closest I came was my fiftieth birthday – 19 July – but even then I ended up overseeing the management of an outbreak at an office complex in Lanarkshire.

My physical exhaustion wasn't the issue though. I was mentally worn out too. The weight of the responsibility day after day, the fear of what the consequences might be if I took the wrong decisions, had taken a heavy toll. My perspective had also changed. I was not the politician after Covid that I had been before it. I had little appetite for a return to politics as usual, for the cut and thrust of it all, and none whatsoever for the increasingly toxic discourse that dominated my final months in office.

However, if all of this seems obvious to me in retrospect, it certainly wasn't obvious at the time. I went into the 2021 Holyrood election fully intending to serve a full term, or close to it. I had always vaguely assumed I would lead the SNP through another UK election, likely to be sometime in 2024. By then, I would have served a decade as First Minister. It would be a milestone moment and a good time to exit the stage. I figured that standing down then would also give my successor time to get established ahead of the 2026 Scottish election.

The 2021 election was fought in the shadow of Covid. The fallout from the Salmond saga, which led him to set up his own party, gave it a slightly unpleasant edge. But there was never any doubt that the SNP would win handsomely. Public perceptions of my handling of Covid cemented the certainty of victory. Yet again, though, we fell just short of an overall majority – sixty-four seats instead of the sixty-five needed.

Given the scale of our win, and the near impossibility of winning a majority under the Holyrood system, it is irrational to harbour a sense of failure. But I did. It was the one thing electorally that Alex had achieved as leader that I didn't. The fact that I had achieved a great deal that he hadn't made no difference to me. My regret about falling short wasn't just some weird inferiority complex vis-à-vis Alex, though. More importantly, I knew it would make it harder to secure the transfer of legal power needed for an independence referendum. There was no guarantee that the UK government would have yielded if we had secured a majority, but, without it, it was virtually certain that they wouldn't.

As 2021 wore on into 2022, the sense that I was banging my head against a brick wall on independence began to wear me down too. I felt I was caught between the impatience of some of my supporters on the one hand and the increasingly nasty vilification of my opponents on the other. My time, and my patience, were running out.

Even so, there were some triumphs and dramas yet to come. I wouldn't have wanted it any other way.

———

Towards the end of 2021, Glasgow played host to the annual United Nations summit on climate change. COP26 had been due to take place the year before, but Covid had forced a delay. The UK had secured host status in late 2019, not long after Boris Johnson became Prime Minister. Without doubt, part of the UK government's motivation for bringing COP26 to Glasgow was political. It was about flexing the UK's muscle in my and the SNP's backyard. The subliminal message was that Scotland had much more clout as part of the UK than it ever would as an independent country.

Given that sticking it to me and the Scottish government was part of the purpose of hosting the summit, it has always perplexed me that when COP26 eventually came around, Johnson did not do more to capitalize on it. Instead, he ceded the ground almost entirely to me. Perhaps it is just another example of his short attention span. He had already lost interest in something that, just a couple of years earlier, had seemed to be a big priority.

For all that base politics was part of the reason the summit ended up in Glasgow, it would be wrong to say it was Johnson's only motivation. This was also a period, all too brief in retrospect, when there seemed to be genuine seriousness of purpose on the part of both the UK and Scottish governments about tackling climate change together.

In April 2019, I had declared a climate emergency, making Scotland one of the first countries to do so. There is a lot of scepticism about such grand declarations, and understandably so. Undoubtedly they involve an element of performance, but there is also a practical point. For me, it was about trying to focus the entirety of the Scottish government on climate change as a mission, preparing the ground for the tough changes it would entail, and also sending a signal to green investors that Scotland was open for business.

My increasing determination to prioritize climate action was also the main driver of my decision to strike a partnership agreement with the Scottish Greens after the 2021 election. There were other reasons at play too. At the tail end of the last Parliament, embroiled in the Salmond saga and worn down by Covid, I had become weary of the opportunism and perpetual game-playing of opposition parties. It was partly a result of electoral frustration, but they had become impervious to any attempts to build cross-party consensus. Instead, every issue was judged for its potential to bring down a minister. Having again fallen just short of a majority in 2021, I knew that five more years of deeply dispiriting trench warfare was a likely prospect. The majority cemented by the Green deal – a pro-independence majority into the bargain – changed that.

I also wanted to champion or at least try out a more constructive style of politics. The SNP and Greens don't agree on everything, but surely what we did have in common was worth working together for? There was an unspoken aspect to this, which I didn't even share with some of my closest advisers. If we could make a success of the partnership agreement, might an electoral pact at the next Scottish election be desirable? With the SNP focusing on constituency seats and the Greens on the list, could we maximize our combined seat tally? I wasn't yet sure in my own mind about it and, even if I had been, I knew it wouldn't be easy to convince my party, but I thought it might be a possibility.

However, as COP26 loomed, it was the desire to force the pace on the climate crisis that was at the front of my mind. I regularly attended COP summits as First Minister. I had been there in 2015 when the Paris Agreement had been struck, binding countries to limit the global temperature increase to 2 degrees Celsius above pre-industrial levels, and had attended all bar one of the subsequent gatherings. I don't think it is an empty boast to say that I had established a degree of international profile and credibility for both me and the country on climate issues.

I care deeply and genuinely about climate change and I see tackling it as both a moral imperative and a massive economic opportunity. The countries with the boldest ambition will reap the rewards in innovation, investment and jobs. I wanted Scotland to be at the front of the queue. I also wanted COP26 in Glasgow to be a roaring success.

Had Boris Johnson asked me to be part of the formal UK negotiating team, I would have agreed in an instant. I also think I would have brought something positive to the table. As co-chair of the Under 2 Coalition, one of the organizations which brings together so-called subnational governments, I had different contacts and influence to leverage. It would also have been a more effective way for him to make his political point about the combined clout of the UK.

Instead, he or those around him chose to brief the media that I would be kept on the fringes and away from the main event (something which, as it turned out, they failed to do). Hilariously, they even briefed that one of the UK government's main objectives for the summit was to prevent me getting a photograph with Joe Biden. It was childish and pathetic.

Those on the ground in Glasgow for the UK government were impressive and collaborative. Alok Sharma, the MP chosen by Boris to head up the UK Presidency, was excellent. He worked tirelessly and pulled off an agreement which, though disappointing in many respects, achieved more than many thought possible. His civil servants briefed me and my team regularly, occasionally asking us to push certain issues with the key players we had good relations with, and, in turn, we fed back any intelligence we had gathered.

Johnson himself was an embarrassment. He seemed disengaged and disinterested. He should have spent the final few days physically present, using the power of the Presidency and his own political capital to drive the best deal possible. Instead, having been at the opening ceremony, he parachuted in for an hour or so in the middle of the second week and was not seen again. It was an abdication of responsibility.

I was present every day of the two-week event. I was criticized by opponents for grandstanding and neglecting other responsibilities. I wasn't. Even while there, I was dealing with the myriad of issues that cross a First Minister's desk every day. In my judgement, though, it was worth it. COP26 was a massive opportunity to showcase Scotland as a climate leader and destination for green investment, and I did so relentlessly. I did what I could to push the negotiators to a good outcome, particularly in cementing 1.5 rather than 2 degrees Celsius as the target limit for global warming.

Much of the focus in climate change discussions is, understandably, on mitigation, addressing the root cause by reducing carbon emissions. There is also lots of attention given to adaptation – for example, building flood defences to help communities cope with the impact of climate change. What has never been given the attention it merits, despite the efforts of many brilliant campaigners in some of the most vulnerable countries in the world, is the loss and damage associated with the already unavoidable and irreversible impacts of the climate crisis. Some low-lying island states will become uninhabitable no matter what action is taken now. Many other countries will suffer unavoidable loss of biodiversity, ecosystems, crop yields and property. Much of the loss and damage is economic, but some of it is less tangible – displacement, loss of cultural heritage and forced changes to traditional ways of life.

The emissions now causing climate breakdown were caused by the economic growth of developed countries, growth which made us wealthy. By contrast, countries in the global south which have done least to cause the climate crisis, some of the poorest on the planet, are suffering the lion's share of loss and damage. Perhaps understandably, there is an acute sensitivity in the international community about the language of obligation and reparation. There is a fear that if the principle is conceded, the quantum will be overwhelming. Indeed, in all of the discussions I had with John Kerry, President Biden's climate envoy, it was probably the only issue we didn't see eye to eye on. Financial recompense for the impacts they are now being forced to deal with is, in my view, exactly what countries in the global south are owed.

At COP26, I consciously chose to use this language. More significantly, I made Scotland the first country in the world to commit hard cash to helping developing nations deal with loss and damage. Together with long-time campaigners on the issue, we forced a step change in awareness and attitudes and paved the way for the decisive breakthrough on loss and damage that was achieved at COP27 in Egypt the following year.

Looking back, COP26 was one of the highlights of my years in office. I felt that I had made a small but tangible impact on the most important issue of our time. I was under no illusion that Scotland, like all countries, had a long way to go to bring our action anywhere close to our rhetoric, and a big regret is that I wasn't able to close that gap more while I was in office. However, we were well and truly on the map as a climate pioneer. I always believed this to be an important step in achieving the progress needed. Unfortunately, it's a position I fear Scotland is now in danger of squandering.

The Russian invasion of Ukraine, the subsequent spike in energy prices and the ensuing cost-of-living crisis opened the door to a ferocious pushback against climate action. Powerful vested interests, chiefly the fossil fuel industry, which to a very large extent is responsible for the climate crisis, reaping eye-watering profits in the process, have sent governments in many places into retreat. It is a grave mistake, not just for future generations, but even for those who still work in the fossil fuel industry.

North Sea oil and gas is a case in point. Not to put too fine a point on it, North Sea reserves are running out. Within just a few years, production will be a tiny fraction of what it is today. Even without a climate crisis, there is an urgent need to pivot away from fossil fuels to alternative sources of energy and employment.

As the fossil fuel pushback gathered steam in the wake of COP26, ruthlessly taking advantage of the turmoil in the energy markets, I was increasingly criticized for 'abandoning' the 100,000 or so people in Scotland whose jobs depend on oil and gas. As climate politics started to fall into the culture war abyss, it was also one of the issues cited by my opponents, and some of my internal critics too, to 'prove' how out of touch I had become with supposedly mainstream opinion.

In fact, the reverse is true. My political outlook was shaped by my experience of growing up in the shadow of laissez-faire deindustrialization, watching so many of my friends' parents thrown onto the economic scrapheap by Thatcher governments which made no effort to ease their transition into new jobs. I feel deeply that the same must not be allowed to happen to workers in the oil and gas industry.

The way to avoid that, though, is not to extract every last possible drop of oil and gas. Every new oil or gas field under exploration sucks in money, labour and expertise that should be devoted to developing and deploying green alternatives such as wind, wave, clean hydrogen. The energy benefit to the UK of new fossil fuel exploration will be marginal, given that most of the North Sea production is already exported. It will be the profits of the fossil fuel majors which are maximized, but as soon as they decide there is no more money to be made from the North Sea they will up sticks. The cost to society of their profit margins having been inflated in the short term will have been failure to ensure investment in the green transition at the scale and pace needed to replace the jobs lost. Just as in the 1980s, it will be workers who pay the price.

As a footnote to COP26, I took some childish pleasure in getting the photo with Joe Biden that the UK government had boasted about preventing. My private secretary, Nicola Dove, one of the best I ever worked with, managed to snap the picture on her phone. The President was effusive in his praise for Scotland when I spoke to him at the leaders' reception in Kelvingrove Museum. So was Angela Merkel. COP26 was one of her last international engagements as Chancellor. I had long been a huge admirer of her leadership and was pleased to have the opportunity to tell her so in person.

———

At heart and by instinct, I am a republican. There is something truly absurd about hereditary power, and deeply discomfiting about the vast accumulation of wealth that so often accompanies it. However, being an instinctive republican doesn't mean I don't feel empathy or admiration for members of the Royal Family. Whether the UK has a hereditary monarch or an elected head of state is not up to them.

Almost all of my interactions with members of the Royal Family have been positive. I know it is part of their 'training' ('breeding' is probably the more accurate term), but they are always engaged and engaging, polite and courteous. I can imagine that Prince Andrew might be an exception, but, thankfully, I've never had much to do with him.

There was only one occasion when I had cause to feel slightly aggrieved towards a senior royal. In 2021, I had a private meeting with Prince William at the opening ceremony of the General Assembly of the Church of Scotland. The meeting was cordial. We chatted about the Covid situation. I asked after his grandmother. We discussed football, as the Euros were only a few weeks away, and various other current issues. What we did not talk about was Scottish independence. In fact, we didn't talk about politics at all.

A couple of days later, it was revealed by *Channel 4 News* that he'd had a private meeting with Gordon Brown at Holyrood Palace. On the face of it, there was nothing untoward about an heir to the throne meeting a former Prime Minister. However, the fact that the meeting had been unpublicized and had taken place in the wake of Gordon setting up the anti-independence think tank, Our Scottish Future, inevitably raised questions. Following the Channel 4 revelation, William obviously felt the need to explain the reason for the meeting. However, the comment issued by his office was, to put it mildly, disingenuous.

I am paraphrasing, but the thrust was that he had wanted to talk to politicians from across the political spectrum, obviously meant as code for both sides of the independence debate. As far as I am aware, though, I was the only senior pro-independence politician he had met while in Scotland and he and I hadn't discussed independence or politics at all. If he had done so with Gordon, that was his prerogative, but, in my view, it wasn't right to suggest that his discussion with me had provided any balance.

And so, to the late Queen . . .

I imagine that every leader who interacted privately with the Queen came to believe that their relationship with her was special. That was one of her qualities. I am under no illusion that, to her, we were all just part of the amorphous cast of politicians who crossed her thresholds over the course of her long reign. To me, though, and no doubt to all of us leaders, the relationship was special. Over the course of my tenure as First Minister, I spent hours with her. The audiences I had were biannual. One took place at the start of the summer in Holyrood Palace, and the other in the autumn during overnight stays at Balmoral Castle.

The exception was 2020, during Covid, when, instead of an in-person audience, I spoke to her on the phone. If anything, chatting to the Queen on the phone as she walked around the gardens at Windsor Castle was even more surreal than seeing her face to face. It was the Balmoral audiences I enjoyed most. She was always relaxed and chatty, and these sessions would typically last for around an hour.

Conversation would range far and wide. She would talk about the goings on in the Deeside communities around the Balmoral estate, as well as current issues in Scotland, the UK and internationally. She was incredibly well informed about everything, from the very local to the truly global. In some ways, prepping for one of these audiences was more nerve-wracking than getting ready for First Minister's Questions. I always tried to anticipate what she might want to talk about and make sure I had all the facts at my fingertips. Invariably, though, she would raise something I hadn't expected. What I loved most was hearing stories about her interactions with different world leaders down the decades. Chatting to her was like being given a private window onto all the big events and key personalities of twentieth-century history. It was remarkable.

The conversations weren't all serious, though. She talked a lot about her family, her grandchildren and great-grandchildren especially. I remember telling her once that I thought Princess Charlotte looked like her and immediately panicking that I might have strayed too far into the personal. I needn't have worried. She lit up with a beaming smile, clearly thrilled that the resemblance had been noted.

She also loved a bit of gossip. She always wanted to hear the stories behind the political headlines. I recall my audience with her at Balmoral just a couple of weeks after the allegations about Alex Salmond had become public. I had assumed she wouldn't mention it, but was worried that it might then be an elephant in the room. I couldn't have been more wrong. She asked me about it almost as soon as I sat down. She wasn't being trivial in any way, but it was clear that she wanted to know more of what was going on. I think she was also trying to put me at ease. That, in fact, was the most remarkable thing about these discussions. No matter how nervous I was in advance, she always made me feel comfortable. I felt able to talk freely, to open up and share whatever was on my mind. I also don't recall a single moment when I thought the conversation might dry up.

At Balmoral, the audiences would be followed by drinks in the drawing room. The Queen would play cards while the rest of us milled around her. I usually got to the drawing room just ahead of her and was always struck by the aura she exuded as she entered the room. Maybe it is because so much of her reign was in the days before twenty-four-hour news, and certainly before social media, that there seemed to be a dignified distance between her and the public. She also came from a time when people had a greater sense of deference. In short, there was a mystique around her that no other member of the Royal Family comes close to having.

After drinks, we would have dinner, usually a barbecue at one of the bothies on the estate. One of these had been built by Queen Victoria to give Prince Albert somewhere to sleep if he went out hunting and left it too late to get back to the castle before dark. This story was recounted to Peter and me by the Queen herself as she drove us there on our first visit, in 2015.

Until the last year or so of his life, the barbecue would be cooked by Prince Philip, who could not have been more different in private to his public persona. He and I would usually sit together at dinner and the conversation would always be dominated by our shared love of books. As he cooked, the Queen would set the table. We were given strict instructions not to try to help her. At the end of the evening, she would clear up and pack any leftovers into Tupperware boxes.

The last time I saw the Queen at Balmoral was in September 2021. I was struck by how frail she was. This was the day that she had started using a walking stick, though it would be another couple of weeks before she appeared in public with it. Despite her obvious fragility, she soldiered on through dinner. There was no question of her not fulfilling her duties.

The final time I saw her was at Holyrood Palace in June 2022. She was in great form and seemed much stronger than during our last meeting. She had just celebrated her Platinum Jubilee and we chatted about how much she had enjoyed it. She told me that, when she had filmed the Paddington Bear sketch, she hadn't really known what it was about. It was only when she later saw it on TV that it made sense. She was quite exercised that day about an ugly structure that had been erected in the Holyrood gardens to stabilize the twelfth-century abbey that sits in the grounds. I promised to make the Chief Executive of Historic Environment Scotland aware of her concerns and did so when I got back to my office.

As I left her, she asked if we had a date for Balmoral yet. I said we did – 19 September – and that I was looking forward to it. Graciously, she said she was too. Those were the last words I exchanged with this extraordinary woman.

————

The day of 8 September started out unremarkably. At 12 noon, I was in the Scottish Parliament chamber for First Minister's Questions. Just a few minutes into the session, as I was being quizzed on overdue ferries and the cost-of-living crisis, John Swinney passed me a note. The Permanent Secretary had texted to say that Buckingham Palace was about to release a statement about the health of the Queen. It was one of those messages that said very little and absolutely everything at the same time. In that moment, there was no doubt in my mind that the Queen's death had either already occurred or was imminent. The rest of the session passed in a blur.

Sitting on my desk when I got back to my office was the briefing folder for Operation Unicorn, the blueprint to be followed in the event of the Queen dying in Scotland. I had been updated on these arrangements periodically since becoming First Minister, but, as when I was first told about them, I had never believed they would be needed while I was in office. Sadly, I was wrong.

Later that afternoon, as I chaired an emergency meeting to make sure all necessary steps were being taken to implement Operation Unicorn, we received informal confirmation that the Queen had died. The emotion in the room was raw. John Swinney was there, as were a handful of senior officials. The Lord Lyon King of Arms, a lovely man called Joe Morrow, who amongst his other duties oversees ceremonial occasions in Scotland, was sitting next to me. I could tell Joe was on the verge of tears, understandably so, as he knew the Queen well. I sensed that everyone needed a moment, so I suggested a short silence for us to reflect and remember. Afterwards, I said a few words in tribute. We resolved to do everything we could to give Her Majesty the send-off from Scotland she deserved. We were determined that Scotland would do her proud, and I think we did.

She left Balmoral for the final time on Sunday, 11 September, and arrived at Holyrood Palace a few hours later. The route was lined with people from Scotland and further afield, all there to witness history and pay quiet respect. The TV shots were beautiful, the Scottish countryside playing its part in a fitting farewell.

The service at St Giles' Cathedral the following day was deeply moving. She lay in state there overnight, with thousands queuing for the chance to walk past her coffin. I gave a reading from the first lesson of Ecclesiastes 3:1–15: 'For everything there is a season, and a time for every matter under heaven. A time to be born and a time to die.' I have made many high-profile and high-pressured appearances over my career, but I had rarely been as nervous as I was on this occasion. On Tuesday, I went to a much smaller ceremony in St Giles', attended mainly by members of her family, to witness her coffin begin the journey to Edinburgh Airport. Watching the RAF plane take off from Edinburgh and slowly disappear into the distance as Queen Elizabeth departed Scotland for the final time was, for me, the most moving moment of the whole week of mourning. Not even her funeral, a few days later, surpassed it.

Queen Elizabeth II was an incredible woman (the 'II' has always been controversial north of the border – Elizabeth I was never Queen of Scotland, as her reign was prior to the Union of the Crowns). Having had the opportunity to observe the Royal Family up close, I have little doubt that history, however long the sweep of it might be in this respect, will look back on the day of her death as the beginning of its end.

―――

During the 2016 Scottish election, I had taken part in a hustings arranged by the LGBTQ+ campaign organization, Stonewall. Alongside me were Tory leader Ruth Davidson, Labour's Kezia Dugdale, Patrick Harvie for the Greens and Willie Rennie of the Lib Dems.

Someone in the audience asked us if we would commit to reforming the process for a trans person to obtain a Gender Recognition Certificate and legally change gender. The existing process, enshrined in the UK-wide Gender Recognition Act 2004, was considered to be intrusive, overly medicalized and deeply stigmatizing. A trans person had to live in their acquired gender for at least two years, obtain two medical opinions confirming a diagnosis of gender dysphoria and then submit evidence to a panel for review and decision.

That night, there was unanimity amongst the various party leaders on the general principle that a process of self-identification should replace the existing requirements. A move towards self-identification was not putting Scotland in the vanguard of social policy. It was already the reality in many other countries, including the Republic of Ireland. It was also being considered by the UK government. It was in this context that, ahead of the 2016 Holyrood election, all parties in Scotland pledged to reform the 2004 Act.

From a more recent perspective, it seems hard to believe that political consensus once prevailed on this issue, but it did. Even when we consulted on possible legislation in 2018 and the volume of media commentary increased, and became more critical, there was no sense that this was an issue worrying people to any great extent. That remained the case for some time. I remember being asked by a journalist towards the end of the 2021 Scottish election if I was concerned about the impact the issue might be having. I was genuinely confused. It had been raised with me on the doorstep just once in the entirety of that campaign, by someone intending to vote for Alex Salmond's new party.

However, by the time the Gender Recognition Reform (Scotland) Bill came to be considered by the Scottish Parliament, it had deeply divided the body politic. The legislation was finally passed on 22 December 2022, after the most toxic few days I had ever experienced in the almost quarter of a century that I had served as a Member of Parliament. For two consecutive nights, MSPs sat well into the early hours of the next morning. The 'debate' was a bin-fire of filibustering, fearmongering and insults. It wasn't all in one direction, but, whether this was the intention or not, it gave vent to the open demonization of trans people, already one of the most vulnerable and stigmatized groups in society.

I cannot begin to imagine what it must have felt like to be a trans woman listening in to these exchanges and hearing it implied that you were, almost by definition, a sexual predator, a danger to women. And for the countless men out there who are predators, rapists, domestic abusers of women, it must have felt like one big 'get out of jail free' card, as attention turned away from them and towards a tiny minority, out of which an even tinier minority have ever behaved in such a way.

It was deeply unpleasant. After the second night of debate, I got back to Bute House around 3 a.m. I was exhausted, but knew

I wouldn't be able to sleep. The nasty, shrill, toxic rhetoric was ringing in my head. I needed to dislodge it and so, as I have done throughout my life, I turned to books. I lay in bed for a while reading a novel called *Our Wives Under the Sea* by Julia Armfield and allowed some beautiful prose to cleanse my mind.

And yet, horrible though it all was, it seemed to me that the issue still wasn't stirring strong public concern. It was much higher up the news agenda and certainly much more talked about than it had been before. People were more likely to offer strident opinions, for and against, but there was no sense amongst the general population of the anger, bordering on hysteria, that was being displayed by campaigners.

Of course, this would be cited by some as evidence of how out of touch I had become, and maybe there is an element of truth in that. However, in that moment, I don't think I was entirely wrong in my analysis.

I left Parliament on 22 December 2022, at the start of the Christmas recess, feeling depressed by the experience of the preceding days, but also hopeful that the worst was behind us. The law was on the statute book, it would come into force in due course, and, when the dire predictions of those opposed to the change didn't come to pass, the controversy would settle. Or so I dared hope.

My optimism was bolstered the following day when I went to buy my mum's Christmas present at her favourite wool shop. I remember feeling a bit nervous as I went in, wondering if I would get a hostile reaction from other customers in light of the previous days' debate. Instead, I had a truly uplifting conversation, which reduced me almost to tears. On the shop counter as I made my purchase was a tray with four champagne glasses. The owner of the shop explained that after the legislation had passed the day before, the mother of one of her staff members, a young trans man, had turned up with a bottle of champagne and they had celebrated the positive difference he believed the new law would make to his life. A customer then said she thought I should be proud of making Scotland a fairer place and hoped I would stand strong in the face of all the hate. I couldn't have asked for a better Christmas gift.

My optimism was short-lived. In the early weeks of 2023, it was shattered, and with it any notion that this was an issue only exercising the political bubble. In mid-January, the UK government re-ignited the controversy with a decision to deploy the never-before-used section 35 of the Scotland Act to challenge the new law on the grounds that it interfered with Westminster powers.

It was preposterous, but suited the Tory agenda perfectly. Not only did it undermine the authority and autonomy of the Scottish Parliament, increasingly a Tory tactic in the fight against independence, but it also exacerbated the kind of culture war the Tories saw as motivational for their natural support.

That move was incendiary, but it was a different spark that set things properly on fire. At the end of January, a trans woman called Isla Bryson was convicted of raping two women and was immediately taken to a female prison. This was a development that gave a human face to fears that until then had been abstract for most people. According to opponents of the law, here was a real-life example of a dangerous sexual predator gaining access to vulnerable women by virtue of 'pretending' to be a woman.

It also completely blindsided me. I had no advance warning that the case was pending. To this day, I don't understand how it could be that no one in the Scottish Prison Service or Scottish government officialdom thought it important to flag it up to me. It isn't for a First Minister to decide which prison an individual goes to, as that is an operational matter, but with some advance warning I could have been ready to explain, and hopefully calm, the situation. Maybe it wouldn't have mattered, the damage might have been done anyway, but at least I could have tried.

The new law had no bearing on which prison Isla Bryson was taken to – and wouldn't have done even if it had been in force. The Scottish Prison Service was simply following long-established procedures in dealing with trans prisoners. The prisoner would be assessed, if necessary in isolation, and, if considered a risk to female inmates, taken to a male prison and looked after there. The SPS had been dealing, appropriately and effectively, with situations like this for years. The challenge of trans prisoners was not a new one. However, by the time any of these points could be made, the story had gone nuclear and I was on the back foot, fighting a fire that was already out of control.

There haven't been many times in my career when my communication skills deserted me as utterly as they did in the face of this controversy. Maybe my confidence had been damaged more than I realized by the intensity of the vitriol flung at me. Or maybe I was just losing my touch. Whatever the reason, when confronted with the question 'Is Isla Bryson a woman?' I was like a rabbit caught in the headlights. The fact that I wasn't the first, and certainly not the last, politician to be felled by this 'gotcha' question was no comfort.

Given what Bryson had been convicted of, I knew that saying yes would enrage people and inflame the situation. Saying no, though, would allow the opponents of the new self-identification law to say that they had been right all along about the impact on women-only spaces – which, in my view, they absolutely hadn't been. Moreover, it seemed obvious to me – media frenzy aside – that the gender question was not the relevant issue in this context. What mattered was that Isla Bryson is a rapist. Identifying as a woman did not confer any automatic right to be accommodated in a female prison. Any convicted trans woman considered a risk to female inmates would be sent to a man's prison, as in fact Isla Bryson quickly was. This all seemed very rational. The problem was that, in a febrile atmosphere, I was unable to communicate it in a way that cut any ice. Because I failed to answer 'yes', plain and simple, to the basic question, I seemed weak and evasive. Worst of all, I sounded like I didn't have the courage to stand behind the logical conclusion of the self-identification system we had just legislated for.

In football parlance, I lost the dressing room. From then on, I was on the defensive. What I had told myself was the situation – that the public weren't concerned – was no longer true. The Isla Bryson case was the break that opponents of the law had been waiting for. The fears they had been trying, and largely failing, to stoke were brought vividly to life in the face of a 'monster'.

The trans debate was one of the most bruising episodes of my time in politics. That might seem an odd thing to say, given the many other 'controversies' I have been involved in over the years. I helped lead a campaign that almost broke up the United Kingdom. I had a brutal falling-out with my political mentor. Yet never before had I received the type or intensity of vitriol – much of it deeply misogynist – that was and still is thrown at me over gender recognition reform.

Obviously, I ask myself now if it was all inevitable. Could the toxicity have been avoided – not just for my sake but, more importantly, for the sake of the trans community which is now under so much attack? Could I have handled things differently? In truth, I don't know if it would have changed anything. Almost everything I have ever said on the issue of trans rights has been twisted and misrepresented in some way. However, if I had my time again, there are things I would certainly try to do better.

I think my belief – until Isla Bryson – that the issue was not troubling the public in any significant way meant that I didn't engage as early or as effectively as I should have done to reassure people on the aspects of the reform that had the potential to cause concern. By failing to do so, I ceded the ground to those making the counterarguments and left the door wide open to the weaponization of the Isla Bryson case.

To be more precise, I failed to engage substantively enough with the concern that making it easier to legally change gender also made it easier for dangerous men to access women-only spaces, that it would make women less safe. The fact that I don't believe that to be true perhaps made me complacent.

The case I made was often technical and, perhaps, too general. I argued that since there is no need for a man to claim to be a woman to commit acts of abuse or sexual assault, changing the process of gender recognition would make no difference to women's safety. I pointed out that the threat to women comes from predatory, abusive and misogynistic men, not from trans women. And I maintained that since men have never needed a gender recognition certificate to access our 'spaces', making it easier to obtain one wouldn't open these spaces up any more than they already were.

These arguments are not wrong, but none of them properly addressed the 'ah, but what if?' fear. They also didn't engage with the more fundamental and visceral concerns some people had. If anyone could be a woman, did being a woman mean anything at all? If anyone could claim the rights that had been won for women down the years, how would they offer any meaningful protection?

I should have recognized that the concerns people had extended beyond the letter of the law. I should have been more explicit in understanding – as I absolutely do – that the language and experiences of womanhood matter; and why single sex spaces and services are, in certain circumstances, important. I should have taken more time to explain the protections already in place. And, perhaps most importantly, I should have been more open to the question of whether, in light of reforms to the gender recognition process, any strengthening of these protections might have been necessary. I do not believe that women will be 'erased' or made less safe by the tiny number of trans people in our society, but I should have been more alive to the fact that some people genuinely do.

The question I ask myself most when I reflect on this period is whether I should have hit the pause button when I realized, sometime in 2022, just how polarized the issue was becoming. With hindsight, I wish I had. Not in the sense of giving up, but to provide space to explore if the aim of making life better and easier for trans people could be achieved without the rancour and division that had come to characterize this debate. So, why didn't I? Perhaps because it had come to feel like a battle about much more than trans rights, I didn't believe there would be the will to find common ground. Perhaps I also felt that it would be giving in to prejudice.

I know that many, probably the majority, of those opposed to the legislation were genuine in their concerns. Even though I believe those concerns to be ill-founded, I have never doubted the sincerity of those who hold them.

But for *some* of the loudest critical voices on this issue, it wasn't just about gender recognition reform or even trans rights more generally. However firm the views they might have on the issue itself, it also served as a weapon in bigger battles.

To me, it is beyond argument that the trans debate has been hijacked by voices on the far right, by some of the more radicalized followers of leaders like Putin, Trump and Orbán, for example.

And yet any time I say as much, I spark howls of outrage and denial from certain campaign organizations who claim, completely and utterly wrongly, to speak for all women and all feminists. There is a brittle defensiveness to this, of course. They assume I am talking about them, when I am not. Much as I disagree with their views, I have never doubted that they hold them sincerely. But how highly intelligent people can fail to see who is standing alongside them is beyond me. I am not expecting it to change their minds, but I do think acknowledging it is important.

For some others, the bigger battle *is* about pushing back against minority rights more generally. The inconvenient truth is that many of the most vocal deriders of trans rights, when the surface is scratched, turn out to be raging homophobes too. Some are also racists. And, ironically for those who claim that their opposition to trans rights is all about protecting women, more than a few are also deeply misogynist. They would take away women's rights, such as abortion and other reproductive rights, in a heartbeat. In some countries, they are already doing so. For these people, trans issues are just a soft underbelly, a socially acceptable way of re-normalizing the language of hate and prejudice, and it is the thin end of a very ugly wedge.

Of course, there is also a more peculiarly Scottish angle too. For some, it is about undermining the SNP – and demonizing me.

Not all opposition voices succumbed to this. To their credit, both Scottish Labour and the Liberal Democrats, and even a handful of Tories, backed us on gender recognition reform. And I am not accusing those who did succumb of being part of the homophobic/racist/misogynist far right cabal that I refer to above. The motive of our Scottish opponents was often much more mundane: opportunism.

By stoking fear and suspicion of trans people, implying that they were all potential predators, and accusing us, and me especially, of prioritizing their rights over those of the majority, they could paint us as out of touch, with warped priorities.

It was entirely legitimate, of course, for people to argue against our proposals, to point out what they believed to be the dangers to women, and to seek to mobilize public opinion in their favour. I would have expected nothing less.

But the tactics deployed by some, however sincere their views might have been, suggested that there was another agenda at work. There are many examples I could cite, but the one that attracted most attention, not surprisingly, was J. K. Rowling's donning of a T-shirt bearing the slogan 'Sturgeon, destroyer of women's rights'. I obviously don't know what her intentions were, but it seems blindingly obvious that a stunt like that was never going to elevate the debate or illuminate the issues at the heart of it.

It certainly marked the point at which rational debate became impossible and any hope of finding common ground disappeared. As the head of the government proposing this reform, I was fair game for robust and uncomfortable challenge, but it went beyond that. It resulted in more abuse, of a much more vile nature, than I had ever encountered before. It made me feel less safe and more at risk of possible physical harm. And it was deeply ironic that those who subjected me to this level of hatred and misogynistic abuse often claimed to be doing so in the interests of women's safety, to be the standard-bearers of feminism. Nothing feels further from the truth than that.

Nevertheless, as I look back now, I can see that it might have been wiser to take a step back than to dig my heels in. Of course, for some it would have made no difference. To those for whom opposition to trans rights has become ideological, nothing short of the total abandonment of gender recognition reform would have been enough. I have asked myself often if this would have been the better course. It would certainly have made my life easier and spared me a great deal of upset and unpleasantness. There are few issues I care more about than protecting and advancing women's rights, so to hear myself described as a destroyer of them wounds me deeply.

What would it have said about me, though, if for the sole purpose of giving myself an easier time I had abandoned an attempt to make life a bit easier for some of the most stigmatized people in the world? It would have run counter to every instinct that brought me into politics in the first place. Despite the hate and prejudice the debate has poured down on them, no trans person has ever said to me that they wish I hadn't tried. Trans people are not an inherent danger to women. Predatory and abusive men are. Some of these men will be found within, or choose to attach themselves to, the trans community. There are bad people within every group in society. Amongst biologically born women, there are some who pose a danger to children. However, for no other group in society do we argue that the way to deal with the bad apples is to withhold rights from the rest. We deal with the bad apples instead. The same should be true for trans people.

This should be true, but manifestly it isn't. And, sadly, it seems to be even less so now than when gender recognition reform was first mooted. At the time of writing, the backlash against what some might call the 'extreme' of gender self-identification has ricocheted us to the opposite 'extreme'. We seem to be at a place now where it is becoming almost impossible for trans people to live their lives in peace and with dignity.

The 2025 ruling of the UK Supreme Court that the terms 'man' and 'woman' in the Equality Act 2010 refer to biological sex has brought this into sharp focus. The Court's ruling speaks for itself (contrary to what seems to be the case for some of the most vocal commentators, I have actually read it). There can be no question that it is a definitive statement of the law as it stands – the Supreme Court is the highest judicial authority in the land – even though it seems to overturn the previously accepted understanding of the 2010 Act. But it is not a moral judgment. Nor is it a statement of what the law *should* be. That is a question for parliaments and politicians. Once upon a time – not so long ago, in fact – the criminalization of homosexuality was the law. So was Section 28. Laws that stigmatize and exclude people can always be changed.

In my view, it is not inevitable that the Supreme Court's ruling should render it impossible for trans people to live their lives with dignity. However, some of the early responses raise concern that this will become the reality. Is that really what we want? I don't believe that to be the case for the majority of decent people.

So where do we go from here? I hope we can now do what I failed to do a couple of years ago. Take a step back and start with a blank sheet of paper. Find ways of protecting women against those who pose actual risks to us – abusive men – while allowing trans people to live safe, happy and accepted lives. Surely that can't be impossible. It may need people like me to acknowledge that self-identification as previously proposed does not have sufficient public consent at this time. In turn, it will take the other 'side' to agree that trans exclusion or segregation is not acceptable. There will doubtless be some who will not want to engage on that basis, but, with goodwill and some basic human empathy, it is surely not beyond the rest of us to find a decent way forward. It must, of course, be based on the acceptance that trans people exist – they always have and they always will – and that their existence is legitimate.

I strongly believe that one day we will look back on this period in history and be collectively horrified at the vilification trans people have been subjected to. In times past, gay men and lesbians suffered the same hate and hysteria, and while prejudice has not been eradicated, society did eventually come to its senses. I have faith that the same will happen for trans people. Whether it will take five, ten, twenty years, or longer, I don't know. I just hope it happens much sooner than feels possible right now.

———

A few months before the Gender Recognition Reform Bill was passed by Parliament, I had attended King Charles's Accession Council in St James's Palace. It took place on the Saturday immediately following the Queen's death and was a moment of genuine historic significance. It was also the only interaction I had with Liz Truss during her short and ill-fated premiership. Our communication amounted to barely more than a hello, but it was enough to convince me that building rapport between us would have been an uphill task. Thankfully, it was never required.

I didn't have much time to interact with Rishi Sunak as Prime Minister either. The main opportunity I had to get to know him was at a private dinner he and I had in Inverness in January 2023. I was shocked by how removed he seemed from the concerns and preoccupations of ordinary people on issues like the cost-of-living crisis. He also showed no interest in even discussing, let alone reaching an accommodation on, the issue of a referendum. I was not surprised by this in the slightest. But I was frustrated.

In terms of my own leadership, I had started to fear, deep down, that I might have reached the end of the road on the issue. That was a hard place to be. For me, independence had always been a means to building a better country, never a holy grail to be pursued for its own sake. I had, however, spent a lifetime arguing and campaigning for it. So, to reach a point, as leader of my party, when I started to think I could not deliver it, or take Scotland any closer than we already were, was a difficult reality to reconcile myself to, and, at times, it still is.

A persistent criticism of me throughout my years as First Minister was that pursuit of a referendum was a distraction, an obsession that put me at odds with mainstream opinion. Obviously, it came from those firmly opposed to independence and keen to see it disappear from the political agenda. They also argued that I was deluding my own supporters in claiming that a referendum was even attainable. While I made missteps along the way, I don't think this criticism, overall, is fair.

Independence is not an abstract. It isn't a distraction from the big challenges Scotland faces. It is how we better equip ourselves to overcome them. Whether it is growing the economy more sustainably or tackling deep-seated inequality, Scottish governments are heavily constrained by the fact that so many economic, welfare and fiscal powers lie at Westminster. Of course, transferring these powers to Holyrood won't automatically make Scotland a better country. As with all nations, it is how well successive governments deploy them that will determine success. However, without these powers, we are often hamstrung, and that is just a fact.

There was also the very strong reason of a democratic imperative – in the form of a Brexit we did not vote for – to offer Scotland a fresh opportunity to consider independence. During my leadership, support for independence was consistently around 50%, and much closer to 70% in younger age groups. Indeed, at certain points, such as after the Brexit vote and again during Covid, overall support came within touching distance of 60%. Of course, not everyone who supported independence favoured an early rerun of the referendum – a point that I didn't always take enough account of, perhaps. However, to claim, as many of my opponents did, that

I was simply ignoring public opinion is not true. In pursuing independence, I certainly put myself at odds with many amongst the 50% or so who opposed it. However, not pursuing it would have alienated many amongst the other half.

Within the Westminster establishment there is a realization that, in a second referendum, Scotland is very likely to vote for independence. The only way, then, to save the Union is to never allow the choice to be made. This blocking position forces independence supporters to bang on about the process of achieving our goal. It is when we focus on this rather than the big-picture arguments for building a better country through independence – when we talk more about the 'how' than the 'why' – that we end up sounding obsessed and a bit out of touch with the realities of people's lives. But this is exactly where we were stuck.

I had zero appetite for trying to stage a referendum that did not meet the standards of 2014. It would have been seen as a Catalan style 'wildcat' vote. Even if it had been practically possible, which it wasn't, it would have lacked democratic legitimacy and failed to secure international recognition. It would have set the independence cause back decades. I was always crystal clear about this.

The question of whether or not the Scottish Parliament has the legal competence to legislate for an independence referendum had always been fudged. In 2014, the Edinburgh Agreement meant it was an issue that didn't have to be confronted at all, yet there had never been much doubt in my mind about which way the cards would fall if the question was tested. For that reason, I knew it was highly unlikely that I would ever get law officers to agree that legislation was within Holyrood's competence, a prerequisite for any government bill.

I was in a bind. Many of my party members and supporters

were unwilling to accept that I lacked the power to bring about a referendum; but, without Westminster agreement, I knew that it was, in all likelihood, impossible. It was this conundrum that made me start to contemplate a move that I had previously ruled out. Around the spring of 2022, I started seriously considering if we should end the ambiguity ourselves by asking the Supreme Court to make a ruling on legal competence.

It would be a big move. Some would say it was a stupid one, as what next if the court decided against us? However, I increasingly felt we needed to break free of the process quagmire we were in. Up until then, the fudge on legal competence had suited us, but now I felt that it had become a handicap. It was contributing to something akin to a collective delusion, allowing too many independence supporters to ignore the reality of our situation and to avoid focusing properly on how we might actually overcome our challenge.

I agonized for weeks. I talked it through with close colleagues, mainly John Swinney and the deputy leader of the party, Keith Brown, as well as Ian Blackford, the leader of our Westminster MPs, and some of my key advisers, Liz Lloyd, Colin McAllister, Stuart Nicolson and Ewan Crawford. Much of the deliberation, though, happened in my own head. It was a criticism regularly levelled at me that I internalized too much of my decision-making rather than consulting far and wide. It is certainly true that on big decisions, I needed to feel I knew the arguments inside out and back to front. I also needed to be at peace with whatever conclusions I reached, so that even if I ended up getting it wrong, I had no one else to blame. What is not true is the claim that I didn't take advice and listen to other points of view. I did. I just also happened to believe that being the leader meant the buck stopped with me. One of the many things I learned over the years, though, is this: strong leadership, when exercised by a man, is a virtue; in a woman, it will more often be described as a character flaw.

Eventually, I made a decision that it was time to escape the limbo we were in. I asked the Lord Advocate, Scotland's senior law officer, to use powers she had under the Scotland Act to refer the question of legal competence to the Supreme Court. If, against expectations, the court decided that the Scottish Parliament did have legal competence, the path to a referendum would be clear. I even named the date on which we would seek to have it as 19 October 2023.

If the court decided against us, we would know the score. The clarity would focus minds on what we needed to do, which was develop the substantive case and build support to a point where it would be impossible for Westminster to stand in our way. In my moments of doubt, I also comforted myself with the fact that if I had tried any other way out of the impasse, for example, by attempting to legislate for a referendum without agreement, we would have ended up in the courts anyway.

I set out my decision in a statement to Parliament on 28 June 2022. There was a genuine sense of shock and surprise. Opinion was split on whether I was a genius or an idiot. When the Supreme Court handed down its ruling on 22 November, I suspect a few more thought I had been an idiot. The judgement was emphatic. The constitution was a reserved matter. The Scottish Parliament had no competence to legislate for a referendum.

The 'Blow for Sturgeon' headlines were predictable, but they missed the point. I had hoped that the court might surprise us with a positive ruling, but I hadn't expected it. The clarity we got was the clarity I had anticipated, and it was the clarity I had come to believe was vital.

We could no longer delude ourselves that if we just wanted a referendum badly enough, we could somehow make it happen, no matter what Westminster said. We had to deal with the world as it was, not how we wanted it to be.

Which is a long-winded way of saying that I don't regret the decision I made. Has it had the desired effect? At the time of writing, it has in part, but not in full. The endless wrangling over process has definitely abated. My successors as First Minister haven't faced the same calls to 'just call it' that I did. That is a good thing, but what hasn't yet taken root is the spirited debate about the opportunities of independence to make Scotland a better country. Partly that reflects the state of the world: global instability, a cost-of-living crisis, the impact of austerity on our public services, and broken politics have left the population too worn down to lift its eyes to the horizon.

It is also because my party has not yet fully seized the opportunity to galvanize opinion and focus minds, to inject some hope in a time of despair. Which brings me, in conclusion, to the second part of my last big decision on independence.

———

When the Supreme Court decided against us, I pledged that the SNP would fight the next UK General Election on the issue of independence. We would make the case and ask people to vote SNP specifically to show support for Scotland becoming an independent country.

I said we would turn the election into a de facto referendum. Was I right to do so? I'm not sure the answer is straightforward. I do think I was right in my belief that independence should have been at the heart of the 2024 campaign. The General Election on 4 July 2024 was the first time since 2010 that the SNP did not win in Scotland. The loss of thirty-nine seats was a brutal reversal of fortunes. The reasons for it were varied, of course, and I carry a hefty share of responsibility. My resignation just over a year earlier and the turbulence that came afterwards, including the developments in the police investigation into the party's finances, played a part. The biggest factor, though, was the desperation to see the Tories kicked out of office. While this led many people in Scotland to vote Labour, most seemed to do so with little enthusiasm. In my view, if the SNP had fought the campaign more squarely on independence, if we had invited the Scottish people to see it as a better way of facing the future than a half-hearted shuffling of the deckchairs at Westminster, our core support would have been more energized and we might have polled more strongly. Independence would have been a powerful motivation in a difficult election.

More fundamentally, if the SNP believes, as we do, that independence is both necessary and urgent for Scotland, our task is an inescapable one. We must build and demonstrate such overwhelming support for it that Westminster can't stand in the way. To do that, we must have the courage of our convictions, win the argument and, crucially, give people who want independence a way to express their support at the ballot box.

While I think I am right that independence should have been central to the 2024 election, I accept that I was probably wrong to seek to brand it as a de facto referendum. I allowed my desire for snappy communication to cloud my judgement. It was terminology that made me seem to be doing what I had always rejected: staging some kind of wildcat referendum with no legitimacy. It also risked setting an impossibly high bar for the party. If winning an independence referendum was hard, winning an election masquerading as one would be even harder. Even in the 2015 landslide we hadn't quite managed 50%.

It would have been a no-win situation. If we had somehow

prevailed, Westminster would have said it wasn't a real referendum and refused to recognize it. If we had failed, they would have claimed that we had now had our referendum, that the issue was settled.

Even if many in the SNP had reservations about my approach, as they did, I knew they would follow my lead. Loyalty to me and faith in my judgement would have sealed the deal.

Perhaps my biggest mistake, then, was setting my party, and the cause I had devoted my life to, on a make-or-break course when I did not have the reserves of energy to lead the charge. In my defence, I did not appreciate this at the time. However, as 2022 gave way to 2023, I came to the realization that I had no more to give as party leader and First Minister. This was when I knew I had to get out of the way; that I had a duty to let the SNP decide the path it wanted to take, unencumbered by its allegiance to me.

CHAPTER TWENTY

The End

At the start of 2023, I did a Sunday morning BBC interview with Laura Kuenssberg. Using the language Jacinda Ardern had used when she had announced her own resignation a few days earlier, Laura asked me if I still had 'plenty in the tank'. I laughed and said that I did, and that I wasn't going anywhere. In the moment, I wasn't lying, I meant it. Or I thought I did. However, in the aftermath of this interview, thoughts which must have been circulating in my subconscious for some time started to rise to the surface.

I suddenly realized that the overwhelming emotion I had felt as I listened to Jacinda Ardern call time on her leadership of New Zealand had been envy. Weeks of soul-searching followed. One day I'd be convinced I was going, the next certain I wanted to carry on, or, at least, that I had a duty to do so, that I had too much unfinished business to walk away now.

I'm not sure when the impetus to leave finally eclipsed any desire to stay, but somehow, by early February, my mind had turned from the 'if' to the 'when' and 'how' of resignation. I told my closest colleagues and advisers over the weekend prior to the announcement I then made in Bute House on the morning of 15 February. The media had been speculating for months that I was about to quit, but that didn't stop their overwhelming reaction being one of shock and disbelief, which of course then led to a sense that there must be more to my decision than I was admitting.

On one level, I understood that. Until very recently, I had been insisting that I would carry on. But, whatever the speculation, the reasons for my decision were exactly as I set out in the speech I gave that morning in Bute House, a speech that I poured my heart and soul into writing, and one of the hardest I have ever delivered. In short, I was exhausted. Covid had taken its toll on me both physically and emotionally. I had served more than eight years as First Minister, but the pandemic made it feel much longer. Indeed, it had only been in the previous few weeks, as I started preparing for the public inquiries, that I had even begun to comprehend the scale of the impact on me. Added to it were all the other pressures of leading a government and country, the turmoil of the Alex Salmond scandal, and the stress of eight election campaigns in eight years. My reserves of energy were drained.

I also believed the time was right politically for me to go. I trust my political instincts as they have served me well. They were telling me that this was the right time for my party, the government and the country for me to make way for someone else. I believe that the independence cause advanced under my leadership, but I had also come to feel that I had taken it as far as I could. My efforts to secure a second referendum had failed. I feared that I was now in danger of driving the independence car, the cause I had devoted my life to, into a brick wall. I didn't want to do that and I preferred to give a new leader the option of finding a different way forward.

That feeling was compounded by a sense that I was becoming

an increasingly polarizing figure in Scottish politics. The approximately half of the population who supported me (if I say so myself, quite extraordinary approval ratings after so long in office) would have been enough for me to keep winning elections, but I increasingly doubted if there were enough open minds amongst the other half for me to have any chance of building a sustainable majority for independence.

That polarizing effect was also, I feared, starting to affect debates around other issues too. The gender recognition reform legislation was a case in point. In short, I wanted to quit at a time when people would still ask why I was going, rather than wait until they were desperate to see the back of me.

Lastly, there was a personal midlife assessment at play. Even though this wasn't a factor in my decision, I had been struggling with menopause symptoms for a while. One of my deepest anxieties was that I would suddenly forget my words midway through an answer at FMQs. My heart would race whenever I was on my feet in the Chamber, which was debilitating and stressful. It was also this experience which made me want to speak out about doing a job like mine while going through the menopause. I had been struck by the total absence of any 'role models' for me to look to. Leaders like Angela Merkel and Hillary Clinton must have gone through similar experiences while they held high office, but they had never talked about it. I don't mean that as a criticism, but I want women coming after me to know that it is possible to do challenging, public-facing jobs while going through this stage of life. Even if only in a small way, I hope I can help de-stigmatize an experience that is still so scary and bewildering for many women.

For all that it wasn't one of my reasons for stepping down, the menopause did prompt me to think more deeply about my life and what I wanted from it in the years to come. For virtually all of my adulthood, I had been Nicola the politician. As I approached my fifty-third birthday, I was starting to worry that I didn't really know who Nicola the person was, and that if I waited much longer it might become too late for me to find out. I had started to confide in a few close friends about my increasingly insistent yearning for a quieter, simpler, happier and more private way of life. One of these friends encouraged me not to wait until I had decided whether to quit to start doing some stuff that might bring me joy. She persuaded me to go hillwalking with her. I loved it. It gave me a sense of peace and perspective, and yet the presence of the police protection officers who had to accompany us was a constant reminder of the constraints on my privacy and personal freedom that being First Minister would always entail.

I delivered my resignation speech in the drawing room of Bute House and answered questions from a shell-shocked press pack. It went as well as I could have hoped. Most importantly, I got through it without crying. I hadn't been sure I would manage that.

I was just about to leave the podium and make my way back upstairs when a journalist shouted an extra question at me about the ongoing police investigation into SNP finances. I sidestepped the question in the moment, as answering it would have entailed commenting inappropriately on a live investigation, but, though it wasn't framed in this way, the subtext of the question was obvious: was the investigation the real reason I was stepping down?

Given what has happened since, it would be hard to blame people for wondering if that was indeed the case. But it wasn't. My attitude towards it at that point was one of frustration more than concern. Why was it taking so long to come to a close? If it was a factor at all, even around the edges, it was as a symbol of the polarized politics I had grown weary of. The complaints that had prompted the investigation initially seemed to have their roots in the Salmond saga.

The idea that I had known, or even suspected, what was about to happen, and that is what had prompted me to stand down, is seriously wide of the mark. In fact, had there been the merest inkling of what would later unfold, I would have been unable to function in the weeks following my announcement, and nor would I have felt the sense of peace that I did on my final days in office.

When I walked out of the Scottish Parliament chamber on 23 March 2023, having just answered my last round of First Minister's Questions and delivered some valedictory remarks – the last words I would speak in there as First Minister – I felt calmer than I had in a long time. I was under no illusion that the transition ahead of me, moving on from almost twenty-five years as a front-bench parliamentarian, sixteen years as a senior government minister and eight years as First Minister, would be difficult. It was going to take time for me to adapt to a different way and pace of life. I was expecting ups and downs. But as I signed my resignation letter to the King on the morning of 28 March, my final day in office, I was excited about the next phase and harbouring no doubts whatsoever that I had made the right decision.

Learning to Dance in the Rain

The sense of peace I felt as I left the Scottish Parliament chamber for the last time as First Minister was quickly and brutally shattered. Around 7 a.m. on the morning of 5 April, just eight days after stepping down as First Minister, my home doorbell rang and my world was turned upside down.

I obviously cannot comment in any way on the substance of the investigation which had triggered what happened that day. At the time of writing, the matter has not come to a conclusion. However, no account of my life so far would be complete if it didn't try to explain in some way the impact that these events, many of them already played out across the media, have had on me. It has been the most difficult experience of my life, certainly of my personal life, and it is not over. Yet, and this seems miraculous to me, I am a stronger, happier and more contented woman today than I was on that fateful morning in April 2023.

Eight days out of office, the novelty of a long lie-in hadn't worn off. At 7 a.m., I was still in bed, half asleep and only vaguely aware that Peter had gone downstairs to answer the door. Within seconds, though, I was wide awake. It was with a sense of utter disbelief that I realized the police were in my home, that they had a warrant to arrest my husband and search the house.

I think I must have gone into shock. What happened next is a blur. I recall a police officer explaining what was going to happen and then Peter leaving. I was told that my protection team, which I still had at the time, was on standby to take me wherever I wanted to go. I also remember a sharp sense of panic about where that should be.

The obvious place was my parents', but my instinct was to shield them from what was happening. I didn't yet realize that there was no chance of doing so and that, within the hour, what was happening would be headline news. My first call, then, was not to my mum and dad, but to Liz, my former Chief of Staff, who had been by my side through so much. As fate would have it, Liz was at the gym and missed my call. With hindsight, I am glad, because it meant I did end up with my parents, and, over the next couple of days, I came to realize that there was nowhere else I would have wanted to be.

By the time I got there, the story had broken, and images of my house were being beamed around the globe. With police tents all around it, it looked more like a murder scene than the place of safety it had always been for me. I was devastated, mortified, confused and terrified. For the rest of that day and for some time after, life felt surreal, as if I was outside myself looking in. A support network of friends quickly formed, phoning, texting, offering places to go. I found out that day and have been reminded ever since just how amazing my close friends are. I will never be able to repay them for the kindnesses they have shown me.

It would be two more days before I returned home. I had felt a sense of comfort and security at my mum and dad's that I was reluctant to give up, but I had to go home sometime. Unlocking the front door and stepping back inside my house was incredibly hard. To all intents and purposes, it was just as we had left it, but it wasn't the same, and never really has been since.

The days after were awful. I was in despair, struggling to comprehend what had happened. Although my house no longer felt like home, I also couldn't bear the thought of leaving it. It didn't help that what seemed like the entirety of the UK's media was camped outside. Apart from being dragged out for a walk by Liz, which I was grateful for, I didn't step out the front door for days. I had only just started to recover a sense of equilibrium when another bombshell dropped. On 19 April, the SNP's Treasurer, Colin Beattie, was also arrested. The media was suddenly full of speculation that, as party leader, I would surely be next. I felt like I had fallen into the plot of a dystopian novel. The next six weeks were excruciating. I tried to live my life as normally as I could, reminding myself all the time that I had done nothing wrong. But I woke up at the crack of dawn every day, having barely slept, with my stomach in knots, wondering if this would be the day it happened. When it eventually did happen, I was horrified and devastated, though also relieved in a strange sort of way. At least the ordeal of wondering and waiting was over. Arrangements were made for me to attend a police station on Sunday, 11 June.

At that point, a depth of resilience I didn't know I had kicked in. The day before attending at the police station, I sat and passed the theory section of my driving test. My first instinct had been to cancel, but, in deciding not to, I did what has helped pull me through ever since. I willed myself to keep going. Indeed, getting my driving licence a few months later is the most concrete illustration of my dogged determination to carry on living my life. Of all the many extraordinary things I've done over the years, passing my driving test has to be one of my proudest achievements, and not just because I did it at age fifty-three. The circumstances I did it in bordered on surreal. My early lessons took place with the media still outside my house. My brilliant instructor, Andy MacFarlane, was unflappable. He would arrive to pick me up in the full glare of media scrutiny. There were days I didn't think I had the strength to do it, but, each time, I would physically and mentally steel myself to open my front door, get into the car and drive away, with the cameras recording my every move.

Sunday, 11 June was the worst day of my life. Being arrested and questioned by the police is an experience I'm not sure I will ever really get over. When I eventually left the police station, late that afternoon, I was in a bad state mentally. I went to a friend's house in the north-east of Scotland and stayed for a week. It was during a heatwave, some of the nicest weather we'd had for years, and yet I was stuck inside, terrified that the media would find me. I badly needed peace and quiet, time to piece myself back together. I read a lot and started to write this book. I also spent hours sitting by a window, looking out across the North Sea. At first, I wanted to somehow disappear into its vastness. Slowly but surely, though, the sea calmed me. As I watched the tide go in and out, regular and steady, I thought about the people who might have sat there a century ago, watching the same tides, feeling that they too had the weight of the world on their shoulders, and of those who would do so again, decades from now. It gave me some perspective.

When I eventually returned home, a new normality kicked in. It was obviously impossible to put it all out of my mind. It was always there, but I carried on with life as best I could. However, I always carried a sense of dread and anxiety about what might lie ahead. For almost a year, aside from stories about the ongoing investigation appearing regularly in the media (sourced from where, I don't know), nothing happened. And then, in April 2024, almost exactly one year on from the search of our home, Peter was re-arrested and, this time, charged. It was another dark moment in what had started to feel like a nightmare with no end.

Even so, it did bring me a brief glimmer of hope. Would I now be formally cleared? It took only a few hours for that possibility to be extinguished. A statement issued by the Crown Office confirmed that the investigation into me was ongoing. I was distraught. I couldn't understand why it was taking so long for the justice system to accept what I knew beyond doubt to be true. I had not committed any crime. I also didn't know how much longer I could cope. As it turned out, I had no choice. The worry and uncertainty had to be endured for another eleven months.

The only new information came in September 2024. It was gleaned from media statements rather than any formal communication, but the substance was that the report of the investigation into me (and Colin Beattie) had been passed from the police to the Crown Office. It is hard to describe how difficult these months were. The investigation was the first thing I thought about when I woke up in the morning and the last thing in my mind before I fell asleep (if I fell asleep) at night. On some days, I could lock it away in a corner of my consciousness and carry on, almost as if everything was normal. On others, it paralysed me.

I was frightened. The rational part of my brain told me that as I had done nothing wrong, there could, by definition, be no evidence to the contrary. But the longer it dragged on, the more scared and paranoid I became. I worried that the 'system' might reach the conclusion that I was guilty of something. Or, at the very least, that I would be forced to prove my innocence in court.

At times, it was very hard to hold on to reason. I felt embarrassed, ashamed even. Not because of anything I had actually done, but because of what many people would suspect I had done. 'No smoke without fire' is a strong human instinct.

I felt robbed of all the things I had looked forward to doing once I stood down as First Minister. It felt as if this new phase of life I had been so excited about had already been snatched away. I oscillated between anger and self-pity. 'Why me? What have I done to deserve this?' were questions I would scream silently to myself in the dead of night when I couldn't sleep for the worry and frustration of it all.

I am not saying any of this pejoratively. I know how these things work. I understand that investigations take time. I accept that the police and Crown Office were doing their jobs. I retain both faith in and respect for our country's criminal justice system. However, none of that changes this fact: being the subject of a high-profile criminal investigation for almost two years, especially having committed no crime, was like a form of mental torture.

The moment of exoneration arrived, finally, on 20 March 2025. It was a day of deeply mixed emotions. Peter appeared in court, and, of course, nothing I say here is meant as commentary on the situation he is in. That process will take its course. However, around the middle of the day, I received the news that I had waited almost two years for. My lawyer called with formal confirmation that the investigation was over and I would face no further action. I came off the phone and burst into tears. The feeling of relief, and release, was overwhelming.

I am writing this just a few days on from that moment. It hasn't properly sunk in yet that the black cloud I have been living under for so long has gone away. I can finally make plans without wondering if they will be torpedoed by a development in the investigation. I can look to the future again with optimism and excitement. I have been given my life back.

———

Given all that I have just written, to say that the period since I stood down as First Minister hasn't been easy feels like a massive understatement. Indeed, it is only since emerging from the darkness of the investigation that I have begun to appreciate just how heavy the toll has been. I have had to dig deep every day, sometimes even just to get myself out of bed. I have done a lot of soul-searching. Given the nature of events and the state of mind I've been in, it is probably not surprising that most of my thinking has been about the mistakes I've made, real or perceived. Some of that has been reflected in what you have been reading. For some of my loudest critics, I know that no amount of self-flagellation will ever be enough. However, I have tried to be frank about the things I got wrong. On decisions I still stand by, even though they may be deeply controversial, I have done my best to explain my reasoning. Even if you are someone who still disagrees with me on one or more of these issues, I hope I have at least given you a better understanding of what motivated me. Even if I haven't changed anyone else's view of me, though, the process of writing this book has helped me arrive at a more balanced sense of myself, and that has been important.

Just to have got through the period since April 2023 would have been an achievement, but I have done better than that. The woman I am today is stronger, with a much keener appreciation of what, and who, makes her happy, than the one whose life was upended the morning the police turned up on her doorstep.

I am a resilient person in my own right, but I wouldn't still be standing without the support of those closest to me. My family, obviously. And my friends. Given the media glare I still live under, being my friend is not always easy, and yet my real ones have never flinched. Val McDermid and Jo Sharp, in particular, have been rocks, but they have all given me shoulders to cry on and reasons to laugh. They have poured me (too many) glasses of red wine. They have given me keys to their homes for any time I needed an escape. They have stopped me hiding away. Most of all, they have never doubted me.

Of course, there is one relationship, at least in its old form, that hasn't survived: my marriage. It is possible, and maybe even likely, that as we left frontline politics behind, Peter and I would have grown apart. However, the strain of the past couple of years took away any chance that we would stay together. The weight of it has been impossible to bear. He will always be part of my family. I love him. But by the time we publicly announced that our marriage was over – on 13 January 2025 – we had been living separate lives for months. It was a relief, for both of us, to finally say it out loud.

What, then, of the future? While I don't know exactly what it holds, I know I am looking forward to it. Even more so, I am trying to enjoy the here and now. I am living in the moment in a way I have never managed to do before. I see life differently now. In the past, while it might have been a constant feature of my job, I always struggled to deal with uncertainty in my personal life. I always had to resolve whatever was worrying me before I could relax and enjoy myself. Moreover, my single-minded focus on work and politics meant that my attitude to fun and joy was often sternly Presbyterian. My mindset was a 'glass half empty' one. No longer. I've learned now, no matter how tough things are, to make the most of every day, to see the upside in every situation, to find moments of joy even when things feel heavy and dark. I've learned to dance in the rain.

As a result, and in spite of everything, I am probably happier now than I have ever been. I am looking forward to new opportunities. I want to write more, maybe even fiction. I am determined to see more of the world. I might live outside of Scotland for a period. I think the perspective shift would be good for me, even though I can't imagine staying away for very long. Scotland is where I belong.

And what about politics? I love the SNP and my loyalty to it will never waver. But I am enjoying not having to view every issue through the prism of party politics. I can't deny that this was a straitjacket I was starting to feel too constricted by. I want to think and speak, as well as live, more freely. This means that the life of an elected politician will soon be behind me – for now, and probably for ever. The caveat isn't designed to tease, but if recent years have taught me anything, it is that we don't know what the future holds.

Politics more generally, though? It is in my blood. The sixteen-year-old girl who rang Kay Ullrich's doorbell is still inside me, still desperately wanting to make the world a better place.

Like many, I am deeply troubled by the state of humanity today. The threats posed by the rise of the far right and the ascendancy of demagogue populists like Donald Trump are grave. Democracy and peace; the freedoms of women and the rights of minorities; the very existence of a habitable planet: all are in peril. I also can't help despairing at the timidity of some of those on the left of politics. In the face of the charlatans hellbent on stoking fear and division, on destroying democracy and upending the world order, progressive liberals seem paralysed or, worse, craven. The Donald Trumps of this world won't be defeated by flattery and imitation. People must be offered a clear and compelling alternative to the snake-oil they peddle. On all of this, and more, I am unlikely to stay quiet for long.

I still desperately want Scotland to be independent. I am also confident that it will happen. I predict that in twenty years, perhaps sooner, the UK in its current form will no longer exist. What will emerge in its place will be stronger, healthier and more democratic. An independent Scotland, a more autonomous Wales and a reunified Ireland will join England, enjoying the benefits of the home rule it will gain as a result, in a new British Isles confederation of nations.

Nothing will stop me playing my part in trying to bring that about. For as long as I have breath in my body, I will fight for a fair, equal, inclusive, outward-looking Scotland; an independent country, relatively small in size perhaps, but with the potential to make a big, positive impact on the world.

That, after all, is what my life has been about.

Acknowledgements

Writing this book has been an often solitary experience, but building the life it recounts was a team effort. One of my anxieties about penning a memoir was knowing that it would be impossible – unless the book was to become an unreadable roll-call of names – to mention or give due credit to all of the many people who have contributed to my story so far.

Even in the paragraphs to follow, as I say thank you to the cast of family, friends and colleagues who have done so much for me along the way, I know that I will inevitably omit some individuals whose presence in, and contribution to, my life have meant a great deal to me. At the outset, therefore, I want to extend my gratitude to everyone who has supported me on my journey up to, and through, my years as First Minister and in the period since, in whatever manner or capacity that has been. This includes the many thousands of people amongst the general public who have sent me messages of support and encouragement over the years. These messages have always lifted my spirits and given me strength to keep going. If you are one of these people – thank you.

As in any life, though, there are some people who stand out – people without whom my achievements, such as they are, would simply not have been possible. It is to them that I now turn.

First and foremost, my immediate family. My mum and dad and my sister, Gillian, are the foundation stones of my life. Being the parent or sibling of a high-profile politician – particularly in today's world – is not easy and, unlike me, they never had any choice in the matter. They have had to deal with loss of privacy, disruptions to family life and the stress of seeing my every up and down played out across the media. And yet they have never complained or made me feel guilty about the sacrifices they had to make. They have only ever loved and supported me and done so with a forbearance I'm not sure I would have managed had roles been reversed. I will never be able to repay them or find words to adequately convey how much I love them.

My sister, especially, has always had my back. I may be the older sister, but I have always looked up to Gillian. I am also fiercely proud of her. Her children, Ethan and Harriet, my nephew and niece, are a credit to her. They are also the loves of my life. They have brought me unquantifiable joy and happiness, and watching them grow into the wonderful young adults they are today has been a privilege. So thank you, Gill, for bringing them into my life and for putting up with all the drama that comes with being my sister.

My immediate family was extended through my marriage to Peter. Over the past twenty years, I have been so lucky in the love and support I have had from him, his mother and late father, Margaret and Harry, and his sister, Lynn. Like Ethan and Harriet, Lynn's children, my nephews, Cameron, Ross and Finlay, have given me endless joy. I love them very much and am so proud of the fine young men they have become.

ACKNOWLEDGEMENTS

Even though I don't see much of them these days, my wider family has shaped and supported me too. I have talked a lot already about my grandparents and how important they were in my younger years. My aunts, uncles and cousins deserve mention too.

On my dad's side, that is his younger sister, my Aunt Dorothy, and her husband, Matthew, and his older brother, my Uncle Leslie, and his wife, Kathleen.

My Aunt Dorothy in particular has been a constant support to me over the years. This is my chance to tell her how much it has meant to me.

On my mum's side is her late brother, my Uncle Iain, and his wife, Elaine, and her younger brother, my Uncle Scott. Scott is just nine years older than me and was more like an older brother than an uncle when I was growing up. I thought he was the epitome of cool. Iain was in many ways my idol. He worked in local media in my childhood, and I think my news addiction came partly from him. We also shared a love of books. Iain died in the summer of 2023 and his funeral took place on the day it was announced I had signed with Pan Macmillan to write this book. I know he would have been excited to read *Frankly* – indeed, his journalistic skills would have been a great help in the writing of it – and the dedication to him at the start of the book reflects the massive impact he had on my life.

It is hard to think of my childhood and teenage years without memories of times spent with my cast of cousins – so to Richard, Jason, Jennifer, Lesley, Alison, Amy, Emma, Lorna, Linzi, Caryn and Laura, thank you for the fun and games.

As well as my family, I am also lucky to have the love of some wonderful friends. The last couple of years have really taught me the value of friendship. I would not still be standing without the support I have had from some of them. I only hope I can be half as good a friend to them in future as they have been to me in recent times. Special mention must go to Val McDermid, Jo Sharp, Susan Stewart, Jeane Freeman, Anne McLaughlin, Liz Lloyd, Sarah Masson, Claire Mitchell, Jenny Gilruth, Kezia Dugdale and Mairi Gougeon. And just to prove that men can be great friends too, Ian Blackford has also been a tower of strength.

Every senior politician is supported by thousands of party and constituency workers, advisers and civil servants. I am deeply grateful to all of them, even if it is possible to name only a few. My heartfelt thanks go to:

Those who have worked over the years in SNP headquarters and for our parliamentary groups – in particular Sue Ruddick, Ian McCann, Lorraine Reid, Trudi Logan, Beverley Murray, Claire Bennett, Ria Robertson, Richy Edwards, Kevin Pringle and Jim Henderson. Thanks too to all of my parliamentary and ministerial colleagues down the years.

My brilliant constituency office staff – past and present – and in particular to those who supported me during my years in government, when the workload was even greater and my time stretched more thinly, in particular Mhairi Hunter, Caroline Scott, Paul Leinster, Nikita Bassi, Carolyn McConville, Irfan Rabbani and Helena Demba.

I am also hugely grateful to the hundreds of SNP activists who have volunteered their time to help get me elected over the years. In my debut as a parliamentary candidate in Shettleston in 1992 that included John Adamson, Bob and Agnes Bothwell and the late Jamie Williamson and Alex Livingstone. Mark Coyle and Joe Rocks were with me at the very start of my Govan/ Southside journey. The late Allison Hunter and her daughter, Mhairi Hunter, served as my election agents over many contests.

Colin and Margaret Pennycook are the best fundraisers I have ever encountered – and they have also been the source of much kindness and support to me over the years, as have Hamish and Ann McPherson and Qasim Hanif, to name just a few of many. There have been countless SNP members from outside my constituency who have gone above and beyond the call of duty to support me over the years – people like Stuart and Betty Farquharson, Colin and the late Davina McKellar, Lachie McNeill and the late Allan Angus.

All of the private, diary and correspondence secretaries who supported me in my various ministerial roles and, in particular, those who headed up my First Ministerial Private Offices – Joe Griffin, Lisa Bird, John Somers, Michelle Quinn and Chris Mackie – and also Clare Hicks, Beth Elliot, Nicola Dove, Patrick Crolla, Gary McGhee and Martin Ward. Martin was with me from my days as Health Secretary right through to the final phase of my time as First Minister. He was also one of the only people who could raise a smile from me first thing on a Monday morning.

John Somers and Nicola Dove merit special mention. John was my Principal Private Secretary for almost half my tenure as First Minister, and Nicola, with me for seven of my Bute House years, probably spent more hours in my company than anyone else in the Scottish Government. Their professionalism, compassion and dedication to public service was indispensable to me. They helped sustain me through some tough times – not least the Covid years – and could always lift my spirits, no matter how heavy the burdens of office might have felt at times. I owe them a huge debt of gratitude. They might have come into my life in a professional capacity, but I am lucky now to count them as friends.

My Special Advisers provided me with excellent advice and counsel to help me reach decisions. The good decisions were down to all of us, the bad ones entirely on me. I am immensely grateful to Liz Lloyd and Colin McAllister, who served consecutively as my Chiefs of Staff. Chief of Staff to the First Minister is a tough, high-pressured, often round-the-clock job, and both Liz and Colin did it magnificently and gave me more support and friendship than I can ever repay them for. They – and me – were supported by my other Special Advisers: Noel Dolan, Katy Bowman, Stuart Nicolson, Ewan Crawford, Davie Hutchison, Ross Ingebrigtsen, Jeanette Campbell, Kate Higgins, John MacInnes, John Macfarlane, Emily Macintosh, Leanne Dobson, Callum McCaig, Stewart Maxwell, Malcolm Fleming, David Miller, Mairi McAllan, Catriona Matheson, Jennie Gollan, Harry Huyton and Gavin Corbett.

The legions of civil servants who supported me over the years. In particular, the four Scottish Government Permanent Secretaries I worked with – Sir John Elvidge, Sir Peter Housden, Leslie Evans and JP Marks – and also, out of many thousands, Kevin Woods, Derek Feeley, Ken Thomson, David Rogers, Chris Birt, Joni Smith and David Fleetwood. I am also grateful to those who kept me safe over the years, in both Police Scotland and SecuriGroup.

This book would not have made it past first base without the guiding hand of my literary agent, Andrew Gordon, of David Higham Associates. Andrew's support over the past couple of years has been invaluable and hugely appreciated. The team at Pan Macmillan have been fantastic in guiding me through my first foray into the book world as an author. I am grateful to Joanna Prior and Lucy Hale for having faith in me and my book. However, I would not have made it to the point of writing acknowledgements without the skill and expertise of my brilliant editor, Mike Harpley. The first draft that I delivered to Mike was clunky, unwieldy and around fifty per cent longer than it needed to be. He was masterful in helping me shape it into the book it has become, and made the editing process much more enjoyable than I had expected it to be. The fresh editorial eye that Mike Jones cast over a later draft also made the book better than it would otherwise have been. On the communications side, Poppy North, Kimberley Nyamhondera and Laura Sherlock have been truly wonderful at helping me get the book to as wide an audience as possible. Thanks also to Kate Tolley and Neeharika Nene on the production side, to Claire Bush and Gillian Mackay, who oversee marketing and liaison with booksellers, and to Rachel Vale who was the creative mastermind behind the front cover. The cover photographs were taken in the magnificent surroundings of Edinburgh's Signet Library by Charlotte Haddon, assisted by Lucy Rooney and George Zenko. Julie McGuire, as she has done for many years, did my hair and make-up, and Amy Albertine Andrew worked her magic as the stylist. As for my dulcet tones on the audiobook version, that is down to Melissa O'Brien at Pan Macmillan and to the skill of Iain McKinna and Olivia Caw at Offbeat Studios, Edinburgh – a massive thanks to them.

Steph McGovern, part of the wider Pan Macmillan family and fellow debut author, who became a good friend during the writing process, agreed to read some of my earlier drafts and was able to give me a valuable perspective from outside Scotland and the world of Scottish politics.

I am also grateful to Fiona Duncan for giving me the initial inspiration for the title, *Frankly*.

Finally, my thanks to three overlapping groups of people without whom none of the events recounted in this book would have been possible.

Firstly, to my extended family of SNP members, now and down the years: thank you for showing faith in a shy, awkward teenager and supporting her all the way to becoming your leader.

Second, to my constituents past and present: thank you for the privilege of being your representative in the Scottish Parliament for twenty-seven years.

And last, but not least, to the people of Scotland. Whether you voted for me or not, being your First Minister was the biggest honour of my life. Thank you from the bottom of my heart.

Photo Credits

Images 1, 2, 3, 4, 5, 6, 24 and 39 courtesy of Nicola Sturgeon

Image 7: Alan Wylie / Alamy Stock Photo

Image 8: Colin McPherson / Corbis News, 9: Christopher Furlong / Getty Images News, 12: Colin McPherson / Corbis News, 13: Pool / Getty Images Sport, 20: Handout / Getty Images News, 22: STEFAN ROUSSEAU / AFP, 26: JACK TAYLOR / AFP, 31: Universal History Archive / Universal Images Group, 32: Duncan McGlynn / Getty Images News, 34: WPA Pool / Getty Images News, 35: Pool / Getty Images News, 36: WPA Pool / Getty Images Entertainment, 37: Cameron Smith / Getty Images News, via Getty Images

Images 10, 11, 14, 15, 16, 17, 18, 23, 27, 28, 29, 33: Jeff J Mitchell / Getty Images News, via Getty Images

Image 21: Scottish Government via Flickr

FRANKLY

Images 19 and 25 by Peter McNally

Image 30 by Liz Lloyd

Image 38 by Nicola Dove

Index